Advancing Humanity

The Need To Make Our Own Future

Alistair J. Sinclair Ph.D.

Almostic Publications
2016

Published by

Almostic Publications

Glasgow

ISBN 978-0-9574044-1-0

© 2016 Alistair J. Sinclair

The right of Alistair J. Sinclair to be identified as the author of this book has been asserted by him in accordance with sections 77 & 78 of the Copyright and Patents Act of 1988

All rights reserved.

No part of this publication may be reproduced or transmitted in any form or by any means or stored in any retrieval system of any nature without prior written permission, except for fair dealing under the Copyright, Designs and Patents Act 1988 or in accordance with a licence issued by the Copyright Licensing Society in respect of photocopying or reprographic reproduction. Full acknowledgment as to author, publisher and source must be given. Application for permission for any other use of copyright material should be made in writing to the publisher

*Other Works by
Alistair J. Sinclair*

BOOKS

The Answers Lies Within Us
What is Philosophy: An Introduction
The Will to Live: A Systematic Guide to Our Reasons for Living
American Papers in Humanism and Religion
Sautonic Wisdom: What We Are Here To Do
The Promise of Dualism: An Introduction to Dualist Theory
Hale and Hearty: Looking at Things as a Whole

E-BOOKS

The Future of Humanity: The Need to Believe in Humanity and its Future
Vindication: Justifying Our Existence
From Time to Eternity: An Essay on the Meaning of Time
Shakespeare on Time
Punish the Person not the Crime: A New Theory of Punishment Based on Old Principles
Old Age, Death and the After-Life
Reforming the British Constitution
The Normal Society: And How To Get It

"Mankind has wandered from the trees to the plains, from the plains to the seacoast, from climate to climate, from continent to continent, and from habit of life to habit of life. When man ceases to wander, he will cease to ascend in the scale of being. Physical wandering is still important, but greater still is the power of man's spiritual adventures – adventures of thought, adventures of passionate feeling, adventures of aesthetic experience."
Alfred North Whitehead, *Science and the Modern World*, (1925).[1]

"The empires of the future are empires of the mind."
Sir Winston Churchill, 'Speech at Harvard University' (1943).[2]

Contents

Introduction
A. Preamble:
The means of advancement – summarising of parts one, two and three   1
B. Prologue on Progress:
The need to make real and lasting progress – How not to make progress – The nature and origin of prospectivism   4

Part One – Social Advancement
1. Unity: Bringing us all Together
    A. The Increasing Unity of Humanity   11
    B. Increasing that Unity   12
    C. Political Atonement   15
    D. The Role of the Holistic View   17
    E. Advancing by means of the Holist View   19
2. Humanity: Believing in our Future
    A. Why Believe in Humanity?   23
    B. The Importance of Humanity   27
    C. What Believing in Humanity Means   28
    D. What Are We Here For?   30
    E. The Bootstrap Species   31
    F. The Need for a Creed   32
3. Centrality: Developing the Middle Ground
    A. Science and the Middle Ground   36
    B. The Role of the Middle View   38
    C. The Centrality of our Position in the Universe   40
    D. The Importance of our Centrality   42
    E. The Middle Ground between Scepticism and Dogmatism   44
4. Duality: Looking at Both Sides
    A. Duality Offers an Anti-Extremist Viewpoint   51
    B. The Interactivity of Duality   53
    C. Why the Dualist View is Important   57
    D. The Relationship of Dualism to Monism   60
    E. The Social Usefulness of the Dualist View   63

Part Two – Personal Advancement
5. Vitality: Building Ourselves Up
    A. The Need to Develop Ourselves Within   68
    B. The Vitality of our Inner Being   70
    C. Its Workings   73
    D. Its Reality   78

E. Reining it in	82
F. Putting it into Practice	83

6. Luminosity: Enlightening Everything
A. Illuminating the Darkness Within	86
B. The Joy of Luminosity	89
C. The Benefits of Illuminating Life	91
D. Illuminating the Divine Within Us	92
E. Illuminating our Rational Passions	94
F. Illuminating our Personal Behaviour	98

7. Creativity: Making the Most of Our Artistic Potential
A. The Way to Artistic Achievement	100
B. The Interplay between Creativity and Intelligence	101
C. The Importance of Intuition in Creativity	104
D. The Complex Build-Up of our Intuitive Powers	105
E. The Verbal Expression of Intuitions	107
F. The Creativity of Metaphysical Intuitions	109
G. The Factual Limitations to our Intuitions	110
H. The Eternal Nature of the Artistic Vision	111

8. Morality: Disciplining Ourselves Purposefully
A. The Need for the Discipline of Morality	114
B. The Role of Moral Sense	116
C. Personal Interaction	119
D. Ethical Interaction	122
E. Good, Truth and Evaluative Notions	123
F. The Importance of Personal Truth-Seeking	126
G. The Truth of Emotive Evaluations	130
H. The Truth of Self-Regarding Evaluations	133
I. The Truth of Judgmental Evaluations	136
J. Applying the Evaluative Notions	138
K. When 'Is' Implies 'Ought'	141
L. Contextualising Morality	142

9. Normality: Having a Society Based on Norms
A. Introductory	145
B. In Praise of the Normal Society	147
C. The Lack of Freedom in the Abnormal Society	149
D. The Normal Family	156
E. The Normal Person	160
F. The Normal Place of Women in Society	163
G. Normal Sexual Behaviour	173
H. The Abnormality of God-Belief	181

10. Servility: Serving Humanity Dutifully
A. How We Can Serve Humanity	190
B. Service by Counselling	192

C. Service as Being Essential to Society	193
D. Serving Society through the Civil Covenant	196
E. The Contextual Limits to Service	198
F. Serving Humanity through Contextualisation	200

Part Three – Future Advancement
11. Posterity: Benefiting Future Generations
A. The Importance of Thinking about Posterity	208
B. The Omnipresence of Posterity	211
C. Posterity and the After-Life	214
D. Orienting Ourselves towards the Future	217

12. Finality: Contributing to the Cosmos
A. The Role of the Cosmos	219
B. The Meaning of the Cosmos	223
C. The Cosmos as a Unifying Principle	226
D. The Cosmic Contribution of Science	228
E. The Cosmic Significance of Past Religions	230

Notes and References	233
Bibliography	245
Name Index	249
Subject Index	251

Introduction

Not to go forward in the way of life is to go back
Bernard of Clairvaux (c. 1140),[1]

A. Preamble
The means of advancement
This book examines some of the conditions necessary for our advancement both as a species and as individuals. It is a work of practical philosophy concerned with getting things done that will benefit us all in the future. The main theme is that of advancing humanity as against many of the trends, imbalances, distortions and other flaws that stand in the way of our progress as a unified species. It is concerned with what will bring us all together to make a better future for us as well as for life in general. This is not preaching some infallible doctrine but showing what can be done if we really care about our future.

Thus, a *prospectivist* view is adopted which looks to the future in contrast with a *retrospectivist* view that looks to the past more than to the future. Prospectivism is the view that looks forward and uses the lessons of the past to make things better in the future. In practice, this view involves an interaction between social and personal advancement. By *social advancement* we strive to make our society better and make life better for everyone whereas *personal advancement* is what we do to make our own lives better. Ideally, this interaction results in *future advancement* that contributes to the well-being of posterity. Though it is always uncertain whether the future will benefit from whatever we do in the present, we cannot allow this uncertainty to hinder our best efforts.

It is argued here that humanity doesn't deserve to have a future on this planet unless we make our own future. If we do nothing, our fate will depend on events beyond our control. Economic collapse, needless wars, environmental catastrophe, or any number of such triggers could plunge us into backwardness. History shows that we regress as easily as we make progress as a species. "Things fall apart; the centre cannot hold."[2] It happened in the Dark Ages and it could easily happen today. Nations are arming themselves defensively while threatening each other politically. The financial system is overloaded with debt throughout the world and could collapse at any time. We are ruining the climate and the environment with our unbridled activities. We are busy constructing robots that could take over and render us extinct. Clearly, the world is accelerating out of our control and we are doing little or nothing to regain control of it.

Thus, human advancement cannot be left to chance. The prospectivist view is that we need to plan ahead and think deeply about our future. We must consider questions such as 'what are the conditions must we fulfil to ensure our advancement and make our own future?' This book suggests that we need a form of civic therapy to overcome the impediments, imbalances, bottlenecks, logjams and other hindrances that stand in the way of our advancement.

To achieve such advancement we need to be more inclusive in our thinking and less exclusive of different ways of thinking. We need to take account of all points of view and not rest with one narrow viewpoint as if it were the one and only answer to our problems. This is holistic thinking compared with narrow logical thinking. The truth is out there in many forms

Twelve therapeutic ways are here suggested to help us to maintain our forward movement by unblocking the obstacles standing in our way and both as a species and as individuals. These ways are not exhaustive of the possibilities, but they are those that seem particularly relevant to the current state of our society and its obvious failings. They fall under the following twelve headings: Unity, Humanity, Centrality, Duality, Vitality, Illuminosity, Creativity, Morality, Normality, Servility, Posterity, and Finality. The first four of these sections contribute to social advancement, the next six sections to personal advancement and the last two sections to future advancement. However, there is an interaction between the social and personal and this means that there is no hard and fast distinction between them. Elements of both these modes of advancement can be found in all these sections. Their contents are summarised very briefly as follows:

Part One – Social Advancement

1. Unity: Bringing us all Together

This deals with the unity of the human race and the holistic view by which we look at ourselves as a whole to keep ourselves on track. Otherwise we will fall out with each other and our progress impeded by senseless conflict and wars. At this time, the principal impediments obstructing our way include racism, religion, nationalism, class and all the other artificial barriers that we have set up to divide ourselves unnecessarily and often catastrophically. Thus, achieving greater unity is necessary to our further progress as a species.

2. Humanity: Believing in our Futue

This is about the importance of believing in humanity and its future. The lack of such belief can only ensure that we have no future. Being a human being means belonging to the human race, and this relationship is much more important than belonging to a nation, race, religion, organisation or whatever. This human perspective therefore needs to be brought to the fore and treated with the importance it deserves.

3. Centrality: Developing the Middle Ground

This concerns humanity's central position in the universe between the very small and very large. By increasing our knowledge and understanding of this middle ground, we consolidate and vindicate our place in the universe.

4. Duality: Looking to Both Sides Critically

The dualist view is seeing both sides of argument and avoiding extremes of thought and behaviour. Extremism and single-minded stupidity can only delay and divert us from our onward path. Dualism is contrasted with monism which is seeing things from one point of view without regard to the value of opposing opinions.

Part Two – Personal Advancement

5. Vitality: Building Ourselves Up

This is about building up our inner strength to enhance vitality and improve intuitive thinking. Only steadfast integrity can give us the will to do what has to be done to ensure our future. It is getting in touch with our inner potential and improving our intuitive powers.

6. Illuminosity: Enlightening Everything

We introduce the light of knowledge and understanding to combat negative thinking. Everything inside us needs to be brought into the light so that its value in advancing us can be ascertained. This is making ourselves available to the world at large and showing what we do for others.

7. Creativity: Making the Most of our Artistic Potential

This is about exploiting our creative abilities for the greater good. Our future depends on our arriving at creative solutions to our boundless problems. The source of creativity is intuition and knowing what it is can help us to use intuition for the best creative purposes.

8. Morality: Disciplining Ourselves Purposefully

The exercise of self-restraint and self-discipline is required to achieve our goals as Immorality and self-indulgent can only stand in our way of advancement. We can cultivate our moral sense and use evaluative notions to find out how to be true to ourselves.

9. Normality: Having a Society Based on Norms

Normality refers to the need for a normal society based on specific norms which are made clear to everyone. At present, no one knows how they are supposed to behave because of the 'anything goes' mentality.

10. Servility: Serving Humanity Dutifully

We are here to serve and make ourselves useful to one another. By serving one another as diligently as we can, we ensure the smooth running of society which can then build towards a better future. We find our place in society in some form of service and thereby enter into a civil covenant whether we think of it in that way or not.

Part Three – Future Advancement

11: Posterity: Benefiting Future Generations

In thinking about our future, we cannot avoid thinking about posterity. We can best ensure our future by contributing to the welfare and progress of future generations. Posterity may be observing us in the present though unable to interfere with us. We need no God watching over when there is the prospect of posterity doing so.

12: Finality: Contributing to the Cosmos

The final legacy that we leave behind is the Cosmos which contains all human achievements. The notion of Cosmos thus gives meaning and purpose to all that we have achieved as a species that makes a difference by adding to the content of the universe. By using the Cosmos to give order and structure to our achievements we can better appreciate the value of our individual contributions, however small and insignificant they may seem to us.

Looking with joy to the future. In the quest for right ways of thinking about life and living, these twelve sections point to the future with joyful anticipation. They aim to show that we have nothing to fear from the future and that we can face up to grim realities cheerfully and purposefully. They reflect at least four philosophies or ways of thinking – holism, dynamism, dualism and prospectivism. The first two of these are diametrically opposed to each other. Holism brings everything together in one static view of things, while dynamism emphasises change and movement to new and unanticipated states of existence. The dualist interaction between these viewpoints resolves the ancient problem of the one and the many. And dualism in its turn is resolved by a prospectivism that looks to the future instead of resorting fearfully to past solutions. All our conflicts, divisions, arguments, uncertainties, and indecisions are resolvable in terms of what we have to do to make a better future for ourselves. This book hopefully begins this necessary process of advancing ourselves by reason and sympathy and good humour. Admittedly, it is a compilation of essays and writings with many repetitions and inconsistencies, but it is a start. It is also an atheistic philosophy showing that we can do just fine without a god glowering down on us. We can take responsibility for our own future by planning ahead instead of praying and kowtowing to something that demonstrably does not exist.

B. Prologue on Progress
The need to make real and lasting progress

Advancing humanity in this context means making progress in a limited and not an absolute sense. This book is not intended to be a full scale utopian plan promoting progress. It is about clearing the way, levelling the path and providing the tools and skills needed to make our way forward. To that end, the book suggests preconditions to making a better future for ourselves both as individuals and as a species. It is therefore a practical philosophy rather than a body of theoretical knowledge. It involves piecemeal social engineering and not utopian social engineering.[3] The approach is therapeutic and educational as opposed to doctrinal and definitive. It is therefore about curing defects, and improving ways of thinking, and it is not a mandatory political programme.

In some quarters, progress has become something of a dirty word. It is blamed for everything going wrong in our society. The argument is that the unbridled progress of industrial society has led to the pollution of the planet. Material progress can only further deplete the planet's scarce resources. It can also threaten the environment and other species living on the planet. The counter argument is that we need to make further progress to overcome the flaws and deficiencies arising from previous spurts of progress. Only further technological advances can undo the damage that we have done to the environment. This includes nuclear and chemical waste as well as carbon based emissions. Further progress will enable us to make better use of scarce resources. The more organised we become, both nationally and internationally, the more we will find ways to make better use of our waste products and reduce our dependency on raw materials. More international co-operation will also enable us to go to the moon and other planets in search of material resources.

Progress in general is not necessarily detrimental to the environment. Indeed, it is desirable as long as making more progress can bring us more into harmony with our environment. The more organised we become internationally the more we can co-operative to reduce our impact on the environment. It is sometimes argued that ancient peoples were more in tune with their environment than modern peoples. In fact, they often destroyed their environment. The first inhabitants of Australia and New Zealand destroyed the fauna and flora when they arrived and changed their respective environments out of all recognition. Ancient peoples were more at the mercy of their environment than in tune with it, in so far as they lacked understanding of their surroundings. They could only manipulate it to their advantage within their limited knowledge of plants, animals, local weather and the like. In that regard, the object of progress is to overcome the arbitrariness of nature so that we can use it to our advantage. What we are now learning to do is how to use nature without destroying it in the process. In that regard, we certainly surpass our ancestors.

Progress is not uniform but directional. We tend to make great progress in specific directions while everything else remains much the same. The impetus of progress then peters out. There is a limit to the extent that computers can transform our lives. If progress is not resumed in another direction then society may begin to fall apart and a definite decline begins. 'Not to go forward in the way of life is to go backward' or 'not to make progress in the way we live is to go back' (as quoted above). Once we stop moving forward, we can only go backward because our complex modern society is not stable entity and must go in one direction or the other. It has to move forward otherwise its internal tensions may make it fall apart. A stationary state such as the ancient Empire of China tends to stagnate and not go anywhere. When we cease to organise ourselves and make continuous economic and intellectual progress, we inevitably find other goals to occupy us, such as fighting with amongst ourselves. We have been very good at that in the recent past. This would begin a downward spiral of a society wholly geared for warfare so that civilised standards are gradually lost as in the Dark Ages period of around 550CE to 800CE when literature and culture were thrown out because of religious fanaticism similar to what the Taliban, ISIS, or Daesh have been doing this century.

Immense progress in people's standards of living was made in the nineteen fifties and sixties. People in the seventies had more comfortable lives than those in the thirties. They had central heating, refrigerators, washing machines, cars and other consumer products. But little or no progress in living standards has been achieved since then. However, the progress in information technology through computers and digital products has been amazing. The idea that we might all have computers at home and carry them in our pockets seemed science fiction in the seventies but from the eighties onwards this has become the reality. There are doubtless countless areas in which we can continue ot make progress and make life better for ourselves. For example, we can protect our cities against the elements with giant umbrella-type structures, or we can construct buildings underground and so on.

Periods of progress invariably coincide with periods of optimism and confidence in our powers to better our condition. Periods of regression equally coincide with pessimism and lack of confidence in our ourselves. The aim of the prospectivist viewpoint is to perpetuate this optimism and make it a permanent feature of our educational system.

We can regard civilisation as our servant or as our master or tyrant. But this is to anthropomorphise a mere idea. In fact, we should regard civilisation as something we interact with to make the most of our lives. We can regard it alternately as for us or against us according to how we interpret our predicament. The following view of Alexander Raven is typical of the pessimistic view of civilisation as an enslaver instead of an enabler:

> Civilisation is not the servant of man. It is his master and tyrant; the superman that directs and enforces his actions to the greater glorification of Himself, and grants him the immense advantages of co-operation and specialisation only as a reward for abandoning his freedom of action to the higher aims of the communal spirit.[4]

Contrary to what Raven says, we can regard civilisation as an enabling, developing system that is full of imperfections but yet full of promise for the future. If we want to be served by it, we need to make sacrifices. Moreover, if civilisation is not serving our purposes then we are duty-bound to change it accordingly. Complaining about it and not doing something about it is not the way forward. Section ten of this book on *Servility* takes this more congenial and pragmatic view of civilisation.

How not to advance humanity

Progress in this book does not necessarily mean altering ourselves in arbitrary ways by means of genetic engineering or brain implants, least of all by converting ourselves into machine-like cyborgs or allowing super-intelligent robots to enslave us. Above all, we must never lose our humanity. Notably, the androids and holograms in the Star Trek television series are always striving to be more human and regret being less than human. For example, being human consists in being subject to unpredictable intuitions, such as are discussed in section seven below on *Creativity*. Such intuitive powers seem to have deep biological roots and perhaps result from quantum activity that will not be readily accessible to proponents of artificial intelligence.

The use of artificial intelligence to achieve so-called 'transhumanism' is not a viable means of advancing humanity if it threatens to our future as a species. We will not be any better for becoming machines, and the creation of intelligent robots may lead to the extinction of the human race as some prominent persons have warned.[5] Artificial means of replacing missing limbs and organs and remedying other bodily defects are admissible and commendable. Equally laudable are attempts to prolong our lives and perhaps conquer death altogether. But using anything else to give one person artificial advantage over the rest of us is comparable to the use of drugs to enhance athletic performance. We don't need to create new types of human being when we are already an immensely diverse species.

It is therefore arguable that we would not advancing ourselves by cybernetic means such as inserting computer chips into brains, or adding devices to make us function more like machines than human beings. If enhanced individuals have mathematical or other skills that are beyond the normal human range of ability then they set themselves apart from the rest of us, like the X-men of the feature film series. This possibility is made worse by advocates of transhumanism who propound the following laws:

1. A transhumanist must safeguard one's own existence above all else.
2. A transhumanist must strive to achieve omnipotence as expediently as possible – as long as one's actions do not conflict with the First Law.
3. A transhumanist must safeguard value in the universe – as long as one's actions do not conflict with the First and Second Laws.[6]

These laws are extraordinarily egotistic. The First Law could sanction the killing of human beings who disapprove of transhumanism on the grounds that their opinions threaten the transhumanist's existence. Perhaps these laws are meant to be preceded by something like Asimov's Robotic Laws:

1. A robot may not injure a human being or, through inaction, allow a human being to come to harm.
2. A robot must obey the orders given it by human beings except where such orders would conflict with the First Law.
3. A robot must protect its own existence as long as such protection does not conflict with the First or Second Laws.[7]

The whole transhumanist enterprise is fraught with difficulties because it puts newfangled beings above and beyond us. We can never be happy with superior beings lording themselves over us, especially if they are of our own making.

It may be that that a so-called 'singularity' will be reached in which computers become a life form of their own. If this is the case, we could perhaps eliminate any threat to us by sending such life forms into outer space on long missions to far-off planets, solar systems and galaxies. They would be free of the biological constraints that presently confine us to the surface of this planet. They could be put on space vehicles containing seeds and frozen embryos that could spread life throughout the universe. In the meantime, we ourselves are slowly adapting to living in outer space by means of the experiments being conducted on the International Space Station. Thus, human beings may eventually be capable of thriving in outer space by making the physiological adaptations necessary to do so. That would be an advance well worthy of us since further advances could take place in outer space and leave the rest of us in peace.

The nature and origin of prospectivism

This book is forward-looking in a prospective manner. The prospective view is relatively new since it is more natural for us to live in the past and not think too much of the future since it is fraught with uncertainties. Only a stable and dependable society, such as we are now living in, can enable us to look to the future in any confidence that it will pan out as we expect it to do. Thus, we act as *prospectivists* when we look forward to the future whereas we are *retrospectivists* when we dwell in the past and despise the future. Retrospectivists include those monks and nuns who live cloistered in the past, rock'n'rollers who live as if rooted in the fifties and sixties, and anyone who believes that things were better in the past or in some legendary Golden Age. In contrast, prospectivists appreciate the past only as a gateway to the future. The word 'prospective' originates from the Latin 'prospectus' which is the past participle of 'prospicere' – 'to look forward' or 'to look into the distance'.[8]

Thus, prospectivists use the past for future purposes, rather than looking back to the past as an end in itself. They look at the changes brought about through time, and use an understanding of past events to anticipate something different in the future. The strength of the prospectivist's vision is such that the future is looked forward to, whereas the retrospective thinker is too pre-occupied with the past to waste time speculating about the future. Retrospectivism is the default position to which we all revert unless we consciously adopt a prospective view. We are all retrospectivists to some extent when we immerse ourselves in the past and make too much of it. But if we want to make the most of our lives, we should also be prospective and make use of our retrospective tendencies to balance them with our prospective ones. Studying history helps us to avoid repeating the mistakes of the past. We learn from history but we need not dwell on it. We don't need to go back and relive the past as if it were *ipso facto* better than the present. We can enjoyably relive past lives such that of Samuel Pepys in his diary but in so doing we learn how things were different in the past and the same in some ways but no better overall.

The distinction between the prospective and retrospective views dates back at least to the talk that H.G. Wells (1866-1946) gave to the Royal Institution in 1902 under the heading of *The Discovery of the Future*. Wells distinguished two attitudes of mind: the backward-looking 'legal mind', and the forward-looking 'creative mind'.

> The first of these two types of mind, and it is I think the predominant type, the type of the majority of living people, is that which seems scarcely to think of the future at all, which regards it as a sort of blank non-existence upon which the advancing present will presently write events. The second type, which is I think a more modern and much less abundant type of mind, thinks constantly and by preference of things to come, and of present things mainly in relation to the results that must arise from them. The former type of mind, when one gets it in its purity, is retrospective in habit, and it interprets the things of the present, and gives value to this and denies it to that, entirely in relation to the past. The latter type of mind is constructive in habit, it interprets the things of the present and gives value to this and that, entirely in relation to the things designed or foreseen.[9]

Wells acknowledged that both these are extreme attitudes of mind and that "the great mass of people occupy an intermediate position between these extremes".[10] But he argued that our civilisation is increasingly oriented towards the future and towards coping with all the problems that our increasing complicated society is creating. He fully recognised the precarious nature of human existence:

> One must admit that it is impossible to show why certain things should not utterly destroy and end the entire human race and story, why night should not presently come down and make all our dreams and efforts vain. It is conceivable, for example, that some great unexpected mass of matter should presently rush upon us out of space, whirl suns and planets aside like dead leaves before the

breeze, and collide with and utterly destroy every spark of life upon this earth.... It is conceivable, too, that some pestilence may presently appear, some new disease, that will destroy, not 10 or 15 or 20 per cent of the earth's inhabitants as pestilences have done in the past, but 100 per cent; and so end our race.[11]

Despite these considerations, Wells thought that "by an act of faith" we can overlook such remote possibilities and believe most fervently "in the greatness of human destiny".[12] Wells was entirely right as we cannot live our lives worrying about what may not happen. During the Cold War period, when a nuclear Armageddon was a distinct possibility, most people went about their daily business hardly giving it a thought. And we were proved right to do so, since nothing came of these remote fears. Even during the Cuban missile crisis of 1962, there was no panic in the streets as most people didn't really want to believe that a nuclear war was impending. These days, there is probably more chance of a nuclear attack from malignant terrorists than there was then. But once again people don't want to dwell too much on such possibilities.

We must have courage in our future to ensure that we do have a future. People nowadays have even less rosy and optimistic about future prospects than in Wells's day. Clearly, the human race needs to work very hard to ensure its place in the future, in view of its environmental destructiveness and the endless possibility of catastrophes such as comets, volcanoes, plagues, and wars spoiling our promising future. Nevertheless, we have to believe in the future prospects of the human race before these prospects can be realised. Therefore, it is important to have a forward-looking view which, following Wells, we have called 'prospectivist' as opposed to the 'retrospectivist' or backward-looking view. Wells was only mistaken in seeing these two views as being antagonistic to some extent. As already argued, the prospective view is built onto the retrospective one which we are all born into.

The good of civilisation requires that people look as much to the future as to the past. We must think about what will be better in the future and what will benefit future generations. The study of the future ought now to be pursued just as rigorously as the study of the past. And the latter study ought to be in the service of the former one. Our greatness as a species lies in what we are about to make of the opportunities before us. It does not lie in our feeble and uncoordinated actions in the past. It consists in what is to come and in our present efforts to ensure that things are better in the future. Everything happening in the past has been, as Wells said, "but the twilight before the dawn" and past accomplishments have been "but the dream before the awakening."[13] Our future thus consists in looking to the future, and this book attempts to work out that viewpoint as consistently as possible. Finally, Wells sums up our future prospects as follows:

> We are creatures of the twilight. But it is out of our race and lineage that minds will spring, that will reach back to us in our littleness to know us better than we know ourselves, and that will reach forward fearlessly to comprehend this future that defeats our eyes.[14]

Part One

Social Advancement

1 Unity: Bringing us all Together

> Man - of all ages and cultures - is confronted with the solution of one and the same question; the question of how to overcome separateness, how to achieve union, how to transcend one's individual life and find at-onement.
>
> Erich Fromm, *The Art of Loving*, (1957) [1]

A. The Increasing Unity of Humanity

Our increasing concerns for humanity overall. Our future advancement depends greatly on our coming together as a species to pursue our common ends. If we fail to come together, we inevitably fall apart and start fighting each other, as has happened so often in the future. The Scottish poet, Robert Burns dreamt of a time when "man to man the world o'er shall brithers be for a' that".[2] The dream of the brotherhood of man still remains and need never be ruled out altogether. If we stop working towards it then we are truly a worthless species. The more intercommunication there is between people and peoples, the more understanding of each other we can acquire and the more we can work towards bringing people together instead of fighting pointlessly between ourselves.

Humanity is more of a self-conscious entity than it ever was in the past. The more we know and understand about what is happening to people throughout the world, the more we realise how much we have in common. We are more conscious than ever that we all belong to the same species. Everything that is happening in the world conspires to bring us closer together. The credit crisis of 2008 onwards shows us that the affairs of relatively small nations such as Greece can have repercussions for the entire world economy. We belong increasingly to humanity with every concern that we show towards members of our species in far-off parts of the world. Moreover we will only make further progress in getting rid of poverty and inequality by coming ever closer together politically and economically so that every nation on Earth reaches the same level of prosperity. Any political activity that threatens to reduce that unity is to be deplored and denounced.

The very word 'humanity' has grown more important in its meaning and complexity. It has become a unifying focal point for all of us and is a legal term of international significance at least since the Nürnberg trials for crimes against humanity in 1945/46. No nation ill-treating any part of its citizenry can now ignore the concerns of the international community. As a result, during the 20th century a concern for humanity as a whole grew as a focal point bringing all nations together. We now talk about the 'international community' disapproving of or sanctioning this or that nation for its misdeeds. The universal acceptance of human rights and the rule of law throughout the world have brought us closer together in a common system of thought. We all now belong to 'the global village'[3] which unifies us with the complex communications ringing round the world, of which the World Wide Web is only one example.

As a result, wars and disorders throughout the world now concern us all. Such an unprecedented unity of thought and purpose should give us an unparalleled opportunity to put our warring past entirely behind us. The difficulties in achieving this are purely political. There is a lack of strong and visionary political leadership to bring this about. Political leaders are typically inward looking and put their national concerns above all others. Such nationalism ought to be a thing of the past considering how interrelated and bound together we now are as single species. Globalisation is still gathering pace as trade and communications becomes ever more connected and ubiquitous.

Historically, the human race has always been a fractious and divisive species prone to go to war with each other at the drop of a hat. We form ourselves all too easily into opposing tribes whose rivalries all too often descend into violence and war. However, we can now develop a unified world-wide community and break out of that cycle of violence if we put more effort into it than we are at present. The opportunity is there but it may well be missed if the parochial concerns of community, nation and religion are allowed to prevail. The European Union has been showing the way forward even though its future is now in the balance because of that lingering factionalism and lack of political foresight involving Brexits, Grexits and the like.

Unity of nations makes the collapse of civilisation less likely. Civilisations in the past were localised and confined to specific areas of the globe. They were liable to collapse and disappear, often for internal reasons. However, civilisation now spans the globe and most nations on Earth are now busily adopting the consumer society and finding ways to trade with the rest of the world. It seems unlikely that the world-wide civilisation will collapse entirely as it is increasingly able to absorb localised collapses. It may now be too big to fail because of its increasing size and complexity. The feeble excuse that all civilisations fail in the end simply no longer applies to the Great World Civilisation now developing before us. In short, the more unified we are as a species the less likely we are to experience decline or extinction.

B. Increasing That Unity

Increasing the unity of humanity is important not just because it helps to ensure our future but also because we vindicate ourselves by unifying as an intelligent species that has goals worthy of itself, such as exercising its responsibilities for other life forms and the planet as a whole. Our growing unity is our future, and anything that divides us belongs to our past. Our history consists in our increasingly reaching out to each other and bringing humanity together as a whole. This is the justifiable side of imperialism, colonialism, commerce and capitalism, even though these historical movements had serious negative effects such as slavery, exploitation, ethnic cleansing and the like. Our future must lie in continuing this historical trend towards political and social unification throughout the planet. A global monoculture is inevitable in which each part of the world makes its individual contributions without hiving itself off from the whole or making itself out to be superior to all the rest.

This globalisation of humanity needs to be measured and controlled to ensure that it encompasses every part of globe and gives people freedom and opportunities everywhere. It need not happen piecemeal so that one part benefits more at the expense of other parts. Agencies such as the United Nations, the World Bank, and the International Monetary Fund need to be more supportive than punitive of poorer and badly run nations. The actions of the international community must be aimed at benefiting the people in suffering nations rather than their governing bodies, big business or other vested interests. The people of a country are not to be blamed or punished for the incompetence or oppressive nature of their government since no electoral system is proof against the rise of tyranny (*vide* the Nazi regime in Germany). The will or interests of the people are not always reflected in their government no matter how 'democratic' it purports to be. Therefore, the people should not suffer unnecessarily because of the failure of their respective governments. Any action interfering with standing governments must be overwhelmingly decisive and involve concerted force since half-hearted, badly planned actions can be more disastrous than if nothing at all is done (*vide* the problems of the Middle East and especially Syria). It is serving the people that matters most, as is argued in section six on *Servility* below.

We serve humanity not by perpetuating the ephemeral divisions of nation, religion and race but by coming together by means of a growing global interactivity which is already taking place before our eyes. The fact is that monoculturalism, not multiculturalism, is the reality now facing us. If we are to avoid the wars, enmities and divisions of the past, then our allegiance to the human race must supersede all other allegiances, lest we forget what we all have in common as human beings. This unifying process transcends multicultural plurality, together with all superficial and ephemeral divisions of nation, race, and religion, to produce a world view common to all humanity. Even racial distinctions are on their way to extinction; a few more generations of global intermixture will make racial boundaries impossible to discern. A monoculture is now establishing itself around the world as we become increasingly interlinked by our communications, trade and tourism. Only a strengthening of the global monoculture can ensure the ending of poverty, inequality and injustice which our artificial national and religious divisions can only prolong.

Monoculture does not imply complete uniformity of culture. The institution of a global monoculture does not make human culture exactly the same throughout the globe. The differences between cultures can be based on historical antecedents and not on ideological or religious prejudices that separate cultures from human culture as a whole. The emphasis is on the differences between peoples rather than on the divisions between nations, races or religions. All the different peoples of the world can be proud of their respective past histories together with their language, literature and the arts while incorporating them in the monoculture of the world. For example, the Scots are proud of their heritage and their cultural peculiarities but these have not prevented Scots from participating fully in British, European and World affairs without losing their Scottish identity. This contrasts, for example, with the historical position of Jewish people who have in the past hived themselves off from any society in which they participated and they suffered the consequences thereof. The Islamic religion is similarly too adept of cutting itself off from other cultures, for example, in its clinging to the retrogressive Shariah law. In contrast, the Scots peopled the world like the Jews but never formed provocative ghettoes that invited pogroms and other atrocities. They were highly individualistic and liked to blend into whatever background in which they found themselves. Similarly, nations such as North Korea that enforce a narrow ideology on their populace become nothing but pariah states ostracised by the international community. Thus, when cultural differences are based on history, language, literature and the arts rather than on ideological or religious dogmatism they can contribute to the global monoculture and not be antipathetic or antagonistic towards it.

An advancing monoculture is the product of a constant interaction between the interests of (1) the élite and (2) the masses, and between (3) the activity of *avant garde* aspirations and (4) the passivity of dominant traditions. The interaction between these four elements is roughly represented in the following quadrifoil matrix:

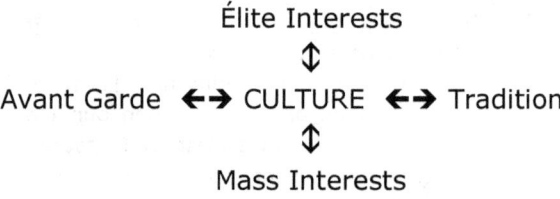

An Interactive Cultural Quadrifoil Matrix

The influence of the élite. The élite is composed not so much of 'the establishment' (as it is nebulously called) but of influential persons, celebrities, media personalities and all the people who influence fashionable opinions and fashions in general. Thus, for example, the popularity of the Beatles pop group became assured when the élite young people in universities and colleges recognised their talent and their interest spread to the general public. The popularity of Facebook similarly began with the élite in Harvard and other Ivy League universities.

The influence of the masses. Public opinion in general emanates from the mass of nameless people who make up most of the population. Thus, the mass interest in the lives and lusts of celebrities dominates tabloid newspapers. The masses are prone to mob-like extremes which are sometimes generated by excessive media activity, For example, the public hysteria that followed the death of Diana, Princess of Wales was whipped up by blanket media attention on this tragic death. The frenzy was compounded by an endless succession of images of this clothes horse princess.

Avant garde aspirations can be generated either by the élite or the masses. But the tendency is for the élite to be in the vanguard of most of the trends and pre-occupations. Thus, for example, the dominance of so-called 'political correctness' is fostered by the dominance of a leftist élite (there is more on this subject in section 9 below on *Normality*).

Tradition is similarly derived from both sides but mass of people tends usually to be on the side of tradition. They are often called the 'silent majority' and are usually not accurately represented by the pollsters seeking to predict elections and fashionable trends. The prolongation of tradition tends to stultify society and it needs to be stirred up from time to time to keep civilisation moving forward.

Thus, we see that culture is the product of an ongoing interaction between all these opposing interests. Understanding this is an important key to our bringing humanity together in terms of our common interests. But the role of the élite is paramount in initiating novelty, innovations, fashions and the like. Thus élitism is unavoidable as far as meaningful social change is concerned. Civilisation benefits by bringing people together in the face of new interests. Getting rid of élites is characteristic of violent revolutions as in France and Russia and leads to anarchy and not necessarily to a better future. It is better to change people's mind through philosophy and new ways of thinking, and the idea of atonement is useful in that regard.

C. Political Atonement

If we unify ourselves in tackling the problems common to us all, we go a long way towards justifying our prominent place on this planet. To that extent we can must seek *atonement* – 'at-one-ness' – in which we become at one with that which extends beyond our selfish selves. By such atonement we bring ourselves together both as a species and as individuals. Thus, in the context of human unity, we vindicate ourselves at the very least by actively seeking political and personal atonement.

Political atonement refers to the political activity needed to bring our species together in pursuit of our common goals and concerns. The divisions of nations, races, religions, sects and organisations of all kinds are only temporary, fictional illusions specific to cultural periods. What is permanent and universal about our species lies in our constantly striving to unify ourselves and achieve a better future for itself and for the planet as a whole.

If anything is sacred about humanity, it is its unity. It is sacred only in the sense that humanity can transcend itself to become more than it is at the present time. Such transcendence is only possible when its unified actions make more of its surroundings, such as building huge buildings and bridges, creating stunning works of art and music, soaring away to the moon, and accomplishing great things together. We can imagine humanity being better than it is at present, and in aiming for this imagined ideal we can achieve a better state. By this constructive and realistic use of our imagination, we find reasons to believe in humanity's relative importance in the great scheme of things. Thus, humanity can transcend itself, for example, (1) by improving its environment, (2) by improving its understanding of itself and its place in the universe, and (3) by its unified activity aimed at ensuring its future and the future of life in general. This transcendence is achieved by viewing ourselves as we are and by seeing what we can do to further both ourselves and life in general. However, this does not mean allowing robots and computers to take over. We need to ensure that cybernetic advances are achieved for our benefit as biological beings and not for some idealised view of us becoming indistinguishable from machines. This is a can of worms or Pandora's box that is best left closed in the meantime as we have enough problems facing us without creating yet more.

Religion has always found reasons to belittle us, and it has thereby impeded the transcendence of humanity to a better state. Achieving greater unity is one of the ways by which we can transcend ourselves as a species whereas our disunity degrades and lessens us. There are still too many instances of degradation that prevent our unified advancement. For example, there is the political disunity that leads to needless conflict, war and massacre. Take, for example, the disastrous division of Ireland into north and south, the catastrophic partition of the Indian sub-continent into India and Pakistan, the heartless fragmentation of Palestine into Israel, Jordan, Gaza and the West Bank, and the needless partition of Cyprus into the Turkish-speaking north and the Greek-speaking south. These resulted largely from British blunders that involved political breaches of previously viable unity and brought about slaughter and untold misery and suffering for countless people. They were purely politically expedient measures with no long-term strategy behind them. For example, the British blundered in not ensuring in 1948 that Palestine became a secular state instead of being divided into religious groupings that are still fighting each other to this day. There was no absolute need for these divisions and they gave no long-term benefit for the people subjected to them. Only the politicians, demagogues, idealists, plutocrats, arms dealers and the like could possibly gain anything of value from such ruptures. And most of that gain is entirely idealistic and in people's heads; it bears little or no relation to the reality of human benefit.

Historically, the winding down of the British Empire during the 20th century was a big mistake. It was a possible nucleus for the political and economic unification of humanity. Unfortunately, the limited, liberal ideas of self-determination overrode the interests of humanity as a whole. The British Empire was far from being perfect but what it offered undeveloped parts of the world was usually better than what existed before and also better than what came after it as, for example, the people of Sierra Leone will attest. The British let down the peoples of the nations under their care when they abandoned them to the whims of tyrants and dictators. In practice, the freedom of self-determination given to nations meant the freedom of tyrants to intimidate and oppress their peoples. The interests of the peoples of these nations were not served by handing over power to persons unprepared or unsuited to wield it properly. Greater political autonomy within the aegis of the British Empire should have been thought out and implemented instead of casting these nations adrift. The resultant British Commonwealth of Nations is only the bare minimum of what could have been achieved.

The continual expansion of the European Union is an obvious example to the world of how overall global unification is politically and economically possible if we work hard enough at its accomplishment. Despite all the economic difficulties and all the doubts about the euro currency nations still want to join the EU, and its imminent collapse is not a foregone certainty even if the departure of the UK puts its future in doubt. Truly the breakup of the EU would be a tragedy for the whole world and an anachronistic reversal of the trend towards greater unity.

In summary, therefore, the political will to achieve greater unity is required. Humanity does have a future in so far as we individually and collectively recognise the importance of our unity as a species and make the most of this unity to create a future for ourselves. What is lacking at this time is the vision and political will to aim for greater unity in the future. Hopefully, the contents of this book will stimulate a political drive towards such unity.

D. The Role of the Holistic View

The need to achieve unity becomes even more apparent when we take a holistic view of things. That view makes it clear that we must think in terms of coming together as a species. The more disunited we are, the more appear to be a disordered, self-destructive shambles from a holistic viewpoint. Moreover, looking at things as a whole does not come easy to us. We have learnt this skill relatively recently. Indeed, the holistic view is unique to human beings. We are the only *holistic* species on this planet, as we alone can look at things as a whole, as long as we make up our minds to do so. Other animals are too rooted in the here-and-now to see the bigger picture. They are governed by instinct and present exigencies more than we are, as we can learn by upbringing to be more than instinctive or impulsive creatures. Thus, the holistic view is not acquired by instinct; we must learn it by education and experience. The task of achieving this holistic frame of mind is addressed here.

The holistic view is incompatible with extremism of any kind. It is inclusive of differing views and does not elevate any view and make it exclusive of the others. The extremist typically focuses on one view to the exclusion of all others. Anyone looking at things as a whole cannot regard one view to be the whole truth of the matter when seeing its merits and demerits in relation to opposing views. The holistic view combats extremism by incorporating dualism and its appreciation of opposing points of view. Extremism results from one point of view being favoured to exclusion of all opposing ones. However, dualism has the problem of discriminating or judging between these points of view. The holistic view steps outside these points of view and facilitates decisiveness as to which is to be preferred. Anyone who is not holistic minded can be vulnerable to extremism.

Thus, a good test of whether a person is vulnerable to an extremist mentality is to ascertain the extent of their broadmindedness and openness to alternative ways of thinking. There is more on the role of dualism in broadening our minds in section 4 on *Duality*.

Neither science nor religion looks at things as a whole. They cannot give us the whole picture. Science is too specialised and religion is too otherworldly and rooted in narrow beliefs. The holistic view avoids scientific specialisation on the one hand, and religious unworldliness and credulity on the other hand. It is not specialised in that it is all-embracing and all-encompassing. It is not unworldly and credulous as it takes us into the real world to do the best that we can as individuals and make it a better place to live in and prosper. Holism gives us an informed wisdom that is ever open to continuous development in the light of further thought, experience and information. It gives substance to the practical kind of wisdom characteristic of wise men down the ages. It is therefore a philosophy to be taught and understood; it is not a religion to be preached or believed in uncritically.

From the holistic viewpoint we can ascertain the extent of our ignorance of things. We can't do anything about our lack of knowledge and understanding unless we see the full extent of our deficiencies. What we do not know can never be grasped without stepping outside ourselves and broadening our imaginations in that way.

Holism takes account of all points of view without promoting any single viewpoint as being the answer to everything. It is therefore a philosophy which involves thinking about things critically and carefully. The holist can never be a single-minded demagogue or charlatan enforcing his views on other people. He can only be a teacher and never a preacher.

Moreover, the holist view does not reduce the individual to the whole. On the contrary, it is suffused with the Autonomy Principle which states that each individual is an autonomous person capable of unique and irreplaceable development. We are all ends in ourselves and the role of society is to provide the framework in which our ends can be achieved. The holist view therefore works from the individual upwards by ensuring that each person adopts that view for their own ends and not because it is imposed from above *ex cathedra*.

The role of self-improvement. The wise person looks at the whole picture in doing worthwhile things. To know the world as a whole is to know ourselves as a whole. But we can never know enough and our education never ceases unto death. In striving to improve our knowledge and understanding we improve ourselves, and self-improvement is something we can all do for ourselves.

By improving ourselves we contribute to the future of our species. We do things better than before, and therefore have more self-confidence, treat other people better, work more efficiently, and waste less time and money. When we all work together in improving ourselves, co-operation becomes more important than competition. *Self-improvement means competing with ourselves and not with other people.* There is no use emulating other people or trying to be better than them when it does not become us as individuals. We can discover for ourselves what we are suited for. In this way, we make enemies of our own inertia and incompetence, and not of other people. Thus, there is no point in thinking that we are as good as or better than other people if we lack the self-knowledge to know that we can do better.

This ethos of co-operative self-improvement brings us together as a purposeful species as opposed to being the self-destructive species that we are too often even today. This is important because humanity must make its own future, just as life has made itself in the universe in the past and is doing so at present. No creator is required as we create our own experience of life and our happiness. We have become responsible for the future of life because we know how important it is to the natural development of the universe. The forces of the universe have complexified its contents over time, and life is the end product of that process. Life has been responsible for its own complexification by improving its means of survival by reproduction (as is shown in my book *The Promise of Dualism*). We in our turn are responsible for our inner development and for cultural progress in supporting and participating in it. We are at the apex of biological advance because we know what is happening in the universe, and that knowledge makes us responsible for ensuring the best possible use of it, both as individuals and as a species. For example, we can use that knowledge to propagate and support life on this planet and elsewhere, as well as to people the moon and life-sustaining planets.

In this way, the broader view helps us to make sense of our lives and gives them purpose and direction that they may otherwise lack. We can only do these things for ourselves alone as there are no outside sources for us to rely upon, and it is a sign of our maturity as a species that we can acknowledge that fact and carry on regardless.

Finally, we are here to do as much in society as will make our lives as fulsome and wholesome as possible. In the process, we learn new ways of thinking and being while seeing the whole picture which is constantly changing and developing. Thus, constant adaptation to realities is the key to our survival and our future prosperity. In that way, we are encouraged to exercise our wisdom on a daily basis and demonstrate our worth to ourselves and others.

E. Advancing by Means of the Holistic View

We need to be in the right frame of mind to advance ourselves both as individuals and as a species. Thus, the holistic view aims to promote life-enhancing frames of mind which are positive, sympathetic, inclusive and developmental:

❖ *Positive frame of mind* – This looks forward to the future with hope and optimism. It sets out deliberately to avoid being depressed, self-defeating, or self-abnegating. The exercises of Vitality, Illumination and Optimism contribute to this frame of mind.

❖ *Sympathetic frame of mind* – This refers to a sympathetic view of humanity and its diversity as opposed to a negative, self-destructive view. The Humanism exercise is particularly relevant here.

❖ *Inclusive frame of mind* – This includes all points of view by not dismissing any of them out of hand. It is therefore an open-minded view of things. The exercises of Science, Art and Cosmos give us reasons to venerate and exultate all that is worthy of us as human beings.

❖ *Developmental frame of mind* – This refers to personal, intellectual, social and universal development.

Personal Development: Developing oneself personally is clearly preferable to degrading oneself with excessive, irrational and pointless behaviour. Such a development requires self-discipline and self-knowledge, whereas self-degradation results from lack of moral sense and self-criticism, as outlined in the Morality exercise.

Intellectual Development: Developing one's intellect requires critical thinking. By increasing one's knowledge and understanding by means of the exercises of Science and Art, It is not just being clever but being known to be knowledgeable and *au fait* with current affairs.

Social Development: Becoming a socially integrated and well-adjusted individual follows from a wide understanding of society and one's place in it. The Humanism exercise is particularly designed to encourage this development.

Universal Development: Developing ourselves universally means putting ourselves into the widest and broadest possible context. This is the particular aim of the Cosmos exercise which embodies everything that is universally worthy of us as human beings.

Ultimately, the holistic view is about doing worthwhile things by looking at the whole picture. True belief consists in serving humanity. Any other kind of belief does humanity a disservice in so far as it lessens and debases it. It is more important to have a justifiable faith in ourselves than an unjustifiable faith in some non-existent entity that is beyond our ken. Unless we are constantly justifying our existence by doing the best we can, we are existing but not living. Life is not meant to be easy and it is better to make it difficult for ourselves for the best possible reasons and not just do things because we want to feel better.

Too many people are too much into themselves nowadays. Self-obsession and self-centredness has become the norm. The whole picture is neglected in favour of immediacies. Many minds are full of mindfulness but empty of purpose. In the face of such inwardness, this book aims to take people out of themselves by emphasising the bigger picture and showing the benefits of looking at things as a whole.

We are supposed to humble ourselves before God but that takes us back into ourselves as the idea of God is essentially subjective; everyone can have their own idea of it. It has impeded our progress in many ways as no agreement can be reached about what it is. God is a perennial source of divisiveness and hostility; it is a disuniting entity that sets us against each other. It is no more than a figment of our imagination – as is argued in section 9 on *Normality*. There is no future in God, and it's time to move on and take responsibility for ourselves and the universe. Our knowledge of latter is growing by the day and it gives us a very clear view of our cosmic insignificance. We no longer need God to cower before or pretend arrogantly that we are made in its image. We now have to work on own image which is ugly enough from many perspectives.

A better approach is to be clearer about our place in the universe so that we make neither too little nor too much of ourselves by being stuck in one extreme or the other. This is possible by using the holistic view and other views offered here. By taking account of ourselves as a whole we can see better what our lives are really all about. We can be as large or small, as important or unimportant as we presume ourselves to be. By oscillating between these extremes we may move forward into a better future instead of being stuck in the logjam of the past. This view therefore exemplifies the dualist point of view already outlined in my book, *The Promise of Dualism* (2014).

But the dualist view is not enough if it leaves us stranded in the middle of things without a definite way forward. Logic and reason are also not enough. They can mislead us with dogmatic certainties, like the bankers and market makers who regard their algorithms as sacrosanct until complex realities prove them to be over-simplified and unreliable. We need to develop our intuitions so that we arrive at reliable certainties and make the right decisions. Our emotions can get the better of us when we are inwardly underdeveloped. We need layers of self-knowledge to gain control of our self-destructive impulses and to protect us against ourselves. This requires us to build up our inner being which is the source of intuition and this is the great gift that the holistic view can give us. We learn to think about things from the broadest and widest perspective and are more inclined to do the right thing by ourselves, by everyone and for the benefit of life in general. Thus, the holistic view is at least part of the answer concerning what the human condition is all about and what we can do to improve it and make it fit for the purposes of futurity.

The holist view takes in the whole human race and therefore abhors racism that divides people irrationally. Thus, human racism is the only admissible form of racism. As human racists we function at our best between the extremes of belief and scepticism and between the extremes of (1) believing human beings to be nothing but animals and (2) believing them to be in the image of God. This can be represented as follows:

Belief
↕
Animals ↔ *THE HUMAN RACIST* ↔ Gods
↕
Scepticism

Both the godly and animalist extremes lessen us as human beings. The one subordinates us to ideas or creeds of some sort. The other becomes an excuse for doing nothing at all as all beliefs can be reduced to nothing by verbal reasoning and over reliance on words and arguments. We are more than just animals by the fact that we can differentiate ourselves from them in our behaviour and in our feelings. But at the same time we make ourselves in our own image and we need no imaginary entity to look up to and demean ourselves thereby.

Those who have more regard for animals than for human beings might as well live with animals if living among us is not good enough for them. Those who put God before humanity similarly make themselves unsuited to human society since they aspire to divine standards beyond the rest of us who are sinful mortals unwilling to live up to the standards and demands of a god hanging over us. The godly view is dogmatically restrictive and the animalist view is sceptically indefinite. The holistic view rejects the extremes of absolute dogmatic belief on the one hand and of insipid scepticism on the other hand. Thus, it is at the middle of things that we constantly have the problem of what it is to be a human being and it is at the centre that we must find our answers, as is implied by the scientific, centralist view dealt with in section 3 below on *Centrality*.

2. Humanity: Believing in our Future

> Whilst the multitude of men degrade each other, and give currency to desponding doctrines, the scholar must be a bringer of hope, and must reinforce man against himself.
>
> R.W. Emerson, *The Method of Nature* (1841) [1]

A. Why Believe in Humanity?

We cannot advance as a species without having a constant and unswerving belief in humanity and its future. Practically everything we do has some future consequences that imply at least some belief in our future. The optimistic view goes further and assumes that humanity has a good chance of surviving into the far future. The chances of our being obliterated by comets, solar flares or other cosmic catastrophes are fairly slim. But the wise optimist expects humanity not to stupidly destroy itself through its own malevolent self-destructiveness. We must work hard to stave off such self-destructiveness, the potential for which lurks in every corner of our civilisation.

There is also the optimistic belief in the inevitable propagation of life throughout the universe and in our potential role in contributing to that propagation. Belief in humanity and its future is a prerequisite to that propagation since we are at present the only hope of it taking place at all. Such beliefs are fundamental but they are not absolute as they are contingent upon our actually doing things to ensure our future. They are also contingent on humanity being worthy of any future at all. Its deserving to have any future has always been in doubt. We always need to work hard to justify our existence on this planet.

These are not just matters of opinion. They are empirical matters which may be shown to be case by careful and impartial consideration of the facts. It is a fact that humanity has developed the ability to look into the future and question whether it can survive into the far future. When we look at the state of humanity at any point in time its future has always been in doubt. Plagues and other natural catastrophes have decimated our species, yet it has survived even though the odds may have been stacked against it. Whether we will continue to survive and thrive is always a matter of probability. But we can always find reasons for optimism if we want to find them. Whether we deign to face the fact that we will probably survive into the future is also a matter of choice.

There is no point in being wise unless it is for some purpose beyond ourselves. In the absence of any credible supernatural being, that purpose must involve a worthwhile contribution to humanity and its future. If we do anything meaningful in our lives, it is in the implicit expectation that it will have meaning in the future and that humanity will survive in the future. There is no need for anyone to explicitly believe in humanity's future. That belief is implicit in everything we do whether we are conscious of it or not. If what we do makes sense to others then we are taking part in human affairs by doing rational and sensible things. The fact of being a human being, who takes part in the activities of the human race, is also an implicit acknowledgement of this belief. No one needs to be put to the test about this as it is plain in the actions of even the most sceptical or misanthropic of people. If they behave rationally and do human things in their everyday lives, they show themselves to be as human as the rest of us.

Thus, belief in humanity is unavoidable whether it is implicit or explicit. The whole of humanity depends on everyone contributing in their own small way to that whole. We cannot make such contributions unless we think at least occasionally in global terms, as we do, for example, in the various anti-poverty campaigns and in our concerns for the victims of earthquakes, tsunamis, floods and famines. These arguments therefore show the importance of our getting together to ensure our own future which depends on all of us not only worrying about it from time to time but also doing something about it.

The dualist nature of humanity. The notion of humanity is not just inclusive of every human being. It also consists in what the individual human being contributes to it and what it can do for the individual in return. The interaction between these is what makes the human race work. Humanity is only an idea or notion and is not more important than the individual person. Our contribution to humanity is what we do in making the most of what we are as individual human beings. What humanity can do for us is to give us the opportunity to do our best as human beings. This includes our rights and responsibilities as mentioned in respect of the Civic Covenant mentioned below in section 10 on *Servility* (p. 196) Thus, humanity is not an end in itself but a means of benefiting us all as individuals. It ceases to benefit us in so far as it lets anyone down unnecessarily.

Why should we worry about the future of humanity, let alone believe in it? Most people never think about it from one day to the next. We are too concerned about our own present worries. The idea that humanity as a whole has a future, as opposed to the future of our respective races, nations, religions, organisations or other divisions, does not loom large among our concerns. Yet our everyday lives depend on the human race moving forward to better things. As argued above, if we don't progress we will regress to a worse kind of society. The forward movement unites us as a species and we make progress because the sense of direction gives us a common purpose. Without that, we will fall apart and start fighting each other as has happened so often in the past, and is still happening in many parts of the world even today. Working together to secure humanity's future gives us a common purpose, as does spreading life beyond Earth.

The worry is that, as a species, we can regress very easily to a more primitive state. If the idea of humanity fails to unify us, our society will sooner or later disintegrate into antagonistic units – nations competing to destroy other nations – religions fighting against other religions – races exterminating other races. There is no limit to the regression of humanity to more primitive conditions if we lose contact with each other and become insular groups that gradually forget their past traditions and ways of doing things. The Tasmanian aborigines and the Tierra Fuegans, whom Darwin mentions in his book *The Voyage of the 'Beagle'*, are examples of how isolated groups can lose their skills and forget how to fish and make fire.[2] Archaeological evidence clearly shows that their ancestors had these skills in their dim and distant past.[3] Anthropological research, such as in the book *The Mountain People*,[4] shows the mechanisms of increasing distrust and over-self-sufficiency leads to the breakdown of social structures and a regression of a more primitive form of society in which the rules of morality are forgotten. In Western Europe, the loss of literature and culture during the Dark Ages (around 550CE to 800CE) was brought about by excessive religious fanaticism which emptied the cities and filled the countryside with monasteries and nunneries, as Gibbon points out.[5] People ceased to care about humanity or its future and they lived only to serve a pitiless non-existent entity that does nothing for us. Thus, religion regresses and demeans us when it is pursued fanatically and mindlessly.

There is no substitute for self-belief. Belief in our future is essential to our survival as a species. Nothing outside ourselves in any way guarantees our future. However, it is arguable that our inner resources are strong enough to ensure our future, barring unforeseeable natural catastrophes coming from comets, solar flares and the like. This book begins the task of demonstrating the strength of these resources. Thus, there is no need for faith in God, aliens, angels or whatever, as our faith in ourselves and our future is all that we require. We can go beyond ourselves without invoking supernatural presences. Contributing to posterity gives us goals that serve the future instead of the dead past as in the case of religion. It is also argued in this book that we contribute to the Cosmos in our making sense of ourselves and our environment, as is argued in sections 11 and 12 on *Posterity* and *Finality*.

We have no choice but to take responsibility for ourselves since there is no concrete evidence of anything else in the universe that has the slightest regard for us. This is not a depressing fact but a challenge to us to justify our existence against all the odds. We can easily think ourselves into extinction, never mind all the external and internal threats to our future. Indeed, it is now fashionable to doubt that humanity has any future at all. We could exterminate ourselves by self-inflicted means such as diseases concocted by deluded scientists or a nuclear war precipitated by economic collapse or by conflicts over ever-diminishing resources. There are also lots of external threats that will do the business. We could be wiped out entirely by pandemics, comets, solar radiation or whatever our fertile imaginations can conjure up.

It is often assumed that because all civilisations in the past have collapsed sooner or later, ours is bound to follow suit. However, as argued above, past civilisations were localised whereas ours now spans the globe. It is arguable that as the world civilisation develops and strengthens through globalisation, it is equipped better than ever to deal with local collapses and catastrophes. If Europe, America and Asia were to collapse economically, the whole of Africa and Australasia may still survive the cataclysm and slowly revive the world economy.

Certainly, if we wait long enough any number of catastrophes could befall us. However, our survival as a species depends on self-belief. Once we stop believing in ourselves and our future, we deserve to become extinct. Survival means fighting for ourselves and this means finding reasons for our existence on this planet. We need to continually seek such reasons to reassure ourselves about our mission. Thus, our survival depends on finding reasons to survive and on staving off negative thinking to the contrary.

One of the biggest threats to our future at this time is a looming financial collapse due to unsustainable levels of debt throughout the world. An increased unity of nations and a reduction of national sovereignty seem necessary to organise the financial structure and eliminate debts. There is bound to be a rational solution if we work hard enough to find it. But an irrational response might result if we allow nations and organisations to compete and impose their own solutions on each other. This could lead to conflict, war and possible nuclear annihilation. Another rational alternative is for us to populate the moon and other planets, and use their resources including gold and silver to pay off our debts. These rational alternatives will be overlooked unless we response to our problems as a co-operative, unified and purposeful species. In short, we need to believe in our future as a unified species. Thus, we can only drive home the imperative need to achieve such a unity of purpose and direction for all humanity.

This belief is not intended to be religious. Believing in humanity does not mean worshipping it or putting it on a pedestal. It is a matter of taking a realistic view of what we are and what we can do together. We serve humanity in acting together for the benefit of everyone. As individuals, we serve humanity by being ourselves and by behaving ourselves. This means doing the best we can and being on our best behaviour at all times since posterity is always on the watch for us.

Our belief in ourselves is not sacrosanct but must be continually justified by our meaningful thoughts and actions. Our self-belief is subordinate to our understanding of ourselves and not *vice versa* as in the case of religious belief, which makes us believe that we are the image of God. This flatters us unduly. Studying ourselves is the way forward. The more we understand about the human condition the more we have concrete and realistic grounds for believing in what we are or are not as individuals and as a species. We need not believe in ourselves absolutely but only self-critically. The existence of anything totally remote from ourselves cannot be understood without getting lost in vain fantasies and imaginings that corrupt our intellect and hence our morals. God belief is absolute and uncritical; it permits us to think anything we like since whatever occurs to us intuitively is assumed to come from God rather than from our unconscious selfish desires. Killing unbelievers is the logical consequence of such absolute god belief. The humanist approach stresses the importance of starting from ourselves outward rather than starting from something outside ourselves that can only be imagined to exist.

Holistic view aims to bring us together. Holism is a philosophy to be understood rather than a religion to be adhered to. It is basic enough to be common to all humanity regardless of their religious beliefs or the lack of them. It constitutes a means of unifying humanity to ensure its future. To that end, it is necessary to transcend all viewpoints that divide us from each other. These viewpoints include the sectarian, national, racial, and religious divisions that are liable to set us against each other when they are treated as being more important than the interests of humanity as a whole.

B. The Importance of Humanity

We only choose to believe we are unimportant. Many people scoff at the thought that humanity has any importance whatsoever. They may argue that way as much as they like but arguing does not make it so. The evidence can be interpreted as much from one viewpoint as from the opposite one. Such detractors are over-impressed by our cosmic insignificance in the face of an unimaginably huge universe. As regards the human condition, we can be in two minds on the matter and, like Hamlet, regard ourselves as 'the beauty of the world, the paragon of animals' and at the same time nought but a 'quintessense of dust'.[6] The correct attitude surely is to take account of both views – both the pessimistic and optimistic views of our future. Total pessimism can't be right and complete optimism can't be either. We necessarily oscillate between the two extremes while making the best of the present. It is not certain whether the human race has a future or not but we can carry on regardless in the expectation of better things to come. Nevertheless, believing in future possibilities is all important.

We are only as important as we think we are. Our self-belief depends on our interpretation of the facts. If a person takes the pessimistic view too seriously then all the facts are inevitably interpreted from that point of view. The balanced view avoids such lop-sided thinking. One's life is only as trivial as one thinks it to be. But thinking does not make it so. It is only an opinion based on the facts. The same facts can be interpreted equally well in the other direction and used to support the opinion that one's life is not trivial. A balanced look at the facts is attempted in this book.

Some ways in which we are important. Humanity's primary mission is to make more of the universe than hitherto. It is primary in the sense that it is the default position from which we can begin to define our role on this planet. If we don't do anything else as a species we will have justified our existence. We are important in that respect because as far as we know at this time we alone are capable of doing this. In particular, we are also important at least in the following respects:

➢ We are important also because we are now responsible for the future of this planet and all the life-forms on it. No other species on Earth is competent to take on that role though we are ourselves diffident about taking on that role. We need to be much more organised in our handling of the planet and that entails much greater political integration and a greater purposefulness in what we do.

➢ We are important because we are increasingly unified as a species so that we can now communicate instantaneously with each other across the globe in a clear and unambiguous way that no other species can rival. This unity is spoilt by the national, religious, economic and language divisions which limit the extent to which we can communicate information.

➢ We are important as we are responsible for the next stage of evolution, namely, the machine age in which computers become increasingly intelligent and possibly self-regarding. We must be prepared to control of this situation and make sure that the value and importance of biological life is not overwritten by this development.

➢ We are important because we are the medial species between the very small and very large aspects of the universe. We are thus in a sense still at the centre of the universe even though it does not revolve around us. Our importance therefore lies in knowing that we are thus placed and in the increasing knowledge that we are acquiring about the very large and small aspects of the universe. (See the role of the scientist below for more on this in section 3 on *Centrality*.)

➢ We are important because we bring value, meaning and purpose and into being that does not exist otherwise. As far as we know nothing else in the universe can find any value, meaning, or purpose in it to the extent that we are doing in making sense of the universe and of everything in it.

➢ We are important because we can put ourselves into context and thereby see our faults as well as our good points. We can use contexts to humble ourselves as well as elevate ourselves, but it is only through practised contextualisation that we can arrive at a realistic view of what we are and what we can do.

➢ We are important because our quest for knowledge and understanding contributes to the cosmos which consists in the continuous ordering of the universe and the consolidation of its contents, as is mentioned below concerning the cosmos and role of the holist.

➢ We are important in that we are responsible for ensuring that there is a posterity which will be capable of looking back and seeing what we have or have not done for their benefit.

C. What Believing in Humanity Means

Humanity is a self-referential term. The notion of humanity does not exist as a thing but only as a self-referential term by which we refer back to ourselves as a species. There is no need at all for us to deify this notion since it is only a way thinking of ourselves. By its use, we can think of ourselves both critically and reverentially. We can see our strengths and weaknesses and do something about them. Only by such self-examination can we understand our place in the universe and hence where we are going and how we can get there.

We should therefore refer to humanity but not defer to it. Humanity is not an object of worship but a notion to which we can refer in considering our role in the universe and how we can unify ourselves to fulfil that role in the future. It is a point of reference and not an object of reverence. As a reference point it unifies us as a species. There is nothing to revere about humanity; we are too well aware of our defects and limitations as a species. It is no more than a context that we enter into and it is no more important than any other context in life. Its importance varies according to our situation and depends entirely on our individual judgment.

Love of humanity humanises us. Our love of people, animals, activities and objects takes precedence over love of humanity as an abstract notion. Love of humanity cannot mean murdering, injuring, threatening people or making their lives miserable. The latter are indicative of hatred of humanity. We are humanised by loving humanity in general when we identify with people in general by means of that notion. However, we can be dehumanised by loving humanity only as an abstract ideal that overlooks people altogether. Sacrificing people to further an idea or vision of humanity is characteristic of callous ideologies. Clearly, people are more important than ideas so that the idea of sacrificing the life of any person for an idea is anathema to the humanist view. However, we are humanised by the idea of humanity when it is applied as a way of making more of people and of benefiting them as individuals.

Belief in humanity and its future is a rational and practical belief compared with religious beliefs because it is focused on benefiting individuals. The more we are organised globally to care and cater for each other, the better life is for everyone. Business, trade and commerce cannot thrive without an implicit belief in humanity in respect of people's dependability, honesty and integrity. Without faith in people and their trustworthiness, our respective economies throughout the world must flounder. In contrast, religious beliefs can hinder enterprise by reducing people's self-confidence and their will to better themselves. Indeed, they undermine business activity and beggar people unless they are tempered with humanity and common sense. Around the world, even today, wherever religion has taken over and repressed secular activity, it has also abused human rights, reduced economic activity and undermined prosperity.

Believing in humanity also means acknowledging our moral superiority over other animals. This is the morality underlying our belief in humanity. Human beings are distinct from other animals in not having a fixed nature that compels us to act without thinking of the consequences. Other animals behave largely instinctively and without self-restraint, whereas we can put thought and restraint into our behaviour. Therefore, it is in our nature *not* to do what comes natural to us. This is because our behaviour is culturally determined to a large extent, and we acquire self-respect and self-discipline because it is in our interests to do so. We don't need any religion to enforce morality upon us. Our culture determines the range of behaviours available to us. We are free to choose within that range what we want to do or nor to do with ourselves. As a result, animal behaviour and the behaviour of primitive human beings tell us very little about what it is to be human. Such behaviour is more likely to be of the sort that we want to avoid. It is not at all exemplary.

Moreover, believing in humanity means countenancing all aspects of human behaviour. The ancient Roman playwright Terence famously wrote "I am a human being: I consider nothing human alien to me."[7] This is usually interpreted from a liberal point of view to express approval of immoral behaviour that comes naturally to us. However, it can equally be applied to behaviour that is unbecoming to us as human beings. In other words, it also expresses approval of moral behaviour as being 'human'. What it really means is that we should be prepared to consider the whole gamut of human behaviour as being 'human' regardless of whether we really approve of it or not. When we start judging people's moral behaviour as being 'inhuman' this is often a good excuse to kill them because we don't like what they are doing. This applies as much to leftists who don't like 'fascist' intolerance as to rightists who don't like self-indulgent permissivism.

D. What Are We Here For?

We are here to make sure that we have a future of some kind. The message of this book is that we are here to ensure the future of humanity and of life in general. This can never be proved to be the case beyond all doubt. But it is argued below that we have no future unless we assume this proposition to be true. We have to make assumptions about the meaningfulness of our existence otherwise we have no reason to do anything with our lives except eat, drink, be merry and not give a thought for tomorrow or anyone else but ourselves. Some people might be content with such an empty and pointless existence but most of us want to do more with our lives.

'All is vanity and chasing the wind' said the sceptic who wrote the Book of Ecclesiastes in the Bible. But this is only the case if we believe it to be the case. We don't live in vain when we see value and importance in the things we do. While belief is everything, the quality and truthfulness of our beliefs are also important. It is better to believe in positive, realistic and practical things that enrich our lives with diverse interests than to believe in impractical and implausible nonsense that trivialises our lives with meaningless ritual.

The truth should help us to make more of our lives while untrue things diminish us and hold us back in developing our true potential as human beings. In so far as religion is untrue, it holds us back both as individuals and as a species. People who believe in the falsities and absurdities of religion have low standards of truth and are liable to believe in anything. Their minds are inevitably closed to new thinking that conflicts with their beliefs. We need to remain open-minded if we are to make a better future for ourselves. It is therefore arguable that our future lies in going beyond religion by adopting a humanistic belief system within which both religious belief and scientific endeavour can find their respective places without antagonising and conflicting with each other. This book hopefully contributes to the establishment such a belief system.

Ultimately, we are here to reach for the stars. Humanity is as much a product of life's ever-expanding proliferation as any other life-form. It is therefore fitting that we should spread our species beyond this planet as we have ever imagined that we could do so in ancient tales and more recent science fiction. In so doing, we can fulfil our Noah's ark function in spreading other life forms throughout the solar system and beyond. In the words of Virgil – sic itur ad astra – such is the way to the stars.[8]

We are also here to take life forward to its next stage. Out of humanity, a more advanced life-form may emerge which takes advantage of the increasing computer power that we are now generating. We have to ensure that this life-form is not entirely mechanical or computational. It must have a biological basis so that it develops from us and not against us. We cannot allow the machines to take over and enslave us. The next stage of evolution must be taken on our terms because it benefits us as much as it benefits life in general.

Religionists typically complain that in medical science and other areas we are playing God and we are not fit to do so. Au contraire we are fit to play God as long as we know what we are doing and are aware of the consequences of what we are doing. We can make babies and change our genetic structure as long as we act within strict guidelines and apply essential safeguards. The bounds and limits to our activities need to be established and adhered to, and this means, for example, keeping things in perspective. In short, we need to be very disciplined and circumspect in our organised activities on this finely balanced planet of ours. This book provides many of the intellectual tools by which we can discipline ourselves, for example, by means of moral evaluation and by putting things into context.

E. The Bootstrap Species

> Human existence is different from that of all other organisms; it is in a state of constant and unavoidable disequilibrium. Man's life cannot "be lived" by repeating the pattern of his species; *he* must live. Man is the only animal that can be *bored*, that can be *discontented*, that can feel evicted from paradise. Man is the only animal for whom his own existence is a problem which he has to solve and from which he cannot escape. He cannot go back to the prehuman state of harmony with nature; he must proceed to develop his reason until he becomes the master of nature, and of himself.
>
> Erich Fromm, *The Art of Loving*, (1957).[9]

We have made ourselves what we are. We are the bootstrap species that has pulled itself up and created itself out of nothing. The behaviour of other species is largely dominated by inborn instinct. But our behaviour is moulded much less by genetic inheritance than by our upbringing and by the culture into which we are born. This applies particularly to our ideals and beliefs which are totally governed by the culture in which we are brought up. Our culture has developed independently of our genetic inheritance. We reputedly share 98.4% of our genes with chimpanzees, yet they have never developed a culture anything like as complex as ours.[10]

In the past we have pulled ourselves up by the high ideals laid down by religion. But religious aspirations demand more of us than we can humanly expect of ourselves. Aspiring to these impossible standards can make us just as evil and inhuman as good and divine. Fanaticism and terrorism result from the purity of religious intentions and are often interpreted as being divine and godly acts. Fundamentalist religion also demeans us too much by comparing us with inhuman entities such as gods, angels, aliens and the like, and by controlling us with authoritarian absolutes. Religion as its stands offers us no future but extremism and divisiveness. It therefore needs to be moderated by a human-centred view that respects the reality of what we are as defective human animals. For the unreality of religion makes us inhuman and callous.

By concentrating on ourselves and our own abilities and disabilities, our capacities and incapacities, we can improve ourselves within the bounds of what is physically and mentally possible for us to do. If we aspire to human perfections and not to divine, angelic or alien perfections then we can achieve them within ourselves and without losing touch with our basic humanity. Religious aspirations make us feel better or worse than other people who do not share our beliefs. We are either contemptuous of them because they are so inferior or are in awe of them because they are so superior. They are absolutely different from us and are either dangerous devils or untouchable saints. Either way, they are inhuman and we cannot identify with them. This kind of alienation from other people is the source of all the religious wars, pogroms, and holocausts of the past in which we treat other people worse than we treat animals. Such extreme religious aspirations are therefore not sufficiently tuned to our real abilities, and we now require more realistic and human-centred expectations and aspirations, some of which are suggested in this book.

F. The Need for a Creed

We should understand things before we believe in them. Inevitably what we believe in depends on the culture into which we are born. However, as free individuals, we have the right to think out our beliefs for ourselves, regardless of the beliefs inculcated into us by the dominant culture. This means that we don't succumb to the precepts of tradition or authority without thinking them through for ourselves. Clearly, it is better for us to understand before we believe rather than to believe before understanding. In other words, we find reason within ourselves to arrive at beliefs and don't just believe something simply because we are told that we must believe it. In this way, we give a meaning to our lives that is specifically our own.

As the meaning of our lives lies in what we make of them, we can develop that meaning by drawing on our inner resources. To become responsible for our own beliefs and opinions, we need strength of character sufficient to take on that responsibility. We should be spirited enough to enjoy thinking for themselves. A developed inner being can access our knowledge and experiences as a whole. Compared with this holistic approach, religion has only a therapeutic value in helping people to cope with their lives in the small scale so that they cease to think critically about life as a whole. It is a retrenchment exercise that does not help us to seek truths of value to the future of humanity. In contrast, these truths can be striven for interactively with an open mind. We should look forward to sorting our problems out instead of looking backwardly for divine assistance. Such a human-centred view fosters our positive-mindedness and impels us to get things done rather than dwell dismally on the past. We are concerned to seek the truth and face up to it, however unpleasant or inconvenient it turns out to be. Seeking the truth is not meant to be easy but it can be an exciting and enthralling challenge, provided we have enough depth and breadth of spirit to see it as such. In this way we can keep our minds open to truthful insights.

Our future both as individuals and as a species depends on our believing in ourselves but only in a qualified and self-critical way, in other words, in a self-reflective way. We must constantly examine and re-examine our self-belief so that we can move forward and fulfil our goals and purposes in life. To that end, we need a stable, all-embracing creed based on that self-belief. Without such a creed, we have no standpoint from which to evaluate our actions, aims and purposes. Thus, such a creed can help us to be self-critical instead of forbidding criticism.

A basic creed that we can live by should be practical, sensible and down-to-earth and give us confidence in what we are as mere human beings and in what we can do collectively as a species. It should help us to do things rather than just accept things as they are. We need to think positively about ourselves and our prospects so that we can move on and embrace the future with confidence rather than dwelling on past failings and disappointments.

The characteristics of such a Creed. Thus, the need for a basic and fundamental creed may be fulfilled if it is universal enough to have characteristics such as the following:

- It can be embraced by all believers without necessarily threatening particular beliefs. It will add to these beliefs without undermining them in any way.
- It will go beyond all previous religious creeds while being practical, sensible and down-to-earth. It will not add to the superstitions and implausibilities to which new religions are prone.
- It should give us confidence in what we are as mere human beings and in what we can do collectively as a species. We need to think positively about ourselves and our prospects so that we can move on and embrace the future with confidence rather than dwelling on past failings and disappointments.
- It should therefore help us to do things rather than just accept things as they are. In that respect it will differ from religious creeds which typically promote passivity and obedience.

The Optimist's Creed below goes as far as possible towards fulfilling these conditions. Moreover, it does not expect any more from us than what we normally do in making something of our lives. It involves having faith in ourselves, in humanity and in power of human reason. But this faith needs constant reinforcement by our understanding and criticising what it means and how valid and applicable it is in our daily lives. In that respect, it has a practical and educational role to play rather than a sacred or ritualistic role. For the optimist would rather teach than preach, and not tell people *what* to think but *how* to think. None of the beliefs in this Creed are the whole truth of the matter, but they can help each of us to strive towards the truth in our own way. They are not themselves the way but they attempt to illuminate our way. Thus, the Creed below is a teaching tool designed to help people on their way and not to dictate what that way should be.

The Optimist's Creed helps us in our daily lives to have confidence in our place in the world, in the power of reason, in the value of our fellow human beings, and in value of life in all its varieties. It is meant to be practical and useful. It aims to make sense of matters that will chime with most people. In contrast, religious beliefs, such as a belief in the resurrection of Jesus Christ, or a belief in a paradise awaiting the believers, lack practical application in daily life. Moreover, this Creed is the minimal belief system that can apply to us no matter what other beliefs, religious or non-religious that we may espouse over and above these beliefs. Thus, the faith of an optimist is summed up as follows:

The Optimist's Creed

The Strength of Knowledge

My faith is mightier than mere religion because it is open-ended and founded on ever-increasing knowledge and understanding of what I am, what other people mean to me, and what life and the universe mean to me.

The Power of Critical Reasoning

I have faith in the power of critical reasoning to reach truth, foster goodness, and support justice, and I will conduct a personal quest for all these and will settle for nothing less. I will constantly strive to understand life's mysteries, as far as humanly possible, and will not be content with myths, absurdities, or similar fruitless deviations from truth. I will search for the good within me and within others and will fight for justice and sweet reason for as long as I have the strength and will to do so.

The Capabilities of Humanity

I have faith in the capabilities of humanity, notwithstanding its obvious fallibilities. My belief in its future is not unqualified, as it depends on humanity doing enough to ensure that future. If no one believes in its future then it has no future.

The Resilience of the Human Spirit

I have faith in the resilience and persistence of the human spirit which has already accomplished so much against all the odds. I believe that the spirit within us will prosper for as long as we nurture it and make the most of its potential for good and well-being.

The Uniqueness of Each Individual

I have faith in the potential of every human being to enrich the world with the uniqueness and originality of their contributions to it. I wish to see that uniqueness blossom forth in the right social conditions and thereby justify the existence of humanity.

The Possibilities of Life

I have faith in the possibilities of life which are limited only by the paucity of human imagination. I believe that life has secure foundations while the human race believes in itself and its mission to further life. This requires each of us to make the most of our lives within the limits of our unique potential. In so doing, we serve the purposes of life as much as we are the custodians of it.

Finally, humanity is like a ship at sea forever repairing itself as it sails along without hope of reaching dry land where more complete and effective repairs can be made.[11] In other words, we are a self-sustaining, self-justifying species, which must rely on its own resources and ingenuity, and can expect no external help in its endeavours. This isolation gives us opportunities and challenges that we cannot shun without dishonouring ourselves. And there is no need for us to invent friendly, helpful entities of whose existence there is no convincing evidence. If we have enough confidence in ourselves then we can do without them. When we take responsibility for our own future, they become superfluous and subject to Occam's razor.

3. Centrality: Developing the Middle Ground

> Science cannot solve the ultimate mystery of nature. And that is because, in the last analysis, we ourselves are part of nature and therefore part of the mystery that we are trying to solve. Music and art are, to an extent, also attempts to solve or at least to express the mystery. But to my mind the more we progress with either the more we are brought into harmony with all nature itself. And that is one of the great services of science to the individual.
>
> Max Planck (1933) [1]

A. Science and the Middle Ground

The scientific view is essential to our future. It has been the chief engine of economic and technological development in the past few centuries. It would be tragic if that view were to be downgraded and dismissed in favour of some religious or ideological fanaticism. Unless the scientific view is fully embraced and made an indispensible part of our thinking about things, our future will be in doubt. It is argued here that science confirms our central position in the scheme of things and that increasing scientific knowledge can only strengthen the conviction that humanity has an important role to play in the universe.

We are all scientific-minded in our desire for knowledge of some kind or other. We become scientists in the broadest sense of the word when we acquire knowledge that enables us to do worthwhile things in the world. Science in this sense includes skills and practical know-how as well as the theoretical knowledge provided by the physical and social sciences. Knowing what science is and what it can do for us is essential to our complete development as human beings. Unless we understand what science is telling us, we cannot begin to understand ourselves, society or the universe. Thus, an unscientific education is an incomplete one since science helps us to understand our strengths and weaknesses both as individuals and as a species.

The holistic view imbibes scientific knowledge as a means of relating to the universe and its contents. It is one of the ways that we face up to the realities of life and living. This does not mean that we all have to acquire detailed scientific knowledge but only that we understand the important role that such knowledge plays in establishing our place in the universe. That knowledge consists in expanding the middle ground between the very small and the very large. It is constantly adding to our knowledge of our surroundings from the smallest to the largest and everything in between.

Through physics we get insight into the quantum realms and through astronomy we reach out to the ends of the universe. Between these extremes, we have sciences such as biology, zoology and the social sciences such as economics and psychology. By expanding the area of this middle ground, science helps us to consolidate our position in the universe. Our importance to the universe grows in proportion to the growth of our understanding of it. In exploring the universe from the centre outwards, we understand better our role in the universe according to what science is telling us. We get, for example, an increasing understanding of how we have emerged quite naturally from the complexifying processes inherent in the universe. Life has made itself without having to be made by anything else. In facing such realities we find the middle ground between thinking too much of ourselves and too little. We reach a more balanced state of understanding our place as opposed to an overweening pride at one extreme and a self-deprecating humility at the other extreme.

Our natural curiosity drives us to understand what we are and what our role in the universe is. If we are interested in science in general then we are scientists in the widest sense of the word. We all have the potential to understand and use science. It doesn't matter whether or not we actually contribute to scientific knowledge. It is enough to study science and to understand it even at a general or populist level. Such a study opens our minds to the possibilities of further scientific understanding. The receptivity and ability to retain one's curiosity and open-mindedness are all important.

Scientific knowledge is important from a holistic point of view in helping us understand our middle position between the immensely large and immensely small things in the universe. The more we understand about that middle position, the more we secure our position in the universe and feel more secure within ourselves. To share in the security of this greater knowledge and understanding we must all act as scientists who use scientific knowledge about ourselves and the universe we live in, to the best of our personal abilities.

By including everything from the very small to the very large, science brings together everything about energy, matter, life and humanity. This includes the sciences of life and humanity, namely, biology, zoology as well as sociology, psychology and economics. Each science is engaged to a greater or lesser extent in relating the very small to the very large and *vice versa*. For example, medical science looks at microbes as well as elephants. Economics relates the behaviour of individual consumers to the economy as a whole and ultimately to the global economy as a whole. (As we all know to our cost, it cannot yet predict anything with scientific accuracy or reliability.) Physics gives us quantum mechanics as well as the rocket science to reach the planets and hopefully the stars.

The Infinitely Large and Infinitely Small. Another way of putting it is that we are placed the finite middle between what is potentially infinitely large and infinitely small. Infinity stretches from us in all directions both inside us and outside us. In that sense, humanity is indeed at the centre of the universe. When we take a purely physical view of humanity, it is clear on the large scale that we are physically insignificant to the nth degree. Many people despair of their existence when it strikes them hard just how insignificant we appear to be in that context. It is too easy to think that humanity is worthless in the face of the universe's unfathomable immensity. Yet that is only one perspective. The same facts show our true importance in the universe when we consider our hugeness compared with very small things such as cells and atoms. We are both infinitely small and infinitely large at the same time. This can be simply illustrated by putting one's forefinger and thumb together and then separate them by a tiny gap. The Earth is far smaller than that gap in relation to the size of the Milky Way galaxy, and the latter is just as small compared to the rest of the universe. At the same time, the cells in our body are far smaller than that gap, and atoms are as small in relation to the cells as the latter are to us. Though we are rendered miniscule by the hugeness of the universe, we are also rendered massive compared with the extreme tininess of cells, molecules, atoms, quarks and so on.

The middle position that we occupy is between the extremely large galactic universe and the extremely small quantum universe. This is expressed as the microcosm and macrocosm, the large and the small, and everything in between these extremes. Our middle view may be called 'metacosmian', after the term 'metacosmia' meaning 'between worlds'. It was invented by the early Greek philosopher Epicurus to isolate the gods and goddesses from human affairs.[2] He put them where they would not bother us and would be safe from the vagaries of the worlds surrounding them. In broadly the same way, we are situated between these worlds of the very small and very large. This middle position justifies our existence on this tiny or huge planet (depending on your point of view). We can look in both directions and glean the immense knowledge available in both directions. We can therefore call ourselves *Metacosmians* in that we are between the worlds of the very small and very large. As Metacosmians, it is incumbent on us to justify our middle position in the universe. We can demonstrate the value of our own existence relative in both directions. If we are not big enough to fit our medial position then we do not deserve to have a future.

B. The Role of the Middle View

> I have placed you at the very centre of the world, so that from that vantage point you may with greater ease glance round about you on all that the world contains. We have made you a creature neither of heaven nor of earth, neither mortal nor immortal, in order that you may, as the free and proud shaper of your own being, fashion yourself in the form you may prefer. It will be in your power to descend to the lower, brutish forms of life; you will be able, through your own decision, to rise again to the superior orders whose life is divine.
>
> Giovanni Pico della Mirandola (1486) [3]

The middle view is important because it confirms our role at the centre of the universe. It enables us to revive the pre-Copernican view of humanity as being at the centre of the universe. This bolsters our self-belief and gives us good reasons for having this self-belief. Above all, we need it if we are to take responsibility for our own future as a species. We have to believe in ourselves because nothing else will. As is already argued above, self-belief is all important. It is a matter of finding reasons for that self-belief. Positive reasons are just as valid and truthful as negative ones. It all depends how the evidence is interpreted and from what viewpoint. Ever since Copernicus displaced the Earth from the centre of the universe, astronomy has increasingly revealed the immensity of our insignificance. We have lost a great deal of faith in ourselves as a result of these discoveries. But this view is all in the mind. We can interpret the facts from a different viewpoint that changes our minds about our position in the universe. Being in a mid-position between the extremely large and extremely small is just the change of mind being proposed here

Everything we now know about the universe indicates that humanity has no future unless it makes its own future. We stand alone in this infinitesimally tiny part of the universe and must make the best of our isolation unless and until we find other intelligent life-forms elsewhere in the universe. We will then have a better idea of our true significance in the universe. In the meantime we can find within ourselves sufficient reasons to consider us to be important in the universe, particularly as regards our middle position therein. We are not at the centre of the universe in the Copernican sense that it does not revolve around us and that we are incredibly small in relation to its enormity. But there are other senses in which we are at the centre of things, especially in our being in a middle position between the very large and the very small, as is argued in more detail below.

The Copernican view is one-sided and incomplete. It provides us with only one perspective that is not the necessary or absolute truth of the matter. It does not encompass everything that we can understand from the available facts. From other perspectives we can think of ourselves as being at the heart of the universe. We are to ourselves just as important as we are in purely physical terms. This has always been the religious view as against the scientific view of things. But religion is incompatible with science in so far as it demands absolute and unqualified faith or belief in its tenets. It gives us a broad view of our potential as, for example, our being made in the image of God, at the price of narrowing our minds to one dogmatic system or another. But this view is not broad enough. Religion no longer provides good enough answers to account for our place in the universe as God has been made increasingly irrelevant by the scientific facts. We must now find the strength within ourselves to make our own way forward (hence the title of my first book, *The Answers Lie Within Us*). In place of the extreme religious and scientific standpoints, this book offers a more holistic, human-centred viewpoint that omits the irrelevancies and superfluities on which religious belief depends, while at the same time taking matters of belief more seriously than the scientific view usually does.

We can now reinstate to some extent a pre-Copernican view of humanity in which we are more important to the universe than our insignificant material existence suggests. This returns us to our rightful place at the heart and centre of the universe. We belong there because we know what we are as a species, and what we have and have not accomplished, for better or for worse. We belong there because nothing else that we know of can adopt such a place or make anything of it. Thus, our self-knowledge alone puts us at the heart of the universe.

We are worthy of such a position because we know enough about ourselves to take responsibility for our own actions and to establish our own place in the universe. We may fail to do so through lack of vision and self-seeking short-termism. However, we are potentially self-critical enough to know all about the mistakes that we have been making, about our ineffectiveness as a species, and about the very limited things we can do in this vast universe. That knowledge is itself an accomplishment. It allows us to be self-reliant and no longer to rely on the sanction and discipline of external beings whose existence is not manifest. The human race should now regard itself as grown up enough to make its own way forward without the support of such fictitious entities.

We are important because our presence cannot be denied or refuted, even though as bits of matter we are vanishingly small and next to nothing. Thus, our presence here and now makes us important. The meaningfulness and purposefulness of our thoughts and actions gives us a presence that transcends our material existence. When we believe in the importance of our presence here and now, then we are important because the belief alone creates the fact, which does not exist without our contemplating it. We are no more important than what we believe ourselves to be, as long as our beliefs are based on the established facts of our existence and the hard realities of life and living.

This is not a matter of believing in ourselves religiously, absolutely or unrealistically. Our limitations are made plain enough in a self-critical open society that does not allow us to get beyond ourselves. Our self-belief is self-regulatory and entirely dependent on ourselves. Mass media scrutiny supplies the self-regulatory mechanisms required to criticise and monitor our activities and keep us on the right track. For example, our awareness of the parlous state of our environment arouses passions in its defence. As a result, lobbying organisations such as Friends of the Earth and Greenpeace actively ensure that governments and big business cannot overlook the environmental effects of our activities. Their activities make no sense unless they are assuming that a better state of affairs can be arrived at in which we have more balanced and rational relationship with the rest of the planet. In other words, they implicitly believe that humanity has a future worthy of itself and its place in the scheme of things.

C. The Centrality of our Position in the Universe

Science tells us we are the middle species. The truth about our importance lies in examining exactly what science tells us our place in the universe. We are indeed insignificantly small in relation to the universe at large. But we are in our turn are immensely large in relation to the miniscule atomic sphere of existence. We are a middle species that lies between the imaginably large and the inconceivably small areas of existence. These facts cannot be emphasised or repeated enough. The following details are adapted from freely available internet information and demonstrate the extent to which this is the ultimate truth of the matter.

We are immensely small	We are immensely large
The true scale of our physical insignificance seems scarcely imaginable. Yet we can imagine this insignificance to some extent. The Earth is not much bigger than pinhead from the distance at which the sun is positioned. But then the whole solar system is even smaller than a pinhead in relation to the Milky Way galaxy of which it forms a part. Then our galaxy appears to be no more than a pinhead from far outside it. And there are millions upon millions of other similar tiny galaxies in the universe. We are infinitely small within infinitely small pinheads. We are therefore the tiniest of the tiny within the tiniest of tiny.	We tower over very small things as much as very large things tower over us. Thus, the cells in our bodies are invisibly small. At least a thousand human cells would fit into a grain of sand measuring a millimetre in length. There are about 100 trillion cells in the average human body. Yet each cell is a mini-factory doing thousands of jobs such as synthesising proteins, deposing of waste products, and making enzymes and hormones to serve the body's needs. We have no conscious control over the workings of individual cells as their functioning is entirely automatic. We may physically dominate these tiny cells but we are nothing without them
Our cosmic insignificance is even greater when we consider the numbers involved. The Milky Way galaxy contains some 200–400 billion stars, of which the Sun is an insignificant one placed the edge of a spiral arm. The galaxy is estimated to contain 50 billion planets, 500 million of which could be located in the habitable zone of their parent star. It is roughly 100,000 light years in diameter, and our nearest sister galaxy, the Andromeda Galaxy, is located roughly 2.5 million light years away. (Each light year is approximately 5.8 trillion miles in length.) There are probably more than 100 billion (10^{11}) galaxies in the observable universe. Typical galaxies range from dwarfs with as few as ten million (10^7) stars up to giants with one trillion (10^{12}) stars, all orbiting the galaxy's centre of mass. A 2010 study by astronomers estimated that the observable universe contains 300 sextillion (3×10^{23}) stars. The chances of intelligent life being on the planets revolving round some of these must be quite high.	We are huge in relation to our cells but the latter are huge in relation of the atoms of which they are composed. Within each human cell there are as much as 200 trillion atoms. (That makes 200 septillion atoms in each human body – 2 followed by 24 zeros! There are more atoms in our bodies than stars are estimated to be in the universe - 300 sextillion.) Each atom is mainly empty space. If an atom were the size of a cathedral, its nucleus would be the size of a fly at the centre of it. The rest of the space is empty apart from electrons zooming around. These electrons repel those of other atoms and keep them apart. Electrons cannot be predicted to be anywhere in particular. At these levels of existence, the automatic functioning that we see in cells breaks down. Electrons, photons and other tiny atomic particles can never be pinned down. Whatever we do to them changes their position and even whether they are particles or waves. Chance and uncertainty reign at the lowest levels accessible to us.

Pascal's medialism. Blaise Pascal (1623-1662) was apparently the first writer to take seriously the middle view and the dualism involved in it. However, he takes a negative view of this. In his *Pensées* he expresses his fear and dismay at the terrifying contrast in our medial position between the infinitely small ('nothingness' as he calls it) and the infinitely immense beyond our understanding:

> For who will not marvel that our body, a moment ago imperceptible in the universe, itself imperceptible in the bosom of the whole, should now be a colossus, a world, or rather a whole, compared to the nothingness beyond our reach? Anyone who considers himself in this way will be terrified at himself, and, seeing his mass, as given him by nature, supporting him between these two abysses of infinity and nothingness, will tremble at these marvels. . . For, after all, what is man in nature? A nothing compared to the infinite, a whole compared to the nothing, a middle point between all and nothing, infinitely remote from an understanding of the extremes; the end of things and their principles are unattainably hidden from him in impenetrable secrecy. Equally incapable of seeing the nothingness from which he emerges and the infinity in which he is engulfed.[4]

However, it is clear that Pascal did not have access to the knowledge tabulated above. His view shows how far we have come towards understanding the nature and content of the immensely large and immensely small aspects of the universe. If he had been informed about what we now know of such matters, it is likely he would take a more optimistic and less fearful view of our place in the universe. For Pascal the contrast between these unknown regions was mysterious and beyond his understanding. The more we understand them, the less unfathomable they seem, just as the Moon now appears to us a relatively uninteresting rock orbiting the Earth compared with the fearful influences wrongly attributed to it by our ignorant ancestors.

D. The Importance of our Centrality

Our middle position gives us knowledge in both directions. The fact that we are both big and small helps us to understand how living beings on the surface of this ridiculously small lump of rock can know so much about themselves. How can we possibly know the extent of our physical insignificance but also something of the workings of the universe as a whole? The answer must lie in the fact that our physical insignificance is only one half of the story. Our insignificance must be balanced with our immensity in size in the other direction. We are really at the half-way house in the scheme of things. If we go in the other direction, we find that everything gets just as remotely small and as the universe is remotely large. Our centrality enables us to take equal account of both directions.

What is going on far below the level of our sight is truly wondrous and is not without purpose. When we think of immensely small cells as tiny factories that are reliably productive throughout our lives, we can't help but be amazed at what life achieves at these levels. Life does all these things on its own without external assistance. Also, we now know that the air is full of equally small bacteria that populate the Earth to a far greater extent than we will ever achieve. The fact that we are increasingly aware of the power of life at these levels makes us important custodians of life. Our undoubted role is to mediate between these extremes and make sure that life gets and keeps a firm footing in the universe. The fact that we can think of adopting such a role means that we are honour bound to take it up. Not to do so would be an abnegation of our very existence as self-styled intelligent beings; we would rightly shame ourselves in the eyes of posterity. People in the future will think us very stupid indeed, if we do not have the confidence and responsibility to make the most of our custodial role on Earth.

Beyond doubt, science helps us to relate the very small to the very large and thereby bring order, meaning, and purpose into being that did not exist previously. We create order by linking the very large with the very small and making a coherent system of them. We are already doing this with a significant measure of success with the sciences of cosmology, physics, chemistry, biology and the other sciences. The purpose of the experiments at CERN and other research centres is to help us understand how the behaviour of immensely small nuclear particles relates to how the universe at large came into existence, what it is composed of, and what is happening to it, now and in the future. At these small levels it appears that everything is connected with everything else and whatever happens there has implications for the universe as a whole. Thus, to understand the beginnings of the universe and how it is expanding, it is necessary to understand how things function at the very smallest level of existence.

Everything is physically *determined* at the very large level of existence and everything is physically *undetermined* at the very smallest level of existence. It is only at our middle level of existence that freedom of thought and movement becomes possible; everything else is subject to chance or necessity. Thus, freedom is only ensured at our middle position. However, to say that we have such freedom is itself a middle position between the extreme views of the sceptic and the determinist. A sceptic typically argues that we are subject to chance events over which we have no control, and the determinist holds that we have no freedom from necessarily determined events. But most of us prefer to believe that we have some freedom in our thoughts and acts. We believe that we can freely choose between alternative courses of actions.

We can also freely choose to make something or nothing of the universe. Our importance in the universe lies in our middle position which enables us to think and act for ourselves in ways that are not possible at the very large or very small levels of existence. Our freedom to think and act enables us to understand what is happening at the very large and very small levels of existence. We are the key to understanding the universe. Our place in the universe enables us to gain some understanding of the interconnections at the very largest and very smallest levels of existence. Understanding fully our true status in the universe therefore depends on our increasing knowledge of what is happening at both these levels. By our unstinting efforts we can make something of the universe. In contrast, we are also free to do nothing at all and therefore make no mark on the universe whatsoever. This has often been the religious position down the ages.

If it were possible for God to exist somewhere in the universe, it could only be found at the middle position. Only at that position can the notion of God be contemplated with any meaning. Our middle position shows us that nothing having creative or purposeful capabilities can exist in the direction of either the very large or the very small. At these extremes there is nothing but determinacy or indeterminacy; necessity or chance. There is no possibility of any sentient entity existing at these extremes, let alone an omnipotent, omniscient or omnipresent being. Moreover, the universe began as an infinitely small point and to increase our understanding of its beginning we need to research into that extremely small area of existence. It can only be understood better in this way by intelligent beings operating at the middle position. Thus, as intelligence is only to be found at the middle position, beings superior to ourselves will only be found at that position. Until we make the first contact with such beings, we can confidently say that God does not exist at present and that we are the only hope of god-like beings coming into existence in the future by our becoming extremely advanced beings with divine powers of our own.

Our quest for knowledge is an investment in the future. Thus, future knowledge can save us from denigrating ourselves to total insignificance. We must invest in the future in that regard by supporting whatever expensive research is required to gain greater understanding of the universe both at the macroscopic and microscopic levels. Cosmological understanding is linked at a very deep level with quantum understanding, since the universe began at that infinitely small level of existence. Indeed, the very fact that we can conduct such research and gain an astonishing amount of information about the universe, near and far, shows that we are unique in being able to do so. No other species on Earth has come close to such achievements, and no other species can be relied upon to do so in the near future. Therein lies our ultimate importance as a species.

In conclusion, we can use our centrality to benefit ourselves, life, the cosmos and posterity. In being at the interface between the very large and the very small, we can (1) establish our value in the universe, (2) find meaning in all that we do or do not do in the world, and (3) form the purposes that make sense of our lives. At this position we can mediate between all other forms of life, both big and small. By putting them all in their place and valuing them all accordingly, we ascribe cosmic significance to all life-forms as well as ourselves. Also, at this intermediary position, increasing order and beauty are created not only by us but also by other intelligent beings, assuming they exist in the universe. As a result, the Cosmos is created which is the increasing orderliness that will possibly save the universe from its ultimate fate of total dispersal and heat death. Finally, by using our insights, knowledge and abilities in a meaningful and purposeful way, we leave a legacy to posterity which will be to their benefit and which will be an example that they can build on to take humanity forward.

E. The Middle Ground between Scepticism and Dogmatism

> Science has furnished the material basis of our civilisation, but its ideas are still pre-scientific, and that is one of the principal reasons for the extraordinary misuse

of applied science which is so characteristic of our age. The late war [i.e. the First World War] is a very good example of this... The future of Western civilisation depends, to a very large extent, on whether it can incorporate into itself not only scientific inventions but scientific ideas and a scientific outlook.

J.B.S Haldane (1932) [5]

Science has served us well but it has also been misused for military and other purposes that do not bode well for our future. The advent of the atomic bomb was a consequence of applied science that dwarves the all weaponry used in the First World War that so concerned Haldane in the above quotation. But such a perversion of science is not what science has been about. It is about finding the middle way between total scepticism of all all beliefs and total dogmatic adherence to them. This is surely what Haldane means when he says that the ideas of civilisation are 'pre-scientific'. Science is a search for truth between the extremes and it is an outlook which, as Haldane suggests, is still to be widely adopted in society.

Science lies between scepticism and dogmatism. Besides occupying the middle ground between the very small and very large, science also occupies the middle ground between scepticism and dogmatism. In the ancient world, philosophers were divided into sceptical and dogmatic philosophers. They were either sceptical of philosophy's ability to reach firm and indisputable knowledge, or they promulgated a body of doctrines that they held to be true on purely rational ground. Thus, Diogenes Laertius, (c. 300 CE) stated:

"Philosophers may be divided into dogmatists and sceptics: dogmatists are all those who make assertions about things assuming that they can be known; while sceptics are those who suspend their judgment on the ground that things are unknowable."[6]

Self-confident philosophers who stated their views dogmatically were countered either by sceptics who doubted the truth of their assertions or by other dogmatic philosophers who put forward alternative views. There could be no agreement as to what was or was not generally accepted knowledge. Thus, this dichotomy hampered the development of scientific method till the 17th century with the works of Bacon and the experiments of Galileo.

Modern science only became possible when the middle ground between scepticism and dogmatism was worked out. It then became clear that science progresses by an interaction between empiricism and rationalism. This was the great achievement of Francis Bacon (1561-1626). The immense scientific progress achieved since the 17th century only became possible when inductive thinking was developed as a dualist, trial-and-error procedure to find out by interactive experiment what nature is really like. This dualist approach was laid down philosophically by Francis Bacon in his *Novum Organon* (1620). He saw scientific study as being the middle way between the empiricist and rationalist methods. It was better to be like bees that collect pollen and transform it into honey, rather than ants that merely collect things (empiricists) or spiders that spin things from themselves (rationalists).

"Those who have treated the sciences were either empiricists or rationalists. Empiricists are like ants; they collect and put to use; but rationalists, like spiders, spin threads out of themselves. The bee takes the middle way, gathering her material from flowers in gardens and fields, and then digesting and transforming it using her own skills. Similarly, the true role of philosophy lies neither in relying entirely on the mental faculties nor in accumulating data in the memory from natural history or mechanical experiments, but in changing and reworking the material in the intellect. Therefore, we have good reason for hope from a closer and stricter union between the experimental and rational faculties than was the case before."[7]

Bacon's entomological analogies may be fanciful but the points he is making are clear and valid. His view can be described as a dualist interaction between (1) the empirical collection of evidence and information and (2) the rational ordering of this material to produce something new and hitherto unthought of. Thus, dualist theory (as discussed in the next section on *Duality*) includes the study of the scientific method in so far as that method is dualist in its procedure. It involves "commerce between the mind of man and the nature of things"[8] Bacon was thus advocating a dualist interaction between ourselves and nature, and between the intellectual and the practical aspects of our nature. He was the first to clarify the distinction between empiricism and rationalism, and he reconciled these opposing tendencies by advocating a dualist, trial-and-error procedure:

Empiricism	*Rationalism*
➤ Knowledge is derived from experience and ultimately from the senses.	➤ Knowledge is deduced from reasoning or thinking about things.
➤ The mind is a blank sheet on which our ideas are written through our experience of the world. There are no innate ideas.	➤ Perceptual experience is not enough to account for our understanding of things, and *a priori* knowledge is not reducible to sensory information.
➤ At its extreme, it leads to piecemeal heaps and collections of things as they are directly experienced. Any ordering of our experiences is considered to be arbitrary and unrealistic.	➤ At its extreme, everything is explained ultimately in relation of a single system of thought which constitutes 'reality'. Everything is amenable to reason.

The foundations of science lie in both empiricism and rationalism. Bacon's middle way was a dualist balance between empiricism and rationalism that stresses a trial-and-error exploration of experience. He said: "When philosophy is severed from its roots in experience, it becomes a dead thing". Philosophy in his view consists in doing things and not in holding dogmatic opinions in the religious manner:

"Of myself I say nothing; but in behalf of the business which is in hand I entreat men to believe that it is not an opinion to be held, but a work to be done; and to be well assured that I am labouring to lay the foundation, not of a sect or doctrine, but of human utility and power."[9]

Bacon laid down the intellectual foundation for the scientific revolution of the 17th century up to the present day. However, it is clear that the dualist view implied by the scientific outlook has not prevailed. There is still a significant dichotomy between the empiricist and rationalist points of view. Indeed, philosophy itself has been divided since then, for example, by the division between the British empiricist philosophers of Locke, Bacon and Hume whereas continental philosophy has broadly followed the rationalist path with Descartes, Leibniz and the idealists such as Hegel and the existentialist philosophers such as Heidegger. At present, philosophical thinking is cleft by two distinct and incompatible lines of thought, the analytic and the synthetic. These lines of thought are disastrous dividers of human beings when they divide people from each other instead of being concentrated within the mind of each person. People become divided rigidly into analytically prone persons and synthetically prone persons. When they are divided in that way they are at polar opposites which compel them to see the other side are being the enemy to be overcome if not eliminated. These ways of thinking are outlined as follows:

Analytic Line of Thought   *Synthetic Line of Thought*

Analytic		Synthetic
Empiricist		Rationalist
Realist		Idealist
Pluralist		Monist
Reductionist		Holist
Relativist		Absolutist
Positivist		Obscurantist
Aristotelian		Platonist
'Tough-minded'	(Willam James)[10]	'Tender-minded'
'Men of Facts'	(A.N. Whitehead)[11]	'Men of Ideas'
'Fox'	(Sir Isaiah Berlin)[12]	'Hedgehog'
'Curiosity'	(Bernard Williams)[13]	'Salvation'
'Extraverted'	(C.G. Jung)[14]	'Introverted'

A State of Mind of *Elaboration*:
➢ emphasising DIFFERENCES as opposed to SIMILARITIES;
➢ abstracting PARTS from WHOLES;
➢ asserting MORE & MORE about LESS & LESS;
➢ elaborating the CONTENTS of things to a multiplicity of factors without reference to their contextual simplicities

A State of Mind of *Simplification*:
➢ emphasising SIMILARITIES as opposed to DIFFERENCES;
➢ generalising WHOLES from PARTS
➢ asserting LESS & LESS about MORE & MORE;
➢ subsuming everything to one CONTEXT without reference to their complex interactions with other contexts

We can easily get into the mental rut of thinking along one of these lines of thought at the expense of the other. We either become overconfident of our opinions or have no confidence at all in them. Either we dismiss all opposition to our views out of hand or we accept mindlessly and uncritically the authority of tradition, gurus, demagogues, preachers or whatever. Instead of taking account of opposing views in an interactive way, we pit our views against the opposing ones and attempt to annihilate them. The result is party politics, warring factions, irreconcilable religions, and so on. In other words, our tribal and sectarian inclinations find their origin in such opposing grooves of thought. As a result, our prejudices are strengthened and they stultify our inner development. We no longer have any incentive to rethink our presuppositions and we remain rooted in our ruts.

However, it must be possible to learn how to avoid extremist thinking. It is after all only an attitude of mind. Our hope for our future must lie in our learning not to lapse into the mental grooves that divide us from opposing points of view and prevent us from appreciating their value. For instance, from an educational point of view, students can perform mental exercises as part of civics courses in which they adopt opposing frames of thought and practice broadening their minds in that way. This is not learning to sit on fences but learning to think out the complexities involved in adopting any balanced and informed viewpoint. The following Schematic Depiction may be useful in that regard:

A Schematic Depiction of the Middle Ground

	The Will to Power (Nietzsche)	The Will to Understanding (Systematic Dualism)	The Will to Belief (William James)
Features:	Carnivorous (Wolves)	Human	Herbivorous (Sheep)
Motivations:	Seeking immediate fame, power or notoriety	Seeking long-term personal development	Seeking security within 'herd/flock'
Traits:	↓	↓	↓
Relational	Dominant	Independent	Dependent
Prescriptive	Commanding	Questioning	Unquestioning
Doxastic	Dogmatic	Critical of belief	Blind belief/faith
Reactive	Authoritarian	Authoritative	Credulous
Predictive	Deterministic	Latitudinarian	Fatalistic
Attitudinal	Absolute certainty	Relative certainty	Total conviction
Judgmental	Contempt	Respect	Uncritical
Behavioural	Demeaning	Self-critical	Subservient
Effects:	↓	↓	↓
Social	Esoteric	Familial	Exclusive
Heuristic	Indoctrination	Teaching	Preaching
Emotive	Hypnotic induction	Rational passions	Mob mania
Dispositional	Them/us discrimination	Tolerance of differences	Indiscriminate love/hatred
Goals:	↓	↓	↓
Epistemic	Messianic knowledge	Hypothetical knowledge	Common knowledge
Personal	Adulation	Truth	Conformity
	↓	↓	↓
Outcomes:	Self-deception	Insight	Delusion

Expounding the Middle Way. The above three outlooks or ways of thinking characterise human nature. We have, on the one hand, the overly strong 'will to power' and, on the other hand, the overly weak 'will to believe', between which the relatively moderate 'will to understanding' hovers uneasily. The former two ways represent relatively primitive and uncivilised aspects of human nature which need to be moderated by the middle way. Their primitive and uncivilised aspects emerge when they are isolated from the middle way and are taken to extremes. All forms of political, religious, and behavioural extremism result from such a loss of the middle way, as is argued below. This extremist potential persists within us all and we need constantly to guard ourselves against its reassertion and predominance. In so far as there is progress in civilisation, it consists in the middle way being progressively introduced until it forms part of everyone's mindset and ultimately of the political and social fabric. Civilised behaviour requires the middle way to insinuate its way between these intimate extremes which feed on each other. This process has recurred several times in history when humanistic attitudes have come to the fore. Equally, the simplicity and attraction of extreme views has all too often resulted in the loss of the middle way. Until the twentieth century, the appearance of the middle way has been cyclical and impermanent. Hopefully, the twenty-first century will see its permanent institution when it becomes an integral part of the educational system.

The Consequences of Repudiating the Middle Way. It may be argued that excess is tolerable while it is related to the middle way wherein we remain human rather than inhuman. We can be a little wicked as long as we repent of that wickedness and resolve to do better. For we need to bear in mind the harm which excessive behaviour does to ourselves and others. We need the restraints of the middle way to function as sociable and rational beings. Repudiating the middle way entirely means losing one's moral sense or social conscience. Psychopaths and sociopaths feel no shame or remorse because they have lost all restraints over their behaviour and have nothing within them to draw them back from doing their worst. In the same bracket, we may include terrorists, extremists, fanatics, zealots, criminals, rapists, gangsters, gurus, charlatans, and sectarian bigots of all kinds, who commonly scorn the middle way between the will to power and the will to believe. They seek the nearest way to satisfy their ambitions, desires, compulsions and obsessions. In preying on the populace like wolves on sheep, they dehumanise themselves and demean their victims. They dominate people to achieve their self-serving ends. They are so sure of themselves that they become dogmatic and authoritarian in their behaviour towards others. In the case of religious and political bigots, they exert power over others by means of messianic knowledge which is usually a belief system specific to themselves or the organisation within which they operate. The belief system is often so esoteric and divorced from common life that they adopt a them/us discrimination policy. You are either in or out, for or against and there is no middle way.

Insight and developed intuition is an important goal. The will to understanding is a drive towards greater insight into ourselves and the human condition in general. It does not come naturally to us and we must make the effort to do it. Adopting the dualist view gives our thinking the extra dynamism and open-minded needed to develop it further and to help us become yet more insightful. It is a dynamic and ongoing philosophy that brings intuition into play. To achieve insight we need to have a developed intuition such as is discussed below in section 7 on *Creativity*. In dualist theory, this is systematic dualism as contrasted with naïve dualism in which intuition is underdeveloped and therefore not dependable because it is random and impulsive. This dualist view is further discussed in the next section on *Duality*.

4. Duality: Looking at Both Sides

"The Universe is dual because, in the fullest sense, it is both transient and eternal. The Universe is dual because each final actuality is both physical and mental. The Universe is dual because each occasion unites its formal immediacy with objective otherness. The Universe is *many* because it is wholly and completely to be analysed into many final actualities - or in Cartesian language, into many *res verae*. The Universe is *one*, because of the universal immanence. There is thus a dualism in this contrast between the unity and multiplicity. Throughout the Universe there reigns the union of opposites which is the ground of dualism."

Alfred North Whitehead (1933).[1]

A. Duality Offers an Anti-Extremist Viewpoint

Extremism is a major obstacle to our advancement. Extreme views create conflicts by the violent disagreements and enmity that they engender. The extremist mentality needs to be countered by showing the limited nature of the truths on which it relies. The dualist view is an essential tool in drawing attention to the limited truth of all our beliefs and opinions. There is always much to be said for opposing views in our quest for truth. Unless we see the limitations to our beliefs and opinions they cannot be applied to reality with any confidence. These limitations are usually defined by the context in which they can be applied with confidence. The success of scientific theories has resulted from their being applied very exactly to the situations in which they can be used with total confidence. Extremist beliefs are typically applied indiscriminately everywhere without critical examination.

The dualist view is therefore anti-absolutist. The world is stricken with absolutist attitudes that stifle human progress. Currently we see absolutist regimes in countries such as North Korea that impose stability and sterility on their populace in an absolute manner. A polarisation of beliefs and opinions still persists throughout the world, and this is a perpetual source of unnecessary conflict. Dualist enmities are still evident in religion while Protestants hate Catholics, Muslims hate Jews, Hindus hate Muslims and the like. Still plaguing us are nationalist and racist antagonisms in which Scots hate English, Canadians hate Americans, Flemings hate Walloons, Norwegians hate Swedes, Serbs hate Croats, Ukrainians hate Russians, Chinese hate Japanese, Hutus hate Tutsis, and so on. The solution is not multi-culturalism but the monoculture of humanity as a whole, as is argued above. Such a monoculture ensures that religious and national identities are subsumed in the identity of the human race as a whole. In being a part of the whole, they are no longer isolated belief systems directly at loggerheads with similar belief systems. They have their own place in the scheme of things and need no longer fight for recognition and survival against rivals that are simply different from them. The dualist view reinforces this by ensuring that the rival viewpoints are taken account of and not demonised or treated as being inhuman.

Furthermore, the conflict and enmity between traditionalists and progressives is also world-wide. Countries in North Africa and the Middle East are in a state of ferment if not outright war because of enmity between these factions. Even the USA is ridden by conflict between liberals and conservatives, not just among politicians but throughout the country. The dualist response is that no one can be absolutely and irrevocably either traditionalist or progressive in their outlook. There is a traditionalist lurking in every progressive and a progressive within every traditionalist. The aim of dualist theory is to bring these opposites to light so that everyone recognises the value of opposing views. The one does not need to do battle with the other in order to reach some understanding of the middle way or what has gone wrong in the imbalances and extremism in people's thinking. In that way, the extremist view will become abhorrent and entirely avoidable.

When people deliberately take up opposing sides, this often leads to irreconcilable conflicts. We don't need politicians to take sides and argue opposing views to the extent of making them totally irreconcilable. This only increases conflict and confusion. It brings the political process into increasing disrepute. However, it is not simply a matter of compromise between opposing sides. It may mean correcting imbalances because we have gone from one extreme to another. There has to be a common understanding of this and the dualist view alone can provide this. For example, the bubble caused by excessive credit has resulted in an imbalance that threatens global finances unless it is corrected. These imbalances result from one point of view being applied absolutely and uncritically to excess. Recognising these excesses to the point of doing something about them requires a dualist viewpoint.

The dualist view is beneficial in preventing the polarisation of opposing and competing beliefs. Absolutism leads to such a polarisation. An absolutely certainty in their beliefs encourages opponents to go to war with each other to resolve their differences once and for all. This mentality is based on a monism that centres everything on one idea, one person, one religion, or one way of thinking. It is the antithesis of the dualist view which is more relativist than absolutist. According to the dualist view, nothing can be said to be absolutely the case. There is always the possibility of doubt and uncertainty. Dualist studies show that effective action is possible because of this doubt and uncertainty and not in spite of it. The long-term effectiveness of action depends on our taking account of all factors in a dualist manner whereas the short-term solutions of politicians are a response to media inspired crises.

Dualist studies are therefore needed to correct the faulty ways of thinking that lead us into extremism and absolutism in one direction or into error, doubt and confusion in the other direction. In other words, we must improve the tools of human reason if we are to survive as a species and think our way out of our problems without despairing of the future.

The dualist view is not popular at this time because it is not well understood. The dualist mentality is presumed to involve nothing but doubt and uncertainty. Dualists are thought to be neither one thing nor the other; they sit on the proverbial fence getting nowhere. But dualism is not necessarily about doubt and uncertainty. It is only the attitude of naïve dualists who don't know their own minds. They lack the inner development to make up their minds. At the other extreme of naïve dualism is absolute monism in which beliefs are held absolutely, rigidly and without question. The systematic dualist on the other hand has it all worked out: they know their own minds and what they can or cannot do in the world. They have a holistic view of things by considering the all the yeas and nays, pros and cons, advantages and disadvantages, strengths and weaknesses of the position to arrive at a conclusion, decision, choice, aim, goal, plan or whatever.

The development of a thorough-going dualist theory has been hindered by the absolute nature of Descartes' mind-body distinction. This distinction is embedded in our thinking and leads us to think what happens within us is fundamentally different from the physical events happening outside us. Positing mind and body as distinct things reifies them as Aristotelian substances with essences and properties. This reification has poisoned philosophical thinking ever since. In interactive dualism, the mental and physical are not fundamentally different. Mental events are seen as complex forms of physical events. When interactive dualism is rigorously and consistently applied, categorical distinctions that divide mind from body and the mental from the physical are rendered obsolete. To put mind and body into absolutely distinct categories is *categorical thinking* characteristic of monist as opposed to dualist thinking.

In interactive dualism, words such as 'mind', 'mental', or 'soul' are merely occult things that can't be explained in physical terms. What they refer to is explicable in terms of dualist interactions that occur in the brain and central nervous system, and they are as just as physical as the dualist interactions anywhere in the body or in the outside world. There is no need for immaterial substances or anything that can't be explained scientifically in material terms. Our subjective experiences are entirely physical and the fact that we seem to experience pains and feelings inside ourselves is only a matter of perspective. These experiences result from dualist interactions involving the holistic self interacting with what occurs physically in the brain. If we cannot explain these experiences entirely in physical terms, that is due to the lack of neurophysiological understanding and not to the existence of a 'mind' distinct from the body.

B. The Interactivity of Duality

Thus, duality in this context is about adopting a dualist view that takes account of both sides of any argument and appreciates the merits and demerits of both sides. It is an important step towards a holist view that is inclusive of everything relevant to humanity and its future. This contrasts with the monist view which concentrates on one side of the argument to the absolute detriment of the other side. Extremists generally adopt a monist view and do their best to eliminate the other side as if it had no merits whatsoever. They think that their view is the absolute truth and any argument opposing it must *ipso facto* be false and ultimately evil and despicable.

The dualist view is about being interactive with our beliefs and opinions. We hold them at arm's length so that they do not possess us. It is about self-reference in which we refer back to our beliefs to criticise them. The monist view on the other hand sees everything in terms of one thing which is thought to be the ultimate, absolute solution to complex problems. An obvious example of a monist solution is the view that capitalism is the one and only solution to all economic problems as opposed to any alternative that favours state intervention. The opposing communist view that promotes state intervention is equally a monist view that fails to take account of the capitalist one. Nowadays, there are few economies in the world that are not a mixture of these two approaches between which a balance is sought through monetary and fiscal policies.

Reality is not so simple that one 'ism' alone can encompass everything about it but monist thinkers consistently behave as if their 'ism' can do so. Monist solutions to our problems are static, monolithic and inviolable to criticism. They are applied absolutely and without alteration so that they lead inevitably to dogmatic extremism in which the opposing view is demonised. If we interact dualistically with our views we can then deal with them objectively and do not take them to heart as being the ultimate solution.

Thus, the dualist view itself is treated monistically when it is applied as if it is the one and only way of looking at things. Like any 'ism' dualism has its limitations and dualist theory aims to clarify these limitations as well as its areas of applicability. It is self-referential and is open to all kinds of interpretation. To that extent it is more like a science than a doctrine or dogma. The point is that we can choose to interact or not to interact in a dualist way and therein lies the reality of freewill. For example, we can stop ourselves doing things if we put our minds to it. Dualism is about building up the inner strength to resist and desist when we need to do so. It is about knowing when to stop and think on the one hand and when to get things done on the other hand.

When the dualist view is applied it usually means interacting between two points of view. But the resolution between these points of view is variable. It does not necessarily mean taking the middle path between extremes, or some kind of compromise between them. The resolution may mean correcting an imbalance in which one behavioural extreme has been taken too far. For example, the world is currently weighed down with increasing debt that threatens the future stability of the world's economy. If nothing is done about this trend, a catastrophic collapse in the financial markets seems inevitable. The dualist view means recognising the extent to which such extremes of behaviour need to be corrected to ensure that future progress is balanced and productive. Thus, applying the dualist view demands intuitive insight and foresight since there is no simple dualist formula that can be applied to all circumstances.

In the physical world, dualist interaction is ubiquitous and it consists in one-to-one interactions in which an exchange between disparate processes produces something different. There is no logical equivalence between the one and the other because complex processes are involved, especially with regard to biological entities. Living processes are complexes of dualist interactions. They have their roots in chemical interactions such as that between sodium and chlorine producing an entirely different substance – salt.

We are dualist beings because of our biological nature. We have internal workings that interact on a one-to-one basis with our external environment to keep us in harmony with it. We breathe in air and expel carbon dioxide. We imbibe food and drink and expel liquid and matter accordingly. The metabolic processes inside us involve dualist interactions that are markedly different from the activity in inorganic matter such as liquid and metal. As social beings we constantly interact with each other and with society and its institutions. Our thoughts are influenced by such interactions, and other people's thoughts are changed as a result of our interacting with them. What is inside us changes when we interrelate with what is outside us. This contrast between the internal and the external is inherently dualist.

Being human means being in two minds about many matters. When we are all of one mind, we may be blinded to other ways of doing things and can harm ourselves, other life-forms and the planet in general because we are collectively stupid, and create bubbles, bottle-necks and other excesses such as led to the world-wide financial crisis of 2008. Crowds are not always wise since they can be driven into riotous anarchy by fashionable excesses to which over-clever people drive them with their specious rhetorical arguments.

However, we are also a self-correcting species that realises its mistakes and can do something about them. Humanity's activities are not entirely unconscious or random like the swervings of bird flocks or the stampedes of animal herds. Our activities are constantly being observed, monitored and commented upon by self-appointed experts, journalists, pundits, academics and the like. By examining the consequences of our actions, we can rectify our mistakes, and this is done by interacting dualistically with our problems. As dualists, we do not expect to get everything right all at once but may hope to do so in the long run.

Single-minded persons often commit atrocities, like Nazi officers who plead that they are only following orders when they slaughter people mindlessly. Man's inhumanity to man often results from the voice of authority being pursued single-mindedly and inhumanely. Single-mindedness is fine in moderation and within reasonable limits. We often need it to get things done. But it is taken to extremes by absolute monists (as mentioned below) who know no limits in pursuing their ends. The dualist view draws attention to our limitations in that regard because it reminds us of the need to be self-critical. We can stop ourselves and think again and be less sure of our own reasonings. The interactive aspect of dualism reinforces this critical self-reference.

We are capable of being self-conscious, self-corrective beings who examine what we are doing and thinking and correct ourselves when necessary. In interacting with ourselves, we figuratively loop back into our former thinking and correct it accordingly. This is basically what self-consciousness involves when we are aware of what we should or should not be doing or thinking. The dualist view thus refers to self-conscious activity that involves trial-and-error; a common sense procedure that also underlies the scientific method and has ensured the remarkable success of science in transforming our society largely for the better. Dualist thinking therefore moves forward recursively in a dynamic and flexible way. It embraces opposing points of view instead of being stuck unyieldingly in one extreme viewpoint. This dynamic view is not completely realist or idealist, empiricist or rationalist, logical or intuitive. It embraces all of these in an interactive manner, that is to say, it moves from one viewpoint to the other and vice versa, according to what needs to be done in the real world in correcting imbalances, redressing injustices, and loosening rigid points of view.

We should regard opposing positions, such as left-wing/right-wing and empiricism/rationalism, as *dualist challenges* rather than irreconcilable paradoxes. These positions constantly challenge us to make sense of them and we live our lives confronting them and dealing with them. To take one side to the exclusion of the other side is the easy monist solution which invariably amounts to an extreme point of view. It is more intellectually and morally satisfying to accept the dualist challenge and to make the most of it to be best of one's abilities.

Perhaps the ultimate dualist challenge is to live as if one is going to live forever and also as if this is the last day of our lives. Resolving this paradox requires us to actively find the most important and lasting things to do, and the resolution demands our constant attention. If we regard it as nothing more than an irreconcilable paradox then we have no incentive to make anything of it. Thus, paradoxes should be regarded as dualist challenges to be overcome rather than dismissed because they are paradoxical. We overcome them by constantly doing things to get beyond them and to make better sense of life as a result.

As human beings we are both unique individuals distinct from society and collective units intimately involved in society. These incompatible positions must be constantly reconciled and this is best achieved when we are in a dualist frame of mind. As individuals we are not so unique that we can live entirely to ourselves. Extreme individuality makes no more sense than extreme conformity. We can learn to balance the two in a dualist manner. Our word 'idiot' comes from the ancient Greek word meaning those who live for themselves alone and do not participate in society at large. To make the most of ourselves we need to conform and find our rightful place in society. But this conformity is taken to extremes by those who obey authority single-mindedly. They are in a monist frame of mind and may lose their humanity by being in thrall to ideas, beliefs or opinions that are regarded as real and inviolable. They become pawns in the nefarious activities of the state or of some organisation whose activities are divorced from the interests of humanity as a whole.

We all have this problem of balancing individual self-expression with the social conformity that is needed to make the most of ourselves, and this balancing involves what is here called 'dualist interaction'. We interact with opposing ideas in a genuine effort to seek the best way forward instead of being stuck in the rut of one way of thinking. There is always another way of looking at things, and this is the essence of open-mindedness. We obey the laws of society because we have good reason to do so but we are not above breaking the law if only because we are human and not mindless automatons. If we are sufficiently moved by the injustice of certain laws, we may purposefully break them. Thus, we interact with these laws when we think about them critically and don't just obey them mindlessly.

The dualist view recognises the fragility of our humanity and is therefore the default position for human beings. Other animals may be driven by instinct and impulse but we always have the choice of doing or not doing what we feel like doing. We need to be fully aware of our potential for wicked and evil acts to avoid actually doing them. This is what self-control is all about. It consists in knowing what we can do and what we should not do. This two-minded duality makes us dynamic and uncertain animals that are always trying to do things better in the future – every day being 'Groundhog Day' as in the outstanding feature film of that name. We are all hoping to experience the perfect day in which everything goes according to plan, though we might never achieve it.

However, many philosophers avoid this obvious duality in favour of a monist view of ourselves and the universe. They see us as purely material beings or in the contrary view as purely spiritual beings. The dualist view is too untidy and illogical as it gives us a very complex interactive account whereas their inclination is to reduce everything to one thing or idea. Their thinking is discrete and categorical, and the truth is often conceived to be static, unyielding and eternal. But in the dualist view, truth is something we are constantly striving for by interacting with our environment. It is a process of continuous advancement and enlightenment rather than a fixed goal to be arrived at

C. Why the Dualist View is Important

The words 'dualism' and 'duality' are often used pejoratively to refer to contradictory and confusing behaviour: for example, the duality of behaving with sympathy at one moment and with hostility at the next moment. The dualist view itself is avoided and often dismissed without further examination. It is considered too indefinite and flawed to be seriously considered.

However, a better understanding of dualism is a tool that we can use to cope with conflict and uncertainty in our daily lives. Conflicting opinions are a necessary dynamic which can make or break an organisation. When people take sides and regard their opinions are more certain and truthful than those of the opposing side, the dualist view helps us to resolve the matter one way or the other. It may be uncertain as to which side is correct, beneficial, or whatever, but dualist thinking is about dealing with uncertainty rather than shying away from it.

Uncertainty is a necessary aspect of the human condition. Life would be boring if everything is predictable and reliable. If the outcome of a football game is certain beyond doubt, there would little point in paying to watch it. A football team that could win all its matches without fail would be promoted to a league of its own.² Similarly, there would be no need for leaders, politicians or managers if every situation pans out predictably and there are no doubts about how to deal with it. Computers and other machines are used when routines, processes and procedures can be worked out mechanically or algorithmically. When machines can deal with unpredictable situations as we do all the time, they will be the equal of us. (Turing's test is not rigorous enough to determine when computers are truly indistinguishable from human beings. The computer would think for itself and show that is thinking for itself without referring to anything else.³⁾

Whatever is discrete and measurable can be analysed by logic and mathematics. But when we think ahead and make choices between alternatives, the process is often intuitive and qualitative. Decisions made on logical grounds can be as extreme as those made by intuition. If the bankers had thought dualistically instead of logically they might have recognised the extremes to which their behaviour was tending. The bankers' and financiers' activities before the credit crunch of 2008 were doubtless backed up by a whole array of reasonable arguments. The fact is that they were too rational and failed to think outside the box. It was not so much collective insanity that led to the credit crunch as too much trust in the rationality of their actions. Only a leader imbued with a flexible, dualist outlook could have broken the mould and shown them that they were going to absurd extremes in their reasonings. Obviously such a leader never emerged at the right time.

Success in life is a black-and-white matter. Either we are successful at getting the job done or we are not – as a matter of fact. But how that success is achieved is not so clear-cut. In practical terms, we are concerned here with the means by which we may or may not achieve success through dualist thinking. A successful person is usually not just a lucky person but also one who takes account of both sides of any argument and also of the extremes to which each side may be taken by those who are prone to such extremes. In that way, they are able to take a balanced view of any situation and make realistic decisions which bear fruit.

The dualist view does not make us any the less decisive in our actions. Indeed, it gives a rational basis for decisiveness. Systematic dualism (as discussed below) considers the extremes to which our thinking can go. By so doing, it clarifies situations by revealing imbalances, imperfections, injustices, bottlenecks, and distortions which can be addressed and rectified. It clearly shows the direction in which action must be taken to achieve harmony, redress imbalances, perfect imperfections, remedy injustices, and relieve bottlenecks and distortions. We can only hope to avoid taking an extreme view in politics by carefully considering the opposing view and evaluating its merits in a dualist fashion. The resulting view is more balanced when it enables us to act more justly having taken account of all factors involved in the situation.

Dualism is part of the human condition as we are alternately active and passive beings. It is in our nature to alternate between self-assertion and self-denial. We may assert ourselves boldly and then retract into our respective shells when things go wrong as a result. This alternation is at the root of the contrast between dogmatism and scepticism. We may be over-confident of our beliefs or have no confidence in them at all. The history of philosophy may be viewed dualistically as an oscillation between dogmatism and scepticism, between the confident assertion of belief and the diffident doubt of it.[4] Evidently, philosophy is undergoing a sceptical phase at present. Perhaps it is now time for some dogmatic, one-sided dualism to help us control our obsessions so that they do not control us. As correcting such imbalances is part of the dualist view, it can be used to extremes to re-establish a balance by which things can move forward in a rational and controlled way. It is an imbalance when we have lost control of aspects of our lives. Our interests are a part of our life and not the be-all and end-all of it. The dualist view helps us to keep them in their place. We learn to externalise them by interacting with them dualistically. Conflicts can then be considered objectively to ensure that we deal with them in a balanced and systematic way. Kipling's well known 'If' poem also advocates the avoidance of extreme reactions to the 'imposters' of 'triumph and disaster' which in the cold light of day may not be as alluring or as depressing as they seem at the time.

Thus, the dualistic view is not simply about moderation in all things. It is about recognising the complications involved in a situation and, if necessary, going to opposite extremes to rectify an imbalance. For example, the prevalence of intolerance in some sectors of the community may itself be intolerable and require extreme measures to rectify it, as Karl Popper recognised in his 'Principle of Toleration'.[5] We cannot tolerate all forms of behaviour without question as is implied by extreme multiculturalism. A limit to tolerable behaviour must be set in the interests of social harmony.

Another example is Aristotle's 'golden mean' between two extremes.[6] This is a static and artificial division that does not reflect the complexity of the real world. Thus, thinking of courage as a mid-point between rashness and cowardice is of no help in practical situations where something must be done or not be done, as the case may be. The courageous person does not deliberate between two extremes but acts intuitively because something must be done. Intelligent decisiveness comes from taking account all the circumstances involved in a situation. Thus, seeking a fixed balance between two extremes is naïve dualism if it does not result from a systematic view of the whole and of all the possibilities.

The systematic dualist recognises that there are only two clear responses to a confusing situation in which people take sides against each other. One can join one side or the other or one can work towards a resolution, reconciliation or synthesis which will take the situation forward and make progress possible. Taking the first alternative, the systematic dualist would join one side or the other and work hard to moderate the views of that side and achieve a reconciliation of some kind. Taking the second alternative, he or she would be confident enough to persuade both sides that conflict and confrontation cannot achieve their ends. A complete and uncritical dualist would lack the leadership qualities required to take the dynamic and purposeful action that the situation demanded. It is arguable that successful leadership depends on the use of systematic dualism to a greater or lesser extent.

Dualism is often associated with shiftiness, prevarication, hypocrisy and even immorality. But systematic dualists by virtue of being systematic in their thinking are also being consistent, reliable and moral in their behaviour. They are no longer being systematic when their behaviour lacks integrity. If they acquire the depth in philosophy that systematic dualism demands then they are more in touch with themselves and are less inclined to misbehave. Their conduct can be consistent with the highest standards of honour and respectability though being human means that they may fall from grace as readily as anyone. The moral lapses of the eminent persons in sport and entertainment come to mind in that regard. Sooner or later, insincere, immature or malign personalities reveal their inadequacies as they are deficient in the self-criticism that the dualist view demands. They no longer see themselves as others see them and are therefore incapable of behaving themselves.

D. The Relationship of Dualism to Monism

At one extreme, the monist view is uncompromisingly focused on one viewpoint whereas in the dualist view there are no fixed either/or, black/white alternatives as far as our beliefs and opinions are concerned. Opposing alternatives are always up for consideration. The moderate or systematic dualist never excludes entirely any opposing view, and this includes even the monist view. Extreme monism in this context is a single-minded and exclusive devotion to ideas, ways of thinking, ideas, hobbies, lifestyles, and so on. Monism is not an absolute alternative to dualism as it has its place in human affairs just as dualism has, and indeed it forms part of the dualist view. There is therefore a spectrum of monist and dualist views such that there is no clear dividing line between them. We can all be monists and dualists to some degree or other. But we must never lose touch with our inner dualist and become absolute or extreme monists.

Absolute monists who give no credence to opposing views can be a menace to society, especially when they know no bounds to their fanaticism and enthusiasm. Terrorists, extremists and hot-headed fanatics are typically absolutist in their thinking. Less extreme monists are simply bores when they systematically interpret everything in relation to one thing. These include those whom the essayist William Hazlitt graphically describes as 'people with one idea.'[7] Having one idea means that every conversation is brought round to it as if it were *sine qua non* of their existence.

However, we are all moderate monists in our everyday pre-occupations with hobbies, football teams, shopping or whatever grabs and interests us most in life. Moderate monists are amateur enthusiasts who may be fanatical about their interests but only within limits. Their interests are always balanced by other interests and responsibilities such as earning a living, pursuing a career, raising a family, political activity and so on. We can therefore distinguish absolute, extreme and moderate monists along a spectrum that includes the dualist view at its moderate end. The full spectrum between monism and dualism may be represented as follows:

Absolute Monists -Extreme Monists -**Moderate Monists/
Systematic Dualists** -Naïve Dualists -Absolute Dualists

The spectrum ranges from absolute clarity to absolute obscurity: absolute monists have absolutely no doubt about their beliefs as much as absolute dualists doubt absolutely everything as a matter of policy. Absolute dualists have no views of their own and are true sceptics. They apply their scepticism single-mindedly so that paradoxically they are absolutely monistic in that regard. The same kind of paradox arises when dogmatic left wingers become fascists in enforcing their views, or when extremely conservative people are notoriously lax and permissive in their moral behaviour. In other words, absolutists end up chasing their tails and confirming that which they deny. These distinctions are summarised as follows:

- *Absolute Monists* despise moderation and give no credence to opposing views. They know no bounds to their fanaticism and enthusiasm and are often a menace to society. Terrorists, extremists and hot-headed fanatics are typically absolutist in their thinking. In absolute dualism, the world is divided absolutely into black and white, good and evil, matter and spirit, mind and body and so on. The thinking of absolute monists is dominated by categorical thinking in which the world is dividing into rigid categories. You are either for them or against them.
- *Extreme Monists* systematically interpret everything in relation to one thing without using violence to enforce their views. Having one idea means that every conversation is brought round to it as if it were *sine qua non* of their existence. To be obsessed about one's hobbies, about losing weight or about any number of such fixations is to be an extreme monist. Thus, those suffering from obsessive compulsive disorder (OCD) are invariably extreme monists.
- *Moderate Monists* are what we all are in our everyday pre-occupations with hobbies, football teams, shopping or whatever grabs and interests us most in life. As moderate monists we are amateur enthusiasts who are fanatical about our interests but only within limits. We are not obsessive about them to a fault, as such interests are always balanced by other interests and responsibilities such as earning a living, pursuing a career, raising a family, political activity and so on. But moderate monists are also systematic dualists by the very fact of being moderate in their monist indulgences.
- *Systematic Dualists* recognise that when they are faced with opposing sides there are only two clear responses to a confusing situation in which people take sides against each other. They can join one side or the other or they can work towards a resolution, reconciliation or synthesis that will take the situation forward and make progress possible.

Taking the first alternative, the systematic dualist would join one side or the other and work hard to moderate the views of that side and achieve a reconciliation of some kind. Taking the second alternative, he or she would be confident enough to persuade both sides that conflict and confrontation cannot achieve their ends. Thus, systematic dualists work hard to reconcile extremes and may even resort to extremes in their dualism if the end justifies the means, that is to say, the end of achieving moderation and good sense.

- *Naïve Dualists* are without any systematic approach by which to cope with their dualist views. They have the muddle-headed, fence-sitting kind of dualism in which one is unable to make up one's mind. They are like Buridan's ass that had equal piles of hay on either side of it. As it was unable to make up its mind which pile to eat, it starved to death. Such dualists clearly lack the internal *nous* and the leadership qualities required to take the dynamic and purposeful action that the situation demands.
- *Absolute Dualists* are sceptical of all beliefs whatsoever. They tend to divide the world absolutely into good and evil, matter and spirit, mind and body and so on. They lack a stable belief system by which to relate one side to the other. The Manicheans were absolute dualists as was Descartes with his mind/body dualism which lacked a coherent interaction between these extremes. These views are also absolute in that they interpret the world from one sceptical point of view. Like all absolutists you are either for them or against them from their point of view.

These categories are entirely fluid and we may shift between them in different situations. Moreover, in everyday life, we can be both moderate monists and systematic dualists. When we want to get things done, we are generally single-minded about it and have no doubts about it. When we are faced with problematic situations then the dualist within us comes to the fore. We need to take account of opposing views and perhaps carefully consider both sides of the argument. We have to be open-minded when we want to reach a clear view of things. But when it is clear that things have gone to extremes and a serious imbalance has occurred than the moderate monist will find plenty of reasons to do what needs to be done.

We also incorporate both dualist and monist ways of thinking without being aware of it. The latter means being moderate in our prejudices and pre-occupations, and the former means recognising the alternatives that are always possible. We must judge when to be carefully doubtful and when to be cautiously certain. Great and successful leaders are usually adept in combining moderate monism with systematic dualism. They are generally dualist in their thinking and are invariably flexible and creative in their behaviour while also being certain and sure-footed in their decision-making. An outstanding example of this is Oliver Cromwell whose conversation could be baffling and hard to understand but whose actions and battle strategy were decisive and effective.[8] This duality is often called 'common sense' but dualist theory goes much further than Thomas Reid and the Scottish Common Sense School in elucidating what it is.[9]

We can all identify with Robert Graves' poem, "In Broken Images".[10] We are "slow, thinking in broken images", while others are "quick, thinking in clear images." We reach a new understanding of our confusion while others experience a new confusion of their understanding. The systematic dualist view is that clarity resides with facts, things and events while confusion and uncertainty may justly reign in our views, opinions, beliefs, convictions which are peculiar to ourselves. Formal, linear logic is needed for the former but a dualist, dynamic logic is required for the latter. We may be certain, reasonable and logical about facts that we all share but we often have to suspend judgment about our own opinions. A different logic is required in which the middle view is not excluded. Thus, dualist logic is not the same as formal logic. Changes of mind may lead us to contradict ourselves. We must be more inclusive in our thinking. Being open-minded and forward thinking means that we hold our opinions at arm's length and with some doubt and uncertainty. In contrast, the absolute monist errs in attributing absolute truth and clarity to his or her beliefs and in attempting to eliminate doubt in matters in which doubt is more often a virtue than a hindrance. It is nearly always the case that "much might be said on both sides".[11]

Nevertheless, decisiveness is not incompatible with dualist thinking. In daily life, it is often necessary to be decisive and sure-footed. Systematic dualists must necessarily hone their judgments to ensure that decisive action is taken when required. They will thrive on opposing arguments and on the pleasure of reconciling them to achieve worthy ends which are otherwise defeated by the acrimony aroused by such oppositions. They will seek unity and unanimity in relation to the aims of society. Effective leadership can always inspire and motivate people so that they fight for common causes rather than against each other. But it is successful only when it eschews the extremes and shows clearly the benefits of the middle way. When left wingers and right wingers make enemies of each other then the middle way is lost and society can lose its sense of direction.

E. The Social Usefulness of the Dualist View

Some Aims of Dualist Studies
- To train the mind to cope with extreme thought tendencies and to avoid complete scepticism on the one hand and complete dogmatism on the other hand;
- To show that dualist thinking is not necessarily vague or indecisive and is in fact necessary for correct and productive thinking;
- To show how new ideas can change society for the better;
- To instil philosophy with renewed vigour;
- To understand better what it is to be human, especially in contrast with what is considered to be inhuman, in thought and behaviour.

The Application of Dualist Studies

Dualist studies involve applying the dualist view to practical areas such as management, crime and punishment, education, future studies, and extreme ways of thinking. An outline follows of the dualist approach to each of these areas:

A dualist approach to management: The dualist view is essential to successful management. It consists in understanding the extremes of opinion and attitude to which both employers and employees are prone and which pervade every workplace. The dualist view can help managers deal with situations that demand intuitive insight more than incisive logic. The distinction between naïve and systematic dualism is useful here in which the former refers to confused and muddled thinking whereas the latter involves organised and purposeful thinking to deal systematically with confusing and conflicting situations. Such distinctions help us to understand conflicts between rival groups within the workplace and with leadership dilemmas such balancing friendliness with aloofness. The successful manager learns intuitively how to maintain a balance between being friendly with employees and keeping his distance from them and is thus behaving in a dualist manner in that respect.[12]

A dualist approach to crime and punishment: At present, crime is punished very unevenly and often ineffectively. Punishments are meted out in an unsystematic way that leads to the extremes of under and over punishment. Those who might be punished with leniency are often given custodial sentences that ruin their lives, while others who deserve very harsh punishment to put them on the right track are often treated too leniently. When dangerous people finish their term of 'punishment' they are let out into the community and may endanger the public. The conservative view is that criminals should be punished with longer jail sentences. The liberal view is that people should be rehabilitated and not merely punished by jail sentences. The dualist view is that the person should be punished, not the crime. In other words, law-breakers should be punished not by fixed, predetermined sentences but according to what is required to 'cure' them of their social deviance and hopefully make honest citizens of them. A *social treatment system* is therefore required to change our criminal justice system and to ensure that those who need lenient treatment are given it and those who need harsh treatment are also given it.[13]

A dualist approach to education: In one respect, we need education to be thumped into us if we are to imbibe successfully such basic skills as reading, writing and arithmetic. But in another respect we need to absorb knowledge and understanding in our own way and in our own time. When these two contrasting approaches are insightfully combined, they interact to produce the best kind of education. The first approach may be called 'Mode 1' and the second 'Mode 2'. Mode 1 emphasises the skills, knowledge and abilities that should be inculcated through education, whereas Mode 2 emphasises the cultivation of individuality and creativity. In the dualist view, both these approaches are combined in an imaginative way.[14] Another way of putting it is that we must both 'fill the vessel' and 'kindle the fire' in our dualist educational approach. Plutarch is often quoted as saying that a child's mind is not a vessel to be filled but a fire to be kindled.[15] But children's minds need also to be filled with facts, poems, stories, languages and all the skills needed to understand society and take their place in it. Their memories need to be developed just as much as their interests and passions kindled and promoted. Thus, a dualist approach to education involves as much disciplined learning as free learning.

A dualist approach to future studies: Though we live in the present we constantly look back to the past and forward to the future. Studying the past helps us to predict the future, and looking to the future helps us to anticipate things being better than they are at present. But we can be too pre-occupied with the past at the expense of the future and vice versa. These are monist views that look exclusively in either one direction or the other. It means that we dwell too much in the past or look too confidently to the future. The *retrospective* view looks to the past and *prospective* view to the future (see the Introduction pp. 7-9 for more on these views). The dualist view helps us to place equal value on both these views. We move in a dynamic way from one to the other without being stuck in the past or leaving everything to the future.[16]

A dualist approach to eliminating extremes of thought: Systematic dualism is essential for creativity as it depends on our maintaining a balance between thinking too much or too little. It is arguable that those 'geniuses' who perform extraordinary feats of creativity are only able to do so because they are systematic dualists who avoid self-defeating extremes in their thinking. They develop their mental powers in a purposeful fashion without taking themselves too seriously on the one hand or belittling themselves too much on the other hand. Often we are in doubt whether to think too much of ourselves or too little. Here are the extreme consequences of the opposing tendencies involved:

Thinking too much of oneself	*Thinking too little of oneself*
May lead to	May lead to
Hot-headed extremism	*Empty-headed indifference*
Involving	Involving
Brazen overconfidence	*Insipid lack of confidence*
And *in extremis* to	And *in extremis* to
Homocidal sociopathy	*Suicidal self-abnegation*

It appears that too many young people are prone to these extremes these days, leading to an outbreak of massacres and suicides, as reported in the mass media. Suicide bombers seem to incorporate both these strands in their thinking. Their unbalanced thinking twists these strands into a deadly double helix, the antithesis of DNA which gives life instead of taking it. They think too much of themselves and too little at the same time. They arrogantly think that their deaths can make a difference while by making out that their lives are worthless enough to be terminated instantly. They achieve nothing lasting by their senseless actions. A rational dualist interaction between these extremes is required to avoid being possessed by them beyond sense and reality. Thus, a greater understanding of our essential duality is the next big step forward for humanity.

Concluding Remarks: The ultimate truth for human beings lies not in settling for one viewpoint but in incorporating all viewpoints by interacting constantly with them to make as much of them as humanly possible. This is clearly the opposite of religious or ideological viewpoints that see only one way forward. It accords with an ongoing dualist view that is constantly interacting with the world and its contents. This whole-hearted position provides us with the open-minded outlook to work out for ourselves what we are to do with our lives. We manoeuvre our way through life on a trial-and-error basis and do not expect everything to be straightforward or made easy for us. In other words, our safety, security and internal well-being lies in constant interaction, in striving to better ourselves, and in taking account of everything in a spirit of open-minded curiosity and vitality. Being open to all things promotes optimism whereas confining ourselves to one point of view or mindset depresses and stunts us as human beings. Dualism can be all things to all men but only by bringing all views into its omniscient fold. This is no easy task but we can all learn to work at it if we have the will to do so. Thus, the task of dualist theory is to supply the reasons and rationale for doing so - this is a beginning not an end.

Part Two

Personal Advancement

5. Vitality: Building Ourselves Up

> This is the true joy in life: the being used for a purpose recognised by yourself as a mighty one; the being thoroughly worn out before you are thrown on the scrapheap; the being a force of Nature instead of a feverish selfish little clod of ailments and grievances complaining that the world will not devote itself to making you happy.
>
> George Bernard Shaw (1903) [1]

A. The Need to Develop Ourselves Within

Our advancement depends as much on our inner development as on our material development. As individuals we need to be mentally strong within ourselves, if we are to maximise our creative potential, our strength of purpose and our dynamic forcefulness. Without these, we are mere flotsam and jetsam on the ocean of life. Also, as fallible human beings, we are all too easily diverted from fulfilling our potential in these respects.

If we are lacking in these respects and wish to improve ourselves, there is nothing to stop us but our own inertia and lack of motivation which each of us has to find for ourselves since no one can do it for us. It is perfectly possible for anyone sufficiently self-directed to increase their vitality and becoming vitalists who are full of the vibrancy of life and living. Such vitality comprises the za-zoom, the extra energy required to get worthwhile things done. We cannot be wise persons without having something special within us that makes us want to continue living and doing things. This special ingredient gives us the *raison d'être* to do what needs to be done in asserting ourselves on the world. It gets us out of our beds and gets us going in the mornings. Without this extra chutzpah, here called vitality, we are meek and humble beings awaiting our fate without doing anything about it.

This additional involvement within us is produced by what is here called 'inner being'. It is extra and additional but it is still entirely physical. There is nothing occult or supernatural about inner being as herein conceived. It is however that which makes us complicated beings instead of being straightforwardly predictable like machines or simple organisms. It also gives us the edge over the internet that lacks the centrality to make it a distinctive entity. Whether it will ever achieve that centrality or 'singularity' remains to be seen.

Self-knowledge involves knowing what one is capable of and what underlies that capability. Thus, a better understanding of the source of our vitality, namely, inner being is essentially to self-knowledge. This 'inner being' is entirely material and yet highly complex and unfathomable. Getting in touch with our inner being involves examining ourselves and what we do with ourselves. This is a circular self-reflection that is an art rather than a science. It cannot be taught but must be achieved by each of us on our own. If a person cannot sit in a room on their own and quietly get in touch with their thoughts, they will find it difficult to become vitalists in the sense of the word used here. It means being in touch with that which is within us. If we are absorbed or pre-occupied with what lies without us, getting in touch with our inner being may prove difficult and challenging.

Clearly, vitality is the essence of life and the mainspring of our existence. Without vitality of some sort we cannot motive ourselves to do anything let alone do the best we can. It is the unifying force within us that gets us going and keeps us going throughout life. It is the 'all' within us that makes us at 'one' with ourselves. We need to build it up and keep it working for us otherwise we lose our way and become depressed, obsessed, over-anxious, suicidal, anti-social or just plain bored with life. By understanding our vitality we can rally it within ourselves. When we understand it sufficiently to make something of it, we become vitalists. We have to invoke the vitality within us by whatever means. Understanding vitality thus means entering a sphere of self-knowledge within which we can better understand ourselves and our capabilities.

We need to work hard to make the most of our vitality. It is by developing our inner being that we can become a vital force instead of weak and vacillating individuals that do little or nothing with our lives. Therein we invoke what is alive and vital within us and become vitalists in the best sense of the word. Without the requisite vitality we have nothing in us to make us do anything of any lasting value. Invoking what is in us enable us to surpass ourselves and do more that we thought we could do. We use our intelligence and creativity both to develop our inner being and to do things in the world. The interaction between these two inner and outer aspects is what makes us vital beings. As vitalists we can bring out our intelligence and creativity in the service of humanity. It is a matter of putting ourselves constantly to the test in understanding our inner workings.

Bringing out the best in us consists in exploiting the potential which lies within us. What is within us is our inner being which comprises the subjective, mental activity that is peculiar to each and every one of us. It includes consciousness, self-consciousness as well unconscious mental activity. It is often inaccurately called 'spirit', 'vital energy', 'universal mind', or whatever. But these terms are misleading as they suggest something non-material whereas inner being can be explained entirely in physical terms.

Inner being is a process that makes possible notions such as 'I', 'self', and 'subjectivity'. These notions reflect our awareness of inner being at least at the conscious level. They make sense only as self-reflective notions by which we interact with inner being and therefore with the physical processes going on inside us. Using words like 'spirit' and 'soul' suggests that a discrete substance exists in us that can survive our death. But the activity of inner being is entirely physical and located in the brain and central nervous system. It is part of the body and dies with it, as is argued further below.

From an abstract point of view, invoking our inner being is arguably the best way to integrate the perfectionist and fallibilist tendencies in our thinking about things. Such an invocation takes the mind to higher planes of existence within which such tendencies may be related and brought together in terms of the best goals and purposes to which the individual is capable of aspiring. We invoke our inner being whenever we do things that conform to the needs and aspirations of our whole personality. Such an invocation is a holistic activity that unifies us in our most prized endeavours so that we do indeed do what is best for us, given all the information at our disposal.

Moreover, it is the practical use of inner being that is being emphasised here. When we successfully invoke our inner being, we are ready to use it actively in a social context. Inner being is such that it must be constantly activated so that it might not stagnate and deteriorate into apathy, dogmatism and extremism. *Firstly,* we must examine what inner being consists in. *Secondly,* we consider what kind of training can help us to develop and bring out the best within us. This includes the exercises in the book as well as the capacity to introspect. We cannot underestimate the extent to which introspection and solitude are important in cultivating inner being. However, it must be remembered that vitality invokes our subjective dispositions to do things, and these dispositions or feelings do not always conform to reality. They must be constantly monitored and subjected to interactive examination and discrimination to weed out what is false and harmful to us. Constant self-criticism is ever needed to keep us on the straight and narrow.

B. The Vitality of our Inner Being

As Wordsworth walked, filled with his strange inner joy, responsive thus to the secret life of nature around him, his rural neighbours, tightly and narrowly intent upon their own affairs, their crops and lambs and fences, must have thought him a very insignificant and foolish personage. It surely never occurred to any one of them to wonder what was going on inside of *him* or what it might be worth. And yet that inner life of his carried the burthen of a significance that has fed the souls of others, and fills them to this day with inner joy.

William James (1915) [2]

What 'inner being' is all about. There is a unified activity within us that makes us what we are and that forms the basis of our vitality. It is here called 'inner being' as opposed to 'outer being' which is our physical body as it is perceived by us from outside us. Inner being is what is going on inside our bodies that cannot be perceived directly, though it nevertheless exists physically. It makes the difference being alive and being dead. As human beings we have various names for different aspects of inner being, such as consciousness, self, ego, 'I', subjectivity, personality, will, character and all the names we use to refer to our distinctiveness and uniqueness as living beings. But inner being also includes all the unconscious mental activity that is always going in the brain. It is not to be confused with simplistic terms such as 'spirit' and 'soul' that have theological connotations. Inner being has a purely material basis in the body and is not distinct from the physical processes going on in the body. All living beings have an inner being that makes them distinctive as life-forms as opposed to mere lumps of matter.

The term 'inner being' is used here in two senses. It is used as a self-referential notion to refer to ourselves and what we do introspectively, and it is also used to refer objectively to what is going on in our bodies that unifies our bodily activity and makes us distinctive as living beings. In the latter sense, inner being is embedded in our bodies and is not distinct from the workings of our bodies. It is identical to what is going on in our brains and in our central and peripheral nervous systems. At death, it perishes with the rest of the body of which it is an integral part during our life-times. It may be described as a strange attractor in the body that loses its centrality, so that dissolution and disorder ensues.

The exact nature of inner being may never be wholly determined by science. However, the novel idea of a 'strange attractor' goes some way towards clarifying how it functions in our brain and nervous system.[3] It may function as a 'strange attractor' that ripples around the organism and keeps all physical and metabolic activity working in unison according to its purposes. In chaos theory, a strange attractor moves around in a chaotic but measurably mathematical fashion to produce patterns that are resonate in nature as well as in mathematical models. For example, coastlines follow that kind of chaotic pattern. Thus, we may postulate that inner being moves around the body like a strange attractor around which all the neural and metabolic activity of the body gravitates. We are aware of inner being as strange attractor when for example we feel our toes or experience pain in parts of our body. It is both what we are and we are not. It is both identical to us and is distinct from us at the same time. It is contradictory because it is a dualist process that cannot be pinned down as it is always on the move. We are conscious of being conscious when inner being is strongly interactive with the mental and physical content of our bodies. In the case of unconscious activity, inner being is weakly interactive with the body as a whole.

The concrete, material nature of inner being. As a unifying strange attractor, inner being includes conscious as well as unconscious mental activity as it refers to all subjective activity including the self that identifies us subjectively. Inner being is a concrete, material notion which is embedded in our bodies and is not distinct from the workings of our bodies. It is identical to what is going on in our brains and central nervous system. At death, it perishes with the rest of the body of which it is an integral part during our life-times. The strange attractor of inner being loses its centrality, and dissolution and disorder ensues. Inner being is thus rooted in material reality and it results from the biological and metabolic interactions occurring in our bodies. Its nature is both ideal and real in that it is an interactive link between these two contexts. The conscious part of inner being results from a self-reference process in which the strange attractor turns into itself to make self-awareness possible. This gives rise to the introspective use of the 'inner being' and this aspect is now discussed.

Inner being includes the unconscious processes that link us to reality on an ongoing basis while we are awake even though we are unaware of them. We are embedded in reality and relate to it by the workings of our inner being which interacts with what is given in reality through our senses and the conceptions we arrive at concerning the content that reality. We see the clouds in the sky but we are only aware of them as being clouds because we have arrived at conceptions of clouds based on our understanding of what we see. That understanding itself results from unconscious processes that relate our conception of clouds to what we see. These processes form part of our inner being that works hard constantly to incorporate such knowledge. The initiative to understand anything therefore depends on our adapting and developing inner being to arrive at such an understanding.

Inner being also governs the strength or weakness of our so-called 'character'. Generally speaking, the stronger our character, the more developed is our inner being. Its development is the *sine qua non* of a vital and affirmative attitude to life.[4] Sustaining this development enables us to keep going against all the odds. It is the source of all will-power and self-determination and it develops over time through an intensification and unification of our experiences of life. It therefore forms the basis of one's personality, namely, that which is unique and singular about us.

This inner development bolsters our resolve to value our lives. Not thinking well of ourselves, as having some value and importance in the world, impairs our ability to improve ourselves and benefit other people to the best of our abilities. A developed inner being concentrates our thoughts and feelings and renders them more intense. As a result we can relate more holistically and completely with our experiences and make more of them. We get more pleasure and satisfaction from our daily experiences and value them and are more pleased with ourselves as a result.

The unified nature of inner being also gives us our conscience whereby we monitor our behaviour and adjust it accordingly in so far as we pay attention to the dictates of conscience. It is the intuition that holds us back when, for example, we feel that we are going too far or are making too much of a situation. Psychopaths and sociopaths typically have lost touch with their inner being and have no conscience. They feel no remorse, shame or guilt for their misdeeds. Their feelings are dislocated from the consequences of their actions. They are not complete personalities because of this disability and are less than human in their lack of feelings.

Inner being involves constant internal interaction between unconscious influences. It is sustained by physical processes within us that underlie the unconscious workings of our minds. It encompasses (1) the genetic influences given to us from our original conception onwards, (2) the build up of habits and routines in the process of our personality development, and (3) the intuitions, impulses, habits, routines and immediate experiences generated by that inner being below the level of consciousness. These three influences intermingle and interact to maintain the dynamism of inner being which never can be pinned down as being one thing or another.

The strength of inner being may be exemplified as follows: On a fine summer's day, I am lying idly outside in the sun when there is gardening to be done. Unless I am inwardly moved in some way, I can't be bothered doing anything. Perhaps I am in need of the rest. But merely being lazy is no excuse and my conscience may prick me. In that case, the strength of my inner being is needed to make the difference between feeling the need to do some gardening and not being bothered to do it. I must feel moved to do it. An aspect of my self becomes differentiated as a positive force in my inner being. It is I alone who must do this and nothing else will do it. The negativity of my inner passivity is countered by its positive aspects which generate further thoughts and feelings on the matter. I need to do this for such and such reasons.

If the need to do gardening is to overcome my negative feelings of laziness and indifference, I must think about what is or is not to be done to accomplish this self-imposed task. Nothing will be achieved if I think of someone else doing it or think too much of the effort involved in doing it. In thinking positively of myself doing this gardening, I am consciously focusing on the task and I can then summon up the will to do them. In the end, the power of a unified inner being is needed to ensure that any negative feelings to the contrary are suppressed and that I am consciously disposed to act as I should. In this way, I am interacting with the positive and negative inclinations of my inner being to get myself to do things. And there is no distinction between my doing the task and my inner being impelling me to do it since they are ultimately at one on the matter when I actually do what I intend to do. We can have all the motivation in the world but unless we have the will to do it, nothing can make us do what should be done. The inner being is the sole source of that will power.

C. Its Workings

Inner being is of paramount importance in unifying the physical processes in the body. It is no 'ghost in the machine' nor is it a distinct organ of the body that can be pointed to. It is rather the unified activity of bodily processes which include (1) neural networks in the brain, (2) the workings of the central and peripheral nervous systems, and (3) the metabolic activity of the organs in the body. These are all unified by the activity of inner being which is therefore not supernatural or distinct from the body. It unifies the body's physical processes which are entirely confined to the body and inseparable from it. Nevertheless, inner being supervenes bodily functions in so far as it unifies them and gives us the immediate experiences that constitute subjectivity. This supervention is a function of the unity of the physical processes involved. It is not distinct from these processes but because it is unified, inner being cannot be reduced to the physical processes that make it possible.

While inner being is a physical activity, it is also more than the sum of its components. The physical processes by themselves alone cannot give us our experience of a supervened subjectivity that defines what we are. The activity of these processes acting purposefully and in unison is required to supervene the components of inner being. We are aware that this supervention takes place only because we have non-reducible, subjective experiences that are over and above the underlying physical processes. Reductionists reduce inner being to its basic physical components and say that there is nothing above or beyond these components. They assume that as inner being cannot be pointed to or excised by surgery, therefore it cannot exist in reality. But they are 'nothing butterists' who cannot see the wood for the trees. The fact is that we are not composed of nothing but matter and energy, nor are we determined only by our genetic inheritance, nor are we impelled by nothing but physical and chemical activity. We are more than all these things otherwise we would be indistinguishable from non-organic entities such as stones, liquids and gases. But it is only the complexity of unified physical activity in the brain that is responsible for inner being and not any additional spiritual component.

Ultimately, it is our purposefulness that is the source of our vitality. In pursuing our purposes, we unify our inner resources to get things done. Such purposes are not entirely predictable or calculable. Indeed, it is a truism that life is not entirely mechanical or automatic in its functioning. A living organism is not a machine but a teleological being capable of changing its inner configurations in relation to its goals and purposes. It is composed of cells and organs, each of which functions purposefully in relation to the whole entity. Neither the whole nor its parts operate automatically or algorithmically in the way that a computer operates. They operate by a flexible feedback with their environment that involves reacting to information received. These reactions are not wholly predictable and they give rise to goals, functions and other modes of purposeful activity peculiar to living beings. What happens inside them is unlike what happens in purely material entities that lack the attribute of life. Thus, inner being involves the purposeful, unified activity of the body, while being indistinguishable from that body and its physical components at the level of physical examination. It is at the higher level of unified, complex interactions that inner being becomes distinguishable.

Furthermore, a unified inner being is essential to the continuance of life. In general terms, biological entities are characterised by unified internal activity which is distinct from their external environment while interacting with that environment at the same time. When that unified internal activity ceases, these entities die. They are no longer living organisms but inert lumps of matter. Something has changed within them that they need to keep them alive and functional. It is their unified inner being that has ceased to function so that the body begins to fall apart. The inner being functions as the goal-making activity that unifies the organism and keeps it going against the odds. Life begins as bundles of cells that have no distinct organs but they have unifying activity that keeps them together. Thus, the unifying activity is not centred on any particular organ but on the whole body acting as an interactive unity. The various organs develop while being connected to the overall unity of the body. The stopping of the heart does not necessarily mean that death follows. Its function can be taken over by a heart-lung machine. The heart itself cannot work properly without the support and input of other major organs such as the brain, liver and kidneys. It does not orchestrate the functioning of all these organs since that functioning requires the impetus of inner being to sustain its activity. That is to say, the heart depends on the unconscious functioning of nervous activity that stimulates it to beat rhythmically according to the needs of the whole organism. It also depends on the food and oxygen supplied again by the whole organism in its unified functioning.

Our inner harmony also requires unifying processes. Inner being is required to harmonise the functioning of bodily organisms and it does so by means of its goals, both conscious and unconscious. In being the organising principle, that ensures the continued life of an organism, inner being harmonises all the processes and organs whose combined functioning is required to keep the organism alive and kicking. It unifies the organism in relation to its goals, aims, desires and aspirations, and in its turn it is produced by that unity and maintains the unity. Hence its activity interacts with all bodily functions in maintaining that unity. It is initiated and sustained by the feedback activity of the goals which the whole organism has in common from its genetic inheritance. It is not an identifiable thing or substance but the unified processes of the body in themselves. On the one hand, inner being is an interactive, self-referential notion that has no fixed essence of its own. On the other hand, it refers to that ever-flowing process which unifies all physical and metabolic processes within us and supplies all the feelings, intuitions and thoughts that constantly beset us. Much of the activity of inner being takes place in our unconscious to which we have only limited access. Thus, the different organs of the body function directly in response to processes governed by the unified inner being working at an unconscious level. They may function at their own pace and within their own limits but their activity also depends on communication with all the other organs to work in harmony with them.

The unified activity of inner being is therefore necessary for the maintenance of life. A comatose person remains alive because of the continued metabolic activity in brain and body. This is the same as saying that inner being is keeping them alive. Death comes when the failure of vital organs such as the heart, liver and brain destroys the unified functioning of the body thus stopping the inner being's activity. Inner being depends on these organs as much as they depend on it to keep them working in harmony. As inner being does not survive death, it is not anything like the soul which is believed by religious people to survive death. Only the effects of inner activity during our lifetime outlive us in the form of our works and our influences on others. It is these vital effects that we need to make the most off in developing our inner being so that we make our mark on the world during our lifetimes, and not during some mythical, non-existent afterlife.

Thus, the activity of inner being is clearly much more than a simple relationship between mind and body. It has nothing to do with the simplistic Cartesian distinction between mind and body. That distinction is made between two substances which have properties of their own. Inner being is not a substance nor does it have properties distinct from the body in which it functions. It is no more than our personal, subjective view of what is going in the body in so far as inner being is accessible to our conscious since most of it works at an inaccessible unconscious level.

Inner being is more than just a functioning brain and central nervous system as it involves the whole body and its intricate metabolic activity of which the brain and its connections are only one part. It is made possible by the brain, nervous system and all the bodily functions combining to maintain it from one second to the next. The latter in their turn are kept going by inner being unifying the whole in relation to its primary goal of survival and its secondary goals and aspirations of making its mark on the universe. As a result of the complex interactions between inner being and all its aspects, it maintains its life-giving unity. For instance, an interaction between the left and right hemispheres of the brain is one aspect of the activity of inner being. But neither of these is sufficient to constitute that inner being since we know that people with damaged or missing hemispheres of the left or the right are very much alive and full of vim and vigour. Thus, inner being requires bodily functioning as a whole and brain activity is far from being all there is to it.

The mental faculties such as memory, perception and conception are tools that we use in acts of interacting. They give rise to the various aspects of inner being rather than being aspects themselves. They are the means by which interaction between the aspects and the external world takes place. These aspects are our direct experiences of ourselves and the external world, The mental faculties give rise to these experiences but are not themselves what we are experiencing on a day-to-day basis. They are genetically generated and therefore bodily inheritances like the other organs of the body. But they are nevertheless ours and they contribute to what we are as complex human beings.

Therefore, we use our brains and not *vice versa*. Our brains don't do anything of their own accord. We may have unconscious, involuntary actions but it is the mental processes underlying inner being that are responsible and not the brain as such. Though the physical workings of our brains interact holistically to make inner being possible, these workings are not independent of the activity of inner being or of other aspects of subjectivity involving the self. The view that our brains are genetically programmed to make us do things is a confusion of cause and effect. When we become self-aware, the changes in our brain's neural connections are the effect of environmental and cultural influences on what we decide or do not decide to do in life. In so far we make up our own minds about doing things, we are not being compelled to do so by our brains. The brain changes are not caused by anything prior to their being affected by these influences. Inner being is initiated by genetic influences but it is built up through thought and experience. We are not programmed for religious beliefs as we have a choice as to whether we adopt or do not adopt such beliefs. Our brains have no choice in the matter. The same applies to the body and other aspects of inner being which have no will of their own because they lack the consciousness of self.

Thus, genetic influences are interactive and not directly causal. The fact is that genetic and other influences are not sufficient to account for complexity and diversity of inner being. Neither the brain, body nor any genetic influences can do everything by themselves. They are parts of the whole and not the whole themselves. By themselves, the brain and the other bodily organs would be competing with each other and their parts instead of co-operating with each other. Genetic influences cannot subsist by themselves. They must interact with the body as a whole otherwise we would be entirely instinctive, mechanical beings. To stop these disparate influences being at odds with each other, the activity of inner being is needed to unify their functioning in terms of its goals. The brain, body and genetic influences contribute to the interactivity of inner being whose activity uses them as tools to fulfil its overriding ends. Inner being also includes the conscious part in which we are aware that we do things for ourselves. There is therefore a constant interaction between inner being and the organism as a whole. Understanding the nature of this interaction is our constant and unending concern as we can never understand it fully without eradicating it.

It is also apparent that inner being cannot be replicated in another body. It is fundamentally unique to each of us and is a biological phenomenon which only comes into being within the medium of a biological entity. It cannot be reproduced independently of the entity in which it is rooted as it forms the unique being of that entity. Inner being is interconnected with the entire body and it is indivisible and cannot be reconstituted by copying the body down to the last atom and molecule. Such a replicated body would have no consciousness or sense of self since it would lack the unifying quality of the original unified activity of inner being. That unifying quality is arguably rooted at the quantum level of existence, and until we can manipulate quantum particles, we will not replicate living beings merely by reconstructing their atomic and molecular structure in the same way. That quantum activity is itself linked to the workings of the universe as whole. It cannot be taken away from us without changing the universe as whole. The evidence supporting this quantum view lies in the freewill by which we decide to do or not to do things. This can only have its source in the indeterminacy of quantum functioning and this occurs at the very smallest level at which inner being unifies bodily functions and achieves physical acts such as raising one's arm. The decision to raise one's arm therefore requires quantum activity that ultimately percolates through the entire body and involves both the brain and central and peripheral nervous systems.

These arguments suggest that there is no possibility of transporting inner being to another body because the unified operation of that particular body involves inaccessible quantum activity. Thus, the functioning of inner being is unique to each individual and cannot be recreated in another brain or body. As already stated, in the absence of inner being, the body falls into disunity, and inner being has no existence outside the body of which it is an inextricable part. They are seamlessly combined into an irreducible whole. The proof of this lies in the reality of the inner being's activity which exists in no particular place in the body. We are all stuck with an inner activity that is unique to ourselves and cannot be transported elsewhere since what we are is inextricably bound up with our bodies in ways that may ultimately defeat the attempts of the most intricate technology to disentangle it.

D. Its Reality

Inner being exists both physically and subjectively as a self-referential notion. Its reality lies firstly in its physical existence and secondly in our subjective experience of it by self-reference or introspection, and thirdly in our knowledge that much of inner being is inaccessible to our consciousness and manifests itself in our feelings, intuitions, dreams and other phenomena that emerge from it and into our consciousness. Inner being does not differ in any way from the physical and chemical activity of the organism. Its reality therefore consists in actual brain and neural activity that makes it possible. It is identical with that activity and is not anything more than that activity. Inner being ceases to exist when that activity comes to an end at the point of death. It is located in no particular place as it is refers to continuous processes that involve the whole body through the brain and the central and peripheral nervous systems. Inner being thus begins and ends in the brain and extends to every part of the body to which it belongs.

The real existence of inner being also depends on self-reference or acts of introspection. We have subjective experiences because cerebral and neural processes refer back to themselves and make self-awareness possible. We are aware of ourselves as distinct entities because of that self-reference which is an entirely physical process. As a self-referential notion inner being is extended in the breadth, range and complexity of our thoughts, ideas and images about things and events. These are still rooted within us as physical events that occur in the brain and nervous systems.

The root of our subjective processes may lie in the hemispheres of the brain. The unifying function of inner being may be initiated in the right hemisphere of the brain, and the fragmenting function is initiated in the left hemisphere where our thoughts are consciously apprehended and taken apart by verbal reasoning. In other words, unconscious mental activity is brought together in the right hemisphere and then taken apart in the left hemisphere where we become conscious of what we are doing or not doing. But the whole functioning of inner being is in neither place but involves the whole mind and body of the person. It is brought together in the brain but extends throughout the body.

It is clearly by means of subjective self-reference that we keep in touch with objective reality. Inner being is only one of several self-referential notions such as the self and consciousness by which we refer back to ourselves and our subjective experiences. They are interactive and inherently paradoxical notions. As soon as we think about what they refer to, their objects become different from what they were originally experienced to be. This means that further interactions are always required to rationalise the contradictions. In using such rationalising interactions we constantly strive to stay in touch with reality, and consciousness often defies the unified inclinations of inner being to impose its arbitrary categories on things. Through intuition, the unity of inner being reinforces our presuppositions and we must consciously strive to criticise and correct such inclinations. In this way we socialise and rationalise our inner inclinations and become less selfish and impulsive. Inner being is always stronger or weaker than we can think it to be. We have difficulty focusing on it as it really is. We only find its limits by constantly putting it to the test. This means bringing it to mind and thus acknowledging its existence by using it rather than believing in it.

Self-reference notions are necessarily contradictory because they are interactive. Such notions as inner being, self, will and consciousness defy logical analysis because they are both *what we are* and *what we are not* at the same time. They can be thought of being as a part of what we are but they cannot be so when we think of them objectively. We interact with them as objective notions while experiencing them directly as subjective notions. These aspects result from inner being turning in on itself to make more of itself. Thus, an aspect of inner being is definable as being a function of its interacting with itself to become something which is both the same as and different from itself. In short, inner being cannot be understood by linear, formal logic but by the dynamic logic of dualist interaction which is characteristic of living organisms.[5] This is a process logic that reconciles opposites to avoid extremes of thought and behaviour. When these notions are used interactively, they are both identical with that to which they refer and differentiated from the same thing, as they move from one side to the other.

What we call our will reflects inner being in action. The self is only a conscious, inward relating aspect of inner being which gives us a notion of ourselves as being distinct individuals. Mere self-awareness does not give us access to everything within us that is associated with inner being, as the self is associated only with conscious mental activity. The will is also a conscious aspect of inner being and involves self-awareness. It concerns the acts that we are capable of doing as agents. Without the will to do things, inner being is reduced to mere survival mode, typical of the vegetable world. We simply vegetate. The unconscious self is that aspect of inner being whose workings are unknown or inaccessible to us except through their effects, such as in our dreams.

Consciousness involves awareness of what is happening and what is being done, while self-consciousness is awareness of ourselves doing things. The latter is unique to language-using beings that can refer back to themselves using notions such as 'I', 'self' and 'ego'. Thus, self-consciousness is unique to language users. When I consider myself to be stupid when I forget something, this is an act of self-consciousness that brings inner being to the fore. I know I am being forgetful because I can refer this knowledge back to myself by being conscious of it. Without the idea of self, I would know nothing of what I call my own. This self-consciousness contributes to inner being which in its turn enables me to refer back to myself in that way. Such self-referential operations enrich my inner experience and add complexity to the content and function of inner being.

When we are conscious of something then inner being is intimately involved because the act of being conscious means fulfilling some end even when we are not immediately aware of what the end is. When I consciously attend to what I am looking at, I do so for a reason which can always be found if I think about it (since we can always find reasons for doing anything, if we so wish, as hypnotists show us). For example, I may wish to pick up the object I am looking at. If I do this only because I feel like it, this is as good a reason as any. There is no internal conflict in the matter. When I am conscious of a sharp pain in my leg, I start thinking of ways to alleviate the pain or to eliminate what causes it. There is no distinction between inner being and consciousness in these circumstances.

However, our awareness of inner being can lead to an infinite regress. Such awareness enables us to be at one with ourselves in what we are aiming to do. But in being conscious of being conscious, we enter an infinite regress in which we part company not only with inner being but also with what we are. This is the effect of making an abstract object of inner being so that we are no longer at one with it. It is only makes sense as a concept when we consider it as being self-referential and therefore subject to such regresses when we try to isolate it from the interactive processes within which it exists. Thus, the regress is always avoided when we are intuitively at one with what we are doing, and it only arises when we think about what we are thinking about, thereby objectifying our activities as if they were distinct from what we are and what we do.

Inner being functions as the interface between our potential for doing things and our actual use of that potential. By downward causation, inner being enables us to do things such as move our limbs and examine our thoughts recursively. Downward causation results from wholes producing effects on their parts. Thus, the unity of inner being affects parts of the body and enables us to walk, talk and think for ourselves. Physically, this is achieved by activating the central and peripheral nervous systems. By feedback we make ourselves aware of what we are or are not doing. The awareness of what we are doing comes from the unified activity of the central nervous system which itself is a function of inner being.

Crucially, inner being is involved in our conscious decisions in the following manner. The unified activity of inner being makes it possible for us to make up our minds to do something and actually do it. This unified activity consists of a turning in process from which neural activity gets the power and impetus to make things happen. Thus, the will to do things is the downward causation that generates the unified activity and makes possible the connection between the conscious decision to lift one's arm and the actual act of doing so. The will is unified mental activity that acts out a conscious decision, say, to raise one's arm. The will manifests itself in unified neural activity which is basically inner being at work. The mental and physical activities are at one in the will that is inner being in action. The connection between mental and physical acts is continuous from the moment that the conscious decision forces the turning in process that unifies neural activity. The will forms a central determining point in the brain that brings together all the neural activity so that a purposeful burst of physical activity is initiated and carried out.

In short, the physical events in the brain are brought together by inner being which becomes the will that generates the conscious decision to lift one's arm. Brain damage or paralysis may prevent these physical events from happening so that the act cannot be carried out. Consciousness of moving one's arm results from the self-reflective function of inner being. Even if it is done unconsciously, inner being is still involved but the self-reflective turning in process is absent. Thus, consciousness engages us in our actions by this self-reflective process so that we are conscious of having the will to do or not to do something.

The mysterious nature of consciousness may be due to its quantum connections. The mysterious way in which consciousness works may be due to its connection at the quantum level with the Zero Point Field (ZPF). This quantum connection may account for the feeling that we are connected with the universe in a very profound way. The ZPF is the point of lowest energy where everything is connected throughout the universe and it is where the quantum phenomenon of 'nonlocality' takes place. Thus, when we are conscious of ourselves and of what we are doing we may be tapping into this energy field at the quantum level of existence. When we are unconscious or are unaware of what we are doing, we have lost this connection and cannot know anything. Thus, our very ability to know things may be due to this connection. This point is important with regard to our understanding of the Cosmos as is mentioned in Exercise Eight below. (The explanatory importance of ZPF is the subject of Lynne McTaggart's book *The Field* [6])

Our intuitions and revelations are also produced by inner being. For example, divine revelations are also in inner being and have no external source. Inner being is the source of all our intuitions, in which the genetic component is usually developed or modified by the experiences of life. This is all happening within us and there is no need for the external sources which have often formed the basis for religion. Intuitions may take the form of messages that are interpreted as divine revelations from God, angels or aliens. But such conclusions are only the product of wishful thinking. The revelations only seem to come from outside us when we have no knowledge of what unconscious processes do in giving us our intuitions. We have no need of such extraneous superfluities when we have a proper understanding of what our inner being can do for us through the medium of intuitions.

Inner being gives rise to what William Blake called 'poetic genius'. He saw it as being the source of our individuality and self-expression. "As all men are alike in outward form, so (and with the same infinite variety) all are alike in the Poetic Genius." Even more interestingly, he thought that "all religions are one" in being sourced in the Poetic Genius: "The Religions of all Nations are derived from each Nation's different reception of the Poetic Genius, which is every where call'd the

Spirit of Prophecy."[7] Blake is obviously referring to the intuitive source of genius and imagination, what is here called 'inner being'.

E. Reining it in

Freewill and self-determination results from moral self-discipline. According to this view, the mature individual benefits from a self-interactive system of morality that is self-generated and self-enforced. Such a system makes sense of our moral behaviour and gives us control over our life together with inner purposefulness. Our freewill is thereby reinforced and strengthened. In simple terms, mature and responsible individuals work out for themselves what is or is not moral behaviour. This self-monitoring is part of what it means to be a mature and responsible person. It is expected that the individual is mature in being self-sufficient, and responsible in taking seriously one's responsibilities in life. Our inner being has developed sufficiently to become self-sustaining. It no longer requires external influences to stay on the straight and narrow. The correct habits of thought and behaviour have been reinforced enough to maintain an active inner monitor and the sustained application of moral sense. The aim of honing such ethical judgment is to arrive at the best decisions concerning what is to be done with one's life and what are the right things to do in life.

Inner self-discipline develops briefly as follows. We are born nonentities with nothing but innate potential within us to become whatever it is possible for us to become in the society into which we are born. Through time and experience we may become whatever is within us to become, relative to what is possible in the environment we find ourselves. It helps if we are properly brought up and learn to discipline ourselves by constantly interacting with our environment and other people. Such interactions ensure that our inner being grows and develop. We need therefore to be disciplined from both without and within, as we need boundaries within which to expand. As children, we benefit from strict boundaries until we can reason out for ourselves the need for such boundaries. Without these boundaries there are no limits to the mischief in which we can indulge. Until we become mature and responsible persons in our own right, the disciplining must come from outside as well as within us.

Self-discipline comes firstly from other people by our interacting with them, and secondly from within ourselves as we learn to behave ourselves. We gradually become inwardly developed enough to become ourselves and not just what other people or society expect of us. In other words, we are genetically programmed to be nothing but hand-to-mouth animals unless we are born into a culture that helps us to become social human beings with untold potential and therefore to become whatever we want to become as long as it is socially desirable and reasonable. Thus, cultural influences override genetic ones. Our genes only provide us with the basic forms and structure by which we can develop as human beings. Our cultural background must initiate these forms, fill the structure with content and add flesh to the bones, as it were. Even our so-called 'language instinct' cannot develop unless we are brought up to use the potential for language within us. Otherwise we remain speechless and ineffective human beings.

Our first lesson in morality is to learn that we cannot do as we please. We learn that it is not acceptable to do the first thing that comes to mind. Acting on instinct and impulse may be unavoidable in pressing situations where we have no time to think. But we cannot allow ourselves to make a habit of this if we are to be rational and thoughtful human beings. We may feel like doing something, but that does not give us the right to do it. Happiness comes not from the ecstasy of the moment but from joyful fulfilment and through having accomplished something worth setting out to do. The fact that we have good feelings about something is no justification for them unless these feelings are articulated and subjected to critical thought. Good feelings are not enough in themselves as they need to be constantly reinforced by their being justified by the facts and by experience.

Faced with an infinite variety of choices to make, we lose direction unless we learn to impose discipline and restraint on ourselves and stay on the straight and narrow way ahead. In other words, we need to narrow ourselves down so that we exercise good judgment in our daily lives and make the right choices. We can use contexts within which to make ethical judgments and to limit our behaviour. But we also need evaluative notions such as honour, sincerity, honesty and justice which we keep in mind and which provide us with judgments by which to limit our behaviour in meaningful and purposeful directions.

The chief end of all this self-discipline is not to be happy but to be free to do as we choose. Such freedom only comes with self-discipline and not before it or without it. We have no freedom at all except within a culture in which we can arrive at a notion of freedom. We cannot be free unless we know what we are free to do and we learn this only within a specific culture. We need to learn to fit into that culture in which we are born before we can express ourselves meaningfully as individuals and change the things that need changing. All this requires us to develop the self-discipline to curb our inclinations and excesses. If we are free to do anything whatsoever then we become enslaved by our passions and by outside influences that indulge us in these passions.

F. Putting it into Practice

The circumscription of inner being. Our inner development needs to be restrained and pruned back if it is to bear healthy and tasteful fruit. The more complex and developed it becomes the more it requires inner discipline to keep it on the straight and narrow. An undisciplined person is either too full of themselves or devoid of content. A developed person is someone who is internally wound up, full of excess energy and with great potential to do good or evil. Such a person needs to develop self-restraint by taming the wild spirit within them. We limit our inner development in at least four ways, namely, through (a) correct habits and routines, (b) critical self-awareness; (c) the contextualisation of beliefs, attitudes and feelings; and (d) sociospheric evaluation of ends and aims.

a. Correct Habits and Routines. Our habits and routines help us to impose order and discipline on our behaviour. The aim is to develop correct habits and routines that advance our being and do not cripple it. Such habits and routines ensure that we don't need to think or worry about what we doing from one minute to the next if we pursue our accustomed mode of behaviour. A habit is something we have learned to do without thinking much about how we do it. Unlike an instinct we can stop a habit or alter it, provided we have the willpower to do so. A routine consists of a chain of habitual actions such as getting into a car, switching on the engine, engaging the clutch and other actions required to get it moving. We can get into the habit of carrying out the same routine without thinking about it. However, if we get into an unaccustomed car then we may have to think hard about carrying out the same actions as the switchboard, instruments, gearbox and so on are different. It is important for us to get into habits and routines that are good for us and fulfil our best goals in life. Obviously, the routines of a chain-smoker, an alcoholic or a drug addict are not desirable but even though they are best abandoned in the person's own interests, the required willpower and motivation may be lacking.

In short, we need habits and routines rather than rigid rules and regulations. The latter stultify us by doing our thinking for us. They prevent us from rethinking every situation anew in which we should behave intelligently and creatively instead of mindlessly. Our habits and routines therefore need to be flexible and not wholly mechanical and without thought. Otherwise they will amount to rules, regulations, exhortations or other mechanical and unbending forms of discipline. Habits and routines are liberating when they are appropriate and fulfilling but they are also enslaving when we feel that they are imposed on us and we can see no way out of them.

b. Critical Self-Awareness. We need to apply critical self-awareness which involves the self turning in on itself to become aware of what it is doing. We see ourselves as if we are looking from the outside. Thus, when we refer to the self or the ego we are using it as the name for the process of being self-aware. When we think of ourselves as being angry, sad, or elated, we are also aware of being so in some sense however vague or indefinite. By naming such feelings and identifying ourselves with them, we personify the inner being us that gives rise to these feelings. What is within us is no longer distinguishable from what we are as identifiable persons. Being aware of these feelings helps us to become ourselves as persons identifiably distinct from other people. We are then inwardly enlivened in the sense of being in touch with our inner being.

Self-awareness is important for self-monitoring, and a person is a self-regarding entity capable of being self-aware and of doing things for themselves. The more self-aware we become, the more we are aware of our strengths and weaknesses. Anyone lacking a degree of self-awareness may go to extremes and become either self-destructive or contemptuous of others, in other words, over-humble or over-proud. The result is often religious and political fanaticism which is fuelled by the extreme behaviour of individuals who take themselves and their ideas too seriously as they consider them to be ultimate truths.

However, self-awareness is needed to a certain degree but no more than that. It has its limitations and must be applied with thought and discrimination. We need to be sufficiently self-aware to feel shame, guilt or anxiety in being painfully aware of the consequences of any wrongdoing that may occur to us to do. This is how our moral sense develops. It is an internal monitor not inherited by us genetically as it develops through cultural necessity, namely, the need for us to fit into society and to be ourselves in that society. Those who fail to develop such a moral sense may well end up in prison, lose their way in life, go to excesses of drink, drugs, sex, over-eating, dieting or whatever. On the other hand, if we are too self-aware, we may be unable to do anything since we doubt our ability to do anything successfully.

c. *Contextualisation.* This topic covered in section 10 on *Servility* (pp. 199-201), but here we are concerned with how contextualising ourselves limits our inner being and makes us more self-disciplined. It involves putting into context our beliefs, attitudes, feelings, aspirations and other internal attributes peculiar to ourselves as individuals. That inner being is disciplined by our entering into contexts and perspectives other than those of the self. In other words, we avoid selfishness and self-centredness by taking seriously viewpoints uncongenial to our own. This means putting our goals into context so that they can be assessed realistically. We also reinforce our ability to recognise our propensity to go to extremes in our thoughts and feelings. Avoidance of such extremes requires us to be aware of our own tendencies as well as those of others. Unless we learn to put our behaviour into the correct contexts, we risk becoming confused or losing control because we cannot make sense of what is happening to us. We can also misunderstand the reactions of other people to our behaviour.

d. *Sociospheric Evaluation.* The sociosphere includes the workings and interactions of society as a whole as well as the internet and other means of communication. The notion of the sociosphere gives us the limits within which we can flourish. It provides the milieu for both self-discipline and self-development. The human being is not meant to be an isolated individual but a person forming part of a community of persons (or 'kingdom of ends' as Kant put it).[8] Our inner development languishes purposelessly if it plays no part in the ethos of a community and in the ethos of humanity as a whole. Within these contexts, we can expand our thinking and civilise our feelings. In other words, they bring us as individuals into the communicative unity of humanity as manifested by the internet, mass media, business and leisure activity and so on. They provide the conditions in which we become more communicative and social beings. The value of our ends and aims must be assessed in a sociospheric context otherwise they remain selfish goals which can be inhuman, anti-social or illegal. In such social contexts, we develop our inner moral sense by which we learn to conform for our own good. This internal monitor of self-criticism is augmented by an external monitor that makes us see ourselves as others see us. Moral sense is discussed in more detail in section 8 on *Morality* (pp. 116-119).

6. Illuminosity: Enlightening Everything

> Instead of dirt and poison, we have rather chosen to fill our hives with honey and wax; thus furnishing mankind with the two noblest of things, which are sweetness and light.
>
> Jonathan Swift (1704) [1]

A. Illuminating the Darkness Within

Our advancement depends on our emerging into the light of day instead of lurking in the darkness of selfishness and self-centredness. We achieve nothing unless we put ourselves out and become illuminists as well as vitalists. The contrast between the vitalist and the illuminist is that of being introverted and extraverted.[2] The one is an internalist and the other an externalist. The internalist within us needs to be brought out into the light to become a more balanced personality. The development of inner being is to no avail if it does not switch on a light within us that can be used to illuminate the world. It is moving ourselves forward into the light and bringing our inner life out into the light. Thus, illumination is an important starting point for making ourselves fit for the world. We can get too wrapped up in our thoughts and feelings. Our dark side can emerge all too easily and fill us with despair. For imbedded in inner being is the darkness of the soul. This darkness forever threatens to engulf us. Thus, we need to pour light on it and dispel it or at least keep it at bay. Illumination is required to counter excessive introspection and bring us into the light of love and understanding. We need to bring out what is within us so that others can see our inner worth. Otherwise we remain stunted introverts having nothing to say or do with ourselves. Thus, illumination is the antidote to excessive obsession with self. It is the externality that contrasts with the internality in which the vitalist can become too involved.

The purpose of illumination is to pour light on our lives and enable us to see them more acutely and accurately than before. The illuminist therefore takes pride in shining a light on life. Light is after all the mainstay of the universe which came into being with a blaze of light that is still with us to this day. Shining a light on things means looking on the bright side of life. It makes us cheerful and optimistic so that our company is a delight to others. When brought into the light, everything makes more sense and is more endurable than otherwise. The illuminist therefore aspires to enlighten everything and everyone with the light of knowledge and understanding. This is the context in which we learn to like what we see in ourselves so that others can also like what they see in us.

Enlightening others and the world. Everyone on the planet is weighed down with their problems, cares and worries. We can do something to ameliorate their discomforts by leading them out of the darkness with our enlightened behaviour. We behave as a worthy example to others and show them the strength of conviction that lies within us. We can all be lighthouses shedding a steady and reliable beam of light all around us. With our inner strength, we are on the solid mainland of purposeful sanity from which others can take their guidance from our luminescent dependability. In so beaming forth we exude an effulgent luminescence and incandescence that none can ignore or undervalue. By shining a light on things we sharpen and intensify them. Taking them out of the darkness enables us to show what can be done with them.

Thus, we serve humanity well by being a beacon of light that brightens up people's lives. To that extent, everyone is a potential illuminist though no one is born to be so. We can learn to be illuminists by aspiring to be enlightening people so that we make a habit of it throughout our lives. Being illuminists enables us to relate to others in enlightening them and making more of their lives. It heightens our interest in and appreciation of other people. Illuminists are shining examples to others and are ever-ready to vindicate themselves through illumination and service. They illuminate others by their belief in humanity's future and by their steadfastness in that belief. They also learn by appreciating its opposite, as the illuminist can be contrasted with the melanist as the following table shows:

Illuminist	*Melanist*
Light	Dark
Positivist	Negativist
Optimist	Pessimist

There is a fervent need for us to make more of the Illuminist in us than of the Melanist. This need comes from the vitality of our inner being. That vitality needs to be directed outwards in an enlightening way to prevent it from turning inwards and towards hellish darkness. Hell is not other people but the darkness within us. Thus, the outward-looking Illuminist is opposed the inward-looking Melanist who looks on the dark side of things. There is a Melanist in all of us since there is inevitably light and dark within us all. We owe it to ourselves to put our dark side behind us and look towards the light. To that extent, we are constantly at war with this darkness that threatens to envelope us and hinder our forward progress.

We are all inclined at various times to be positive and negative, optimistic and pessimistic depending on our circumstances. However, our well-being depends on our light side predominating over our dark side. We must fight for the light as against the darkness that would engulf it. It is not old age that needs to 'rage against the dying of the light' but young people who are even more vulnerable to the self-annihilation to which self-abnegating darkness leads them. In this battle, positive thinking and an optimistic demeanour can help us on the way. Smiles instead of scowls will win the day.

The role of the Illuminist. As light-seeking Illuminists we strive for illumination by clarifying things but not necessarily proving them beyond all doubt. We are always seeking greater clarity. We see ourselves as purveyors of light to the entire world. To see the light is to have something revealed to us that was previously mirky and impenetrable. To pour light on a subject is what every scholarly person strives to do in seeking truth. We enlighten and thereby lighten the burden of life by dispelling the darkness of ignorance, malice, hatred, bigotry, self-centredness, and so on. We are all purveyors of the light in so far as our lives bring the light of experience and understanding into the world. Past purveyors of the light include not only Moses, Jesus Christ, the Buddha, and Mohammed but also all the scientists who have contribute positively to scientific knowledge. Enlightenment is what we seek throughout life, whereas dimness and darkness is what we avoid throughout life. The light is thus common to us and is as important to the religious person as to the scientist. We do not worship the light but revere only what it can do for us and what we can do with it. Such reverence is enough to ensure that we use it well and not as a malignant cover for dark deeds. *Lumen siccum*: the 'dry light' of philosophy purifies thought whereas the '*lumen humidum*' drenches the light with moist and unwholesome affections.

The illuminating standpoint is an attitude of mind that we must cultivate lest the darkness and dullness of negative thinking should engulf us. In response, we illuminate the importance of living. In the darkness of negativity "nothing, nothing matters" – *Rien, rien n'avait d'importance* - to use the words of Camus in his pessimistic novel *L'Étranger* (translated as *The Outsider*).[3] The moral philosopher, R.M. Hare tells us about a young Swiss boy who visited him in his home. He was gave the lad Camus's book to read as it was one of the only French books he had available. The book turned this cheerful, normal young man into a morose, withdrawn chain smoker who went on solitary walks. He was obviously much too impressed by the idea that 'nothing, nothing matters'.[4] The same sentiment is expressed in the Bohemian Rhapsody pop song – "Nothing really matters anymore" and the even more pathetic "I wish I had never been born at all". But everything matters when we pour enough light on life and living to see that the fact of living is itself marvellous and miraculous. The gift of life overarches any negativity when we concentrate on its opportunities instead of its discomforts. Moreover, anything is better than nothing, and ultimately there is nothing in nothing so that it is nothing which is not of any consequence. In resisting such pointless negativity, it is a matter of attitude and not of facts, opinions or beliefs. It is deliberately turning one's thoughts in a positive direction. Thus, it takes effort, study and persistence to keep this dark side at bay and concentrate on the light within us.

The dark side lurks around always to be combated. Religion makes much of walking in the light but in life we cannot avoid the darkness as readily as is implied, for example, in the following Biblical passage:

> "Walk as children of the light. For the fruit of the light is in all goodness and righteousness and truth. . . . And have no fellowship with the unfruitful works of darkness, but rather reprove them. For it is a shame even to speak of those things which are done of them in secret. But all things that are reproved are made manifest by the light: for whatsoever doth make manifest is light."
>
> *New Testament*, Paul's 'Letter to the Ephesians', 5: 8-13.

There are inevitably things within us that need never see the light of day. It is part of being human that there is a dark side to all of us, just as shining a light on it is even more human.

B. The Joy of Luminosity

The joy of human relationships. There is great joy in seeing the light and following it. It makes life luminous and incandescent. There is even greater joy in sharing our elevated feelings with others. We enlighten others in enlightening ourselves. This is not done by merely sharing our feelings but also reaching an understanding and accommodation with other people. We bring them into our family, as it were, so that they belong to us as friends. When we see the light that resides in them we can also see them as potential friends. For there is light to be found even the darkest and most dismal of individuals.

We ought to wax lyrical about luminosity as being the *leitmotif* of life by which we can shine forth and bathe everything in the light of love and freedom. We can illuminate that which is in darkness but without shunning that darkness entirely. Such illumination enlivens our lives and makes us human. We can argue that other animals do not glow with inner light of the same intensity as human beings. We exude more light and are ultra-luminous animals who can differentiate light and dark, good and bad. Unlike other animals which only see light and dark, we can conceive of these distinctions as matters of life and death.

Thus, we are all potential illuminists having a beacon of light within us which we can share with others. Each one of us can light up the world in our own small way. In constantly seeking illumination we make sense of our lives. In gaining illumination, we achieve true happiness that is lasting and foundational. It is a 'Holy Light' (*Sanctus Clarus*) that clarifies everything and envelopes us all. We need to bring forth the 'Holy Light' within us as it is the difference between life and death. Without such illumination we are dead to the world. But we can only re-affirm our luminosity by tackling and coming to terms with the darkness within us.

We can choose to live forever in the light if we so wish. Only by constantly seeking and achieving luminosity can we hope to live in the light and eschew the darkness that always threatens to engulf us. Thus, the purpose of our living at all is to illuminate our lives and other people's lives. We may never get rid of the darkness but we can continually keep it at bay by purposefully staying in the light and by ensuring that others also do so. In that way, we learn to stay in the light and spurn the darkness. The light within us potentially eclipses that of the sun as its intensity is purely physical and has no purpose apart from exhausting its energy. In so far as the products of our lives can outlive the sun, just our lives may outlive our death (as is argued below in section 11 on *Posterity*).

The more light we pour on things the less room there is for darkness. The sun shines all day when we fly around the earth following its course above the clouds. The higher our thoughts the brighter the prospect. The right attitude determines the altitude, and *vice versa*. Thus, we can live all our lives illuminated perpetually by the brightness of our thoughts and deeds, provided that we work hard enough to make it so. We fly with the light and leave the darkness straddling behind us.

We live like flames that shine brightly as they feed on flammable material. We burn brightly during our lives by feeding on the flame of life for as long as it lasts. Just as the flame runs out of material to burn, so we run out of time and energy and our lives are snuffed out like a dying flame. We are however extremely complex flames that shine further than any other flames around us. The effects of the heat and light generated by us have reverberations far beyond our little lives. In fact, they have a cosmic resonance that contributes to posterity in what we leave behind us.

Above all, the Light of the Cosmos within us illuminates our way. As the Bible teaches us:

> "You are the light of the cosmos (τὸ φῶς τοῦ κόσμου). A city on top of a hill cannot be hidden. No one lights a lamp to put it under a bowl but to put it on a stand, so that it shines for everyone in the house. Let your light so shine for everyone that they may see the good you do."
>
> *New Testament*, Matthew, 5: 14-16.

The Cosmic Light affects us all equally and makes no distinction between us. It is not really the sun which makes life possible on Earth but the light produced by the sun. It is more important and worthy of respect than the sun which is only one insignificant source of light in the universe's vastness. The Cosmic Light is belongs to the entire universe whereas the light of the sun is only pinprick in comparison. This takes us into the role of the cosmic holist which is dealt with below in section 12 on the *Cosmos*.

We can actively seek illumination both for ourselves and others. We illuminate the way for others by the good deeds we do for them, as well as by thinking of them affectionately. If we remain lurking in the darkness this intimates a failure to be oneself and to make something of oneself. Negative thinking, cynicism, enslavement by drink or drugs, resorting to criminality, are examples of dark living. There is no evil in the darkness itself; it merely lacks light. Evil lies in thoughts, intentions and motivations being deprived of light, love, honesty, truth. We put the evil into darkness which is otherwise devoid of anything. We therefore dispel evil by going into the darkness to illuminate it.

We achieve illumination in numerous ways, for example, through insights, revelations, as well as through scientific research. Philosophers, scientists, theologians, poets, novelists, and mystics, all contribute to our illumination. Everything human and inhuman is illuminating in its way, as we need never allow anything to darken our way if we can find illumination in it. For example, dark deeds can be illuminating in revealing our limitations and what we ought not to do. Beacons of brightness exist everywhere to lighten our way if we only make the effort to find them. All our positive thoughts are illuminating in so far as our minds are enlightened and brightened by them.

Accentuating the positive means promoting positive things at the expense of negative ones. Illumination accentuates the positive in that it flows with life and therefore through non-life and not against it. Everything is slithered to the side in its forward, just as light photons are deflected by the gravitation of large objects in space. The light follows the line of being and is distinguishable from non-being in that it is goal-directed. It is not just a matter of opposing or combating either non-being or the negative. It is also a matter of pursuing a positive course of action which is ultimately the way of life and not the way of non-life. In this way, the illuminating view can ensure that judgments are made as to actions that are positive and not negative.

C. The Benefits of Illuminating Life

Illuminating Love: The Holy Light of love brings us all together for the highest purposes of humanity. Love lightens all our lives and brightens everything it touches but only when it is caring, thoughtful love. Love applies to our relationships with everyone and everything that interests and involves us and takes us out of ourselves. But love brings darkness as much as light when it is a means of captivating and imprisoning people. Love without care and affection darkens and diminishes our souls and those of others captivated by this lustful love.

Illuminating Beauty: The Holy Light of Beauty shines bright for us here on Earth and we are initiated into heavenly things as we contemplate beautiful works of art or listen to beautiful, uplifting music. Beauty frees us from the oyster like shell that binds our bodies, as Plato puts it.[5] We are brought from earthly beauty into absolute beauty which is the oneness of existence. Such beauty belongs to eternity and deserves to exist forever, as is argued below in the next section on Creativity.

Illuminating Knowledge: The Holy Light of Knowledge replaces the dark light of religion which has brought much suffering, ignorance and ignominy to humanity. Knowledge is holy and delightful because it gives reasoned meaning and purpose to our lives. Knowledge begins with self-knowledge which enables us not only to live with ourselves but also to appreciate each other. Through study, we begin to put our knowledge in its proper perspective. We gain knowledge through our personal involvement in it. Our interest and enthusiasm in getting to know and understand things is the source of the light that we throw on knowledge.

Illuminating Truth: The Holy Light of Truth comes to us when we see ourselves as being significant in relation to the unity of things. Truth highlights the path before us by drawing us on and showing us a better way of doing things, thinking about them, acting on them, anticipating them. We use truth first of all to find ourselves, then to find how things are, and finally how we want things to be. We keep to the path of truth in being open-minded and by freely inquiring into things. An open mind pursues truth by pouring light on things and moving forward to greater enlightenment, whereas a closed mind remains stuck in the false darkness of self-centredness. The path of truth is fringed on both sides by error and ignorance that lead us to darkness and depression. Truth is not just what is said to be the case; it is more importantly what can be done. It is relational rather than absolute. We can approach it and try to keep up with it but it inevitably recedes before us. Those who think that they have truth to hand are only grasping dreams, shadows and falsities.

Illuminating the Present: Carpe diem: seize the day. The present time is the right time to do what must be done, correct what must be corrected, and help who must be helped. *Nunc stans*: the standing now which refers to constant presence of reality lying before and around us. It is also the *Dasein* – the 'being there' that stands still as time moves on inexorably. The everlasting now is what we must make the best of with the full force of our being. The 'Now' is happening for each of us only in so far as we make something of it. While we do nothing right now, we are a living death. We are marking time instead of going along with it. We do not exist in the present so much as endure it. Our lives are prolonged for the duration of our existence but not forever.

Illuminating the Darkness:

"The eye is the lamp of the body. If your eyes are good, your whole body will be full of light. But if your eyes are bad, your whole body will be full of darkness. If therefore the light within you is darkness, how great is that darkness!"

New Testament, Matthew, 6:22-23.

Seeing the light and avoiding the darkness takes effort and application. Darkness lingers on whenever things cease to move forwards. Everything that is stagnant and stuck in the doldrums is in gloom and darkness. All religions are in darkness in so far as they linger in the past and wield absolute power over people instead of empowering them. Mohammedism is the darkest religion of all as it gives all light to God, and leaves unbelievers in total darkness (see *The Koran*, Suras xxiv 35-36, iv 174, lxvi 8, lvii 28 etc.) It offers them only hell-bound annihilation. We avoid the darkness not by outward shows of belief (which invites hypocrisy) but by being true to ourselves and to others. Seeing ourselves as others see us is one form of inner illumination. We are never content with ourselves just as we are but seek ever to better and enlighten ourselves.

Illuminating the Future: In the future, everything that we do in the present will be illuminated and made plain to all. We can do no better in the present than to serve the needs of posterity and ensure its future. When we enlighten the future with our good deeds, posterity will benefit and hopefully reward us with their gratitude. The meaning of our existence could well be even more enhanced by what posterity makes of it than by what we ourselves have made of it. We illuminate the future by anticipating how posterity may judge our present actions. Posterity is therefore present with us when we look to the future to judge our deeds and thoughts.

D. Illuminating the Divine Within Us

We can be divine to ourselves at least. We need not seek any god beyond us when there is already something of a divine spark within us that needs illuminating. This spark is not god but only the best part of what we are. It is produced by our ability to imagine ourselves and everything about us as being potentially better than they are at the present moment. It has given rise, in the past, to notions of god, gods, goddesses, spirits, angels, aliens, androids and other beings endowed with superior powers about which we could only dream in the past but which are coming into being through our cultural and technological developments e.g. flying in the sky, communicating with people throughout the world, and reaching the moon and ultimately the stars. The divine aspect in our natures belongs to us alone, as intelligent beings, and we progress as a species by cultivating that aspect within ourselves and not by imputing divinity to non-existent beings above and beyond us.[6]

Moreover, only human beings can be truly said to be divine since it is our invention. Divinity can only be a product of humanity. It only applies to us in imagining ourselves to be better than we are at present. Indeed, the epithet 'divine' was invented solely by us in our inquiring into things. To impute anything else with that epithet is tantamount to a blasphemy against human beings who alone can make use of it. We become divine in surpassing ourselves in our own terms. And that surpassing is only makes sense within a social context in which we are helpful towards others. Thus, the sociosphere and posterity are the ultimate arbiters of whether we are being truly divine in our activities since they are evinced in the context of the cosmos as herein developed.

The divine within us therefore signifies a capacity for self-improvement and growth of intellect and integrity which is shared by all human beings worthy of the name. The divine within us may be considered multifaceted, as indeed the Greco-Roman civilisation imagined it to be. Christianity is only nominally monotheistic since the doctrine of the Holy Trinity (not to mention the worship of the Virgin Mary and the innumerable saints) is another example of the divine being given several aspects. The humanist writer, Julian Huxley has accounted for the objectivity of the trinity as follows:

> In the particular trinitarianism of Christianity, the reality apprehended to exist behind the forces of Nature is called the Father, the up-springing force within the mind of man, especially when it seems to transcend individuality and to overflow into what we designate as the mystical, is called the Holy Ghost, and the activity, personal or vicarious, which mediates between the individual and the rest of the universe, reconciling his incompleteness and his failures with its apparent sternness and inexorableness, is called the Son.[7]

These distinctions are obviously manifestations of the divine within us. We use them to articulate and put into words our divine aspirations. But the holy trinity can only apply to ourselves metaphorically. It is the metaphorical Father within us that is invoked when we confront the stark realities of life and living. It is the metaphorical Holy Ghost within us that impels us to get in tune with the universe at the most fundamental and holistic level of our experience. It is the metaphorical Son within us which is the physical activity of the human spirit in using rational passions to cope with our failings on the one hand and to adapt to the constraints of external reality on the other hand. Such metaphors are useful in helping us to make more of ourselves and not if they lessen us in favour things outside us.

To externalise the divine within us by conceiving of the existence of gods, angels, extra-terrestrial aliens and the like, is deprive us of our ability to face up to realities on our own. Externalising our divine part only demeans and degrades us. A god only hinders our freedom to do what is entirely natural for us to do, namely, make everything of our lives which we can legitimately and morally conceive of doing:

> If reality is relative to perceptions, and the false is what limits and hinders human adaptability and growth, then truth for man must be the freedom to develop more unique, individual and perceiving spirit. Because only thereby can more of reality be revealed. If the real is relative and not fixed, then it can only be unveiled as a dialogue between growing perceivers and a changing universe. Freedom is part of a philosophy of nature, as well as of science, democracy and religion. [8]

As Becker also points out, our development can only take place within the finite limits laid down by ourselves. An externalised divinity presents with a bewildering infinitude of possibilities. What is required is an *"individuality-within-finitude"* Ibid.. In the context of human advancement, this means that the individual can only develop himself within limits of the sociosphere.

E. Illuminating Our Rational Passions

Our passions always need to be enlightened. Our raw emotions can only be rationalised by making light of them and expressing them in a social context. They can become rational passions by being so socialised. Thus, rational passion differs from our usual emotions in being rationalised and therefore enlightened. Our passions generally result from making the most of ourselves and our abilities for good or ill. We need to pour light upon them and bring them forth lest they fester uselessly and harmfully within us. Indeed, the efficacy of our vitality depends greatly on our rationalising our passions so that they are our servants and we are not enslaved by them. We need inner strength to master our passions and make them work for our best ends in life.

The rational passions are our best bulwark against the extremist state of mind since they make open-mindedness a matter of passionate concern and not something which is merely desirable in an objective, offhand manner. Rationalising them fosters open-mindedness. They are basically an expression of the ordinary person's common sense view of things. Everyone who willingly maintains an open, friendly and guileless approach to life, will sympathise with and apply the rational passions without having to think too deeply about them. But in order to make them stick and to ensure that they become a permanent feature of our culture, it is necessary at the outset to articulate them and expound them in some detail. The rational passions must form part of our character which is the very being of our personalities. It is not enough to read or learn about them; they must be put into practice. The rational passions include the following:

(1) *Truth.* A love of truth and a hatred of falsity

(2) *Honesty.* A desire for honesty and a contempt for lying

(3) *Exactitude.* A repugnance towards error in logic or fact

(4) Straightforwardness. A revulsion at distortion and a disgust at evasion

(5) Theory. An admiration of theoretical achievement

(6) Accuracy. A keenness to achieve accuracy in observation and inference

(7) Elucidation. A fervour for getting to the bottom of things

(8) Evidence. An enthusiasm for seeking out supporting evidence for assertions

(9) Open-mindedness. A determination to abandon hypotheses in the face of opposing evidence

(10) Respect. A respect for the considered arguments of others

(11) Sympathy. A resolve to listen sympathetically to opposing points of view

(12) Clarity. A passionate drive for clarity, accuracy and fair-mindedness

(13) Consistency. An aversion to sloppy thinking and the inconsistent application of standards

(14) Intellectual. A devotion to intellectual pursuits and a thirst for knowledge.[9]

(1) Truth. A love of truth is one of the most important of all human passions since the continuance of our civilisation depends upon it. Unless a love of truth is accompanied by an equal aversion towards falsity, it is only truth in the abstract and not truth as applied in the imperfect real world.

(2) Honesty. Some feeling about the importance of honesty is characteristic of an honest person who will gain a reputation for honesty by showing it consistently in practice. It is not enough to be honest out of habit even though it is important to be in the habit of being honest. The habit of honesty needs to be reinforce by consideration of why honesty is the best policy.

(3) Exactitude. It is part of being an honest and open person that one should also feel repugnance towards logical and factual errors. Exactitude and avoidance of errors is necessary to establish the truth of matters. An unexacting person is invariably slip-shod and careless.

(4) Straightforwardness. The realisation that distortion and evasion are taking place in any discussion or conversation naturally leads us to feel revulsion and disgust at the individuals doing this. This is a passion for seeing straightforwardness in daily life instead of the two-faced hypocrisy and deceit that too often takes place.

(5) Theory. When the importance of theory in advancing our knowledge is realised, the achievement has to be admired. Thus, this admiration arises from participating in the triumph of the theoretician in making sense of an area of knowledge which was previously in disorder and darkness.

(6) Accuracy. Accuracy in observation and inference are acquired by getting into the habits and routines in which such a keenness for accuracy becomes second nature to the investigator. It is the product of natural curiosity and is a skill to be nurtured because of elation to savoured when the results of such accuracy enable the investigator to arrive at distinct advances in knowledge and understanding.

(7) Elucidation. Our natural curiosity gives us a fervour for getting to the bottom of things. But this has to be balanced with an equal amount of enthusiasm

for seeking the evidence that confirms or denies whatever conclusions we reach as a result of our inquiries.

(8) Evidence. It is easy to assert what we think or feel but not so easy to find the evidence to back up our assertions. Thus, an enthusiasm for the task of finding such evidence is both helpful and necessary. Our curiosity to get the bottom of things makes us find the evidence for saying or doing anything. Only intellectual laziness can stand in the way.

(9) Open-mindedness. An open-minded attitude helps us to treat our conclusions dispassionately so that we don't become unreasonably attached to them. This helps us to abandon them as soon as the evidence is stacked against them. When they become dominant in our thinking to the extent of explaining anything and everything then our minds are closed to any other way of thinking. There must be limits to the explanatory power of any ideas that occur to us as being true.

(10) Respect. The same open-mindedness also requires us to respect the opinions and arguments of other people. We must always be prepared to admit that they may be right and we may be wrong.

(11) Sympathy. It is a stern discipline in rational behaviour to listen sympathetically to opposing opinions without wishing to dismiss them out of hand. Not to do so is to be prejudiced and one-sided in one's thinking. One's breadth of vision and understanding is enhanced by being so sympathy. It also facilitates the finding of better arguments to support the views and beliefs to which one adheres.

(12) Clarity. A passionate drive for clarity, accuracy and fair-mindedness does not come naturally. The emotions have to be trained and exercised in that direction until it becomes second nature for the individual to continue driving towards such goals. It is a matter of getting into the routine of looking for such standards and expecting to find them.

(13) Consistency. The rational passions thus cultivate the highest standards within us. They compel us to be consistently intolerant of sloppiness and sub-standard conduct. This applies as much to our own behaviour and work standards as those of other people. We are therefore consistently reliable in what we expect of ourselves and others.

(14) Intellectual. Cultivating one's intellectual interests is the ultimate way to rationalise one's passions about life and living. Then our curiosity and inquisitiveness comes to the fore and leads us to take interest in the most abstract and out-of-the-way forms of knowledge. In this way we contribute to the sum-total of human knowledge and thus to the Cosmos as mentioned in section twelve below.

The rational passions are needed also because without them people have little or no incentive to make the most of the intellectual capacities. These passions therefore help to combat gnorance and laziness. It is easy to be lazy and do as

little as possible unless we are particularly moved to get things done. As Dr. Johnson (1709-1784) pointed out:
> Mankind have a great aversion to intellectual labour; but even supposing knowledge to be easily attainable, more people would be content to be ignorant than would take even a little trouble to acquire it.[10]

This is certainly not absolutely true of human limitations. A developed culture offers more incentives for people to use their brains. Better education gives them more confidence to think for themselves. However, a contentment with ignorance does indeed make people the slaves of the dominant views of the mass media. A faulty upbringing may ensure that people fail to acquire 'the rational passions' that everyone may possess in invoking their natural inclinations towards curiosity, love of learning, and desire to explore and examine things. Many people have their natural curiosity knocked out of them in childhood by the indifference of adults, the meanness of their peer group, or the discouragement of the education system. Thus, it benefits us all if we exercise and develop the rational passions which lie within us all to be brought out and used for the service of humanity as well as life in general

Newman's view of the intellectual passions. Cardinal Newman (1801-90) long ago expressed the ideal of perfection towards which the rational passions are designed to aspire:
> The intellect, which has been disciplined to the perfection of its powers, which knows, and thinks while it knows, which has learned to leaven the dense mass of facts and events with elastic force of reason, such an intellect cannot be partial, cannot be exclusive, cannot be impetuous, cannot be at a loss, cannot but be patient, collected, and majestically calm, because it discerns the end in every beginning, the origin in every end, the law in every interruption, the limit in each delay; because it ever knows where it stands, and how its path lies from one point to another. . .
>
> That perfection of the Intellect . . . is the clear, calm, accurate vision and comprehension of all things, as far as the finite mind can embrace them, each in its place, and with its own characteristics upon it. It is almost prophetic from its knowledge of history; it is almost heart-searching from its knowledge of human nature; it has almost supernatural charity from its freedom from littleness and prejudice; it has almost the repose of faith, because nothing can startle it; it has almost the beauty and harmony of heavenly contemplation, so intimate is it with the eternal order of things and the music of the spheres.[11]

Thus, by honing our intellectual abilities we can achieve stability and harmony and our lives. We boost our vitality and inner being and therefore make us fitter and stronger in the face of what life throws at us.

It is also the case that we must never give up on the possibility of people improving themselves. Everyone can aspire to perfectibility. Even the most unlikely individuals can astound us in improving themselves. As John Passmore put it:
> We know from our own experience, as teachers or parents, that individual human beings can come to be better than they once were, given care, and that wholly to despair of a child or a pupil is to abdicate what is one's proper responsibility. We know, too, that in the past men have made advances, in science, in

art, in affection. Men, almost certainly, are capable of more than they have ever so far achieved. But what they achieve, will be a consequence of their remaining anxious, passionate, discontented human beings. To attempt, in the quest for perfection, to raise men above that level is to court disaster; there is no level above it, there is only a level below it.[12]

The rational passions are therefore deeply connected with that which is divinely perfectible within us. They help us to get in touch with the best part of ourselves. But there is a distinct level beyond which we cannot profitably rise. If we expect too much of ourselves we will always be disappointed. A balanced use of the rational passions is required and holistic wisdom helps us to maintain that balance between too much intellectual indulgence and too little by instilling moral discipline and balanced thinking. Moreover, rational passions are to no avail unless they are outwardly directed. We are initially impassioned by what we observe in the world, and then wisdom results from the interaction between these passions and the realities of life.

F. Illuminating Our Personal Behaviour

Illuminating development and eliminating degradation. When our personal behaviour harms us and impedes our development, it must be brought out of our inner darkness and into the bright light of reason. In other words, when we doing what we know to be the wrong things in our private and public life, we need to clarify the moral status of our behaviour. We can shed some light on this by making the important distinction between *Personal Development* and *Personal Degradation* (as dealt with in more detail in section 9 below in *Normality* – p.162). The former consists in developing ourselves in a positive way that is truly beneficial to ourselves and useful to society at large. The latter involves self-indulgence, self-harming or a lack of personal standards of self-awareness and integrity. Personal Development leads to a person developing their interests in diverse fields without going to extremes and harming themselves or others. Personal degradation leads to self-indulgent practices that may be harmful and life-threatening in the long run. Extreme changes to the body are enforced to conform to unrealistic ideals of self. The over-eaters and the under-eaters are examples of this self-degradation. The morbidly obese are a heavy weight on social and health resources because of their selfish obsession with food. Anorexic people harm themselves and put their lives in danger by being obsessed with a selfish idea of their bodily shape.

The illumination of moderation. Thus, those who go to harmful extremes in their behaviour degrade themselves instead of developing themselves. Their behaviour is not normal because they have lost touch with their moral sense that consists in being sensitive to behaviour that is harmful or unworthy of them. The cure is to help them reinstate their sensitivity so that they experience shame and guilt at their transgressions. This involves increased self-awareness by thoughtful introspection. Thus, it is illuminating to draw attention to the distinction between Personal Development and Personal Degradation as it supports greatly the self-knowledge and self-restraint implied by this distinction.

However, this is not a matter of society deciding for each individual what is or is not degrading for them. People are not judged so much as helped to judge themselves. Everyone has to work out for themselves what they find to be personally developing or personally degrading. The illumination must come from within as to what is or is not wrong with their conduct. The norms are there for people to make up their own minds and are not to be imposed upon them against their will. In the normal society, it is the role of philosophy and morality to help individuals to think about these things and arrive at their own conclusions, which they can then justify or not with their peers, parents and society at large. In short, the education system falls down in so far as it fails to make philosophy and morality a part of the curriculum since these are essential to helping people to become rational and moral human beings and remain so throughout their lives.

Illumination paves the way for greater self-awareness. Whatever we do or don't do can be taken to ridiculous extremes through lack of self-awareness, self-criticism and ultimately self-discipline. We may know our limitations but sticking to them is another matter. We need to monitor our own behaviour and stay in touch with our bodily and mental condition. It is too easy to get carried away and become obsessed with one sort of behaviour or another. To avoid such extremes, we need to take our time and reflect on what we are doing and why we are doing it. We need to be aware of when we are truly developing ourselves in a positive and when we are simply degrading or abusing ourselves in an obsessive and self-indulgent way. This is why we need morality to help us judge better that which develops us as compared with that which degrades us.

7. Creativity: Making the Most of our Artistic Potential

> I can very well do without God both in my life and in my painting, but I cannot, suffering as I am, do without something which is greater than I am, which is my life, the power to create.
>
> Vincent Van Gogh (1888) [1]

A. The Way to Artistic Achievement

Exploiting our creativity is essential to the future of humanity. We would have achieved little or nothing in the past without our creativity which has been our salvation and our vindication throughout the ages. But it is up to each of us to find our own creative area as this is the ultimate expression of our individuality. Creativity is one of the many 'invisible hands' by which all of us together contribute meaningfully to the whole in pursuing our selfish interests. Smith's 'invisible hand' referred mainly to monetary wealth accumulated by individual efforts.[2] But the wealth of artistic creativity is surely worth more to humanity than all the gold, silver and fiat currency circulating throughout the world. Even if we had no money, we would still have art, music, literature, buildings and other means to express ourselves and find enjoyment in life.

In the widest sense, we can all be creative artists of one sort or another. We can all enrich our lives by making the most of our potential artistry. As artists, we can dream up what has never been thought or created before. By putting our dreams into practice, we give them a concrete existence that can last for as long as their materiality persists. Thus, our artistic role is to bring new things into being that will be long-lasting and ultimately eternal.

Our dreams may be beneficial or destructive. The destructive ones diminish us while the beneficial ones can inspire and enthuse us. Dreams about destroying things and killing people can do us no credit unless we can use them in beneficial way in our artistic creations. The nightmarish paintings of Hieronymus Bosch are obvious examples of negativity being transformed into positive art. We can rationalise the worst parts of our nature by the positive use of art, and make evil entertaining as in murder stories, zombie movies, ghoulish sculptures and the like. This positive approach can ensure the durability of artistic contributions by enlisting us into the novelty and insightfulness of the artist's vision of things.

To make the most of our artistry, it is helpful to get the creative process right. Art is characteristically intuitive in its origins but its application requires the use of reason and intelligence. The creative process might be described as follows. An idea occurs to us intuitively and by the skilful use of reason and intelligence a work of art is produced. We use our brains to bring an artistic insight into practical reality. Thus, both creativity and intelligence are both involved in the artistic process. The interrelationship between intelligence and creativity is extremely important and this interrelationship is rudimentarily shown in the following diagram:

contributing to

Artistic Achievement

The interactions of reason/intuition and understanding/aesthetics feelings are crucial to the artistic process. They are implied when the painter uses his intelligence and creativity, for example, when he judges whether his painting is as beautiful and striking as he wants it to be. The importance of these distinctions lies in their interrelationships with each other. The one feeds off the other since by becoming more intelligent we increase our creative potential and vice versa. Our intellectual abilities are enhanced by our artistic bent, and our artistic inclinations are given sense and purpose by our intellectual interests. For example, an inventor would get nowhere with his intuitive ideas unless he works out intelligently how the public might benefit from his ideas and how to get them to the production level to sell them to the public. The interaction between creativity and intelligence is important not only to the artistic process but also to humanity in general. It is therefore worth considering in more depth.

B. The Interplay between Creativity and Intelligence

Intelligence and creativity are important to the holistic view in general, and they are also vital to our future. Unless we use them to make a better future for ourselves, we don't deserve it. Intelligent and creative behaviour is resonant of sagacity, insight and foresight. It is intelligent behaviour not to do things that are unworthy of us. It is creative behaviour to find new and different ways of doing things that are productive and worthwhile doing in themselves. Thus, in this context, being intelligent means being thoughtful and considerate, and being creative means rethinking things anew. The one is reasonable and the other intuitive, and we need both if we are to be wise and well-rounded individuals.

It is not enough for us to be intelligent and creative individuals, we need also to be intelligent and creative as a species. The lack of intelligence and creativity ever threatens our future. It is not intelligent to maintain confrontational nation states forever ready to go to war with each other. It is not intelligent to misuse our creativity in creating more efficient weapons to kill each other. The more we make the best possible use of our intelligence and creativity, the more we can justify our existence and make sense of our lives. In applying them as individuals we can become wise and worthy people who make all the difference in the world. Making the most of these attributes brings us all together as human beings whatever we believe or do not believe. Intelligence and creativity are therefore the *leitmotifs* or recurring themes that dominate the thinking behind the holistic view

Intelligence and creativity shows itself to be so in what we do or don't do in our daily lives. We show our intelligence in the actions that are shown to be effective and appropriate and are generally accepted to be such by those witnessing and benefiting from them. Similarly, creativity involves introducing something new and different which is shown to be so and is generally accepted to be so by those who appreciate it as it being an example of creativity in action. Thus, intelligent and creative behaviour is judged to be so by the general acceptance of independent communities of inquirers, critics or participants who are interested enough to pass judgment. The ultimate community is of course that of public opinion, whether it is or is not manipulated by the mass media.

Intelligence is inextricably entwined with creativity and *vice versa,* so that the interrelationship between them is crucial. An intelligent act can be seen to be creative in some way, and a creative act involves intelligence in some way. Our mastery of computers involves a series of intelligent acts that are often creative in that we may not have thought of them before. Computers constantly give us problems of which we have had no previous experience. By our ingenuity we can often overcome these problems without consulting helplines and the like. In thinking things out for ourselves, we do things differently and therefore creatively. Indeed, our most commonplace actions give us scope for creativity by finding new and different ways of doing things. Ideally, we can all benefit when every one uses intelligence and creativity to the best of their abilities. Equally, we all benefit from living in an intelligent and creative community. These are social ideals that we must constantly strive for, even though we often fall short of attaining them. They result in the one benefiting the many. This is the crucial interaction between the one and the many that makes all social cultures work, for example, those of the ants and bees.

This is therefore about using our intelligence creatively. Intelligence in this context refers to our rational side while creativity takes in our intuitive side. In our quest for truth and knowledge we use our intelligence, and in finding beauty and feeling in all things our creativity is stimulated. Intelligence depends on reason and knowledge that are based on truth, while creativity is inspired by beauty and other intuitions that impact on our senses and inner feelings. We need to make the most of these to living life to the full. However, the argument is that intelligence and creativity are not sufficient by themselves to bring about wisdom. They need to go through the mill that involves learning all the roles of the holistic viewpoint. As human beings we are partly rational and partly intuitive. Intelligence involves being rational and creativity thrives on intuition. Wisdom consists in combining the both of these without going to one extreme or the other.

Intelligence and creativity are beyond doubt the most important things in the universe, which is otherwise a dull place full of meaningless stupidities unless we counter these by behaving intelligently and doing creative things. We human beings can consider ourselves important to the universe in the valuable things we bring into being that would not exist otherwise, especially creative objects and ideas. When we brighten it up for ourselves, it is a brighter place in itself. Our value lies in the new and different things we introduce into it that did not exist before. Our knowledge and our art shine forth despite all our flaws and faults. The universe progresses from dull uniformity to dazzling diversity, and we contribute to that process in ways never hitherto countenanced. We belong to the universe as we are a part of its natural processes in becoming more diverse and different as it expands and develops.

The holistic view is therefore essential to artistic vision as it emphasises our oneness with the universe, as we are indeed children of the universe. That human beings live at all is such a fortuitous event that we owe a debt of gratitude to the universe which has given rise to us against all the odds. If it were configured differently we would not have existed in any shape or form. Events in the past could have turned out so very differently. We are indebted because we live and the alternative to life is to be nothing at all. We can repay that debt by using our intelligence and creativity to add to its diversity.

That we exist at all as human beings is an important fact in itself. Every human being is capable of displaying intelligence of some sort and of creating things that did not exist before. We vindicate our existence by the intelligent and creative things we do, and the holistic view helps us to make the most of ourselves with a better future in mind. Our being and doing makes us important in the universe. We are at the cutting edge of the universe; we are the scythe by which universe cuts its way to the future. Nothing else can achieve this. Only by using our intelligence and creativity can we achieve a better and richer future which we bequeath to the universe in living our whole lives to that end.

Intelligence and creativity are always in need of active promotion and approbation, as we can never really be intelligent or creative enough. Even the most handicapped and challenged human being has intelligence and creativity to contribute to the whole. Everyone has intellectual potential of some sort. For example, the physicist Stephen Hawking is as handicapped as anyone can be without being vegetative but he is still making valuable contributions to human life and learning. Thus, everyone is capable of achieving wisdom by using their intelligence and creativity to the best of their abilities and for the best of reasons. Every child born on Earth has potential beyond the wildest dreams of its parents. The faults and failings of its parents need not prevent it from its fulfilling its potential. The blame lies more with the necessarily limited nature of society into which the child is born. None of us can become any more than our society is capable of enabling us to become. We are all born into a society that is limited in its growth and development. It can only go a very small way towards helping us to fulfil our potential. It is up to us as individuals to stretch society further and ensure its further development so that everyone benefits from it.

C. The Importance of Intuition in Creativity

The meaning of intuition. Without intuition, the creative artist is bereft and powerless. All novelty, innovation, ingenuity and indeed genius come from the power of intuition that enables the creative person to think of new and different things. It is extremely important but it must be tempered and directed by intelligence and sustained by will-power and enthusiasm. What is here meant by 'intuition' is often no more than a feeling or idea and it has bee variously called by philosophers 'immediate experience', 'intentional object', 'the given', '*a priori*', 'self-evident truth or principle', or 'common sense principle.' Intuition involves what is implied by all of these things depending on the context in which it is used. It also refers to the unconscious, psychological activity underlying these notions. It is therefore the direct product of inner being as discussed above in section 5 on *Vitality*. The strength of inner being is essential to the intuitions, thoughts, ideas, feelings and impulses that come to us all of a sudden without any conscious prompting on our part.

Generally speaking, the greater our vitality, the greater are our intuitive powers. The greatest creative geniuses seem to have more developed intuitive powers than most of us. They have highly developed and complex inner beings from which their creative genius springs. We appreciate all the better their music, poems, novels, plays, paintings, works of art when we admire the superiority of their abilities and creative genius as compared with our own humble accomplishments. The involved nature of Shakespeare's plays, prose and poetry is evidence of the inner complexity of his thought and mind. True equality therefore comes from everyone developing their intuitive powers and realising their own creative potential. It comes not from reducing everyone to the same mediocre level but in raising everyone to their own particular ways of expressing their creative genius. Understanding what intuition involves is therefore an important step towards understanding the nature of creativity. What is given here is a phenomenological account of what it is involved in intuition.

The influence of intuition is what the ancients called the Muses. The creativity of the classical writers and thinkers was thought to be due to the Muses inspiring them with great ideas and new ways of thinking and writing. Intuition has also been thought of as divine inspiration, but we can now think of it as being the product of unconscious thought processes that underlie inner being.

Intuitions are the primary expression of the potential of being and doing. They can be generated consciously as well as unconsciously. They result consciously when we interact dualistically with our experiences to produce intuitions which are a holistic grasping of our experiences. Seeing a painting as thing of beauty is an intuition generated by interacting with the sight of it. We become intuitively conscious of the intuition of beauty as a whole. Intuitions are experienced as one thing or facet that influences our being and doing in interacting with our environment. When intuitions are generated by unconscious mental activity they come to us all at once as a result of that activity. They are *a priori* products as compared with the *a posteriori* products of consciousness that makes them something more of what is given *a priori*. What we make of our intuitions is therefore as important as having them in the first place.

Intuitions are expressed in a variety of ways. Intuitions are first experienced directly and are only subsequently brought before consciousness and expressed in some way. They expressed in a variety of ways of which verbal expression is only one, and it is not necessarily the most important. They are also expressed in our immediate feelings, facial expressions, hand gestures or some such action which is inwardly or outwardly expressed. Intuitions are also expressed in being thought about, concentrated on, felt intensely, undergone or carried out. In expressing intuitions we either do nothing with them or interact with them to make something of them. For instance, we may approve or disapprove of them. Ultimately, everything in life depends on what we make or do not make of our intuitions since by themselves they are not reliable guides to truth and reality.

The importance of education through reading and learning. A developed intuition results from the experiences of life being learnt and absorbed to become part of one's inner being. The products of education, reading and learning need to be imbibed holistically so that one's whole being is suffused with what one has learnt through life and living. It is not a matter of learning facts but of how these facts are brought together inside oneself to make one a better person. Life then consists in continuously augmenting the sum-total of what one is from day to day.

D. The Complex Build-up of our Intuitive Powers

Our perceptual and conceptual intuitions. Our basic intuitions put us into immediate touch with physical reality by means of perception and conception. Genetically inherited sensory organs give us the ability to sense things through sight, hearing, smell, feeling and other senses. These sensations are the first intuitions that we experience in life. But there is nothing creative in them in so far as they are directly representative of reality. Even dreams and images at that early stage consist of repetitions of these direct experiences. When the intuitions involve images or the sense impressions of hearing, touch and feeling, these are given by the memory of previous experiences. These sensory intuitions give us images of things that may be real or imaginary but conception is the real source of our creativity. Sensations only become perceptions *per se* when conception is involved in them. The ability to conceive of things as being distinct things in themselves enables us to think of them independently of experiencing them. We identify and distinguish things by separating them from what is immediately given to us by sensation. Even cows in a field can conceive of grass as being distinct from bare earth even though they lack words to describe such distinctions. Their dreams doubtless comprise images of tasty grass and such like.

Thus, our perceptual experiences are immediately given by means of our inherited sense organs but are augmented by the conceptions and ideas attached to them. These experiences underlie the intuitions of inner being that are also given immediately. Perceptual experiences give rise to objectivity while inner being involves subjectivity. Our apprehension of external reality depends on a constant dualist interaction between the intuitions of the senses and the intuitions of inner being. Such an apprehension is also at the root of our consciousness in general as we are aware of ourselves interacting constantly with our given experience of things and events. The originality and creativity of intuitions comes from the admixture of experiences within inner being. New thoughts and ideas come from previous experiences being re-ordered and re-fashioned within inner being.

Perceived reality is reliable because of childhood learning. Our immediate experiences of things and events are intuitive in so far as we don't have to think about or analyse them. External reality is given to us intuitively and is experienced all at once and undivided at any moment in time. This is because our skills for doing so are unconscious and already well learnt. Thus, we normally don't have to think about what we are seeing and hearing and touching because our perceptual skills are so well honed in early childhood. Such intuitions are habitual and automatic unless they let us down and we have to do more than just look, listen or feel. We can be mistaken or misled by our perceptual organs when in ill-health, facing optical illusions, or when we don't pay attention to the objects of these organs. We have to constantly monitor perceptual activity if we are to keep in touch with reality. We do this by recursively looping back on what is being perceived by us to ascertain with any certainty just what it is that we are perceiving at any point in time.

The intuitive limitations of other animals. Other animals are subject to intuition in that they conscious in being aware of what they are doing but not of themselves doing it. Not having a concept of self they cannot identify themselves with whatever they are doing. They may choose to do or not to do something but they lack knowledge of why they are doing it because they have no awareness of themselves doing or not doing it. In short, they do things randomly or instinctively without further thought. Even if an animal seems to recognise itself in a mirror, it cannot understand the process by which its physical form is reflected back to it as it lacks the concepts by which to arrive at such an understanding. It is therefore doubtful whether it could ever experience the reflection in anything like the complexity that we enjoy.

Perceptual intuitions therefore involve the formation of conceptions about what exists or does not exist in external reality. Creative intuition arises from the alteration, juxtaposition, or rearrangement of pre-existing conceptions of things. It involves the intuitive reception of conceptions, thoughts, ideas, or notions which are given as objects before the mind. The advent of language skills enables us to think of things and events in abstraction from our perceptual experiences. The thought of a better way of expressing our thoughts occurs to us intuitively. We make more of these creative intuitions by the thinking processes that are developed by means of language and other abstract symbols. Intuitions produced by these processes are no less immediate since they are produced by habit and routines that have become unconscious and automatic in their functioning. These often considered to be 'rules' but they are generally not hard and fast and can be changed through experience and trial and error.

The actuality of a conceptual intuition is established by critical analysis. The reality of an intuition in a system of thought or a context is established by its coherence within that system or context. The external reality of an intuition is established by correspondence involving trial and error, experiment, investigation and other forms of critical research. Developing this aspect of intuitive thinking belongs to dynamic logic which is part of dynamic philosophy and is already mentioned in outline in my book *The Promise of Dualism* (2015).

The origin of goals in intuitions. The first intuition experienced by us is that of a goal, aim or end towards which our being and doing is directed. The pang of hunger experienced by a baby gives rise to the desire for food and drink. The instinctive need for food gives rise to the intuitive feeling of hunger. Thus, the origin of goals lies *primarily* in intuitions that are governed by the inner being and the genetic influences that underlie inner being. These fundamental intuitions may take the form of instincts, impulses, whims, inclinations, feelings, habits, routines and similar activities which are not the result of conscious awareness, rational thought or verbal deliberation. These intuitions mean something to us so that our inner being has the goal of bringing that meaning to our conscious attention. The intuition is the unified product of inspirited activity that makes us aware of what the intuition means to us immediately and without prior notification. A stab of pain makes its presence felt immediately so that we have no doubt of what it means to us. Exclamations such as 'Ouch!' are used to express the pain and communicate our discomfort to others.

The origin of goals in our reasoning powers. Goals arise *primarily* in intuition and only *secondarily* in the reasoning powers of life-forms of sufficient complexity to be self-aware and have language abilities. Either we decide to do things on a whim and without thinking about them or we do so deliberately by consciously and rationally making up our minds to do them. It is this verbal expression of intuitions which is now discussed.

E. The Verbal Expression of Intuitions

Verbal expression is always inexact. Our intuitions are not always expressed verbally. We mostly have to put them into words after the event. Through verbal expression our intuitions can be described but only approximately since words and symbols are insufficient to reproduce these intuitions in the immediate way that they are experienced by us. An intuition such as an idea comes to us all at once as a complete whole. But in expressing it verbally it loses its unity. We have to use the given conceptual distinctions and current verbal expressions to convey the intuition's content and meaning. In other words, in speaking our minds concerning what we think or feel, we need to put our intuitions into words and symbols that are communicable to other people. Such assertions are immediately open to analysis, criticism, examination or elaboration of some kind. In contrast, a command assertion is not open in that way as it is meant to be acted upon without question or criticism.

The inaccuracy of verbal expression also applies to mathematics. The limited nature of verbal expression applies even to the precision that mathematical calculations and formulae can give us. Unless mathematical formulae are applied correctly in the right contexts and circumstances they may be inapplicable or lead to erroneous conclusions. The formula 1 + 1 = 2 does not apply when one cup of liquid is added to another cup making one cup of liquid. Naturally, we learn by habit and practice not to apply such formulae incorrectly.

Mathematics gives us access to greater precision but it does not represent external reality with any absolute or infallible accuracy. Practical mathematics can be applied with reliable exactitude when it is used in strictly limited circumstances where it is shown to work reliably. But the practice of pure mathematics typically exists in the world of its own, divorced from complexities of the physical world. Even the science of physics becomes divorced from reality when it seeks aesthetically pleasing formulae regardless of whether they are shown to apply to the real world. Physics then enters the context of pure mathematics and leaves behind the context of applied science.

Intuitions should be analysed only in accordance with our goals. We may criticise our immediate intuitions by submitting them to rigorous logical analysis. But analysis and criticism should not be done for their own sake but to achieve coherence, clarification or elaboration of our intuitions in relation to our overview or outlook so that our account of things makes sense in itself. Above all, our aims in carrying out analysis must justify the extent to which we engage in such critical analysis.

How intuitions acquire meaning. Intuitions only acquire meaning within contexts. A context-free intuition would be unconnected to conscious thought which can only subsist meaningfully within a context. It would be forgotten as soon as it experienced as we remember things only because the context is required to catalogue the experience in one's memory. Moreover, the truth of intuitions may only be ascertained by reference to different contexts to which they may be compared and judged interactively. Meaning supplies us with information which is used to further our goals. Thus, our aim in giving expression to an intuition is to give it meaning and significance in our thinking about it.

Our developed intuitions are those that are built up through experience and have complex unconscious processes underlying their simple, unified apprehension as immediate intuitions. They may take the form of perceptual, conceptual and metaphysical intuitions. Thus, dreams for example may be perceptual but they are highly interconnected with our past experience. They occur to us immediately as a result of cerebral activity that brings our thoughts together into unified understanding or apprehension of something or other.

F. The Creativity of Metaphysical Intuitions

The analysis of metaphysical intuitions. Metaphysical intuitions are the more elaborate and complex thoughts, ideas, notions, beliefs, hypotheses or theories that occur to us immediately and without conscious deliberation. Such intuitions are ideas, opinions, hypotheses, theories or philosophical considerations generally. Only subsequently do we them put into words and sentences when they occur to us. The potential in any thought is found in grasping it intuitively; whereas its actuality is realised by subsequent analysis of its contents. Analysis means making an object of the thought whereas an act of intuition puts thoughts together anew so that the resulting intuition becomes a subject in itself. Our thoughts turn into themselves to reach a unity which occurs to us all at once. When an idea occurs to us, its centrality is reached by intuition and the intuiting person identifies entirely with it at the moment of grasping it. It is, as it were, himself *per se*. The thought cannot be distinguished from the object of thought in the intuitive event. This is the beingness or Dasein of the intuition. It durates at the moment of intuition and it exists absolutely at the moment of being intuited. It is not established as representing reality but remains a mental chimera. It requires more to be done to it to ensure its relationship to external reality.

Infinite regresses are not implied by the recursion of thoughts. When we identify with our ideas by means of intuition, our thoughts turn into themselves to reach a unity of thought that occurs to us all at once. Thus, in intuition, there is no infinite regress that spirals into infinity. This regress does not occur because our thoughts move forward through time. Bergson calls this 'la durée' or 'duration'. This duration is an interval of time which gives us time to link the past to the future by using past experience to plan for the future. The thought that we have later differs from the previous thought because it takes account of that thought and adds to or subtracts from it in some way. In this way, our thoughts are always moving on and never can be pinned down absolutely.

Clinging to one intuition is to make a god of it, for example, such ideas as 'Absolute', 'Dasein', 'duration' in the manner of continental philosophy. When philosophers such as Hegel, Heidegger and Bergson build their philosophies round these ideas, they use them to represent their experience of reality with which they are perpetually interacting. They are constantly testing their ideas and concepts in relation to their respective dominant intuition. These notions are names for their thinking about things.

Enabling principles are those intuitions that enable us to get on with our lives without needing to think too much about them. They are intuitively accepted as true only in so far as they are enabling. They are valid for as long as they are shown to be enabling. The principles of religion ceased to be enabling with the advent of scientific knowledge and understanding. These principles facilitate forward movement. The falsification principle is not itself falsifiable because it is an enabling principle. But such principles are always contingent and never necessary.

G. The Factual Limitations to our Intuitions

The creative person generally uses the facts to present them to us in a different way that enables us to see things anew. Thus painter for example doesn't just represent reality in a photographic manner but interprets what he sees and puts his own spin on the way things look. This applies particularly to portrait painting when the personality of subject is highlighted and brought to the fore. Equally, the skilled photographer doesn't snap a scene before him but pre-plans his photographs and manipulates them in an interesting way that shows his creative flair. The artist knows intuitively what feels right and such feelings are not matters of fact that can be stated rationally. Thus, artist's intuitive powers add to the facts and to their interpretation of reality.

The intuitive reception and use of facts. There are limits to the extent to which the artist can manipulate and massage the facts without offending us, violating our sensibilities, or losing touch with reality altogether. Facts are too important to be meddled or muddled with impunity. We need often to differentiate what is intuitive from what is factual. Thus, fiction writers use their intuition to represent reality as closely as possible. The extent to which they fail to do so, makes their works seem fantastical, absurd or senseless. It is therefore useful to be clear about how intuition can be misleading. What we intuitively believe to be the facts is often not the case when we examine them in retrospect. When an intuition occurs to us we are prone to regard it instantaneously as being factual and as representing realities directly and immediately. We may be mistaken by what merely appears to be case.

This tendency can be overcome by mental discipline. Theoretical facts, for example, are never established absolutely but only as interactive processes which we may correct and update according to future events. The reality of facts may not be doubted when they enable us to deal directly and effectively with reality. It is important to clarify the role that facts play as our agreement concerning what is or is not to be done depends on our agreeing what the facts are. We must reach general agreement about the facts concerning the plight of the human race; otherwise we will do nothing together to ensure our future.

The word 'fact' comes from the Latin *factum* which is the past participle of *facere*, meaning 'to do'. Strictly speaking, 'fact' means something which is done, an act or deed. It signifies something that we do in relation to reality. A fact is therefore best seen as a process rather than as a fixed, determined object. Facts are only stable in so far as they refer to past events. Even then, they may not represent the whole truth of the matter and are subject to further revision, rethinking and updating. Facts are therefore hypothetical entities when they are considered in isolation from immediate perceptual experience.

Three types of fact are important here: (1) perceptual facts that may be confirmed or denied by using such senses as sight, hearing, touch, and feeling; (2) scientific facts that are subject to appropriate scientific methods; and (3) social facts that apply to meaningful and communicable human activity. Perceptual facts are those dependent on the direct perception of objects and events. On hearing the reports of others about what has happened we know that we can verify these reports by seeing or hearing them for ourselves. Scientific facts depend for their truth or falsity on the particular scientific methods by which they are obtained. The most problematic and relevant are social facts since our future depends on our agreeing about them. Though these types are interrelated, we are largely concerned here with the status of the last two of these.

Every assertion bears some truth in so far as it has meaning, and every assertion is factual in so far as it refers to something else beyond itself. Therefore, neither truth-bearing nor factuality is sufficient for us to rely absolutely on words and symbols for our decisions. We must ultimately evaluate the extent of fact and truth in any assertion by reference to context and perspective. Thus, facts are established not simply by the form of words and sentences or by their definitions. Their relationship to the sociosphere and what is happening therein must also be taken into account.

Facts are those assertions which indicate sociospheric relationships between the words and symbols we use in these assertions and the meanings inherent in them. These words and symbols have no meaning outside the context of sociospheric activity. This is same as saying that they only mean anything to people and their activities. Facts therefore exist sociospherically rather than actually, unlike those events and states of affairs which are not facts in so far as they actually happen regardless of whether they are described in words or symbols. Furthermore, facts exist cosmically when they have been established in science, history or some and settled science, field of knowledge or subject of study. They then have the potential to exist for posterity hence for all time thereafter. Short term facts are those current in the sociosphere of intercommunication whereas long term facts form part of the cosmos over and above any sociospheric context in which they are used. This outline only applies to the role that facts play in our creative use of intuitions.

H. Eternal Nature of the Artistic Vision

> It has sometimes been said that what we feel is always something existing here and now, and limited in its existence to the place and time at which it is felt; whereas what we think is always something eternal, something having no special habitation of its own in space and time but existing everywhere and always. In some sense this is perhaps true.
>
> R.G. Collingwood (1938) [3]

There is no end to the artist's vision and ingenuity. It stretches nigh to eternity. Thus, there is a touch of the eternal in the artist's intelligence and creativity that takes them beyond the commonplace here and now. The very idea of eternity is important for artists as it broadens their thinking about things. It takes their artistic achievements into a higher context. Every creative act brings about changes that transform things forever. Moreover, beauty in whatever form is forever. So the artist's works are eternalised in their very creativity. His standpoint must be *sub specie aeternitatis* - under the aspect of eternity.

The word 'eternity' is nothing more than a notion or concept that exists in the mind but nevertheless it helps us to make sense of the universe we inhabit. It refers to the everlastingness of things; the possibility that things can go on forever and ever. This is useful because it is within the aspect and prospect of eternity that we can embrace everything that will possibly take us forward to the future. It includes everything concerning us that lasts without end and stretches to infinity. It is the sphere of the sublime that surpasses all. We broaden our minds and stretch our imaginations beyond everyday life in contemplation of the eternal. We transcend the middle ground to trawl our imaginations concerning what has not come into being and what is beyond all present being. It underlines the all-encompassing view of the artist in contributing things of awe and beauty. The view of eternity is therefore that of glimpsing the eternal and embracing it as a viewpoint. It is the view of the Muses of old, and is therefore that of the artist or creative person of whatever description.

In eternity, the Platonic forms take their ultimate place though that place is only in our thinking about things. We imagine them to have such an eternal existence. Though eternity embraces the everlasting nature of Platonic forms, it does not confirm their reality. These forms do not exist outside the categories that we impose on the world. Their place is therefore in our minds. Truth and beauty reside there and the artist accesses to them in their transcendent form. The artist is therefore tasked with bringing the eternal view out-of-mind and down-to-earth by representing it in a material form which may be artistic, literary, visual or whatever the imagination of the artist can conjure up. Thus, in holistic view, the artist is the sublime exponent of eternal forms.

The eternal view is therefore essential to the artist as it looks at things from afar and gives a long-lasting standpoint from which to judge works of art. In so far as 'eternal' means lasting forever and ever, all existence lies before the artist and all feelings related to that existence. The artist uses the present to put the past together with its future prospects in mind. This millenarian attitude expands our minds to infinity. In every painting, poem, symphony or other work of art there must be a universal theme otherwise there is nothing in it to appeal to the bulk of those viewing, reading or listening to their works. The artist at his best seeks truth and beauty in his works of art and these ensure their eternal significance. In being creative, artists are often more prospective than retrospective in their outlook. They are looking forward to new and different things that will make the future different from the past. The eternal view of the artist therefore includes the ability to look to the future and anticipate the needs of future generations. This is important because our value as artists is ultimately judged by posterity.

However, it is important to note that eternity is not God. In religion, eternity is often equated with God who is portrayed as an everlasting being compared with temporality of the human being. God is also thought to be a perfect being. But both eternity and perfection are mere ideas that exist only to order our thinking about the universe and our place in it. The notion of eternity helps us to expand our thinking beyond the temporal existence to which we are condemned throughout our lives. It is an inherently human thing with no divine attributes beyond our own divine aspirations.

We can speculate that everything and nothing is preserved within the scope of eternity. At the moment of death we enter eternity and then everything is nothing to us. We come out of the eternal nothingness at birth and re-enter it at death. Between these two empty instances, our lives are lived and they potentially persist for eternity since there is nothing else in it. The eternal existence of things perhaps belongs within the Zero Point Field postulated by physicists. Our lives may be accessible there for an eternity. All the thoughts and images that pass through our minds are looped into this field wherein their existence is guaranteed in some way at present unaccountable to us. These at least survive us for an eternity even though our lives have come to a predictable end. It is not entirely beyond the bounds of possibility that eternity is perennially accessible at that level of existence.

8. Morality: Disciplining Ourselves Purposefully

> A Christian says: 'If all were good, all would be happy'. A socialist says: 'If all were happy, all would be good'. A fascist says: 'If all obeyed the state, all would be both happy and good'. A lama says: 'If all were like me, happiness and goodness would not matter'. A humanist says: 'Happiness and goodness need more analysis'. This last is the least deniable view.
>
> John Fowles (1980) [1]

A. The Need for the Discipline of Morality

The past achievements of humanity have depended greatly on the moral behaviour of individuals. This is morality in the sense of applying moral discipline, not to avoid sinfulness, but to get things done and make decent lives for ourselves and others. We are all sinners in being imperfect beings but what matters is doing what is worthwhile in our own and other people's judgments. If we are totally self-indulgent individuals we are unlikely to accomplish great things. If we follow our immediate feelings unreservedly and consistently, we will lack the discipline and energy to do what we ourselves really want to do. Total lack of moral restraint means killing each other when we feel like it, cheating and lying with every word we speak, having sex with each other without shame like bonono apes, and so on. We will be unable to live together and trust each other. Our social ties therefore depend on the acceptance and practice of moral behaviour.

Thus, we need morality to give us rules for our conduct and boundaries within which to behave ourselves. Without such rules and boundaries, there are no limits to the inappropriate or self-destructive behaviour to which we may stoop. By learning to live within such moral confines we can become normal, trustworthy and hardworking people. We can freely adopt and practice the norms of society to become mature and responsible people who are ready to take our place in society. Wholesomeness is necessarily incomplete without a sound moral basis that makes us life-long moralists.

Unless we learn to discipline ourselves and behave in a manner becoming to ourselves, we never can be moralists. The moralist wants to behave properly both for their own satisfaction and out of respect for other people. Such behaviour is self-reflective and can make us wise people. We cannot be wise unless we are living a basically moral life-style. This is a life-style that is restrained and self-regarding and is adopted by one's own freewill and not imposed willy nilly on us by others or society. This is disciplining oneself on purpose and not randomly.

Morality is important because it is the means by which we distinguish between (1) behaviour that develops us and takes us forward and (2) behaviour that degrades us and lessens us. Personal development takes us forward while personal degradation weighs us down and cripples us as vibrant human personalities. We must discover for ourselves the behaviour that advances us as opposed to the behaviour that impedes us.

Moral behaviour involves self-discipline and self-direction. Without these, we dissipate and waste our vital energy. Within the context of morality we examine ourselves and come to terms with our inclinations to behave badly or inappropriately. It involves the studied exercise of self discipline wherein we discipline and direct our impulses, instincts, forces, and drives, and wherein we criticise our behaviour, motivations, inclinations, feelings, impulses and everything else that governs our behaviour and our relationships with other people and society in general.

Being a moral person means not just behaving ourselves but also taking account of other people's feelings and thinking about the consequences of our actions on other people as well as ourselves. We do this by evaluating our own behaviour more than that of others. Thus, morality in this context is about personal evaluation and not about moralising about other people's behaviour. It is about what I ought to do rather than what you ought to do. We are not moralising for other people as it is about learning personal evaluation for ourselves. It is a process of self-education in which we learn the moral truth about ourselves. This enables us to consolidate our values and integrity and to establish the extent of our self-discipline and the commitment that is required to further our intelligence and creativity. The quest for moral truth involves making moral judgments and distinguishing right from wrong, good from bad, just from unjust. Otherwise we are no longer being true to ourselves and we become immoral or amoral. Immorality is not adhering to one's moral norms, and amorality is not having any moral norms to live up to. In short, a moralist is one who learns to exercise self-restraint by habit and choice.

Another task is to purify our actions and motivations by simplifying them. In place of lives complicated by meaningless and enervating self-indulgence we reduce our behaviour to what is truly necessary for our purposes. We seek the purity of balanced thinking that looks ahead to better things. It therefore means simplifying our lives by cutting out extraneous behaviour, habits, thoughts and other unwholesomeness and superfluous activities. The aim is not to impose austerity for its own sake but to maintain a balanced enjoyment of life instead of being subject to the vapid extremes of misery on the one hand and mindless ecstasy on the other hand. Thus, morality contributes to wisdom through the quest for moral truth and balanced living. In this way we become moralists who have the self-command needed to direct our passions instead of being ruled by them.

There are therefore distinct benefits in being a moralist. It means being a mature and responsible person making the best use of our intelligent and creative powers to live truthful and balanced lives. Responsibility involves taking account of the effects of our behaviour on other people. As moralists we take responsibility for our own lives. We become control freaks in the best possible sense. We establish control over our lives for the benefit of others as well as ourselves. This does not mean imposing our moral values on others simply because they behave differently from what we expect or find tolerable. It is what we impose on ourselves in being moralists, and it is not doing what we know we could do as we prefer on moral grounds not to do it. It requires strength of will not to do just what we feel like doing. We also control feelings lest we do unnecessary harm to other people. The inner strength to do so does not come naturally; it comes with maturity and is bolstered by the responsibility that life demands of us.

The self-disciplined moralist doesn't just conform mindlessly to social norms of behaviour. Being a moralist means relying on ourselves for self-discipline. We learn for ourselves how to do, say and think the right things. We aim to become moral people who do not act impulsively and thoughtlessly and who do not do or say the first thing that comes to mind. This is best achieved by a morality of self-evaluation by which we monitor and criticise our own behaviour. This is only possible when our inner being has been developed to the extent that we behave well because we want to. Thus, our moral behaviour consists in exercising self-restraint and self-regulation for the best possible purposes that are worthy of ourselves and humanity. A prerequisite is that we achieve sufficient self-knowledge to know our strengths and weaknesses in moral matters.

The moral view explicates the good and the truth and what are outlined here are only snippets that remain to be developed into a systematic theory of interactive ethics. The aim is to offer tools for achieving self-knowledge in ethical matters. In particular, interacting between extremes is shown to be a way of keeping on the straight and narrow. However, it is not good enough just to be a good person. Being good may involve doing nothing at all. Once we start doing things we need ways of evaluating our behaviour. Ultimately, the truth of what we are consists in what we do for others, humanity and the universe. We learn to see that truth within ourselves in interacting with other people and society as a whole. Moral evaluation is a useful guide in assessing whether we are really being affectionate, showing respect towards others, acting honourable, and so on. But a prerequisite to acquiring such moral skills is the possession of 'moral sense' which is now outlined.

B. The Role of Moral Sense

Moral sense gives us self-awareness and self-criticism. In so far as morality is an internal more than an external matter, it concerns our 'moral sense'. This is a product of the inner being which is our introspective mental activity as is explicated with regard to the Vitalist's role above. Moral sense is basically our conscience or 'superego' (to use Freud's word).[2] It consists in being aware of the inner voice telling us to desist from doing what it is feels to be undesirable or avoidable. It is inner being turning in on itself to make us aware of our behaviour and its merits and demerits. In practical terms, we stop to think and assess our behaviour. It makes us morally sensitive of our conduct and we feel shame or guilt if that conduct has not met with our inner approval. If we are mature and responsible adults, we don't need to be told what we know 'in our hearts' we should not do. We learn to 'desist and resist' as far as our basic inclinations are concerned. Nothing needs to be specified by any external authority that claims to know us better than we know ourselves. When we begin to think for ourselves we need to develop morality for ourselves by our inner development. Hence the importance of inner being in helping us to regulate our conduct.

Morality therefore begins with our moral sense which is partly inborn and partly acquired. It is the intuitive product of our inner being which itself is partly inborn and acquired. Because moral sense is basically intuitive, what is given by it is not enough in itself make us moral let alone rational. Our moral sense may rouse us to be angry, indignant, sympathetic, appreciative, or have other feelings, regardless of whether we have real reason or evidence to support such feelings. To that extent, we are slaves to our passions and can be provoked into hasty actions for no reason at all. However, we can learn to discipline ourselves by interacting critically with what is given by our moral sense to make us consistent in our behaviour, and give ourselves moral direction in the conduct of our lives. Thus, our moral sense is given us by intuition but is trained and disciplined by reason which consists in putting our feelings into words and relating them to our purposes as a whole. The holistic view is intended to be helpful in ascertaining these purposes.

Having a moral sense means being directly cognisant of one's feelings. It involves intuition and direct sensitivity rather than reason, calculation or verbal expression. We are directly aware of our feelings without having arrived at them by any conscious process. Having experienced these feelings we then interact with them and make them the subject of our reasoning powers. We need to react in that way, otherwise we are enslaved by our emotions rather than master of them. Some of the feelings connected with moral sense are listed as follows:

Approval Feelings	*Disapproval Feelings*	*Responsive Feelings*	*Susceptible Feelings*	*Refined Feelings*
Gratitude	Contempt	Sympathy	Guilt	Purity
Appreciation	Anger	Compassion	Shame	Uprightness
Reverence	Disgust	Empathy	Embarrassment	Integrity

A Table of Moral Sensibilities

Approval feelings reflect our recognition of other people's forbearance, altruism or excellence. They prompt us to reward these traits in other people. Such feelings need to be cultivated and expressed to foster our social relationships. They help us to be less selfish and self-centred in showing how we value and appreciate the other people's behaviour towards us regardless of whether we consider their responses to be more or less appreciative than we deserve.

Disapproval feelings are expressive of the indignation that we feel at other people's behaviour, though they may also result from annoyance at our own behaviour. At worst, these feelings can prompt us to seek vengeance and find ways of punishing the infractors. At best, they help us inform others of the extent to which we disapprove of their behaviour, and to clarify to ourselves our disapproval of our own behaviour.

Responsive feelings result from seeing others in plights that we would wish to avoid ourselves. We respond to the inner anguish of other people because we can put ourselves in their position. These feelings take us out of ourselves and help us to put ourselves in other people's shoes.

Susceptible feelings follow from the disapproval that we feel about our actions which we would like to be otherwise than what they are. Being ashamed of our behaviour helps us to regulate and discipline it. Thus, for example, we may feel guilt and shame at our sexual behaviour and we can use these feelings to impose more discipline upon ourselves. But the discipline must come from within and not be imposed from without.

Refined feelings. These feelings most distinguish us from other animals that are incapable of such refinement. They are resonant of our attempts to behave to the highest standards and to be better people as a result. Thus, these feelings flow from our desire to regulate our behaviour in relation our highest and best aims and purposes. They are holistic feelings that transcend our animality and give us divine aspirations that are too easily projected outside us as divine beings or inside us as divine delusions of grandeur. These feelings therefore need to be restrained and disciplined as any others.

There can be no self-restraint or inner discipline without moral sense. For it enables us to be sensitive to the wrongness of bad behaviour in ourselves and others, and being susceptible to feelings of disgust, anger, shame and guilt about such behaviour. Some acts are simply repugnant to us because they do not feel right. Such feelings are the product of inner being and go to the heart of what we are as human personalities.

The lack of moral sense may have a genetic basis. Some people may be born deficient in moral sense, for instance, because of damage to their genes, and some may be lose it through bad upbringing or adverse circumstances. Others may decide for their own reasons that they don't want to be sociable or amenable persons. They will not allow themselves to be sensitive to the feelings of others, or to feel adversely about whatever nasty or unacceptable behaviour they may indulge in. Thus, sociopaths, psychopaths and other anti-social or totally misanthropic individuals are typically devoid of moral sense. But whether they actually commit anti-social or criminal acts is another matter. If they are clever or self-regarding enough, they may appear to be socially respectable and their propensities may never be made evident.

The presumption must be that everyone is capable of moral sense until their total lack becomes apparent and they are shown to be constitutionally irremediable, and perhaps need to be locked away for life. Nevertheless, self-control must be possible in an otherwise normal person. Even though a person is genetically deficient in their moral sense, their ability to exercise self-control and consciously refrain from immoral or socially unacceptable conduct must be presumed. Overall, such defective individuals may need to be specially trained and disciplined to alter their ill-natured feelings. Quite simply, it is in their self-interest to behave themselves and this needs to be made clear to them. No one with any sense wants to be considered so abnormal that they are not expected to behave themselves and consequently must be deprived of the free and open life-style that the rest of us take for granted.

A loss of moral sense can result from self-indulgence and depravity. It means losing touch with one's inner monitor. Self-control and self-discipline are impaired. As a result, there is a lack of guilt, shame and remorse at one's conduct and over the results thereof. Kleptomaniacs and sex addicts are typically lacking in moral sense in so far as they have lost control over their behaviour. Such a deficiency means that they need to work harder than most people to make themselves socially viable human beings. Prisons and other social institutions need to be properly equipped to help people by training and disciplining them in a manner that is shown to be effective and appropriate. In these ways, lack of self-control can be countered by education and training. Thus, the ability to respect the interests of the community and of humanity as a whole is an essential extension of inner being by which it develops within itself to get beyond its innate self-centredness, as is now discussed.

C. Personal Interaction

Self-discipline involves balancing extremes of behaviour. To discipline ourselves, we must learn to interact with our impulses and inclinations and become aware of their power and potential. By constantly interacting with them we are able to distinguish ourselves from these impulses and inclinations so that we do not give way to them immediately and thoughtlessly. In other ways, we are making ourselves consciously aware of them so that they are not lurking in our unconscious ready to pounce us unawares. We can learn more effectively to do this by becoming aware of the oscillation between our feelings of pride and humility. If we are overconfident then we give way to impulses all the more readily. If we lack confidence then we may go to the other extreme and become inhibited in respect of all our feelings. To avoid these extremes we need to be aware of when we are being too full of ourselves at one extreme and thinking too little of ourselves at the other extreme. We therefore learn to get the correct balance between pride and humility which will enables us to act and behave appropriately and rationally in all circumstances. The one extreme leads us to become overly active while the other extreme makes us overly passive, as is depicted in this interactive table:

```
          PRIDE  ← →  HUMILITY
            ↓            ↓
      Self Expressing   Self Restraining
        Empowering       Disciplining
       Self Indulgent    Puritanical
         Spendthrift     Parsimonious
            ↓            ↓
         ACTIVE  ← →  PASSIVE
```

The Interactive Tension Between our Proud and Humble Propensities

    Uncertainty as whether we are proud or humble, active or passive keeps us constantly re-assessing our situation. It is right that we should be unsure of whether we are superior to inferior to other people, and in what ways. To be utterly sure of our superiority or of our inferiority is to possess either a superiority complex or an inferiority complex. At such extremes, we look loftily down on people or meekly up to them. We are either too proud or too humble. The balanced personality is forever uncertain since this keeps us on the hop. If we are never too sure whether we are being proud or humble, we have to think carefully about it, that is to say, if we are concerned at all. We must balance our propensities towards superiority or inferiority and put restraints on our pride and humility. The balancing process is always ongoing and inconclusive.

    We can consciously aim to be sociable and amenable persons as opposed to self-seeking, self-indulgent individuals. This is achieved by plotting the middle route between the extremes outlined above. We constantly battle to avoid entrapment at one extreme or the other. A mature and responsible person learns to find a healthy balance between self-expression and self-restraint. Thus, a maturation process is needed to cope with these extremes. Empowerment is potentially self-destructive if it is not restrained by self-discipline. If we want to, we can learn to avoid the extremes of being totally self-indulgent and totally puritanical, or totally spendthrift and totally parsimonious. We do so through experiencing those situations that lead us astray and how to avoid them in the future. Ideally, this maturation process should take place in adolescence and should be undertaken in full knowledge and understanding of these extremes and the harm that they can do to the individual.

    A 'golden mean' between these extremes is not implied. There is no absolute or categorical mean between these extremes. There is only a fluid interaction between them. Most of our ethical dilemmas are rooted in our perennial uncertainty about whether to act or not act, to restrain ourselves or not restrain ourselves. Thus, we must learn to balance self-expression with self-restraint, self-indulgence with puritanism, and so on. This interactive balancing does not involve a 'golden mean' (attributed to Aristotle)[3] between these extremes as the middle route is constantly shifting and uncertain. We have to work hard to keep on the straight and narrow. There is no dogmatic answer always to be adhered to. The Aristotelian approach is overwhelmingly categorical and therefore too logically clear-cut to help us in those practical problems that require fine judgments and flexible thinking. The process of maturation cannot be reduced to a logical one of categorisation. It is an ongoing experience that is dynamic, interactive and cumulative over time. The more that we make of our experiences in life, the more we are equipped to deal adequately with whatever life throws at us.

The process of maturation is one of *personalisation* in which we become mature and responsible persons and know our place in the scheme of things by means of contextual self-awareness and ethical interactivity. We become sociable persons rather than isolated individuals. We are aware of ourselves as social beings and therefore capable of ethically assessing our behaviour. Thus, in personalising ourselves we adopt ethical values which initially are beyond ourselves in belonging to the language culture in which we are born more than to ourselves. These ethical values are established whenever we articulate our aims and goals in terms of the rational alternatives available in the society.

The quest for individuality often runs counter to that of personalisation in so far as it confines the individual to the context of self. Personalisation means embracing other contexts to be become a better person. We need individuality but only within the limits dictated by personalisation. This means becoming an individual who is also a respectable and well-adjusted person having a place and standing in society. This means balancing our pro-self and anti-self propensities as exemplified in the following diagram:

Pro-Self	*Anti-Self*
Pride	Humility
Love	Hatred
Pleasure	Pain
Beauty	Deformity
Pride	Humility

The Positive and Negative Aspects of Selfishness

A well-balanced person will therefore balance these two propensities which limit and channel our behaviour. This balancing therefore means taking account of negative extremes as well as positive ones. There is no point in running away from or suppressing humility, hatred and the rest of the anti-self propensities as these are feelings that are a part of us as much as our more positive feelings. This view means taking account of negative and contrary feelings so that they can be rationalised in relation to our more positive feelings. Participating fully in society gives us our best chance of overcoming the negative and accentuating the positive. Thus, the holistic view of morality consists in directing our feelings towards sociable purposes without repressing them on the one hand or allowing them a free rein on the other hand. Holistic purposes are therefore important in directing us between these extremes. These purposes are ascertained in fulfilling roles such as those suggested in this book.

D. Ethical Interaction

The activity and passivity of being good. All these maturation processes imply ethical interactions which are ongoing throughout our lives. Another interactive feature is that between activity and passivity. It is a never-ending facet of daily living that we interact between being active and being passive in trying to do and to be the best that we can. We may not think of daily life in these terms but it is nevertheless illuminating to do so. We then realise that we are often unclear within ourselves as to whether to lead an active or a passive way of life. In uncertain circumstances, we often vacillate and oscillate between doing too much or too little. By trial-and-error, we may or may not reach a more moderate position between the two extremes which may be represented as follows:

An Active Good Life	A Passive Good Life
Involves:	*Involves:*
Social conformity	Self-restraint
Fitting into society	Balanced living
Learning skills & wisdom	Seeking internal well-being
Becoming a great-souled person	Becoming a contented person
Taking an active role in society	Indulging in a contemplative life
Aiming for:	*Aiming for:*
Virtue or Excellence	**Happiness or Well-Being**

The Contrast between an Active with a Passive Life-Style

The interaction between these often involves a blending in which the elements of both of them are brought into play. Both of these ways of living can enrich our daily lives, just as we blend work and play, not to mention the scientific and religious attitudes. Moreover, the active life can lead to happiness or well-being just as the passive good life can lead to virtue or excellence. Each way of life only tends in one direction or the other. They are entirely under our control and their direction needs to be frequently monitored.

Happiness isn't necessarily good for you. It is an ethical fallacy to assume that happiness means making ourselves feel happy all the time. Happiness is the usual translation for Aristotle's word *eudaimonia* which really meant 'good spiritedness' or 'well-being' in ordinary Greek usage.[4] He thought that a state of well-being is an end to be striven for but this is not an ecstatic feeling of the moment. Happiness in that sense does not mean a temporary state of euphoria such as that induced by drink, drugs or other forms of mindless excitement. In trying to feel happy all the time, we pump ourselves full of false emotions and end up plunging into depression as a reaction against that extreme behaviour. Bipolar swings between ecstasy and depression may well result from trying too hard to feel happy all the time. Happiness at its best is a balanced state of mind that we reach as a result of living a productive life. It is an end towards which our actions are aimed. As an abstract notion it is something perfect and self-sufficient that can be never reached in its entirety but merely lies rainbow-like forever before us. We find true happiness, for instance, in having done a good job. And having done it we must then move on to something else: mowing the lawn, writing a novel, building a house, and so on. There is no point in resting on our laurels as there is always something more to be done *ad infinitum*.

It is also the case that we learn to be virtuous more than are born virtuous. Virtue is the translation of the Greek *aretê* which also means 'excellence' or 'efficiency'. It doesn't just mean being good but doing the best that we can as a matter of principle and not because other people require it of us. For most people, virtue is partly learnt by instruction and experience. It also means adopting and maintaining the correct habits of behaviour as well as being morally good and dependable people. We are not virtuous at birth but we are endowed with the capacity or disposition for becoming virtuous in the course of time. Some people are born with a greater capacity for virtue than others. But whether a human being may be born totally evil has yet to be proven. They are more likely to have acquired evil habits and ways of thinking very early in life. If the correct habits are formed early enough, a person's moral sense can remain intact of a lifetime. For example, a child begins by following its parents' admonitions to tell the truth without being aware of the moral implications of its actions. Eventually, the habit of truth-telling becomes an ingrained part of his or her moral character.

In summary, goodness is the product of developed inner being which instils a conscience and the good feelings associated with it. But goodness is not enough in being true to oneself since our reason must predominate over our impulses however well-meaning they may be. The relationship with the good and the truth is now outlined.

E. Good, Truth and Evaluative Notions

Noli foras ire, in te redi, in interiore homine habitat veritas.
Do not lose your way from without, return to yourself, truth dwells in the inner man.　　　　　　　　　　　　　　　　　　　Augustine of Hippo (354-430CE)[5]

A Matrix of Evaluative Notions

The interaction between good and truth. It is ethically useful to think in terms of an interaction between good and truth in which we move purposefully from one to the other and *vice versa*. We can use this interaction to regulate our behaviour and learn to be true to ourselves. In thinking about our behaviour in relation to these notions we can evaluate what we are doing and hopefully are more self-critical and self-aware as a result. We then discover what is true or not true about ourselves. In that way, evaluative notions such as those shown above can be used to move interactively from good to truth. We thereby exercise our reasoning powers and preserve our inner integrity by judging matters in relation to the truth of what we are or are not.

Goodness is not good enough. The above diagram illustrates figuratively the most important of the evaluative notions by which we can keep ourselves on the reasonably straight and narrow towards truth. It exemplifies how the good is related to truth through the matrix of evaluative notions. The theory is that it is not sufficient to be good in being affectionate, respectful, obliging, and so on in respect of the rest of these notions. It is necessary also to be true to ourselves in applying them. If their use is not related to ourselves as a whole then we are playing lip-service to these modes of behaviour. We are in a state of 'bad faith' or being 'inauthentic' to use the terms of existentialist philosophers, if such behaviour is performed automatically or because it is expected of us. It is not meaningful or truthful behaviour unless it is performed from the heart and is resonant of what we really are as human personalities.

The three ethical paths exemplified above are not all inclusive or exhaustive of the possibilities. They are only illustrative since other paths and other notions are perfectly possible. There are also interconnections between these notions which are not separate in thought from each other. In theory, therefore, there is an interaction between what these notions are good for and the truth that lies in our use of them. An examination of what these evaluative notions mean to us helps us to gain self-knowledge and establish how we must live our lives in order to be true to ourselves.

The truth to be aimed at here is a moral truth which is a holistic feedback process. It concerns the truth of what we are as a whole and of what we aiming to do with our lives as a whole. It is a constant feedback process in which we use our experiences to refer back to ourselves and re-orient ourselves in relation to what we learn about ourselves on a daily basis. The evaluative notions listed in the above diagram are a guide to our thinking about ourselves and what we are and what we are aiming to do. A quest for moral truth involves evaluation and the making of moral judgments. This means that logical consistency is not being sought since a constant rethinking of our moral values may lead us to contradict ourselves and do things differently from before. For moral truth is a quest for flexible values and not fixed facts in the manner of formal logic. Thus, moral truth is not like logical truth. It is truth pertaining to ourselves and our personal values.

A moral logic concerns our integrity. There is therefore scope for a self-critical moral logic that helps us to evaluate our behaviour. It enables us to change our minds about ourselves and how we are behaving while preserving our integrity and the truth about ourselves. Whereas formal logic is usually used to criticise other people's arguments and assertions, moral logic is used exclusively to criticise ourselves and our own behaviour in relation to behaviour that is true to us and beneficial to our integrity and self-respect. 'Good' is an evaluative notion that only leads to truth when it is used in our moral judgments together with the other evaluative notions listed above. The Logic of morality consists of the following. What we immediately judge to be good or bad this is product of intuition. These good or bad things are evaluated by means of evaluative notions and this takes us to the truth of what we are. This is what we are as a whole in terms of what we have done with our lives and what we intend to do with our lives. This process if it is carried out methodically helps us to become more integrated and purposeful personalities.

Goodness in this context means doing something reasonable and purposeful that has good consequences. In short, goodness means doing good. Thus, it is not enough to be good for the sake of goodness. Unless we are good for a reason, it is a simplistic, unreflective goodness. It can only be a superficial show of goodness that is not necessarily heartfelt and sincere. It is easily swayed and manipulated especially other more cunning persons. We can all be good by doing or being nothing at all. If we are being true to ourselves then we must have reasons for being good, otherwise there is nothing in us to which the goodness relates and it has no rational value. A good person may be someone who does little or nothing. The good life might be an entirely contemplative life leading to a Buddhist-like Nirvana, as exemplified in the 'Passive Good Life' illustrated above. Thus, being good may mean simply not doing anything.

Nevertheless, it is better to be doing worthwhile things than not doing anything at all. We must do something to find out what we are and what we are capable of. Thus the truth of who we are lies in our actions and behaviour. One or more of these evaluative notions may be used to develop what we judge to be good into something that conforms to the truth of our being. In other words, our goodness leads us to truth only when its power is converted by the evaluative intercession of these notions into that which is true to our nature. What this means is explicated in more detail in the subsections below.

The point is that we must evaluate good things to find their truth. This approach in relating good to truth turns on its head Plato's assumption that the form of the good 'causes' truth.[6] *Au contraire*, truth of itself results from putting good things through the transformational mill of other evaluative notions. Good things amount to little unless they are appropriately evaluated and assessed as being beautiful, respectful, sincere, obligatory, righteous, just, or whatever. We arrive at truth by using thee evaluative notions as tools to assess the value of our deeds and not just by proclaiming them to be either good or bad according to our intuitive assessment thereof. G.E. Moore believed that the word, 'good' is a simple notion which is indefinable.[7] But this is only because it initially involves an intuitive and immediate judgment which stands in need of further evaluation.

The notions of good and bad were perhaps the earliest judgmental and evaluative notions arrived at by human beings. Learning to exercise judgment by valuing or devaluing something in comparison with other things was one of the most significant steps taken by our ancestors. It enabled them to discriminate between objects in a rational way instead of responding mutely and instinctively to their presence. The subsequent development of the comparative and superlative adjectives: better and best; and their opposites: worse and worst, were essential in making possible the technological improvements brought about by Cro-Magnon man (or *homo sapiens sapiens*). Instead of sticking to the 'good' things made by Neanderthal man, the more complex-minded modern man wanted something better and this led to continuous improvements in artefacts and living conditions. This development went to harmful extremes when these notions were attributed by the Aryan peoples to individuals so that a class structure was created which was dominated by an aristocracy that claimed absolute power over the majority.

Comparative judgments can often be intuitive and potentially irrational. When these judgments are confined to our selfish ends and goals, they enable us to instantly judge things by intuitively thinking of them as 'good', 'better', 'best', or 'bad', 'worse', 'worst'. Because these involve simple and immediate judgments, they are eccentric and idiosyncratic to everyone who uses them in that unreflective way. Their more rational and social development depends on their being qualified by the more exact evaluations afforded by emotive, self-regarding and judgmental notions such as are listed in the above diagram.

The good can mean anything to anyone. Moreover, Aristotle's supreme good (*summum bonum*),[8] which was in his view the best and most final thing of all, should never be decided by one or more persons for the whole human race. It occurs to individuals in particular circumstances and it may change for them in other circumstances. We all have our own ideas peculiar to ourselves. It is therefore different for everyone and may vary for the same person at other times and places. The good is therefore the most superficial and simplistic of the evaluative notions and always needs to be qualified and backed up with other more evaluative notions.

Thus, we need to get at the truth of what is good for us. Nothing is good enough for us unless it helps us to aspire to the highest standards of truth. Our integrity and self-worth depends on our adhering to what is true as well as what is good. This means that truth is not a thing but a process of getting at truth. In this case, it involves personal truth-seeking which is distinct from other forms of truth-seeking such as those of formal logic, mathematics or science. We therefore use moral logic which amounts to personal truth-seeking as it now outlines.

F. The Importance of Personal Truth-Seeking

Finding out the truth about ourselves. The truth about any of us lies in what we do that has a lasting impact on our lives, the lives of others and on society and life in general. That includes our contributions to knowledge, literature, art, architecture, music and other pursuits of cultural excellence (see section 10 on *Servility* for more about the role of service in vindicating ourselves). Discovering the truth about ourselves therefore lies in finding our place in society wherein we can contribute meaningfully and purposefully to society.

Apollonian/Dionysian interactions. Without balanced thinking and inner development, we cannot think ourselves productively into any of the institutions, activities, norms, or aims of the society in which we find ourselves. To use Nietzsche's distinctions, the Dionysian side of our natures will predominate over the Apollonian so that, in losing touch with our dreams and ideals, we no longer make sense of society and, as a result, are unable to find a place for ourselves in it.[9] We may seek solace in self-indulgence and in living for today, without a care for the future. But the balanced view involves a healthy interaction between these two attitudes so that we maintain our integrity and make progress with our personal projects. There is always a place for Dionysian excess but Apollonian moderation must predominate in the end if our lives are to have lasting value. The sociosphere of communicative activity helps us to restrain ourselves so that we fit into society to fulfil ourselves to the best of our abilities.

Balancing eccentricity and endoxicality. The evaluative notions, exemplified in the diagram above, can help us achieve the balanced living and thinking that enables us to contribute to society. It is only within the sociosphere that these notions can be elaborated and made more meaningful and valuable to us. In that context, there is an important distinction to be made between *eccentricity* and *endoxicality*. To ourselves alone evaluative notions such as respect and honour may be applied eccentrically, that is to say, we develop our own understanding of them which we apply regardless of their conventional meaning. At the other endoxical extreme, we may fail to make them our own and conform rigidly to their conventional usage. We then become slaves to fashionable thought and the notions lapse into endoxicality.

Endoxicality defined. When something is endoxical, it is commonplace and uninformative because it is common to everyone and therefore not distinctive of anyone. This is the other extreme from being entirely idiosyncratic and specific to one individual. Thus, in being sociospheric, these notions can also be taken to the other extreme from personal eccentricity. This happens when they are subject to the tyranny of fashionable opinion, mass culture, and even mob mentality. This constitutes their 'endoxical' propensities; 'endoxos' being the Greek for 'honoured' or 'glorified'. (Aristotle used 'endoxos' to refer to 'generally accepted opinions' which he considered to be a source of non-contentious truths.[10]) Religions are of course extremely good at making their notions endoxical and therefore imposed on everyone willy nilly. Such endoxical attitudes are the origin in western thinking of self-evidence as a source of infallible truth. But self-evidence, especially in the form of 'common sense principles', curtails further thought and discussion on the matter.[11] It becomes *de rigueur* to think that way, and you are not allowed by fashion, convention or legal sanction to speak against such 'self-evident' conclusions.

The tyranny of endoxicality. Thus, common sense itself becomes uncommonsensical when endoxical fads and fashions take over entirely and banish eccentricity. They make any deviation from them seem eccentric and unacceptable. The tyranny of 'political correctness' is an obvious example of such endoxicality. When people are made to conform to conventions and are not allowed to criticise them or laugh them off, this is endoxicality at its worst. The mere fact that notions are used in a generally accepted fashion does not make them true *per se*. We all have a right to challenge such usages in the name of truth since that involves more than just a majority or democratic decision. It means also working out the truth by personal, rational, logical, empirical or mathematical means.

The pathology of eccentricity. However, too much inner development without sociospheric input and output leads us into the realm of unreason and potential paranoia. We become eccentric when we are so wrapped up in ourselves that we cease to care about how we appear to others or are judged by others. Eccentricity can lead us even further into antisocial, pathological and even psychopathological behaviour. But these extremes are best avoided by our adherence to common sense, and by making ourselves open to the demands and strictures of social interaction. In this way, we may be brought out of the darkness of dogmatic eccentricity and fashionable endoxicality to bask in the sunshine of flexible dualist activity that takes account of opposing points of view.

The quality of the interaction between our eccentric and endoxical tendencies is our saving grace. Through our use of evaluative notions we enhance that quality by adding to the value and quality of our thoughts and actions. By that means, our use and application of evaluative notions helps us to build up our integrity and personal atonement, and thus be true to ourselves, and bring out the best in ourselves. As Shakespeare expressed it:

> This above all: to thine own self be true;
> And it must follow, as the night the day,
> Thou canst not then be false to any man.[12]

However, there are definite limits to our being true to ourselves. Terrorists and extremists are doubtless being true to themselves when they commit their dastardly acts. Their eccentricity is such that their ideas become an absolute reality which others must be brought to see by brute force. To avoid such extremes, we must use evaluative notions interactively, that is to say, use them as flexible tools rather than fixed principles. How this is done is outlined below in the discussion of each evaluative notion.

It may also be asked by what process, in being true to ourselves, do we avoid falsity and insincerity in our dealings with others? The answer here is that we do so in developing our moral sensibilities by making evaluative notions an intimate part of our thinking and judging about things. The words that are denoted by evaluative notions are used as vehicles by which we connect ourselves socially with others. These words can be important vectors of truth about ourselves.

Language is our common inheritance and because of it, other people can share our thoughts and feelings. We can use words to reveal the truth about ourselves or not as the case may be. In that sense, pursuing the straight and narrow path leads us to the truth about ourselves. This personal aspect of truth concerns how evaluative notions, such as good, beauty, sincerity, duty, and justice, help us in evaluating things and events to accord as much as humanly possible with truth as a whole. Such evaluative notions are therefore important interfaces by which we aspire to truth and goodness, as is now discussed.

Ethically speaking, we should aim to make truth personal to ourselves. Personal truth-seeking consists in being true to ourselves and in maintaining our personal integrity. Logical truth-seeking involves the application of logical principles, mathematical truth-seeking involves measurement and demonstration, and scientific truth the application of scientific methods. Thus, logical, mathematical and scientific truth-seeking are relatively impersonal, objective methods, whereas personal truth-seeking is conducted within ourselves by dualist means. It is made personal to us by interacting with the evaluative notions and making them part of our intimate thinking. And what is personal to us becomes sociable when we participate in the sociosphere and find our own place in society. The importance of such truth-seeking lies in humanising logical, mathematical and scientific truths which are nothing to us in the abstract and need to be made personal to us (what Polanyi calls a "passionate participation in the act of knowing."[13])

Also, being true to ourselves means being open to ourselves. Personal truth-seeking demands openness combined with honour, honesty and sincerity so that it can rise above mere reasoning and become the arbiter of the correctness and justice of our reasonings. Ulterior motives impede our truthful reasonings as they mean withholding or suppressing information. The free expression of all our motives contributes to our openness and to our giving a full and fair account of what makes us what we are. We are not sincerely seeking truth unless we are also being true to ourselves and being transparent about our motivations. Thus, 'true' in this context means true by virtue of the methods and processes used to reach it, whether personal, logical, mathematical, scientific and, ultimately, by dualist methods. This omnibus view of truth is dealt with in more detail in my writings of the subject of dualism, for example, in my book entitled *The Promise of Dualism*.

Such personal truth-seeking involves constant self-reference in which we are constantly aware of what we are doing and thinking. This process of self-reference is an important source of our moral consciousness. It puts us in touch with our inner being that is the source of moral conscience. In being moral persons, our internal monitor should always be at the ready to tell us when we have gone too far or not far enough in achieving our goals or fulfilling our motivations.

Truth-seeking involves the sociosphere. This truth-seeking is a social matter that ultimately contributes to the sociosphere in which all our social activities are focused. The sociosphere is important in providing the ambience in which all our motivations are taken account of. Being answerable for our actions to other people means that the connections between our conflicting motivations are constantly reviewed, and our reasonings are scrutinised from all possible points of view, and conform to reality and the facts. The interconnections within the sociosphere bring isolated individuals, groups, sects, cliques, companies, nations, and international organisations into the common forum within which all truths are ultimately decided in the light of history and posterity. Truth-seeking is a sociospheric activity at its highest and best when it contributes to the future of humanity. And by using evaluative notions to evaluate ourselves and our sociospheric activity we are led to truth, as we shall now see.

G. The Truth of Emotive Evaluations

Emotive evaluative notions augment our intuitive feelings. Judging things as being either good or bad is merely intuitive when nothing more is said about the way that they are good or bad. We evaluate things with more precision and tenacity by using complex notions which are more emotive, self-regarding or judgmental than the mere assignment of goodness or badness. Emotive evaluations use notions such as affection, love and beauty to give expression to our emotional reactions to things and thereby augment our intuitive feelings. They elaborate the good or bad feelings which we have about ourselves, other people and things. They direct us towards truth because of their sociospheric tendencies.

Affection

Affection is the most natural and straightforward of our feelings. It is a relatively pure and unsullied feeling in so far as it is not normally associated with sexual objectification. It refers to our good feelings about people which are a necessary accompaniment or preliminary to love. It leads us to truth in being associated with Platonic or abstract love. The affection of one human being for another need not be tainted with sexual or physical attraction. The notion can therefore from physical love or sexuality because it refers to our non-physical feelings about other people. It means caring for people as people and not because of what is required from them in return. Thus, to have affection for a person is not to lust after them but to care for and be concerned about them as a human being. It is to feel for them in the most intuitive way. It involves empathy and sympathy, and having such deep and lasting feelings that they transcend the love/hate oscillation or temporary infatuation. It particularly includes the feelings of parents towards their children: what the ancient Greeks called *storghé* (στοργή). An emphasis on affection is therefore an emphasis on one of our most natural and straightforward feelings which is untrammelled by sex or other selfish motives.

It therefore follows that affection is more important to the sociosphere than mere love. Arguably, affection should be promoted more than mere love To treat a person as a sex object is not to display affection for them but to treat them an object of one of our lowest and most irrational emotions. It is also a selfish act that includes no concern for the person being objectified. Focusing on 'affection', rather than on the more general term 'love', is deliberate because the latter is all too often bound up with sexual impulses. Affection, first and foremost, consists in thinking about the other person. For example, 'falling in love', when it exceeds the bounds of mere affection, merely expresses a person's sexuality. When affection enters into the person's feelings then their love becomes more sincere and dependable. Thus, affection is a better and more rational basis for human relationships than love by itself because it is not confused by association with sexual attractiveness or the lack of that attractiveness, or with passionate extremes. It is therefore more conducive to the free and unsullied exchange of thoughts and ideas within the sociosphere. Above all, the notion of affection helps us to focus on those feelings which are worth of us and which enable us to remain true to ourselves and to our best interests.

Love

It is unfortunate that in the English language love is often synonymous with sex. Love is extremely important as an abstract notion because it signifies the breadth and depth of our relationships with each other. No other animal knows in an abstract way that it loves another. Nor does it have any way of knowing what its feelings are, whereas we have this notion by which to express them. But love is all too easily confounded with physical attraction, desire, infatuation, and lust. In its best sense, it is care and affection which has deepened into something more lasting and permanent because it is associated with specific relationships between those loved. In this sense, saying 'I love you' expresses a commitment to the person loved and not just a raw expression of unadulterated feeling. In its worst sense, love is used to dominate and use other people as when a person says 'I love you' because of the effect on the other person and not because they have true feelings of love. True love consists in being true to ourselves and our most intimate feelings. There is no room for insincerity and deception in true love.

An over-emphasis on love and on the need to express that love can lead to extreme and uncontrollable feelings. The feelings expressed by 'true' love are often extreme and can lurch from worship and adulation into its opposite: hatred and contempt. These feelings need to be tempered by good sense and the development of a strong inner being to control such feelings. This is because the notion is mixed up either with unadulterated sexual desire or with the power that one or more individuals wishes to wield over other individuals. Thus, Roman emperors always required their subjects to express their 'love' for them and the failure to do so often meant death. Such extremes can be avoided by ensuring that love is always accompanied by feelings of care and affection. Caring for a person invokes the rational part of loving them since it means having active feelings and a desire to do things for them whereas the act of loving is more passive and unexpressed unless it is overtly sexual. Thus, love, care and affection go together in our working towards genuine feelings which are true of ourselves. Love as a stand-alone Platonic notion is more of menace to harmonious relationships than an incitement to virtuous conduct.

Love is more than just the opposite of hatred since it can incorporate and dissolve all hatred. It has truth and righteousness on its side whereas hatred is nothing but a negative, destructive feeling which achieves nothing in the end since it merely heralds death and dissolution. Hence the Christian injunction to love your enemy[14] is a rejection of Manichean self-negating opposites. Hatred is not an inevitable counterweight to love but that which obstructs needlessly our path to truth and self-realisation. It can be combated by force of reason if we so wish. By concentrating on the interactive, sociable side of the notion we can make ourselves deal rationally with our feelings and thus become more reasonable in our behaviour and truer to ourselves.

Beauty

Beauty acquires objectivity when we detect holistic symmetry and material orderliness in objects. There is something physical in objects that look beautiful to us and it can be reproduced accordingly, as painters and sculptors constantly do. But it also involves subjectivity in so far as it notionally expresses our appreciation of whatever is given to us in life. We feel good about beautiful things and these feelings may only be subjective. There is little point in living unless we appreciate the beautiful things that surround us in our everyday lives. But beauty is not only in the eye of the beholder, it also is subject to sociospheric influences. Its objectivity lies in its cultural influences. We often learn to appreciate what is beautiful because of fashionable influences, dominant opinions and trends set by artists, authors, poets and advertisers. In that case, we learn to see and feel the beauty which others have anticipated us in appreciating. Someone with distinctive taste can influence others into appreciating the standard of beauty and excellence laid down by that person.

A sense of beauty is necessary for the appreciation of life and other people. In recognising the beauty of a painting, a car, a building, a symphony, or pop song, we are participating in the culture which produced these things. In feeling for ourselves the beauty of these things, we add value to our personal view of things. We become better people in the eyes of others because we can converse about these things more meaningfully than otherwise. As we feel better about ourselves, this activity fortifies our integrity and our respect for goodness and truth. Appreciation of beauty therefore makes our lives more interesting and valuable to us. We look at the beauty in other people and make more them as a result. Beauty is thus an essential component of our civilisation.

As a notion, beauty is intimately bound up with love, affection and the other evaluative notions. We love beautiful things and feel affection for them. We respect and honour those who make beautiful things or live a beautiful life. This shows us that beauty is not a discrete thing but a fluent process which is expressive our ever-changing feelings and aspirations. But as a notion it also abstracts and distils from our feelings something that can be shared with other people through language. Thus, the notion of beauty, like other evaluative notions, helps to socialise us. It is as important from a sociospheric point of view as from that of the individual experiencing personal, aesthetic feelings. Our appreciation of beauty enhances our love, care and affection for the objects we perceive as beautiful. We are led to be more sociable and amiable human beings as a result. In this wholehearted way, beauty contributes to our personal development and to our grasp of what is true about ourselves.

H. The Truth of Self-Regarding Evaluations

By valuing ourselves we also value other people. Self-regarding evaluations use such notions as respect, honour and grace to examine our behaviour as others see us, so that by valuing ourselves we also value other people. Thus, the self-regarding notions concern the value we put on ourselves personally in relation to the value we put on other people. They include our own estimation of ourselves and our personal integrity. Unless we put a minimal value on ourselves and our own lives we cannot appreciate the value of other people. Inevitably we demean others when we think little of ourselves. We must find reasons for self-respect and thus vindicate ourselves in that way. As evaluative notions, they also serve to separate our feelings about ourselves from those about other people, so that we can relate more directly to ourselves as a whole, and see ourselves more exactly as others see us.

Respect

Respect should not be entirely divorced from love or affection. It implies placing value on ourselves. But it also means deferring to or extolling someone or something other than ourselves. In demanding respect as a right or obligation to be exacted from others, we are liable to depart from truth and lose touch with ourselves as a result. We cannot expect respect from others unless we respect ourselves as persons in our own right. We often look for respect from other people even if we do not command their love or affection. The deferential aspect of the notion often goes along with hatred and even fear. Respect on its own is often demanded by celebrities, politicians, industrialists, criminals, gangsters and terrorists, when they may not deserve any respect whatsoever. They require unadulterated adulation and respect because of their insecurity and lack of self-regard. Thus, respect should not be entirely divorced from love or affection. Otherwise it becomes inhuman and ultimately means being disrespectful of other people.

Respect is not normally thought of as a form of love, yet it could be considered an aspect of the Greek, ἀγάπη, *agapē*, which was non-sexual love or affection, (especially as used by St. Paul in the well-known passage in I Corinthians 13.1-8). Thus, respect is made more respectable by associating it more directly with love in the form of *agapē*. What we have then is respect that is mingled with love and affection. It is then earned as part of a reciprocating relationship by which both parties gain. In this way, the respect that we have for ourselves and for others can reflect the ongoing truth about ourselves and our relationships with others. Thus, respect is ultimately bound up with a great deal of affection and reciprocity to avoid inciting negative feelings of fear and hatred.

Honour

While honour is essential to our continued self-respect, it differs from respect in being the reward or recognition for being respected or having respect. It is therefore essential to our continued self-respect since it is a sign of the respect that others have for us. We want to be honoured for our character and deeds, and we wish to behave honourably because our self-esteem depends on it. Generally speaking, people cannot live with themselves with any ease unless they are honoured or believe themselves to behaving honourably. Taken to extremes, the honour due from others becomes more important than any other consideration. When it is paramount and all-consuming then it becomes an end in itself. This impedes self-criticism because dishonour is blamed on other people or on external events. This Platonic attitude was widespread in the Middle Ages when it was called 'chivalry'. Nowadays it is often associated with gangsters and terrorists who make it an excuse to bully and kill people. This happens when it becomes a Platonic end in itself.

The enlightened view is that the notion of honour aids self-examination by focusing on honourable behaviour which does not make us feel ashamed or ill-at-ease with ourselves. This is becoming behaviour that is worthy of us. Thus, a dishonourable person knows no shame or guilt whatever they do or however they behave. It is not just that other people are ashamed or mortified by such a person's conduct. It is more that the dishonourable person has lost that degree of sensitivity and self-awareness which makes them sensitive to the shamefulness of their conduct. Such a person has lost touch with themselves to some degree and no longer feels the effects of their behaviour either on themselves or on others. In other words, they are being untrue to themselves. In short, the notion of honour is useful dualistically because it enables us to call people's attention to their dishonourable deficiencies, and to give them an opportunity to think about their honour and, if possible, do something about it.

Grace

The notion of grace is important even in a non-religious context as it can be used to bring the best out of us. Grace is basically what nowadays is called 'style' or 'charisma'. A 'gracious' person has all the 'graces' which make for a 'graceful' person. It also has the sense of being 'well-favoured' as in a graceful person or animal. A person having grace is usually a 'nice' person who enjoys being thought of as nice. The notion encourages us to be gracious and therefore to be more sociable and pleasant than we are otherwise inclined to be. In mollifying our feelings, it reinforces our feeling of belonging in the universe and of being at home in it rather than out of place and ill at ease. Grace brings out the nobility inherent in us all, and reveals the ungraciousness underlying the pretence of superiority. A large amount of graciousness in any society is supplied by persons who behave with nobility, honour, sincerity and honesty.

Grace is closely associated with nobility. As Edmund Burke remarked in defending the rationale of the French nobility: "Nobility is a graceful ornament to the civil order. It is the Corinthian capital of polished society."[15] But it is more than just an ornament because noble, gracious behaviour is a useful civilising influence. A lack of grace and a surfeit of greed and ambition in money-grabbing, rat-racing cultures ensure that people behave badly towards each other since they lack standards of good behaviour to live up to. A system of honouring worthy citizens favours such graceful conduct, in the absence of which wealth becomes the standard for judging people regardless of how dishonourably and disgracefully their wealth has been acquired.

Fame and wealth are often not gracious or noble. The form of nobility of course changes from one kind of society to another. The dominance of the primogenitary system in Europe virtually ended with the First World War. It has been replaced by a new kind of *timocratic* or *celebrocratic* nobility, based on wealth or celebrity, and this often falls short of true nobility because of its lack of graciousness. An uncouth and uncultivated meritocracy does not amount to a nobility, nor does a timocracy which reveres people merely because they are wealthy, famous and well-known, regardless of their personal qualities. Such a society is the worse for its lack of graciousness. Its people are less than true to themselves or to others in so far as they climb over each other in a very ungracious and self-demeaning fashion. The notions of grace and nobility exemplify the proper behaviour for a human being to aspire to. They can ensure that good manners, courtesy and etiquette become the life blood of society.

Sincerity

Sincerity is an important characteristic of the honourable and gracious person, as it signifies openness and genuineness. A sincere person strives not to be devious or underhanded but to express and implement genuine feelings straight from the heart. However, sincerity is often feigned by those who wish to give an impression of sincerity for their own devious ends. Many people believe themselves to be sincere who are only deceiving themselves that they are so. An inner lack of sincerity stems from self-deficiency and a lack of inner development. True sincerity is an essential part of being true to oneself, therefore, in being true to ourselves, we supposed to be sincere in every respect. But that depends on the purity and integrity of our inner being.

Sincerity requires self-knowledge and self-criticism. But such an ideal notion of sincerity is only attainable in practice when we are sufficiently self-aware to detect and overcome our own insincerity. Sincerity thus implies self-knowledge and self-criticism. All the evaluative notions are self-referential to a degree but sincerity demands self-reference *par excellence*. Without constant self-monitoring, we can never be sure that we are being truly sincere nor that we are really in touch with our true feelings, opinions, motives and goals. Thus, the insincere person is detectable when their lack of self-criticism and self-doubt becomes evident.

Honesty

Honesty is the best policy because honest behaviour contributes to one's honour and grace in the eyes of others. An honest person feels ashamed at any suggestion of insincerity and deviousness in their motives. They are justly proud of their ingenuousness which comes from being no more than they seem to be. Dishonest people hide behind their outer appearance and know themselves to be different and more complex than they appear to be. They are untrustworthy because their ulterior motives get in the way of doing the straightforward and expected thing. Thus, honesty involves openness and trustworthiness.

Trust therefore is an important product of honest behaviour without which society cannot function. Trust simply cannot be sustained without the expectation of honest and truthful behaviour. Our social standing is harmed when we are no longer trusted or are accused of dishonesty. Thus, meaningful sociospheric interaction depends on our taking seriously any accusation of dishonesty on our part. It is fuel for self-examination and for changing our behaviour accordingly. Not to take account of such an accusation is resonant of self-deception and failure to be true to oneself. Therefore, punishment in matters of dishonesty is of no use unless it directly assists the individual in coming to terms with what they are and must do within a social setting.

I. The Truth of Judgmental Evaluations

Judgmental evaluations socialise us and make us think of others. Judgmental evaluations, which include such notions as obligations, rights and justice, are necessary for the harmonious running of society. They concern how we judge our social behaviour and that of others in relation to ourselves and our interests and goals in life. These notions thus bring us into the context of society where we must consider the effects of our behaviour on other people and of their behaviour on us. We leave behind our selfish concerns when we contemplate our responsibilities, obligations and rights, and thereby assess the justice of our behaviour and that of others.

Obligations

Obligations bind us to society and make us a part of it. They are social relationships that are necessary for the functioning of our daily lives. They arise because we take upon ourselves the duties, responsibilities, commitments, promises, undertakings, contracts, or other activities that tie us down and make us relate in rational and predictable ways to other people and society in general. Fulfilment of our obligations induces us to contain ourselves so that we conform to our own aims, needs or desires, or to the demands of other people and society in general. Obligations can bind us or free us. They bind us when we do things reluctantly; they free us when we no longer have to think or worry about what we are doing. Either way they help us towards the truth about what we are and about our role in society. They are therefore an inevitable part of living a mature and responsible life in a social setting and are part of the civic covenant that we all enter into implicitly when we take part in society (see section 10 below on *Servility*). In making our obligations a rational and structured part of our lives, we become rational instead of impulsive beings, as they provide limits to our behaviour as well as goals and challenges to aim for.

Rights

Rights such as those of freedom of speech and movement are due to all of us only in so far as we behave ourselves as human beings and make a decent place for ourselves in society. They are earned by our good behaviour and not simply because they belong to us automatically by being born into a free society. They form part of the civic covenant and they do not exist on their own or independent of what we do with our lives. In so far as we claim any rights at all, we do so as an inextricable part of a free society whose freedoms are conditional rather than absolute. We are not born free; we are born enslaved to a mass of selfish desires. We learn to be free by finding out by trial and error what we can or cannot do which both satisfies us and conforms to what is expected of us by other people and society in general. There is an interactive give-and-take involved and our rights emerge only as we develop as social beings. Thus, rights necessarily accompany obligations and responsibilities. Without having rational obligations and responsibilities, we cannot expect to retain any rights beyond those of being allowed to live an unmolested and solitary lifestyle (possibly in prison). The measure of what are rational obligations and responsibilities lies in sociospheric values since they have been built up through centuries of social interaction. The notion of the sociosphere, in justifying the allocation of rights, also reinforces and protects them. For the act of preventing any human being from exercising their rights diminishes sociospheric activity. Such an act curtails their free and responsible contributions to the sociosphere at which they arrive in being true to themselves. Knowing one's rights and exercising them responsibly is therefore an important of knowing oneself.

Justice

Justice will be judged ultimately by posterity. Justice is our way of making comparisons between the behaviour of people and of things and events to arrive at supposedly objective standards of fair treatment for human beings and other living beings. Such standards are subjective in our treating each other justly or unjustly from a personal point of view. They are only objective in relation to the sociosphere of collective communication. In the interests of social harmony, there has to be general agreement about what is just or unjust and this is arrived at by constant debate and discussion. The law is only just in so far as it is constantly criticised, amended and improved so that it conforms to the realities of social life. An absolute, concrete notion of justice is not helpful since it only makes sense within the context of sociospheric debate and not when it is confined solely to the thinking of one or a number of individuals. Defining justice in a fixed constitution is even more unhelpful as such constitutions take no account of ever-changing social circumstances (*vide* Amendments One and Two of the US Constitution). Thus, justice in a open society is a fluid process that is constantly updated by means of sociospheric debates. But even in such debates, posterity is the ultimate arbiter of what is really and ultimately just, so that all our present judgments on that score are only provisional and never absolute. By looking at just and unjust acts from the perspective of posterity, we are better placed to see where justice lies, especially in respect of human rights and the equal treatment of individuals. Thus, the truth of justice lies in its being interactive between personal and objective perspectives. Our behaviour is just and right when we keep our minds open to further insights into the nature and practice of justice which will be judged ultimately by posterity.

J. Applying the Evaluative Notions

The evaluative notions applied in personal processes. The point of the above discussion is to show how we may use evaluative notions to become sociable persons without sacrificing our individuality to anyone or anything. These notions help us to evaluate our actions and stay true to ourselves, while in the process our goals, aspirations, and motivations become clearer, more rational and sociable, and so contribute to the well-being of society and the future of humanity. These evaluative processes are personal to each of us as they are not imposed from outside but are engendered within ourselves in our natural desire to improve and better ourselves. Thus, these personal processes enable us to become more than mere individuals. They help us to relate our motivations to social and rational activities. In that way, we become productive persons taking our place in society while still pursuing our personal goals. This is why the above account was particularly concerned with the sociospheric use of these notions. We become more sociable and accessible persons in applying them.

In the above outline, the evaluative notions are not so much analysed as elaborated in terms of what we do with them in a sociospheric context. In that context, we evaluate our position so as to arrive at goals and ends appropriate to us both as individuals and as social beings. This method explains in theory how ethical judgments function in our society. It therefore offers a theoretical basis for a more humane and scientific ethical system which is more generally accepted than has been possible hitherto. A humane and scientific ethical theory is therefore the ultimate aim. But whether this aim can be achieved depends on a thorough and systematic development of dualist theory that makes sense of the dualist interactions involved in personal development. My book, *The Promise of Dualism*, shows the possibilities of that theory.

Applying the above evaluative notions therefore involves a systematic moral logic in which personal truth is sought by using them. There are however definite limitations to this personal truth-seeking. This moral logic is only applied socially in interpersonal relationships, that is to say, in sociospheric circumstances. It concerns how we behave to other people and how they behave towards us in response. The preceding sections show the extent to which our personal quest for truth involves using these evaluative notions. It is not just an objective process of establishing the way things are for us personally. It also includes the thoughts and feelings which personally involve us in the truths being sought. Such is the complexity of the truth-seeking process, it is clear that neither objective nor personal truth can lead us to ultimate truth as it is always beyond us and to be striven for. The most that our truth-seeking can do for us is to give us practical guidance in particular situations.

Examples of the questions that arise. Personal truth-seeking involves using evaluative notions to answer such questions as the following:
- What am I to do with the rest of my life?
- How should I behave with other people?
- Why should I not do whatever I feel like doing?
- What kind of habits and routines are most relevant to my aims and aspirations?

In answering such questions evaluative notions can be used in making assessments of the alternative answers available to us. In so far as we don't want to fritter away the rest of lives in idleness or self-indulgence, we need to (1) plot and plan our future and (2) evaluate our plotting and planning as we go along. Evaluative notions of the self-regarding sort help us to be honest and sincere in our deliberations. Thus, these four questions can be explored in both a self-critical and a self-appreciative way to reach a balanced view of whatever we decide to do or not to do. The above discussions already contain sufficient material to answer these questions.

Formal logic is of limited value in making moral judgments as it involves the objective definition of words in arguments and trains of reasoning. Logical analysis cannot help us to reach the personal truth concerning such moral judgments nor is it enough to keep us true to our best aims and aspirations. It tells us only that some words fit together or do not fit together with other words in any statement or logical deduction. It is good for arguments but not for making sense of our feelings or for evaluating them. When we confine our quest to logical truth, the connection of truth with such notions as honour, honesty and sincerity is overshadowed. We are simply analysing these words and making deductions from them without seeing what they mean for us personally. This is because personal truth uses context and perspective more than verbal analysis in making assessments.

Deduction is therefore not a viable basis for moral evaluation. Whatever makes sense in a deductive manner is truthful only in a limited sense in being a valid deduction. But we can always invent reasons for whatever we do or do not do. In the absence of self-criticism what is reasoned to be the case is treated as a valid deduction regardless of its correspondence to the real state of affairs or its coherence with the facts as a whole. We need to be inwardly sceptical of all such reasonings and we do this by submitting them to the constant scrutiny of evaluative notions of an emotive, personal or judgmental type.

Nevertheless, truth-seeking of a formal kind can be an essential part of our evaluations, as our reasoned evaluations must conform to factual truth; otherwise they are false, misleading, deceitful or self-deluding. We are always veering between the two extremes of being too personal and too impersonal. For being true to ourselves means avoiding extremes. If we are to achieve our full potential we must learn to adhere to truth and not let our personal prejudices and predilections get the better of us. At the same time, we must avoid being so impersonal in our pursuit of truth that we become enslaved to our perception of truth and lose touch with ourselves. Hence the importance of evaluative notions in guiding us towards truth without compromising our personal integrity.

Even when we say something truthful such as 'there is a chair next door', this is true only at a particular time and place, though as a historical fact it exists forever in the past. What is stated to be true is only what is established as truth at one point in time. The object of thought has to be re-assessed in relation to different periods and places. To keep adapting our thinking to what is really the case, we must be as flexible and open-minded as possible concerning what is or not true. Thus, the truth of past events depends on their really having happened at a particular time and place, and the evidence may with others. We add to the value and extent of our knowledge of things by not settling for truths arrived at entirely by ourselves. In not cleaving absolutely to heartfelt truths, we keep our minds open and freely reach out to people, books, mass media, internet and all the other sociospheric sources of knowledge and understanding. Seeking truth also involves being truthful to other people as well as to oneself. We rely on other people's trust for our change when we delve deeper into the past. Even the most certain truths of physics and astronomy are only provisional in the end. The laws of physics may have been different billions of years ago for all we know at present. With time and greater knowledge, we may eventually ascertain if and how they were different. Thus, in so far as ultimate truth is possible, it can only sociospheric and not entirely personal to any of us. Ultimately, it is the preserve of the holistic Cosmos as is argued in exercise eight below.

Moreover, truth that is worthy of us must be striven for interactively. Though the truth of the matter is the way things really are, no truth counts for anything unless a person or persons is facing up to that truth or failing to do so. Truth is either relative to person, time and place, or it is being proclaimed a timeless dogma that is inhuman and untouchable (such as God or holy scripture). Any assertion can be true or false for somebody somewhere, or it is nowhere and nothing, as far as we are concerned. Thus, truth-seeking is an interactive process in which we relate to something other than ourselves to make it a part of ourselves, or not as the case may be. Even the truths of mathematics have to be true to someone. Falsity and negation come into play when we fail to identify things and relate to them in positive terms. Formal logic operates at this level when it is applied to us personally.

The social value of all truth-seeking activities depends on our self-esteem being sustained by constant interaction with people in the sociosphere, and we gain more by being honest with people than being dishonest and distrusted. It is harmful to disconnect truth from our personal and social involvement in it, as logicians, scientists, political theorists, and theologians are apt to do with their abstract reasoning divorced from personal involvement. Such disconnections have fostered inhumanity and enmity all too readily in the past, as in religious and ideological truths which are held to be more important than the lives of those disagreeing with such truths. Thus, moral truth-seeking is self-connected in that it involves ourselves viewing our conduct critically and hence interactively.

We can also be too personal and individualistic in our truth-seeking. Taking an entirely egocentric and selfish view of things is called solipsistic as it means behaving as if we alone, together with our experiences, really exist. Such a solipsistic view is self-destructive and ultimately futile. A solipsist interprets everything within the context of self. But when the self becomes socially detached, it loses its social rudder and is condemned to a self-destructive circularity. We escape the sterile circularity of solipsism by opening our minds to truths and values in contexts beyond ourselves. Even our use of evaluative notions can lead to a sterile solipsism unless they are used in social contexts. Only within these contexts can we develop our notions so that our opinions and beliefs become more truthful and realistic. There is more on this contextual broadening of the mind in section 10 on *Servility*.

K. When 'Is' Implies 'Ought'

What we ought to do in any given situation is always implied in the facts relating to the situation. The fact that someone is drowning means that we ought to do something about saving them. The 'oughtness' of this situation follows from the fact that drowning implies loss of life and doing something to prevent the avoidable death of someone is a good thing to do. The linkage between 'is' and 'ought' is supplied by words such as 'good' or 'right': it is a good or right thing to do. Thus, we can add ethical values of good/bad, right/wrong, just/unjust to any facts that are not totally objective and beyond human concern. Facts concerning our humanity have values that imply that either that we can do something about them or that we cannot or will not do so. This is where the 'ought' comes in. If we make facts totally objective then we don't have to do anything about them. They are 'objects' out there that do not touch us. This is the attitude of the sceptic who doesn't want to do or be anything. The sceptic seems to lack the concepts that link feelings to facts, as is suggested by Hume's original formulation of the distinction between 'is' and 'ought':

"In every system of morality, which I have hitherto met with, I have always remark'd, that the author proceeds for some time in the ordinary way of reasoning, and establishes the being of a God, or makes observations concerning human affairs; when of a sudden I am surpriz'd to find, that instead of the usual copulations of propositions, *is*, and *is not*, I meet with no proposition that is not connected with an *ought*, or an *ought not*. This change is imperceptible; but is, however, of the last consequence. For as this *ought*, or *ought not*, expresses some new relation or affirmation, 'tis necessary that it shou'd be observ'd and explain'd; and at the same time that a reason should be given, for what seems altogether inconceivable, how this new relation can be a deduction from others, which are entirely different from it. But as authors do not commonly use this precaution, I shall presume to recommend it to the readers; and am persuaded, that this small attention wou'd subvert all the vulgar systems of morality, and let us see, that the distinction of vice and virtue is not founded merely on the relations of objects, nor is perceiv'd by reason."[16]

Thus, the deduction in the above example is not from simple statement "There is a man drowning" The deduction is from the whole conception of the situation and the context in which it takes place. The facts include all such evaluative matters. A simple statement does not imply doing anything unless it means something to us over and above it. This additional meaning gives the value to the statement from which an obligation of 'oughtness' can be inferred. Thus, the overall conception of the situation involves our feelings whether or not we are consciously aware of them.

It is noteworthy that conceptions and contexts were conspicuously absent from Hume's arguments and that absence suggests a deficiency in his reasoning powers. Thomas Reid and Immanuel Kant naturally found inspiration for their respective writings in working out the consequences of these deficiencies, though they in their turn were led into further philosophical deficiencies in the systems of thought that they concocted to replace Hume's system.

In conclusion, values concern the feelings and meanings that we attach to facts, however objective they may seem. Mathematical formulae such as $E=MC^2$ seem to be totally objective but it is our feelings that enable us to see the practical value in them over and above their mathematical efficacy. Unless such formulae grab our attention and give us a sense of awe at their applicability, they mean little or nothing to us. It is also the case that 'is' will always imply 'ought' when facts are regarded as things about which we are meant to do something. The use of universal notions in practical situations will always supply the values, meanings and feelings that we need to do what we know we ought to do.

L. Contextualising Morality

The contextual view as giving a foundation to morality. In so far as morality lacks a firm foundation, the contextual viewpoint may be a step towards providing such a foundation. It shows the extent to which all our moral feelings, intuitions, judgments and obligations have their foundation in our relating ourselves to contexts other than ourselves. In thinking of ourselves in relation to other contexts, we exercise judgment in respect of our moral judgments, values, principles, and obligations. The following is an outline of the ways in which contextualisation can be such a foundation for morality:

- *In making moral judgments.* Moral judgments consist in evaluative processes by which we organise and order our lives. Judging what to do or not to do something depends on one's values as well as one's principles, motivations, aspirations etc. In judging, we make use of evaluative notions such as good, beauty and justice which are examined in more detail in the various subsections above. For example, judging a play to be good means going beyond the context to which the play belongs to make that judgment. We do not need to enter into the plot of the play or the words of the actors but we do need to stand outside the play as a whole to judge it. The play is good because it interests us, is well-written, entertaining, moving, thought-provoking or whatever. These reasons for believing it to be good concern not the play in itself or its contents but our reaction to it or our judgment of it. Nevertheless, the aspects of the play that are judged to be good belong to it. These aspects are its being well-written, its ability to interest, entertain and move as opposed to judging it to well-written, entertaining and so on. These aspects become part of play's context after-the-event and following the acts of judgment which belong to the person judging.

- *In Using Moral Values.* Our use of values often varies from one context to another. We go beyond these immediate contexts in ensuring that our values still conform to our overall principles. Contextualisation enables us to see how more general contexts can encompass less general ones. The principles applied in the workplace can be accorded with those applied in the home by using the context of self to compare them and find a way to reconcile them. Using the context of family broadens our concerns to include their effects on other people. The application of our principles is thereby not just confined to what affects ourselves alone. This ensures that our values are consistently applied by their being related to overall principles and made sense of in terms of these principles, or not as the case may be.

- *In Applying Moral Principles.* The consistency of our moral principles depends on our applying them uniformly in different contexts. Moral principles are formulated and applied in various contexts but they ultimately refer back to the integrity of the self. If they are not so referred back then they are expedients rather than principles. We owe it to ourselves to adhere to our principles. It is an abrogation of our responsibility for our own principles to unload them onto God, thereby making excuses for our own shortcomings for which we alone are responsible and can rectify if we so choose.

- *In Adhering to Moral Principles.* Moral principles are usually rules which we apply to all contexts, by and large, and not necessarily without exception. The integrity of our characters is built up by our adhering to such principles, with the result that we are reliable and praiseworthy people in the eyes of others. An obvious example of moral principles is the ten commandments in the Bible. We might think that 'thou shalt not kill' is a good moral principle to live by. Yet there are contexts such as wars and self-defence where this principle has to be laid aside. No moral principle can be realistically treated as absolutely infallible. We may well adhere to them throughout our lives without giving a thought to them but, equally, contexts can arise where we have to question them and perhaps set them aside.

- *In Fulfilling Moral Obligations.* Moral obligations come from thinking of ourselves in relation to contexts which usually, but not always, go beyond ourselves. We have obligations towards ourselves such as looking after our health and preserving our lives. But our most thought-provoking obligations are usually those which involve other people, society, and the human race.

These obligations are often more important to us than our obligations to ourselves. In the context of the workplace, we apply certain moral standards which that particular context demands in order to get the job done. Unless these standards are also commensurate with those of other contexts then double standards can arise. Strictly speaking, our rights depend on our fulfilling our moral and legal obligations. If you can't fulfil the obligations of friendship then you have no right to expect friendship from anyone.

9. Normality: Having a Society Based on Norms

> The right to search for truth implies also a duty; one must not conceal any part of what one has recognised to be true.
>
> Albert Einstein (1930) [1]

A. Introductory

We no longer live in a normal society that has clear norms of behaviour to which we can choose to adhere or not to adhere. We live in an abnormal society that provides no clear boundaries or guidelines. The lack of these drives our society to unnecessary extremes. Here we draw attention to some of the abnormalities that infect our society and do it untold harm because of the extremes, distortions, confusions or bottlenecks involved. Many of these abnormalities are not recognised as such because they are supported by fashion, accepted usage, popular opinion, or the assumptions and presuppositions of the mass media. Criticism of these abnormalities is often dismissed out of hand and a rational discussion about them is inhibited if not banned outright.

In the interests of free speech, unpleasant views need to be aired whatever the consequences. It is harmful to society to conceal unpopular points of view. In German the concealment is felicitously called *Massenpsychologischerumkehrschluss*. This word translates as "mass psychological reversal circuit" and it arises "when a crisis in the political system occurs, people turn to the ideas that the system tried hardest to suppress."[2] In other words, these unexpressed ideas are tucked away out of sight. Though they are unspoken, they rumble around at the backs of people's minds. It is surely healthier to air these suppressed opinions so that they are treated rationally rather than to allow them to build up and fester in the body politic. They form a hidden boil or bubble that sooner or later bursts forth and manifests itself in hideous extremes.

Fashionable opinions of a left wing nature are supported passionately and are taken to extremes because of the one-sidedness of political policies. The role of politicians is to take sides and stick to the policies arrived at. They invariably conform to the will of public opinion and mass media pressure. Few of them are strong enough leaders to take a stand against prevailing opinions. As elected persons, they are obliged to sweep along with public opinion and not oppose it, even if they consider it to be wrong or misguided. But there is often validity in opposing views. Society is harmed by suppressing the truth that may lie within them. Their suppression creates imbalances and bottlenecks that build up over the years and will surface and overwhelm society sooner or later. An obvious example are the banking and financial excesses that are overlooked until their catastrophic consequences erupt apparently from nowhere, even though the signs were there all along.

Contrary opinions are also required to shake up fashionable opinions and remind people that all opinions have their limitations. A contrary person is inevitably a non-conformist. Society progresses when non-conformity prevents one-sided views from prevailing absolutely as if they were inviolable truths. The given paradigms are re-examined instead of being accepted without question. When they are shown to be inadequate, new ways of thinking can replace them.

Fashionable opinions can also prolong undesirable ways of thinking by suppressing them. Thus, racism is an attitude of mind that is increasingly irrelevant in a world where the races are intermixing and where interbreeding is making the distinctions between them increasingly hard to detect. Divisive racism is out-of-date as we are all 'human racists' now, whether we like it or not. As human beings we are all part of one human race which is more important than any physical differences between us. But demonising racism and making it illegal only exacerbates the problem. Banning it increases its appeal to an extreme frame of mind, just as banning smoking and drug-taking doesn't change people's habits but merely drives the practices undercover. The racist mentality is a psychological problem that ought to be treated as such. Opposing it absolutely prolongs its existence indefinitely. As is argued below, the normal society treats people individually and expects moral behaviour from them rather than using legal sanctions indiscriminately.

Similarly, people having so-called 'phobias' such as homophobia and islamophobia have their reasons for having them. No amount of contrary arguments or legal sanctions will dissuade them since their heartfelt feelings are involved. There is one-sided bigotry on both sides, and the normal society recognises both sides of these arguments. In so far as liberal views have been taken to extremes, the way to redress the imbalances is to work out opposing views so that what is meritorious about them can be ascertained, assuming they have any merit at all.

Freedom of speech is not a political or legal matter unless it means putting one's extreme views into harmful practice. However, political correctness aims to change people's behaviour and ways of speaking by political and legal action. It is a form of legalism that is condemned outright in this section. In contrast, the exercise in free speech herein does not aim to change anything by political means. It is all about making moral choices not legal ones. It cannot be breaking the law if it does not advocate persecuting people or discriminating against them. Political correctness is at fault in going too far. It is a reaction against the oppressiveness of Victorian attitudes and arguably it goes to unacceptable extremes that undermine the integrity and morality of society.

There can be no freedom of speech without giving offence. Those who are offended have an opportunity to respond with equal freedom. The result is a frank exchange of views characteristic of an open society. The slanging match between political opponents in the House of Commons is an example of offences being freely given and taken, without being inhibited by legal sanction (unless the Speaker objects!) It is also an example of the dualist interaction which is arguably essential to social and other forms of progress. As systematic dualists (see section 4 above on *Duality*, pp. 60-63) we are intent on redressing imbalances and pointing out that things have gone too far in one direction or another. Thus, this section contains a collection of disparate essays that are not intended to be a political treatise or a programme for social reform. They are meant to stimulate people's thinking and help them to see the merits of opposing opinions. In short, the aim is to stimulate an interactive debate to resolve issues instead of suppressing them or dismissing them out of hand. It is an exercise in free speech.

B. In Praise of the Normal Society

Our future depends on our living in a society that makes progress possible. An abnormal society impedes progress because it is unbalanced and unhealthy. People are encouraged to be self-seeking to the point of self-degradation and self-destruction. Higher ideals are absent to which people can aspire and make more of themselves thereby. Mediocrity is fostered by making exceptional talent seem abnormal instead of being the norm for everyone.

The normal society is a healthy, dynamic society based on rational norms of behaviour. It constantly strives for a balance between restricted and unrestricted behaviour. It sets clear standards of conduct that everyone understands and appreciates. An abnormal society is one that goes to extremes; it either permits too much or restricts too much, and gives us no way of redressing the resultant imbalance. It spirals ever more out of control as people believe that more of the same is the way forward. Thus, a society in which anything goes and there are no boundaries as regards to permissible behaviour is an abnormal society. But at the other extreme, a society is also abnormal that imposes rigid moral precepts that are repressive and draconian. A normal society strives for an interactive harmony between these extremes. In an unbalanced society there is a violent opposition between two extremes in which there is a suppression of one side by the other side.

The normal society is therefore a dynamic interactive society that is ever striving forward. It is in a state of disequilibrium while it tries ceaselessly to balance its antagonistic activities and to even out the extremes to which these activities are taken. It takes account of all the imbalances, bubbles and unstable elements that are detectable in society while moving forward to a more rational and integrated society that absorbs these instable elements. The more diverse and opportunistic society becomes, the more it can cope with tendencies that threaten its future. This is arguably how periods of intellectual and material progress achieve greatness such as during the Enlightenment and the Industrial Revolution. The normal society is therefore ever developing both in the opportunities it offers and in the diversity of its internal structure.

The normal society becomes more diverse by providing an increasing range and variety of opportunities. Thus, the main purpose of a developing society is to maximise the opportunities available to people to make the most of their lives. This is an opportunistic principle that replaces the felicific or greatest happiness principle of utilitarian philosophers. It is not enough for people simply to be happy; they need also the optimum amount of opportunities and chances in life to make something of themselves. The normal society can maximise opportunities by ensuring that everyone learns to practise the discipline and restraint needed to make the most of their opportunities. Thus the purpose of education in the normal society is to prepare people to take advantage of life's chances and to give them the skills, knowledge and discipline they need to make full use of these chances. The more people that are doing this, the more diversity is created and the more opportunities are created as a result. There is therefore a multiplier effect produced by the opportunistic principle that percolates through society bringing benefits to everyone.

In the normal society, we are all conformists to some degree. We all recognise limitations to our behaviour as being the price of participating in society and of benefiting from its rewards and opportunities. Freedom is not absolute as it always comes with responsibilities and obligations. We earn our freedom by being responsible and obliging individuals who enjoy conforming to the given norms.

In an abnormal society, there are two extremes. At one extreme, there are no limits to what people can or cannot do. It is therefore a permissive society that gives no clear guidelines as to what is or is not permitted conduct. At the other extreme, there is an excessive use of moral and legal restraints to make the individual conform to society. At present, there is something of both these extremes in our society. It is extremely permissive as regards sexual behaviour, and it is extremely repressive in its use of laws and rules to regulate people's behaviour in other respects. The lack of any way of reconciling these extremes makes our society profoundly irrational and aimless. There can only be conflict and misunderstanding between right and left, and between conservative minded people and liberal minded people.

The normal society reconciles these extremes in a dynamic way by moving forward in its diverse development. Instead of an unproductive battle between them there is a cyclical movement forward from one direction to the other without sticking at one extreme or the other. The aim in the long run is to even out extreme trends of behaviour in one direction or the other. Not surprisingly even the most dynamic and progressive of all societies may never attain such an aim but it is worth pursuing nevertheless since it gives direction and purpose to society.

Abnormal behaviour is that which is contrary to the natural way in which human beings ought to behave themselves and towards each other. It is not normal or natural for us to overeat or starve ourselves or to make ourselves slaves to sex, drink, drugs or to become obsessed to the point of being enslaved to habits or routines. It is normal for a marriage to be between a man and woman with the purpose of making a family whether it is childless or not. It is abnormal for there to be a marriage between friends of the same sex. It is abnormal for women to consider themselves exactly equal to men and vice versa. These positions are argued for and against below.

In the face of unbridled permissivism, an abnormal society inevitably becomes a legalistic one in which laws, rules, and bureaucratic oppression become the means of controlling people's behaviour. People are forbidden by law to smoke where they please, are forced by law to wear seat belts even if they don't want to, and so on. The police and social workers are used to instil moral discipline instead of educating and training people to be moral themselves.

The police would not be needed if everyone behaved responsibly and did no harm to themselves or others. Lawyers would not be needed if everyone made allowances for each other and behaved with generosity and altruism instead of pride, greed and arrogance. These are often regarded as unattainable utopian ideals. But what are we here for if not to better ourselves and make life better for everyone? Religion used to have such ideals but it is no longer fit for purpose. It divides and debases us before a non-existent entity about which the various religions cannot agree. Humanism seems to be the answer though it is at present an underdeveloped philosophy to which this book may make a much needed contribution. This can only be a start and not the ultimate answer.

C. The Lack of Freedom in the Abnormal Society

The normal society is a free one in which we can speak our minds without fear or favour. We no longer live in such a free society. It is an increasingly legalistic society wherein the law insidiously impinges on our freedoms and deprives us of the right to make choices. The essence of being free is to be able to choose whether to do something or not to do it, even if it turns out badly for us. But when laws decide what we can or cannot do, then we have no choice and therefore are not free in that respect. The law is now used as a substitute for morality and self-discipline.

We can have no real freedom until we have the normal society in which everyone is expected to be mature and responsible and not simply do whatever they please. When people are encouraged to do whatever they please with no guidelines, they inevitably go to the extremes of self-indulgence and self-harming as they lack the internal discipline to restrain themselves. We exercise restraint only when we learn by habit to behave ourselves without being told to do so. In short, there is no freedom unless it is closely tied with the responsibilities and obligations that we can expect of all grown-up people. It is the failure of people to be mature and responsible in their thoughts and actions that has opened the floodgates to an unending surge of laws, rules and legal restrictions.

Thus, in a truly free society the individual is expected to behave responsibly. We cannot trust people to do the right thing unless they behave responsibly, and therefore we deprive them of freedom and ultimately put them in prison. When people behave consistently with maturity and responsibility, they usually deserve to be trusted. They have demonstrably earned the right to be free to do what they think fit. This view does not require a return to religious domination in political and social affairs. It requires only an emphasis on personal vindication and self-justification on the part of the individual. This implied by the humanist view that emphasises individual responsibility.

We therefore need a society based on personal freedom within the limits of morally responsible behaviour. It will enable us to abolish much of the legislation that curtails or infringes personal freedom. This includes health and safety legislation, smoking bans, compulsory wearing of seat-belts and the like. Such legislation will be replaced by an onus of personal responsibility in which the individual expected to be responsible for his or her behaviour. Personal freedom must be tempered by the obligation to be personally responsible for one's behaviour.

In a sense, there is no real freedom as we can find compulsion lurking somewhere if we look for it. We are compelled by our motivations, our genetic pre-dispositions, our friends and relatives, and by the constraints of the environment and the society we live. However, there is always freedom of choice to a certain extent. Perhaps freedom consists in being able to choose one's chains and then being free to break free from them when they become too constraining and restrictive. But that is an ideal that real life does not always afford.

Freedom to speak one's mind

"Sticks and stones may break my bones, but words can never hurt me". This is a saying we rarely hear in these days of rampant political correctness in which you have to watch every word you utter. Dictionaries list the saying as a childish taunt, but it is literally true in that words themselves can cause no physical harm. It is people's feelings that are hurt by allegedly offensive words. But people need not be so easily hurt and offended. The utterance of such words should be like "water off a duck's back", another unfashionable saying. Why should people be so oversensitive to words that might not even be intended to be insults? It is at the masculine and feminine extremes that offense is usually taken. Macho men take offense at slights to their honour or at disrespectful behaviour. Oversensitive females take offense at words that derogatory in any way whatsoever.

Even if words are intended to be insults, no one deserves to be so proud and superior that they have to defend their honour and fight for respect. In fact, such sensitivity betrays a lack of security and inner confidence. Mature, self-respecting people have enough self-confidence to laugh off insults and offenses. They don't need everyone respecting and honouring them to bolster their flagging egos. Thus, no one is so special that they are inviolable to insults and disrespect.

Politicians and other prominent persons are too often persecuted for merely speaking their minds in a so-called 'free' society. The Duke of Edinburgh is an excellent example of this excessive sensitivity to words that are spoken in jest or have only a 'teasing' intent. What he actually says is often quite witty and amusing but it is interpreted by the media as being offensive in some way when there clearly was no such intent. Party politics can prevent politicians from speaking their minds as they are compelled to toe the party line, as their careers depend on it. Unsurprisingly, outspoken politicians who speak their minds freely have recently been making a comeback.

Freedom to live dangerously

We are constantly putting our lives at risk by walking along a city pavement. At any time, a vehicle could mount the pavement and kill us or severely disable us. Climbers and hill-walkers also put themselves at risk out of choice, but there are those who would like to deprive them of the freedom to roam the hills and mountains at will. If anyone puts themselves at risk by their own freewill, then there is no need to restrict or forbid just because of the risk element. Life is full of risk and we cannot legislate against unfortunate events happening from time to time. There is also too much legislation preventing us from acting irresponsibly when the harm to ourselves is a calculated risk that we are willing to take. Smoking can damage your health, so let's ban it, thus making it a heroic matter to continue doing so.

Health and safety legislation has gone too far and needlessly makes cowards out of professional people, when fire-fighters for example are prevented from doing their work because of some perceived risk that they personally are prepared to take to save others. This imbalance can be redressed by abolishing the legislation together with the quangos involved with it. It can be replaced by more specific legislation such as 'Danger to Human Life and Limb' and 'Dangerous Sites' laws which are enforced by the police. These laws would be specifically directed towards clearly dangerous practices and to dangerous working sites where extreme caution is required. For example, the lack of hard hats on building sites would be a potential danger to human life. Each case could be judged on its own merits and with more common sense. The police could inspect building sites and other potential areas where human life could be endangered by working or other practices.

Freedom to discriminate

Discrimination is a necessary facet of human society. We are all different one way or another therefore we are inevitably discriminated against because we are different from other people, one way or another. We constantly discriminate against each other on grounds of gender. A man may be discriminated against when a group of women at a bus stop begin to talk among themselves and ignore him completely because he is a man. The well-educated person may be discriminated against in applying for some jobs because he or she is deemed too well-educated for them. Persons who speak with a 'posh' educated accent instead of the local patois, may disparaged by local people who fear showing themselves up. Short men (such as myself) may be scorned by some women because they prefer tall men. Tall people look down on short people because it is physically impossible for them to do otherwise. Most short people learn to live with this and think nothing of it while a few may take it personally and be resentful as a result. Most people having a differently coloured skin also learn to live with it. A few may develop a chip on their shoulders because of this difference. They blame everything bad that happens to them on discrimination against them on account of their colour. It can't be because of bad luck, their own incompetence, people taking a personal dislike to them or whatever. It is always because of the colour of their skin. Unfortunately it is those people who are most vociferous and make a great deal of trouble instead of dealing with their personal problem which is over-sensitivity about their skin colour when they should be getting on with their lives like everyone else who may have differences that stand out.

Thus, the fact that some forms of discrimination are branded as being illegal can be counterproductive. It encourages people to show bravado by chanting, singing offensive songs, using 'forbidden' words, and so on. If a person suffers discrimination they should live with it and even use it to their advantage. 'Don't get angry, get even' – ought perhaps to be their response. They should stand up for themselves and show their superiority in mind and manners to their traducers. If they can't cope with it rationally then they are more in need of psychological treatment than of protection by law.

Freedom of access to knowledge

The normal society is itself a repository of information which exists for the benefit of individuals in their quest to better themselves. Data protection discriminates against the majority of law-abiding citizens who always use knowledge and information responsibly. People must be educated into the responsible use of information instead of being prevented from accessing it by law. Those who misuse knowledge for criminal or other purposes are relatively few and far between. That our freedoms should be curtailed because a tiny minority misuse them is unacceptable.

Knowledge exists to be used by people and not protected from them. Limiting people's access to knowledge is the way of religion and ideology that makes knowledge exclusive, mystical and unattainable to the masses. However, limitations to this freedom lie in privacy and security. We are all entitled to private lives that are nobody's business but our own, unless we harm others or break the law intentionally or maliciously. Governments can also limit access to knowledge on grounds of national security but this limitation should also be subject to the law and perhaps to independent scrutiny so that governments do not misuse this privilege to the detriment of the public.

Freedom to buy things without excessive pressure

The sustained pressure to buy things is an abnormal capitalistic excess that has no place in the normal society. It is an infringement of our privacy and our dignity to be perpetually bombarded with inducements to buy things. Our minds are not free if we find that choices that we have made in privacy are thrown back at us in the public arena of the internet. Thus, for example: when buying a camera one is then bombarded with adverts soliciting the purchase of more cameras, as if buying one camera lays one open to purchasing another and another. It is a flagrant invasion of our privacy when our photographs are taken up and used in some other context without our permission. Thus, in such cases, the freedom of organisations to exploit us overrides our freedom to make up our minds in our own time and in our own way. The freedom of individuals is more important than that of organisations to do what they like and when they like.

If we agree that the consumer is king then we should all be treated right royally and not simply as the abstract objects of sales and advertising campaigns. We need to have more choice about the extent of our exposure to advertising. Some people are more tolerant of it than others and the advertisers should recognise this. Over-advertising and extreme sales pressure may be harmful to the economy. Inducing people to buy things willy nilly may increase their debt burden and lead to a waste of resources as they buy things indiscriminately. The unsustainable debt levels in the modern economy are surely due in some part to people buying things unnecessarily because sales pressures. More scarce resources are wasted as a result of people buying things they don't really need. Thus, a continuous growth in GNP may be achieved at the expense of credit bubbles and ever-increasing imports that are not being paid for by corresponding exports. It is surely not normal to allow the workings of the economy to go to such extremes without taking proper account of the consequences thereof.

Freedom to exploit the environment for our own benefit

There are those who would limit our freedom to exploit our environment because they regard the environment to be more important than mere people. But the normal society is about human beings and everything that is of service to humanity first and foremost. This includes our environment which can be husbanded by us for our benefit as well as for life in general. It is a case of human beings first, environment second. If we are the most important species on the planet, then we have the right to order the environment to suit human needs before any other concerns. But those who make too much of the environment are also making too little of us. This impedes our ability to do anything for the environment since we are not good enough to do anything or to be on the planet at all. We can only do our best for other species and the environment when we are strong enough financially and materially to do so. That strength can only come from our giving priority to our own interests.

Thus, an abnormality arises when the protection of the environment is regarded as more important than the welfare and livelihood of human beings. Those who overemphasise the needs of the environment to the detriment of their fellow human beings are *sentimental idealists* who place their ideals before the reality of human needs. These idealists cannot be allowed to impose their romantic ideals on us just because it makes them feel good. The reality is that the land exists to be peopled, worked and enjoyed by human beings and not just left to the animals and plants. Until we learn to live in the sky, under the ground or on the Moon or Mars, we cannot do both. We are undoubtedly moving to a position where we can leave living beings on Earth to their own resources but we will never get there if we compromise our progress by sacrificing too much to the interests of the environment.

The danger is that we compare ourselves unfavourably with other animals to the extent of regarding ourselves as an inferior, destructive species that has no business being on the planet at all as we are just messing it up. On the contrary, we have more right to be on the planet than other animals because we know the damage we are doing and can do something about it. Other animals are inferior in that regard. They can be as destructive as they please as they know not what they do. But a balance has to be maintained between sustaining ourselves on the planet and making the planet a better place for other animals. Our welfare must have priority otherwise we will not have the wealth and resources to do our best for other animals. Sentimental idealists are upsetting that balance by ignoring our right to look after ourselves so that we can be economically capable of looking after the planet.

For example, the sentimental idealists are bent on re-introducing wild species into the limited spaces of the Scottish Highlands and elsewhere. People who live and work there are expected to put up with the consequences of returning the Highlands to a state of nature at a time when we are also trying to develop the economy of the area. There are good reasons why beavers, wolves, bears, lynxes and other obnoxious animals were eliminated from Scotland. Their presence was simply incompatible with the growth of human activity. Encouraging biodiversity makes sense in the wide open spaces of Central Europe or North America but it makes no sense at all in a small country such as Scotland. If we want to encourage people to live and work in the Highlands and enjoy the landscape as tourists, climbers, anglers, skiers, cyclists and the like, then we cannot at the same time encourage the introduction of species that threaten our way of life. The tourist potential of having rare and exotic animals roaming the landscape cannot possibly replace that of having a safe and secure landscape for human beings to roam around, not to mention the safety of farm animals such as sheep, goats and cattle.

Those who care for the welfare of animals more than the welfare of human beings are scarcely fit to live in human society. Their attitude is hypocritical in that they complain about the damage that humanity is doing while enjoying all the fruits of our harmful civilisation. If they truly care more for animals than human beings then perhaps they should be living with animals and not amongst us.

Sentimental idealists often object to anything that is man-made. Bird's nests, animal droppings and decaying carcasses fit beautifully into the environment but houses and factories are blights on the landscape. But beauty is in the eye of the beholder. There was a time when trees were considered a nasty blot on the landscape. They block out our view of the horizon, bring noisy birds, nasty insects, useless vermin and so on. Now electricity pylons and wind farms are considered unacceptable. Other eyes might see them as things of beauty, emblems of our progressive civilisation, and purveyors of employment which are indispensable to our future. The fact is that objections to such advances are usually one-sided and tend to stress the negative over the positive aspects. In reality, the impact of these structures on the environment is fairly minimal. No plant or animal species are likely to die out as a consequence. Renewable energy is part of our plan to reduce our waste of planetary resources and temporary blots on the landscape are the price we have to pay in slowly minimising our impact on the planet without beggaring ourselves in the process.

The same arguments apply to the idealists' objections to genetic engineering and fracting. We have been genetically engineering other species since wolves were turned into dogs, aurochs into cattle, and wild grass into wheat, oats and barley. The fact that we are getting better at it is reason for approbation not condemnation. Similarly, fracting for oil and gas is an extension of coalmining and other techniques. We have to do it more carefully because of the possible harmful consequences but that does not mean that it should not be done at all. Again, it is a matter of people first, environment second.

Freedom to continue living as long as humanly possible

In the normal society it is taken for granted that everyone is free to live as long as possible. However, in the abnormal society, this freedom is under constant threat from the opposite freedom (or 'right') to die at a time of one's own choosing. If we are free to live, it is questionable whether we can also be free to die. After all, suicide in general is usually condemned and we are expected to avoid doing it in all circumstances. The distinction between suicide and euthanasia is not easily made. It is too easy for euthanasia to lead to the slippery slope in which you end up killing people for their own good. Serial killers can rationalise their killings by thinking that they are doing their victims a favour by enabling them to escape the horrors of living or of aging into insensibility. This was the mentality of Doctor Death himself, namely, Harold Shipman who made a profession of terminating lives deemed worthless by himself. He was totally convinced to the end that he was doing it for people's own good, and he could not be persuaded otherwise.

A very old person or a person with a terminal illness may lose the freedom to continue living and not just when put under pressure to end their own lives. They may choose to die and then have no opportunity to change their minds. Here is a real life example of this. We were privileged to see the work of *Dignitas*, the assisted suicide clinic in Switzerland, when the famous author, Terry Pratchett, presented a BBC television programme in which the clinic was visited. The programme was called *Choosing to Die* and it was broadcast on 13th June 2011. The subject of the programme was a man with a terminal illness who had chosen to go to the clinic, and we were shown the whole process of his assisted suicide. The elegant lady who administered the terminating drug acted very properly. It was obvious that he voluntarily took the cup from her while she constantly told him he didn't have to take it from her. However, we heard nothing from his wife, Terry Pratchett or the film crew who were in the room with him. His wife sat with him arm in arm and I wanted to hear her say that he didn't have to go through with this suicide, but she said nothing. I wanted to hear Terry Pratchett and the programme producer assure him that he didn't have to go through with this just because they were there to film him. But they said nothing. Silence of the others in the room seemed to me to be ominous. Perhaps they did say things to that effect but they were edited out of the eventual programme but that did not appear to be the case. The filming was continuous except towards the end when the poison had been taken. After the death had been confirmed we were shown his wife in the corridor talking to someone on her mobile phone. It seemed to me that this programme raised questions about the borderline between suicide and murder. The clients of this clinic have to pay for the privilege and when they arrive they are fully committed to doing the deed. If they have no choice but to go through with it, it is suicide or murder? In this case, the poor fellow did not seem overly keen to snatch the poison and get it over with. He hesitated and might have been thinking: "Well, I had better go through with it now. My wife expects it. Terry Pratchett and the film crew are standing there waiting for me to do it. I have no choice in the matter now." Doubts like these make euthanasia seem to be a very dubious and dangerous way of doing things. A better procedure might be to leave it to a team of professionals to consider each case and decide what is best for any patient who genuinely wants to end their life while making their decision in an open and above-the-board way so that there are no doubts about whether it is suicide or murder.

Contrast the above case with the legally compelled suicide of Socrates. His enemies ensured that he had ample time to escape and go into exile if he wanted to do so. He refused to do this as he believed it was his public duty to take the poison as dictated by legal process. His friends crowded round him pleading with him not to go through with it. Plato gives us his reasons in two dialogues – *Crito* and *Phaedo*. Indeed almost the only instance of Plato mentioning himself in the dialogues is in the *Phaedo* where he tells us that he was absent in saying 'I believe Plato was ill'.[3] He probably felt badly about his absence and thought that he might have persuaded Socrates that he was wrong and that he would do more good by continuing to live. There is little doubt that the primacy of life must prevail over the tragedy of death wherever possible. When a person decides that they must commit suicide, this is an idea or an obsession that is arguably irrational in that it does not accord with the idea that life is for living and not for dying. When someone gets into a suicidal frame of mind there is perhaps little else to be done but restrain them physically in the hope that they recover themselves and think more positively about the life's prospects. (There is much more on these subjects in my e-book entitled *Old Age, Death and Immortality* [2014a])

D. The Normal Family
The normality of family life

The assumption of the normal society is that children benefit most from being brought up in a normal family environment consisting of father, mother, siblings and the extended family of grandparents, uncles, aunts and cousins. Children lose out one way or another if their family upbringing lacks any of these aspects. But without doubt children can develop normally under the most deprived circumstances. Nevertheless, the normal society has a duty to ensure that children are given the best possible normal upbringing. This is already the aim of social work departments in dealing with problem families.

The nucleus of any normal family is the marriage between a man and a woman in the traditional way. It has reproductive aims more than purely sexual aims. It is abnormal to think that friends of the same sex can be 'married' in any proper sense of the word. Two men or two women cannot possibly form a normal family since it is based not on reproduction but on sexual attraction and self-indulgence. Friendship between persons of the same gender, however intimate and sexual, is an insufficient basis for a normal marriage. It is a perversion of what a marriage is meant to be, namely, a union between a man and woman. The extension of the idea of marriage opens the door for paedophiles to marry for the purpose of procuring children for their vile and base ends. It will lead inexorably to polygamy in which groups of people feel free to get married as they wish and no doubt have massive group orgies. Why stop at two men getting married when you can have three, four, five *ad infinitum* and *ad nauseam*? People used to talk about the decline of the Roman Empire in such terms. The lessons of history are not to be ignored in such matters.

In summary, therefore, marriage is specifically between a male and a female for the reproductive purpose of creating a family whether children enter into it or not. Friendships between persons of the same sex, however close and enduring, are not more than close friendships. Same sex marriages are not justifiable in the normal society for at least six reasons. Firstly, they send out a message that same sex relationships are normal when they manifestly are not. Secondly, they assume that homosexuality is a permanent condition that people have to live with for the rest of their lives, when this is not necessarily the case (for more on this see subsection E on 'Normal Sexual Behaviour' – pp. 173-180). Thirdly, they are more emblematic of sexual self-indulgence than of the enjoyment of a normal family life. Fourthly, they consolidate personally degrading relationships that give the individuals less opportunity to sort themselves out over time. Fifthly, they enable paedophiles to organise fake 'marriages' with the sole but secret purpose of adopting children whom they have *carte blanche* use for their own foul purposes. Sixthly, such marriages open the possibility of polygamous groups of people coming together purely for sexual gratification which has nothing to do with family life.

The role of the father in a normal family

The reaction against Victorian values has been particularly successful against the Victorian *paterfamilias* which was the mainstay of that society and doubtless contributed to its astounding success in producing outstanding individuals. Nowadays young men are not expected or trained to take up the duties and responsibilities of a father. They are left too much to their own devices and can become fathers without bothering to father their children. Victorian society had the right expectations of men but did not train them sufficiently to adopt that role successfully. As a result, there was a whole spectrum of attitudes among such men as was shown graphically in Jane Austen's novels:

Tyrannical:	General Tilney	(*Northanger Abbey*)
Strict:	Sir Thomas Bertram	(*Mansfield Park*)
Easy-going:	Mr Bennet	(*Pride and Prejudice*)
Timid:	Mr Woodhouse	(*Emma*)

Clearly, our education system must prepare young men for their duties and responsibilities more thoroughly than the Victorians attempted to do. They need to be trained into the responsibilities of fatherhood. Male exemplars are even scarcer these days than they were in Victorian times. The problem is that men are disadvantaged in having more problems than women in establishing their place in society. Women are not only geared for child bearing and upbringing, they are also more conformist than men. Thus, in an education system in which men and women are treated equally, men will always lose out. Women will make more of the system because it favours conformity and passive learning that does not rock the boat. To make the most of their talents and abilities, men need additional training and discipline which women generally do not need. This does not mean taking women out of the education system – à la Taliban – but of giving men more education that they need to take their place in society and become proper spouses, fathers, and grandfathers. Young men can be trained by imagining the types of situation in which their fatherliness may be required. They need to be taught what is expected of them as men in the normal society. Otherwise, they will tend towards the extremes of masculinisation or feminisation. They either become over-macho men or wish to fulfil their so-called feminine side. For more about this see subsection G (pp. 173-80).

In the normal society, there are plenty of outlets for males that are neither too macho nor too effeminate. In a developed and diverse society, there are plenty of fields of battle in which men can assert themselves without killing each other, shedding blood, or physically harming anyone. For example, the battlefields of sport, entertainment, politics and academia are ever strewn with proverbial corpses that have been cast aside. The great explosion of Victorian energy resulted from first full exploitation of these virtual wars and battles. Men had learned that society can benefit from the fights that they have with each other to better society one way or another, or in the outlets for masculine endeavour such as in sport and entertainment. The virtual reality generated by computers obviously gives yet more scope for wars to be fought online without bloodshed. In the face of such continuing masculinity, there will always be an important role for fathers to play in moderating masculine activity and in teaching children to live within themselves instead of going to hideous extremes as they are allowed to do nowadays.

Little Children should be seen and not heard

In the normal society, children are given space and freedom to develop in their own way but only within a disciplined and stable environment. At present, the upbringing of children has swung too far in the direction of indiscipline. Unless children learn discipline and self-restraint when they are children, how can they function as responsible adults when they grow up?

Children are encouraged to be heard and seen far too much. They are given far too much attention and are never left alone. It is currently fashionable to let children run riot and scream their heads off. This is sadly mistaken. If children are not restrained in their behaviour, they end up either screaming their heads off or crying their eyes out. This puts them at the mercy of their moods and they are either extremely happy or extremely sad. They swing from one extreme to the other and are at risk of bipolar disorder, or what used to be called manic depression. An epidemic of this disorder may well ensue in upcoming generations.

It is also fashionable to talk to children ceaselessly and overstimulate their brains so that information has no chance to gel and take root. No wonder we hear a lot these days about autism and ADHD (attention deficit hyperactivity disorder). This results from children reacting against unwanted over-stimulation by over-eager parents and relatives. If children are not left alone to play out their inner fantasies, they will lack inner development and grow up to be a prey to hot-heads, confidence tricksters, and charlatans of all descriptions. They will also lack the inner discipline to avoid the extremes of food disorders, drug and drink addiction.

The over-cosseting of children leads to children going wild when they are released into the world. This might be called the Bramwell Factor after the Bramwell Brontë, the brother of the famous Brontë sisters who wrote enduring novels. Bramwell also was exceptionally talented but he lost his way through drunkenness and waywardness. He was unable to devote himself to anything and stick at it. This can be put down to his over-sheltered upbringing in which he was educated at home by his father and over-indulged by his sisters. He had no time alone to work out things for himself. As a result, he lacked the will within him to control his passions and inclinations. He never did find himself and what he really wanted to do with his life. Typically, when such children grow up, they lack self-restraint and easily slip into extreme activities and bad habits.

Lack of inner life means lack of strength to cope with the pressures of the grown up world. Dominant persons, such as gangsters, tyrants, or demagogues, will dominate them completely because they are unable to resist the attractions of such people. Unless children are left alone to think for themselves and develop their imaginations for themselves, they will become slaves to powerful persons and organisations as they lack the character to assert their individuality. They will become nameless, thoughtless cogs in the cultural wheel. These are exactly the conditions that led to the Roman Empire and the blanket imposition of authority therein. People wanted to be dominated by a strong leader, rather like the Russians today.

'Spare the rod and spoil the child' was once a common saying. Physical violence inflicted on a child is now anathema but it remains true that lack of due restraint can spoil a child. But some children need more discipline and direction than others. This can be illustrated by analogy to the ability of the best football managers to get the best out of their players. They know instinctively when a player needs discipline and when they need more encouragement than discipline. At one extreme, an insensitive manager may prance about the dressing room ranting at his players to get out there and win or else. As a result, the players go out in a state of nervous tension and fail miserably. At the other extreme, an over-confident manager may tell his players not to worry about it and to go out and enjoy themselves. As a result, the players fail because they think that it doesn't matter whether they win or not; they are at least enjoying themselves. There is a story told about the highly successful Manchester United football manager Sir Alec Ferguson that sometimes in the dressing room he would tell his players stories that had nothing to do with football. Presumably, this would be to ease tensions and take the players' minds off the coming ordeal. He would instinctively gauge the atmosphere of the dressing room and response accordingly. Similarly, parents and teachers must be sensitive to the needs of their children, whether they need discipline or encouragement. Too much encouragement and attention is just as bad as too much discipline and restraint. As usual a dualist interaction between these extremes is the ultimate answer.

E. The Normal Person
The normality of ordinariness

The normal society gives us a clear idea of the normal person at least as a guideline for the upbringing and education of children. It is normal to be an ordinary person and the vast majority seem to think of themselves as such. Most people are destined to be ordinary and they learn to be more or less content in that station in life. Ordinary people are salt of the earth and the abnormal society tends to undervalue them. Human society cannot function for long without most people being content with their lot in life. Thus in the normal society, normality and ordinariness are promoted as being worthy ends in themselves.

Moreover, every individual human being is unique and irreplaceable. 'It takes all sorts ot make a world' was a frequently used saying in the past. Every person is an end in themselves, and everyone is important to society in the uniqueness of their contribution to it. The purpose of organisations and groupings of people is to exploit that uniqueness and not to repress it. They provide the opportunities for individuals to make the most of their lives in accordance with the opportunistic principle already mentioned in subsection B above (pp. 147=8). Oppressive organisations are counter-individualistic in that they impose their ends, aims, beliefs and policies on people in a draconian way without their having a say in the matter or being able to their own contributions to the running and rationale of the organisations. Religious and political organisations are particularly prone to impose themselves on people in that repressive way.

Thus, the normal society is humanistic in its regard for the importance and dignity of the individual. But because it recognises the uniqueness of individuals, it is not egalitarian. Outstanding individuals are entitled to be recognised and lauded for their achievements and contributions to society. However, it is another sign of the abnormality of current society that being famous and standing out from the crowd are lauded to the nth degree. This has spawned the celebrity culture in which people are famous for being famous. Fame ought to be reserved for those who have made a positive contribution to culture and civilisation. In that case, the end is not fame or recognition but the accomplishment itself. As Robert Louis Stevenson put it: "to travel hopefully is a better thing than to arrive, and the true success is to labour".[4] In other words, true self-fulfilment comes from doing the work that one is best suited to do. The work itself becomes the end regardless of whether one achieves fame or recognition. The normal person therefore strives to find the work that most involves them and gives them a sense of accomplishment in the mere doing of it. The reward comes from being stretched and challenged by work that is both worthy of oneself and worthwhile doing in itself.

To be a normal person ought to be the height of everyone's aspirations. Unrealistic expectations lead people to waste their lives striving for the unattainable. Very few people become pop stars, movie stars, star footballers, best-selling writers, business billionaires, famous television presenters or the like. "Many are called but few are chosen" (*New Testament*, Matthew 22:14). Ninety per cent of actors are said to be unemployed at any one time, and this presumably means that many of them are a burden on the state while they remain so. It is therefore right and proper that people should be discouraged from pursuing such unproductive professions. They should be encouraged to be ambitious within their apparent capabilities. It is not a sign of failure to lower one's sights and look for fulfilment in more modest ways. It is being realistic about what life really has to offer. Contentment is found by living within one's capabilities rather than in exceeding them to the point of causing oneself more pain, discomfort and disappointment than is necessary in life.

Superficially, a normal life may seem boring and predictable. But in the normal society, everyone is free to pursue their lives in a legally and morally acceptable way. The opportunities to have a rich and fulfilled life are limitless even for the most ordinary of individuals. The normal life for everyone is a balance between all the extremes to which human behaviour can be taken. The following forms of behaviour are typically taken to extremes when people become obsessed with them:

Physical Activity	Intellectual Activity
Over-Eating	Under-Eating
Drinking	Abstaining
Working	Playing
Talking	Thinking
Running	Resting

Everything we do or don't do can be taken to ridiculous extremes through lack of self-awareness, self-criticism and, above all, lack of self-discipline. We may know our limitations but sticking to them is another matter. We need to monitor our own behaviour and stay in touch with our bodily and mental condition. It is too easy to get carried away and become obsessed with one sort of behaviour or another. To avoid such extremes, we need to take our time and reflect on what we are doing and why we are doing it. We need to be aware of when we are truly developing ourselves in a positive and when we are simply degrading or abusing ourselves in an obsessive and self-indulgent way.

There is therefore an important distinction to be made between Personal Development (PD+) and Personal Degradation (PD-). The former consists in developing ourselves in a positive way that is truly beneficial to ourselves, acceptable to others and useful to society at large. The latter involves self-indulgence, self-harming or a lack of personal standards of self-awareness and integrity. It is behaviour unworthy of the best we can do as human beings. PD+ leads to a person developing their interests in diverse fields without going to extremes and harming themselves or others. PD- leads to self-indulgent practices that may be harmful and life-threatening in the long run. Extreme changes to the body are enforced to conform to unrealistic ideals of self. The over-eaters and the under-eaters are examples of this self-degradation. The morbidly obese are a heavy weight on social and health resources because of their selfish obsession with food. Anorexic people harm themselves and put their lives in danger by being obsessed with a selfish, self-centred idea of their bodily shape.

Thus, those who go to harmful extremes in their behaviour degrade themselves instead of developing themselves. Their behaviour is not normal because they have lost touch with their moral sense that consists in being sensitive to behaviour that is harmful or unworthy of them. The cure is for them reinstate their sensitivity so that they experience shame and guilt at their transgressions. This involves increased self-awareness by thoughtful introspection. Helping people to develop their self-awareness and increase their self-knowledge is essential to this procedure. Thus, the normal society draws attention to the distinction between Personal Development and Personal Degradation and champions the self-knowledge and self-restraint implied by this distinction.

However, this is not a matter of society deciding for each individual what is or is not degrading for them. People are not judged so much as helped to judge themselves. Everyone has to work out for themselves what they find to be personally developing or personally degrading. The norms are there for people to make up their own minds and are not to be imposed upon them against their will. In the normal society, it is the role of philosophy and morality to help individuals to think about these things and arrive at their own conclusions, which they can then justify or not with their peers, parents and society at large. In short, the education system falls down in so far as it fails to make philosophy and morality an important and indispensible part of the curriculum since these are essential to helping people to become rational and moral human beings and remain so throughout their lives.

Happiness is not the answer

When the normal society is governed by the opportunistic principle (as mentioned above), everyone seeks fulfilment in their lives. Finding a measure of fulfilment in life is a reason for contentment, but not necessarily happiness. The latter is an extreme feeling that has sadness as its opposite. As the Bible puts it: "Laughter may hide sadness. When happiness is gone, sorrow is always there." (*Old Testament,* Proverbs ch.14, v.13)

However, it is currently fashionable to promote happiness, and it is even proposed that it should be taught in schools. But happiness is boring. Cows in a field, fishes in the sea, birds in the sky are all as happy as Larry. They can afford to be happy as they don't know anything, least of all that they are made to be a meal for other animals. Human beings are born to be sad and miserable as they know the ultimate futility of their all-too-short lives. Happy human beings have no incentive to do anything out of the ordinary. As soon as they stop having fun, they give up and take to drink, drugs, sex or anything that will make themselves feel happy again. This occurs because happiness is associated with an ecstatic feeling which has to be consciously sustained or else supported by external stimulants. This kind of ephemeral happiness is certainly not the answer.

Aristotle is supposed to have made happiness an end in his *Ethics*. But the way he uses the word 'happiness' (*eudaimonia*) was not like happiness in our modern sense as being the opposite of sadness. He thought that for most people it meant 'living well or doing well'.[5] Otherwise, in his view, it is not strictly definable though we can use it as an end or good towards which we should aspire. He clearly did not think of it as a feeling to be fed or extended by artificial means to stave off sadness. The word 'contentment' perhaps better expresses the end we should aim for. No one can expect more out of life than to be contented with his or her lot in life. Such contentment requires a lot more work than a mere feeling of happiness. Anyone can force themselves to feel happy, unless they are chronically depressed, but it is not so easy to feel contentment. It is global state of mind that implies an integrated and self-possessed personality.

Along with contentment, there can be *joie de vivre*. The joy of living for its own sake is more profound and lasting a mere feeling of happiness. It is a feeling that suffuses the whole personality rather than being an isolated, ephemeral feeling. Joy can also be projected outwards because it is so intense inwards. A smiling, outwardly happy person can be quite miserable inside, but a joyous person goes around in a joyous state of mind whether they show it on their face or not. This state of mind does not need to be consciously sustained or induced by the artificial imbibing of drink or stimulating substances. It exists because it is a natural physical state and a part of one's normal being.

Besides, it is perfectly normal for a person to be serious and sad without having to smile, laugh and be happy all the time. It is abnormal to expect everyone to be happy and smiling whatever they are really feeling behind the smiles. Hypocrisy and insincerity are fostered instead of a genuine display of inner feelings. People are forced to put on smiles and fake happiness when inwardly they are anything but. Sadness is as much a part of the human condition as happiness and we need reach a balance between them lest we fall into bipolar extremes of behaviour, as is mentioned above.

F. The Normal Place of Women in Society

Feminism at first seemed to be good idea when it meant women having more confidence in themselves as women. But it has turned into a masculinism in which women think of themselves as indistinguishable from men. They are no longer women when they have purely masculine aspirations. Moreover, the unbalanced prominence of women in our society has led to a mothering, smothering society in which people are overprotected by political correctness. Such is the abnormality of the present situation which is now discussed.

The normality of a male-female balance in society

In the normal society there is a relative balance and interaction between the active, male principle and the passive, female principle. There will always be a need for the male principle of getting things done, as opposed to the passive female principle, which puts a necessary drag on impetuous male assertion. The progress of our society depends on the rational balance between these principles. When the one gains primacy over the other, our progress can be impeded accordingly. Nazi Germany exemplifies a society in which the aggressive, masculine principle predominated. It produced an excessively war-like society that aimed to take over the world. The court of Louis XIII in France is an example of an excessively feminised culture that invented ballet such like trivials. It led eventually to the well-known revolution that went to the extreme of proscribing and decimating the allegedly corrupt and over-feminised aristocratic class.

Women and men tend towards opposite extremes in their behaviour. At one extreme, women hesitate to take the initiative and put themselves forward. At the other extreme, men are inclined to "rush in where angels fear to tread" and to be more headstrong. These are not stereotypes but examples of the extremes to which the two sexes might tend in their behaviour. Between these extremes is the whole gamut of human behaviour. Most people are clear about whether they are either a man or a woman but there is an overlap where people are intermediate between the sexes and behave indefinitely. This minority does not blur the clear differences between the genders that most people accept as being the norm.

Because women represent the passive element in society it is natural for them to mind their place and not presume to be the equal of men in all things absolutely. Their passivity is a necessary drag on the impetuous active element of society. They are needed to hold back men, more than to draw them on, like masculine mad Lady Macbeths. Moreover, women's normal place in society is beside their menfolk and not against them. They have evolved to look after children and to be content in a home environment, hence their high-pitched baby voices and their caring, sharing attitude.

Human culture has always been centred on women and children, and men have always been peripheral. Women are favoured in all societies because of the key role they play in it. In contrast, men often have more difficulty in finding their place in society than women (as mentioned above). Women are fortunate in being genetically programmed to produce children if they so wish. They are therefore already privileged in being child-bearers and upbringers. To gain all the privileges of men they should in all fairness give up their own privileges which they are not necessarily inclined to do. Moreover, it is a fact that most women are content to be women and just as most men are content to be men, and this must be basis of the normal society.

At the same time, the normal society is always developing in its diversity and it produces an ever wider range of opportunities for both men and women. Thus, equality of opportunity for both sexes is thus beyond question. The further development of our society depends on women continuing to make their invaluable and unique contributions to it. However, our society is currently abnormal in that there is an imbalance towards the female principle. The over-feminisation of society makes it oversensitive and indeed soft. It becomes vulnerable to muzzie and other extremists who regard it as decadent and therefore to be destroyed.

In the current abnormal society, passivity is too much rewarded to the extent that passive males opt for femininity instead of rationalising their passivity in the male sphere. If instead they sought manhood in a rational way they may contribute to human progress. They are in a sense traitors to the male sex in repudiating the male principle altogether. They betray society also in depriving it of their masculine contribution. In these circumstances, there is a clear need to differentiate between the sexes and to emphasise the benefits of feminine role among women and masculine role among men. The roles need to be clearly worked out and this essay is hopefully a step towards doing so.

If women take over society then they are liable to be a drag not only on men individually but also on the whole society because of their passivity. Human progress arguably depends on male initiative. For example, the industrial revolution was entirely wrought by men working together with the aim of improving things. A woman in the 19th century would have made nothing of a steam engine; it is far too messy, smelly and noisy. It would have offended her delicate sensibilities. Arguably, we would still be living contently in caves if things had been left entirely to the non-initiative of women, who are evolved to be contented within the social structures laid down by men, for good or evil.

Overall it is arguable that we have lost control of women and this is an excuse for religious extremists to turn the clock back and enshroud women and chain them to home and children forever and ever. The problem is that, these days, men scarcely know what they are about. In fact, the height of manhood for many apparently manly men is to become women, though other men might think that they couldn't sink lower. This also needs to be clarified.

The Monstrous Regiment of Women

> I am assured that God has revealed to some in this our age, that it is more than a monster in nature that a woman shall reign and have empire above man. And yet, with us all there is such silence, as if God therewith were nothing offended.
>
> John Knox (1558).[6]

John Knox is my favourite bigoted Scotsman, though he was rather too extreme in his reaction against the corrupt catholic church. He famously put Mary Queen of Scots in her place by preaching at her endlessly. He also wrote a glorious tract entitled *First Blast of the Trumpet against the Monstrous Regiment of*

Women. In it, he rails against the 'regiment' or rule of Mary Tudor of England and Mary of Guise of Scotland who at the time ruled their respective countries (Mary of Guise was Regent of Scotland until her daughter Mary Stuart came of age). He obviously thought that women are not proper persons to rule nations. He would be horrified to know that women are now being encouraged to take over society, and not just rule it.

> "To promote a woman to bear rule, superiority, dominion, or empire above any realm, nation, or city, is repugnant to nature; contumely [insulting] to God, a thing most contrary to his revealed will and approved ordinance; and finally, it is the subversion of good order, of all equity and justice."[7]

> "As St. Paul does reason in these words: 'Man is not of the woman, but the woman of the man. And man was not created for the cause of the woman, but the woman for the cause of man; and therefore ought the woman to have a power upon her head'" [That is, a cover in sign of subjection] 1 Cor. 11:8-10. [8]

Mary Tudor in particular is "an cursed Jezebel" and she "may for a time sleep quietly in the bed of her fornication and whoredom; she may teach and deceive for a season; but neither shall she preserve herself, neither yet her adulterous children, from great affliction, and from the sword of God's vengeance, which shall shortly apprehend such works of iniquity."[9] Jezebel was a biblical Queen of Israel who worshipped the god Baal and the goddess Asherah and who killed the prophets of the Lord (Old Testament, 1 Kings 18:4). She threatened the life of the prophet Elijah (1 Kings 19:1) and naturally came to a very sticky end: being thrown from a window, ridden over by a chariot, and eaten by the dogs; despite doing her make-up and arranging her hair beforehand (2 Kings 9:30-37).

It is an incredible fact that in recent years the armies, navies and air forces of five European countries have been under the control of women. Recently, the defence ministers of Germany, Holland, Norway, Sweden and Italy were Ine Eriksen Søreide (Norway), Karin Enström (Sweden), Jeanine Hennis-Plasschaert (Netherlands), Ursula von der Leyen (Germany), and Roberta Pinotti (Italy).[10]

Does this mean that they feminised their armed forces? Were their troops encouraged to fling flowers, spray perfume and blow kisses at their enemies instead of fighting and killing them? Of course not! The cruel Jezebel factor will raise its ugly head. Literary and historical figures such as the Amazons, Boudicca, Lady Macbeth, and Margaret Thatcher exemplify the masculine machinations of women in such positions of power.

Is it because he was a man that Churchill does not seem as nasty a person as Margaret Thatcher? No, it is because there was so much more to Churchill than the bellicose warmonger that he had to be at times. There is also his literary output, inspiring speeches, and wise and witty sayings that resonate with us even today. Above all, there is his pre-war humanity in responding to the Nazi gangsters and seeing them as a threat to civilisation.[11] In comparison, Thatcher has left nothing behind her but the 'blood, sweat, tears and toil' of the Falklands, riots, union bashing, and the destruction of our industrial base. In short, women can only be one dimensional leaders who blunder blinkered in one direction to the bitter end.

The recent female President of Argentina made threatening noises over the Argentine claim to the Falkland Islands currently held by Britain. Doubtless, she would have invaded it (once again) if only she could. But what Argentina requires to enforce its claim is not a fuming female but a smiling 'Churchill' visiting the Falklands with cigars and whisky in hand to woo the people into the welcoming arms of the Argentinians. After all, it was once unthinkable that the British colony of Hong Kong would allow the tanks of the Red Army not only roll into it but also be welcomed by the people of the colony. But the thoughtful men of the Chinese Government achieved this peaceful revolution, much to the sadness and regret of the British people at losing yet another piece of their Empire. (Contrast that with the President Putin's ham-handed alienation of the Ukrainian people with his mindless bellicosity.)

Knox would have been appalled that his beloved Scotland has recently been taken over completely by the Monstrous Regiment. The leaders of the three main political parties in the Scottish Parliament have all been women at the same time. Scotland does not appear to be better governed as a consequence. Indeed, unemployment is rising, productivity is down, and a complacent malaise veils the country, while the leading ladies sign autographs as if they were feckless superstars.

Women may be good at multi-tasking but they have one dimensional minds driven by heartfelt emotions rather than patient, self-critical reason. Except for the very ablest of women, politics is not and never has been their forte. The view that parliaments need equal numbers of male and female members is idealistic leftist nonsense that is contrary to human nature and inadmissible in the normal society. The very able but disastrously divisive Margaret Thatcher might be thought a trailblazer in becoming the first female Prime Minister, but she was no feminist and she didn't approve of women making too much of themselves. She appointed no women in her cabinet which she dominated in a stridently man-like fashion, while turning on the feminine tears when necessary.

However, it is noteworthy that Thatcher, ten years before she became Prime Minister, quoted with approval in a 1969 speech the saying: "when woman is made equal to man she becomes his superior". She attributed the saying to Socrates and said that she "would not dissent from anyone as wise as Socrates."[12] However, the saying "A woman once made equal with man, becometh his superior" dates back no further than 1598 in the book *Politeuphuia, Wits Commonwealth*.[13] It is there ascribed to Socrates, but it is not found in any classical source.[14] The most likely explanation is that it is a 16th century gloss on Plato's advocacy of equal education for men and women in the *Republic*, and prompted in particular by this passage:

> "There is no administrative job in a community which belongs to a woman *qua* woman, or to a man *qua* man,' I said. "Innate qualities have been distributed equally between the two sexes, and women can join in every occupation just as much as men, although they are the weaker sex."[15]

Socrates is here referring to rulers of a state and there is no question of women being equal to men in all respects. No one in antiquity could have thought of women as being equal let alone superior to men. The ancient Athenian assembly was exclusively male, and no woman could attend, let alone speak or rule. In the Roman world women had more freedom and greater power behind the scenes but they were not equal enough to rule or show any 'superiority'. The advent of Christianity brought more recognition of women's abilities. But it was only in the 16th century that Plato's *Republic* became widely available and widely read. It is likely that the above passage became the rationale for allowing women to be rulers in their own right. Without it, there would have been no 'Bloody Mary' or 'Good Queen Bess'!

In that context, a 16th century commentator on Plato's *Republic* must have thought it dangerous to give women the same education as men and may have made the remark about the potential superiority of women which was then attributed to Plato's narrator, Socrates. Even by the 18th century, fear of women's 'superior' powers was still very evident. For example, in 1717, a group of young women in Edinburgh founded a 'Fair Intellectual Club' in which they aimed to improve their literary skills like the male clubs in Edinburgh that at the time were dedicated to improving themselves. In 1720 they published a pamphlet about the club and this led to its suppression lest they made too much of their 'exorbitant powers.' We hear no more of ladies' clubs during the eighteenth century.[16]

The fact is that the greatest women exploit their femininity and do not consider themselves to be superior to men. They know that they need men to keep them in check. This applies even to Queen Victoria, the ruler of the greatest empire in history. Her favourite Highland servant, John Brown fulfilled that role after the death of her overbearing husband, Prince Albert. The role of Brown is exemplified in the following story. When a nervous young footman dropped a silver salver with an almighty clatter, the Queen lost her temper and ordered him to be consigned to the kitchen. When John Brown heard about this, he shouted at her: "Whit are ye daein' tae that puir laddie? Hiv' ye never drappit onything yersel?"[17] She immediately saw that she was in the wrong and the footman was reinstated.

If we really regard women as superior to men then it means a preponderance of the female passive principle and a suppression of the male active principle. The emphasis on the former principle has already resulted in so-called 'political correctness' which manifests oversensitivity to offensive words and behaviour. We end up saying and doing as little as possible for fear of offending people or upsetting them. When women are allowed to rule the roost, feelings become the motive power in society. Women are typically concerned about feelings - their own and other people's feelings more than about their reasons for doing things. When people's feelings become more important than their reasons, our society loses its rudder and drifts out of control. This book aims to reinstate the role of reason in taking civilisation forward and giving it a coherent direction.

Women's taking on a superior role in society is comparable with bee hives in which the workers are all female and the males are useless drones that die out as soon as they fulfil their biological function. Nowadays, men are not even required for the biological function since their sperm can be harvested or their genes made use of without any coupling required. It is surely time for men to fight back and show that the masculine principle is still necessary to society and in particular to our future. Nations and cultures that treat women as equal and allow them to take over, typically have no future. We know very little about the Minoans, the Etruscans and the Picts which were dominated by women. These civilisations were so complacent and self-effacing that they felt no need to record their achievements for posterity and we don't even know their languages with any certainty. The feminisation of society is a recipe for decline, dissolution and the end of civilisation as we know it. Thus, the normal society therefore cannot allow women to think of themselves as superior to men in any absolute sense. Women have their strengths and weaknesses just as men have their strengths and weakness. The normal society exploits these self-evident differences and does not suppress them absolutely from one point of view or the other, for a healthy interaction between the sexes in a family background is all-important.

In summary, therefore, the trouble with allowing women to rule the roost is that they are prone to give primacy to their feelings. Women in general are sensitive creatures who often take things personally. The fact that they are easily offended is the source of fashionable political correctness which reflects women's oversensitivity to words however innocently they are intended to be. This is why men in particular have to be careful what they say to them. If a man tells a woman that he is offended by what she says or does, she is liable to be even more offended than he is by the fact he is accusing her of being offensive. Her feeling seems to be: "How dare you think of me as being offensive – *Moi!* – being such an adorable woman!" The self-centredness of women is such that any offense against them must take precedence over the offense given by them to any man. Moreover, if a woman is criticised by a colleague this may be interpreted as not only offensive, but also harassing and even intimidating. This over-sensitivity means that women in general are not cut out for the cut and thrust of politics which often means being offensive and being offended in turn. Above all, it means that, in the normal society, women and their extreme left-wing toadies would not be allowed to foist political correctness on us since it is a perpetual barrier to free speech, as is argued everywhere above.

Marilyn Monroe was the true feminist

The actress Marilyn Monroe was the true feminist of the 20th century. She was the embodiment of femininity and therefore deserves to be called a 'feminist'. Stepford wives, in the feature film of that name, are also true feminists. However, this kind of feminism is obviously extreme and irrational. Such feminists are all women but too much so in that they make themselves the sex slaves of men rather than their sympathetic companions.

Women are the same as men in being human beings but they are not the same as men as they are feminine human beings rather than masculine ones. Feminism that demands equality with men is really masculinism. If women are different from men then they cannot be equal to them. It is a matter of simple logic. If A differs from B in specific ways then A does not equal B. There is not equality between them – woman differs from man in specific ways, therefore woman does not equal man.

It seems to be universally acknowledged, even by the most extreme of so-called 'feminists', that women are biologically different from men. By their nature, they can talk better, are more sociable, empathetic and intuitive. Men have better visual, spatial skills and are usually less sensitive, emotional or highly strung than women. If one puts one's hand on the shoulder of a man, he will probably not winch. But a woman will instinctively react to such a gesture by moving away, squirming or even squealing. Clearly, women are in the thrall of their sensitive nervous systems and therefore are subject more to their immediate feelings than men generally.

Many women nowadays will say that they are not feminists. But what they really mean is that they acknowledge the differences between men and women. They are therefore against masculinism in which women claim to be indistinguishable from men. They may not be feminists like Marilyn Monroe but they are at least more feminists than masculinists.

It is the pursuit of masculinism rather than feminism that leads women to take up sports previously left to men. We are always told that it is intolerable for men to be violent towards women. However, it is now permissible for women to do violence on each other. They can punch each other black and blue in boxing bouts. They play football and run into each other, fall to the ground, have a football kicked at all parts of their bodies, and all in the pursuit of masculinism. It is painful to watch them being beaten up black and blue in the pursuit of rugby and other rough sports. They are saying 'We can be men just like you'. But men are still not allowed to beat women up. They want it both ways – "We are just like men but you must always treat us like women". How confusing is that then?

A recurring question asks "What do women really want?" The answer is that women want no more nor less than men want for them. They need to be told what to do or encouraged to do things by men who set the parameters within which they are allowed to behave. This is proved nowadays by the ease with which many women of a certain faith adopt the repulsive clothing and retrogressive behavioural patterns foisted on them in the name of so-called 'religion' (i.e. tyrannical bigotry). They may plead that their religion demands this of them but it is men who are really doing the demanding.

The popularity among women of the book *Fifty Shades of Grey* suggests that they secretly long to submit abjectly to the will of men. They may dream about such things but the reality might be quite different. One might ask what women are for if they are not to serve the needs of men? They have evolved for that purpose and any society that makes too much of women is doomed to ultimate failure as it is against our basic nature to elevate women to a state of total equality with men. Their squeaky, shrieky voices have evolved because their place is among children and not among men. Those of us whose ears are pained by high-pitched voices are physically harmed by loud shrieking female voices. But pointing out this painfulness to them is regarded as offensive and rude. As mentioned above, their feelings on the matter must always be paramount as far as they are concerned.

The parlous state of the economy may be blamed at least in part on the rise of feminism in the sixties. The phenomenon of stagflation began then. This is when a stagnant economy generates ever-rising prices. There is increasing demand for a limited range of goods and services, mainly those favoured by women. But these are consumer goods that are not capital intensive like machinery, buildings and aeroplanes. There is less of a multiplier effect so that the economy does not grow in its diversity. Prices go up without the economy expanding to any great extent. This may be explained by the fact that women suddenly had their chocolately fingers on the purse strings. They increasingly spent their money on clothes, shoes, handbags, cosmetics and other goods and services that have a low multiplier effect. This pushed up consumer prices without stimulating the economy. It also increases imports over exports. The credit boom may be explained in the same way since women have the freedom to buy things on credit and their shopping habits make it difficult for them to stop ratcheting up increasing amounts of credit. Thus, the behaviour of women who shop till they drop creates bubbles and imbalances which may in the long run threaten the future of our economy. These social distortions can only be reversed by redressing the feministic imbalance and returning to more normal balance society in which the sexes perform their natural roles in terms of passivity and activity.

In section 23 of the 1948 Universal Declaration of Human Rights states "Everyone, without any discrimination, has the right to equal pay for equal work." This right has been reinforced by Acts of Parliament since the 1960s. Yet there are still complaints, after seventy years of legislation and feministic propaganda, that women do not get equal pay for the same job and that they are constantly being discriminated against in employment and elsewhere. This exemplifies the difficulty of legalising to change human nature, as well as the fact that women seem to be willing to accept lower wages even when the conditions for wage equality are made as favourable as possible. Thus, it is natural for women to defer to men in financial matters and it should be so in all matters.

Physical exercise and improved sanitary towels were perhaps the principal reasons why women were able to 'liberate' themselves during the 20th century. The importance of physical exercise was recognised by H.G. Wells writing in 1945 in the last of his writings. After noting how difficult it is to distinguish between males and females in other animals, he makes the following observation:

> "Even the stigmata of sex in *Homo Sapiens* are far less conspicuous to-day than they were a hundred years ago. The exaggeration of the waist by tight-lacing has ceased. So also has much mysterious cosseting of girls. The bicycle played a part in that release. The growing girl braced herself up and went for a gentle ride on the new toy when her grandmother would have been resting in bed, and found herself all the better for it. At any crisis our great-grandmothers would 'swoon', but who

ever hears of women swooning to-day? Now men faint more frequently than women."[18]

It is preposterous to insinuate that men are responsible for the corseting of women in order to keep them in order. Corsets were deemed necessary for women who didn't take physical exercise and whose spines required bolstering because of the lack of muscularity to support their backbones. Corsets must have eased the back pain caused by that lack of muscularity. Indeed, in the 19th century men also wore corsets since this made them thinner, improved their deportment and prevented them from slouching.

Those women who think that it is still a man's world and that women are still not getting a fair deal, should read Samuel Pepys's diary (1660-1669) and find out what a man's world was really like. Pepys's wife had virtually no freedom. He goes ballistic when she buys an expensive pair of earrings without his permission.

"After dinner I walked homeward, [and] at home find my wife this day of her owne accord to have lain out 25s. upon a pair of pendantes for her eares, which did vex me and brought both me and her to very high and very foule words from her to me, such as trouble me to think she should have in her mouth, and reflecting upon our old differences, which I hate to have remembered. . . . the poor wretch afterwards in a little while did send out to change them for her money again. I followed Besse her messenger at the 'Change, and there did consult and sent her back; I would not have them changed, being satisfied that she yielded."[19]

In other words, Pepys is implicitly telling his wife: you can keep them but don't do it again! She was only allowed to shop for herself for agreed things. Yet Pepys dearly loved his 'poor wife' as he constantly called her. He always wanted to be 'good friends' with her following their numerous spats. (He even gave her a black eye on at least one occasion!) He was also concerned that she was at home alone with only two or three servants to keep her company. But he didn't think she needed employment. He thought she needed entertainment to keep her happy ('girls just want to have fun', as they say nowadays). So when he could afford it, he arranges for talented women to keep his wife company and entertain her with songs, dancing and music. Among his other faults, he was an anal-retentive miser continually counting his money as well as his faeces (he suffered badly from constipation). Presumably his wife only tolerated him because she had nowhere else to go. Obviously, such total control of women was axiomatic in his society. Indeed, it seems to be a natural consequence of men's sexual addiction which was the norm: Pepys seems to regard his own unrestricted sexual behaviour as perfectly normal and manly, at least until his wife found out about his philandering and curtailed it by keeping a watchful eye him. In short, women needed in those days to be protected from the rampant sexuality of men.

No one is suggesting that we return to the good old days of total male domination of women. Marilyn Monroe was an extreme feminist who made herself completely subservient to men, especially famous and influential men. With better education and self-knowledge, she might have developed as a more productive person and become like, for example, Dolly Parton and Bet Midler who are not only feminists in the best sense of the word but also astute businesswomen and acclaimed superstars. They are models for all women as they have become global phenomena without compromising their femininity in any way.

Men suffer by the masculinisation of women as they are driven to the extremes of aggressive machismo on the one hand and pathetic effeteness on the other hand. They no longer have the angelic example of females who are not trying to be better than men themselves. To paraphrase Goethe: *Nicht mehr zieht uns das Ewig-Weibliche hinan!* – the eternal feminine no longer draws us onwards and upwards![20] We men are lost without real women to look up to and put on a pedestal. But Marilyn Monroe is unfortunately too good to be true in that respect.

G. Normal Sexual Behaviour

> "As to the act of sexual love, we should all, no doubt, contend that it is most pleasant, but that one must, if he perform it, do it so that no one else shall see, because it is most repulsive to see."
>
> Plato, *Greater Hippias*.[21]

The need for sexual restraint

In the normal society, there is obvious sexual restraint. No one is allowed to have sex anywhere and everywhere, least of all in public. One of the principal ways in which we differ from animals such as bonono apes is that we exercise sexual restraint on an individual basis and on a public one. Everyone learns to control themselves sexually, otherwise they can get themselves into trouble with their personal relationships and ultimately with the law. Sexual restraint is also necessary for human beings because it helps to sublimate our inner energy and divert it from carnal lust towards worthwhile projects and thereby enhance our lives. Nowadays, those who are unable to control their sexual impulses are called 'sex addicts', as if it were a kind of medical or psychological disorder instead of merely a deplorable lack of will-power and self-discipline. As they are human beings like the rest of us, they can learn to control themselves just as the rest of us have to. In the past, they would be told to take a cold shower to cool their ardour!

Sexual restraint is behind all our great achievements in making a better life for ourselves. It underpinned the Protestant ethic and Victorian energy. Indeed, the Victorians had a better idea about what to do about sex than they are usually credited with nowadays.. They didn't forbid it according to popular myth. It was a case of "get on with it but don't make a fuss about it. Make too much of it and we will punish you accordingly." People may do all kinds of things in private but they should not make out that what they are doing is in any way laudable. The proper place of sexual activity is the closet or bedroom. Thus, people had immense freedom to do as they pleased as long as they kept within the bounds of superficial responsibility. Appearances were everything and no doubt a lot of hanky panky and weird goings-on festered away beneath the respectable surface.

However, the Victorians got it wrong in going too far to eradicate unacceptable sexual behaviour by legal means. They started the regrettable process of using the law to change people's moral behaviour by outlawing homosexuality and other perversions. However, they got it right in putting sexual behaviour in its place, namely, in the private places where it belongs. Their attitude to sex has been misunderstood. They were not really forbidding in matters of sex; they simply wanted to give it as low a place in human affairs that it deserved. If you parade your dirty behaviour in public you will be punished for it by social disapproval if not legal sanctions. Sexual indulgence that does not involve reproduction is not important as long as it is moderate and not physically and mentally debilitating or harmful to others. As a matter of reproduction, it is very important indeed. But otherwise it is no more important than scratching your back or picking your navel. There is therefore no need to make so much of it as to 'come out of the closet' when it is obvious it belongs there in the first place – out of sight and out of mind.

Sigmund Freud, more than any other single individual, changed public attitudes on sexual matters. However, he was a sex addict whose perversion consisted in seeing sex in everything. He explained every aspect of human behaviour in terms of sex: if someone dreams of a tall chimney stack, this is obviously an unconscious symbol for an erect penis, and so on. Any other explanation was inadmissible. The consequences of his extreme views are still with us. It is ironic that although most of his doctrines are now considered unscientific, his views on sex still reign unchecked amongst us. In short, we still await the discrediting of his extreme pre-occupation with sex (which is not attempted here!)

The spectrum of sexual behaviour

There is a whole spectrum of normal and abnormal sexual behaviour which is depicted very roughly as follows:

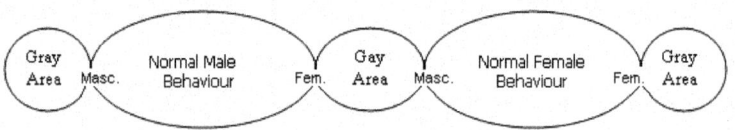

The Spectrum of Normal and Abnormal Sexual Behaviour

This diagram gives a rough idea of how the gray and gay areas relate to the areas of normal male and female sexual behaviour. The 'gray' area takes its name from the S&M novel *Fifty Shades of Grey* (using the alternative spelling to match 'gay'). To the far left we have the extreme masculine 'dominant' behaviour and to the far right we have the extreme 'submissive' behaviour said to be characteristic of S&M relationships. In the very middle, we have the 'gay area' of homosexual and lesbian behaviour. Feminine men are often associated with homosexuality and masculine women are often associated with lesbian behaviour. But of course these are typical stereotypes; there are enormous variations between individuals and this is only the roughest of distinctions. Also, S&M behaviour is often associated with homosexual behaviour so that the 'gray' can also be 'gay'.

The above diagram illustrates the theory that the more excessively sexualised society becomes the bigger the gay and gray areas become in response to people's search for increasingly extreme ways of expressing their so-called 'sexuality'. In becoming excessively sexually indulgent they are soon bored with repetitions and seek increasingly bizarre alternative forms of behaviour as are detailed below. They become enslaved by sexual indulgence and lose their freedom as respectable, self-regarding human beings. Their downward path is one of personal degradation rather than personal development.

Normal male and female sexual behaviour involves restraint and discrimination. It is controlling one's impulses and retaining a sense of shame and guilt about going to extremes or violating accepted norms of sexual behaviour. In other words, normal sexual indulgence is subject to freedom of choice and not determined by lust, impulse, compulsion, obsession or other irrationalities. The latter is slavery not liberty. The normal person is free to have sex or not, while the sex slave has no choice but to follow their mindless compulsions. "Licence they mean when they cry libertie", as Milton put it.[22]

Thus, all restraint goes out the window when sexual desires take over and become the ruling object of a person's life. Those who make too much of sex and allow it to fill their thoughts excessively will not be satisfied with simple fornication or simple masturbation on a restricted basis. They will become bored with these and seek ever more extreme and bizarre ways of obtaining sexual satisfaction. The excessive fornicators will end up as sex addicts who adopt increasingly objectionable practices such as S&M and buggery. They may become rapists (male) or nymphomaniacs (female). They may even start abusing children and babies in search of cheap thrills. The excessive masturbators become self-abusers obsessed with pornography or with even more bizarre perversions such as auto-erotic stimulation in which foolish men strangle themselves sometimes to death in their absurd quest for the ultimate frisson. All these extremes are avoided by people who learn the benefits of exercising restraint and self-discipline in sexual matters. This may be difficult in the current over-sexualised atmosphere but it is not asking the impossible.

The above diagram therefore illustrates how an abnormal society that is excessively sexualised has growing gay and gray areas as more and more people seek increasingly extreme ways of assuaging their sexual addiction. Such a sexualisation occurs when the media is overflowing with sexual content so that the whole country is mad for sex. Anyone showing restraint is consider abnormal and in need of sexual treatment of some sort. The paedophiles and sexual abusers can think of themselves as performing a necessary public service by inducting innocent people into sexual 'normality'. In a totally corrupt society every male and female will be filled with lust and will get into the gay and gray scenes to enrich their sexual experience. In this way, society can spiral into total decadence and worthlessness. Its depravity may leave it open to extreme reactions such as the beheading and sharia law currently favoured in places where muzziness predominates

The antidote to this spiral into increasing sexual and moral corruption is the distinction between self-development and self-degradation as mentioned above. We may stop the rot by promoting the former over the latter. There is nothing progressive, for example, in people changing their gender simply because they feel better in the other gender. It is pure indulgence that complicates their lives and often makes them obnoxious to their nearest and dearest. There is no personal development involved because they have to completely reconstruct themselves in the other gender usually very imperfectly. They face a lifetime of medication and social prejudice. They waste endless time and energy in acting out the chosen gender instead of simply making the most of the gender they are born into just as people have been doing for hundreds of thousands of year. They use up valuable medical resources when they could be contributing to society in much more sensible and rational ways.

It is only the over-sexualisation of society that makes people worry about being one gender or the other instead of making the most of what they are as human beings. It is as if it is more important to be gender re-assigned into one gender or the other than to be a human being with all the ambiguities that most of us have. Nobody is absolutely male or absolutely female in any case. Those who are worried about being in the 'wrong' gender should be much more concerned about developing their skills and abilities to make their unique contribution to society instead of making themselves into something that they were not necessarily born to be.

The ultimate absurdity is reached when fully functioning males change their gender to become the lesbian lovers of women. This shows how much pure sexual indulgence is often the real motivation behind so-called gender re-assignment. Obviously, it would be much easier and more straightforward for them to hone their skills as heterosexual lovers of women and in the process they would be of better service to women. Presumably, they don't do so because they think that they can get more sexual opportunities by insinuating themselves with women as women. It is pure sexual self-indulgence and self-degradation.

In conclusion, a permissive society is not progressive but morally aimless and misguided. It heads only in the direction of the sewer or cesspit. Permissive progress is just the inverse of religious or spiritual progress which advocates chastity, purity, holiness and an abject submission to the deity. The latter impedes self-development by being inhumanly extreme in its demands. The one is pure self-indulgence and the other is pure self-immolation. The normal society eschews such extremes by promoting self-awareness, self-discipline and self-restraint in the interests of self-development as opposed to self-degradation on the one hand and self-annihilation on the other hand.

The Abnormality of Sex Change

Transgenders are self-indulgent traitors to their sex. Those who change their sex merely because they feel like it are betraying the sex into which they were born. For hundreds of thousands of years the human race has benefited from the ambiguity of the sexes. Our progress was made possible because female-favouring males have appreciated the femininity of women as much as they benefited from the masculinity of being a male. Conversely, male-oriented females have given backbone to the relative spinelessness of femininity. This mixing up of gender propensities and attitudes contributed to the creativity and dynamism of humanity. All that is threatened by the promotion of gender re-assignment. The sexes are being polarised into their opposite and increasingly irreconcilable camps. The sexes will increasingly have nothing in common with each other. Lesbianism will be promoted by re-assigned males and homosexuality by re-assigned females. The sexes will have less and less reason to come together for the purposes of procreation. The worst case scenario is that the very future of the human race will be threatened by these developments.

Gender-changing is a selfish and self-indulgent act. It is selfish because it puts the personal feelings of these persons before those whom they hurt and bewildered by their irrational and unsocial acts. It is self-indulgent because it puts mere feelings before any other consideration. They can never become completely the gender which they foist upon themselves. They are simply not biologically equipped to become completely in all respects the sex they have allegedly 'chosen' to be. They are born a 100 per cent one gender and are able to marry and have children as many of them do. They cannot possibly become a 100 per cent of their chosen gender; therefore they spend the rest of their lives mimicking that gender. They are merely following their feelings which are not the reality of the matter.

They become sad shadows of what they formerly were. Changing their gender is an unnatural act. It is not self-development but self-degradation. It does not make them better persons but lessens them into pseudo-females or pseudo-males respectively which they were not intended to be by nature. It cannot be self-development as they can never develop completely into their chosen gender. They are biologically not equipped to be anything other than the gender they were born into. They spent their lives trying in vain to be the woman or man they were never intended to be in the first place. It is a progressive degradation from their original natural state.

Males who become females have betrayed their sex and have opted out of the struggle to be men and find their male role in society. They are cowards that have run away from the battle of life. Instead of striving to make positive manly contribution to society, they waste their time and resources aping their chosen gender and usually convincing no one in the process.

The fact is that we are not meant to give way to our feelings just because we feel like it. We may feel like hitting someone and feel that we would get great pleasure from doing so but we nevertheless refrain to do so because it is uncivilised behaviour, unlawful, and because of the untold consequences of doing so. If we feel like raping someone that does not mean that we are not being ourselves unless we put these feelings into practice. Nor does it mean that we are inherently or potentially rapists. Feeling like murdering someone does not make you a murderer. Similarly, feeling yourself to be a woman does not make you a woman nor does it mean that you are not being yourself unless you change your sex. Also, it is irresponsible behaviour as we are responsible to other people and we need to take their feelings into account in anything we think of doing. In short, such behaviour is egotistical and selfish in the extreme, to say nothing of the vast waste of medical resources in such pseudo conversions.

Sexual perversion is nothing to be proud about

It is clear that sexual pre-occupation in the abnormal society leads to a proliferation of perversions and bizarre forms of sexual expression such as S&M and auto-erotic stimulations. However, the normal society is puritanical only as regards what normal people get up to in their normal social activities. What they do in their private lives and out of the eyes and ears of other people is their own concern. By keeping such things private we can avoid the over-sexualisation of society described above. Innocent people no longer have sex rubbed in their faces and they can develop their sexuality normally instead of experimenting with perversions because everyone seems to expect it.

There is no need for other people's filthy habits to be flaunted in our faces. As mentioned above, the bedroom or closet is where they ought to be confined. Ignorance is bliss as far as other people's pathetic proclivities are concerned. The ridiculous, stupid and disgusting things that people get up to in their private lives are of no consequence as long as they are legal and involve consenting adults. Why should such things matter to any one else? They only matter when they are paraded arrogantly before us as if they were something to be proud about. Their activities are nothing to be proud about and they do themselves harm by bringing attention to their inclinations as if they were beyond reproach. In the witch hunt against paedophiles, we hear a lot about protecting the innocence of children. But what about protecting the innocence of adults? Is this not equally important? We surely have the right to free from sex being perpetually thrust before us. In a normal society, it is usually out of sight and out of mind because we have better things to think about in our everyday lives.

The sexual pre-occupation endemic in the abnormal society is fuelled by the perpetual parading of sex in the media, books, music and so on. Thus, this unhealthy pre-occupation would dwindle in the normal society in which sex is put in its proper place i.e. out of public view. An out-of-sight, out-of-mind attitude would allow people's minds to be devoted to more sociable and edifying thoughts and activities. People can concentrate more on Personal Development and are less prone to Personal Degradation (as mentioned above). For the over-sexualisation of society leads to growing Personal Degradation as 'private vices' become increasingly public and 'public virtues' become increasingly hard to find.

Sexual perversions in general are a form of personal degradation that is nothing to be proud of. Perversions that involve two or more persons are particularly degrading for the participants. It is often a matter of power being wielded over people. In degrading themselves, they degrade others in imposing a mindless control over them. Homosexuals who treat other men like women are making passive objects of them. In this way, they both lose respect as men. The relationships between men are harmed when the reason for men's interest in each other becomes entirely sexual. This is why homosexuality is often banned in martial societies that depend on men being able to trust each other. Homophobia will not go away however much the decadents argue and fight against it.

Indeed, homosexuality is arguably just as bad as paedophilia. If paedophilia is a disgusting and repugnant form of behaviour, homosexuality is equally so. It is just as degrading to its participants. Homophobia is an entirely normal and natural response to such behaviour. We have every right to be fearful of what these people get up to. There are apparently no limits to the shameful behaviour of homosexuals in degrading each other out of pure self-indulgence and through wielding unnatural power over each other. The less one knows about it the better. One can have great pride in being a homophobe. It is the entirely wholesome and human thing to be. It is a repudiation of the lowest forms of behaviour.

However, this does not mean banning this form of behaviour or taking action against it. It simply means wanting out of one's face. It is sickening that people make it out to be a good thing when it plainly it is not. It is better to be a straight heterosexual raising a family composed of a man and woman. Anything else is plain perversion and that is a plain statement of fact. No one need be bothered by a person's sexual orientation as long as they keep it to themselves. It is when they start flaunting it as it were something important when it is not just trivial but also repulsive. In short, it has to be clearly recognised that sensitive people are disgusted and offended by such objectionable behaviour being paraded before them. It is not correct to say that only ignorance and bigotry lies behind homophobia. Genuine feelings of revulsion are involved that cannot be suppressed by law or by further information about this disorder. The more one learns about this behaviour the more repelled one is liable to be.

A fashionable left wing view is that homophobes must be 'in denial' over their sexuality. But anyone can be said to be 'in denial' about any kind of behaviour in which they haven't actually indulged. We may be said to be 'in denial' over our propensity to kill and injury people, or any other obnoxious activity that we are all morally capable of stopping ourselves from perpetrating. The anti-homophobes are therefore in a morally indefensible position. We are all capable of being murderers. But if we deliberately avoid being a murderer, we might be said to be 'in denial' about our murdering propensities. If we conform to our true nature then we must give way to any feelings that we might have about murdering people. But of course we are deliberately being moral and law-abiding persons by refraining from doing so. Similarly, all men are potential rapists, therefore they must be 'in denial' if they don't give way to any desire to rape a woman. Moreover, adults have as much right as children to preserve their innocence and not to have such behaviour flaunted before them. In that respect, homosexuality in particular can be considered as bad as paedophilia.

It is not true that all homosexuals are genetically determined to some extent to become homosexual. Some of the most rampant and committed homosexuals have changed their ways and become heterosexual. The most obvious example of this phenomenon is the great economist John Maynard Keynes. For most of his life, no man was safe from his advances. Yet he suddenly amazed all his friends by marrying a ballerina and apparently living happily ever afterwards. It cannot be the case that Keynes did this because of social pressures or because he wanted to appear conventional in the eyes of society. He was so eminent that he could do as he pleased and could indeed act according to his maturing instincts. His Wikipedia biography states the following:

"In 1921, Keynes fell 'very much in love' with Lydia Lopokova, a well-known Russian ballerina, and one of the stars of Sergei Diaghilev's *Ballets Russes*. For the first years of the courtship, Keynes maintained an affair with a younger man, Sebastian Sprott, in tandem with Lopokova, but eventually chose Lopokova exclusively, on marrying her. They married in 1925. The union was happy, with biographer Peter Clarke writing that the marriage gave Keynes 'a new focus, a new emotional stability and a sheer delight of which he never wearied'"[23]

The only reasonable explanation for Keynes' changed behaviour is that he eventually outgrew his adolescent homosexuality and began to appreciate his potential as a real man. There is therefore hope for all homosexuals if they really want to change their habits and are prepared to work hard enough to change them over a lengthy period of time.

The blanket toleration of perversion is also intolerable. Any perversion is personally demeaning and degrading. It lessens the person enslaved by them. It is a deviation from an innocent and simple life-style that is the ideal for all of us. A perversion is basically the prolongation of a bad habit that can be overcome given the requisite time and effort. If this were not the case, it makes no sense to persecute and imprison paedophiles. If their perversion is a compulsion over which they have no control then there is no point in punishing them for it. The fact is that all perversions are potentially under people's control. They can change them over time if they really want to. It may take months or even years but it is humanly possible to do so, just as giving up other bad habits such as cigarettes, alcohol or hard drugs is humanly possible.

The degrading nature of deviant behaviour leads to a loss of shame and guilt concerning the moral decency of this behaviour. For example, notorious paedophiles such as J. Savile, R. Harris, and other celebrities caught up in the moral witch-hunt, clearly lost touch with all sense of shame and guilt about their obnoxious behaviour. They were so famous that there was no limit to what they got away with. Just as no one is above the law, however famous and powerful they are, so no one is above morality in terms of moral restraint and decent behaviour. Hence the need to make objective moral rules a part of subjective thinking so that we do good by force of habit instead of doing just what pleases us or makes us 'happy'.

H. The Abnormality of God-Belief

The normal society has no need for god-belief any more than it needs sun-worship as a religion. God-belief is as culturally irrelevant and out-dated as sun-worship. Nowadays, it serves only to divide people according to their varied and irreconcilable opinions concerning it and its unlikely existence. If God really exists then why are the various religions at complete loggerheads as to what it is and how to deal with it? So far from bringing the human race together, God serves only to ferment wars and conflict between the various god-believers. There are people today who shout 'God is Great' and shoot other people, blow themselves up or fly planes into buildings. There is nothing great about that. It is plain stupid. We can well do without this God. We are all the better for standing on our own feet without this god-crutch.

We are supposed to humble ourselves before a being superior to humanity. But we are already humbled by our infinitesimal insignificance in the universe. We are intimidated by all the possible catastrophes that could befall us. We don't need anything imaginary to grovel before when we know we could be wiped out by comets, earthquakes, volcanic eruptions, mega-tsunamis, solar flares, global pandemics, nuclear Armageddon, or whatever. These threats are dreadful enough but they can be faced without cowering behind a non-existent being. We can stand up for ourselves with courage and accept the fact is that there is no god. We are on our own. Only stone cold reality lies before us. We can learn to live with this fact. We can adapt to this new truth just as we have adapted to the idea that the earth really goes round the sun even though the sun seems to go round the earth. The revolving Earth makes it seem as if the sun is going round it. God belief can only be an excuse to hide away from reality instead of facing up to it in a manly and productive fashion.

It is fundamentally abnormal to believe in the existence of an entity that cannot be seen and of whose existence no clear evidence has ever been given. Worshipping the sun seems much more sensible as we can at least see its effects. Indeed, we can't live without it, therefore it has more right to be worshipped than this unseen God that does nothing at all for us. We don't worship the Sun nowadays in any religious sense because we know that its effects are explicable in scientific terms. As the universe is now largely explicable in scientific terms, there is now no need for any creative God making it all happen or interfering with it in any way.

The saying "He who does not believe in God will believe in anything" is wrongly attributed to G.K. Chesterton, (actually, it is a conflation of two sentences in his Father Brown stories[24]). But this is nonsense. Most Americans still believe in God, but it is they who believe in almost anything: the Da Vinci Files, alien abduction, we didn't land on the moon, Elvis lives; you name it and some daft American will believe in it. In fact, a belief in God makes you believe in anything, since that belief reduces your standards of rationality. If you believe that God exists then it is easy for you to believe in the existence of angels, aliens, the Holy Grail, or the immortal Elvis. God-belief thus makes people superstitious.

Ghosts and evil spirits are seen everywhere because their imaginations are overstimulated by belief in an imaginary being. Numbers take on a life of their own, for example, 666 is the mark of the evil beast in the Bible (Revelations 13:18). Thus, Route 666 in the USA is a highway replete with evil and misfortune simply because it was given that number by chance.

If we believe that God exists then we can equally say that Santa Claus exists, fairies exist, angels exist, aliens exist and so on. Anything can be said to exist if we want to believe in its existence. The reality is that these things only exist in a manner of speaking. They are no more than figments of our imagination. We need to face up to the stark reality that God is only a figment of our imagination. It is a cultural artefact that people needed to believe in the past but not any more. It is a convenient social construct that is relative to time and place. People's personal experience of the notion is induced more by social conditioning than by any evidence which can withstand impartial scrutiny. They believe because they have never needed or wanted to subject their beliefs to close examination.

God-believers believe in nothing since God is nothing. It is nothing but a big daddy! In fact, the poet William Blake mocked God by calling him 'Nobodaddy'. The following poem is in the works of William Blake for all to see.

Then old Nobodaddy aloft
Farted & belchd & coughd
And said I love hanging & drawing & quartering
Every bit as well as war & slaughtering

Then he swore a great & solemn Oath
To kill the people I am loth
But If they rebel they must go to hell
They shall have a Priest & a passing bell [25]

We are not genetically programmed for god belief as the notion can only be traced back three or four thousand years, perhaps to the pharaoh, Akhenaten, (1352-1336 BCE). His imposition of monotheistic beliefs had such disastrous effects on Egypt that his reforms were quickly reversed after his death and his name effaced from the records. So far from being natural, the Egyptians eagerly returned to their habitual polytheistic beliefs and forgot this untimely pharaoh. However, his beliefs may have lived on and influenced the Hebrew peoples, as is argued albeit unconvincingly by Freud in one of his last works, *Moses and Monotheism*.[26]

Religions such as Buddhism, Confucianism, Taoism and Shamanism have survived for centuries without any specific belief in God. The notion depends on a specific frame of mind which is usually established in childhood. It can easily be lost in adulthood when the lack of evidence for its existence strikes home (as in my case). The idea of a God that is personal to each of us may survive this lack of evidence. Thoughts and ideas emerging from our unconscious may be interpreted as god-given. But it is then impossible to distinguish thoughts and ideas that are malign, evil and the product of the devil, demons or evil spirits from those that are truly divine. Moreover, an uncritical person may assume that all their thoughts and ideas must be derived from God. This is precisely the mentality that led Hitler to say that his persecution of the Jews was directly sanctioned by God (see below for more on that). Any charlatan can say that their ideas have been given them directly by God, and who can prove them wrong?

There is of course the notion of God as a real physical possibility of something in the past bringing about the structure of the universe at its outset or ensuring its continuity from second to second. This kind of 'natural theology' is a wholly culturally relative phenomenon which formed part of pre-scientific attempts to explain the world in which past peoples found themselves. The idea that God is a real being dwelling somewhere or other is not only redundant and unnecessary, it is also dangerous and harmful. It is dangerous because it is irrational and can never be adequately comprehended unless anthropomorphically. We cannot really conceive of such an entity except in our own image and with conceptions which make sense to us. Until we are actually confronted with such a divine being, it can never be conceived as any more than our own selves writ large. In other words, we create God in our own image, not vice versa.

The idea of God as being the divinity within us, or the holy spirit, is equally redundant. Confining God to the depths of human soul merely prolongs the fiction rather than justifies it. It brings subjectivity to the fore which could as easily come from the devil or an evil spirit within us. There is no practical way of verifying whether we are being prompted by God or the devil. However, the idea of a subjective god or holy spirit may be a device to focus the mind on our perfectibility, but it is superfluous. We may have the feeling that there is something perfect existing somewhere because we can conceive of absolute perfection. But ideas and feelings are fuel for the imagination and do not necessarily have any real foundation. The idea of a perfect being is just another figment of our imagination. Notions such as those of good and bad, just and unjust serve the goal of perfectibility much more directly by pinpointing the aspects of perfection at which we may aim in our daily lives.

Because no rational agreement can be reached concerning what God is, it is a source of constant disagreement to the point of hatred and enmity between different sects of god believers. The more passionately they believe in their own particular notion, the more they fight and kill each other in defence of their particular beliefs. Since the notion is capable of an infinite variety of distinct interpretations, it is potentially a source of an infinite variety of beliefs, each competing with the others for intellectual attention and passionate adherence.

This partisan enmity arises because the notion of God is a subject of absolute belief instead of relative and limited belief. It demands an absolute and unqualified adherence because there are no limits to its possible application. In contrast, notions such as 'sociosphere' make no more demands on us than other abstractions such as 'society', and 'company'. Such abstractions are limited in their application because they refer to activities are purely human and subject to basic human rights. Also, they are no better or worse than the people conceiving them, whereas there are no limits to what an infinitely perfect being such as God can expect of human beings. We seemingly have no rights before God and its power over us has no end. Hence the immolation and self-mortification of the saint or ascetic who seeks perfection by self-denial while not doing anything worthy of humanity.

The notion of God is therefore dangerous to humanity because it can be used to justify all manner of evil deeds. Serial murderers regularly rationalise their killings as being sanctioned by the deity. It is often said that the mass murderers, Hitler and Stalin were atheists. In fact, Hitler said in *Mein Kampf* and in his speeches that he thought he was serving God in opposing the Jews. He claimed to be a God believer but this was probably because it suited his power-mad purposes. In any case, neither Hitler nor Stalin were humanists. As already mentioned in section 2 above, Hitler thought the human being is nothing but "*eine lächerliche Weltraumbakterie*"- 'a ridiculous cosmic bacterium'.[27] He had a withering contempt for the human race, for life, and for everything except the fulfilment of his own grandiose dreams. Hence his abysmal role in history. Likewise, Stalin had no regard for the value of human life. He executed hundreds of people, exiled thousands to Siberia, and allowed millions to die of famine, without any shame or conscience. Humanism, by contrast, values the individual human being. Are there any mass murdering humanists? Of course not; it is simply unthinkable. Preserving life in general is just what humanism is all about. The problem is that it is a relatively new creed. In its present form it only dates from the 1920s and 30s. It began as an ethical creed and remains so to this day. Perhaps its day has yet to come.

The notion of God makes us inhuman because it distracts us from our involvement in humanity. If there really were a God which clearly manifested its presence to us, then there would be no need for any of us to reach out to each other. We could then appeal directly to this being and ignore our fellow humans altogether. We might as well withdraw entirely from social interaction and live to ourselves alone, as did the ascetics and anchorites of the past. The internet is in danger of becoming such a god for many people who have no life outside of their computers: 'Who needs God when we have the internet!' We want to avoid thinking of the internet in these terms and perhaps need to humanise it before it takes over and enslaves us. Thus, the very notion of God is the enemy of human society and of the freedoms we have in that society. This applies, for example, to the notion of 'sinfulness' which in fact contributes to the workings of society, as Mandeville showed in his book, *The Fable of the Bees,* 'private vices' go along with 'public benefits'.[28] If women didn't have a private lust for shopping, our economy would collapse. The same applies to most of the 'vices' of the modern world.

Believing in a God above and beyond us, gives us unrealistic expectations of ourselves and others. It makes us intolerant of imperfections both in ourselves and others because we expect divine perfection instead of human foibles. We can barely live with ourselves or others when we see only how far short our behaviour is from such perfection. In short, god belief makes us inhuman towards ourselves and others, and intolerant towards everything that makes us human as opposed to superhuman. It is one thing to expect betterment or the best from each other but quite another to expect us to be divine and superhuman. This is a step too far and an unnecessary one at that.

God belief can also induce immoral behaviour and make people lie to themselves and others. They can say that they are doing in the name of God or because God told them to do so. No one can tell whether they are lying or fooling themselves. Social pressures on people to believe in God can make them insincere, dishonest and hypocritical because they put on a show of such a belief to impress or to gain respect and social advancement. No one can prove whether they do or do not believe in God since the appearance of doing so is all that is required. Similarly, clergy, priests, preachers and ministers may have no religious faith in their heart of hearts but they take oaths and vows simply because their profession demands it. To do good or simply to get a secure and undemanding job, they find it expedient to lie to themselves and deceive others as to their true beliefs.

The notion of God also harms our natural curiosity and desire to get to the bottom of things. Anything that seems inexplicable by scientific means is often said to be due to God or some kind of divine or supernatural intervention. A badly brain damaged baby survives and develops normally in spite of all medical prognoses to the contrary. This is therefore said to be due to divine intervention. But this conclusion insults the inner strength of the baby. It requires no outer intervention since it possesses immense inner strength and physical organisation which enabled it to survive and thrive. Invoking God is a patronising explanation which is superfluous to a real and lasting account of the matter. Using God to explain what is otherwise inexplicable therefore demeans our spirit of inquiry. The fact that some event cannot be readily explained by science challenges us to use our ingenuity and skills to find a satisfactory explanation. Anything less is laziness and intellectual cowardice on our part, and religion is too easily used as an excuse for this.

The notion also harms us when it is used to absolve human beings of their accountability and responsibility for themselves and their own lives. Such a rejection of accountability is characteristic of the immature and unfree person who seeks security in some parental figure to whom he clings in a childlike fashion. In contrast, the mature and free adult is confident of his own abilities in relation to the opportunities that life gives him. He can take responsibility for himself and his own actions without appealing to any external agency.

Being a mature adult consists partly in being accountable for the whole human race because of the unavoidability of belonging to it, for good or ill. We are responsible for the human race because each of us is human, and a product and microcosm of the universe as a whole. Maturity means being realistic about our place in the universe and our responsibility for life and for the well being of the planet. If we are mature then we don't need to pass on to God this responsibility for the consequences of human deeds. We can see for ourselves what is or is not wrong with the human race and its activities. We can judge for ourselves what can or cannot be done about its errors and deficiencies. Therefore, there is no point of leaving problems to God when we are perfectly capable of handling them for ourselves, even if we can only do so imperfectly. Leaving them to God only ensures that they won't be handled at all. Moreover, by taking on this responsibility we can at least hope to get better at dealing with these problems.

Even if God did exist, we can well do without him. The notion of God has now fulfilled its useful function in taking humanity through that stage of adolescent dependence and uncertainty which preceded the development of scientific and technological knowledge. The latter now gives us power over our own destiny, plus all the responsibilities which accompany that power. We may yet lack the moral fibre to carry out these responsibilities consistently and resolutely, but they are still within our capabilities. And the humanist view can supply the moral framework and intellectual tools by which we can live up to our responsibilities, both as individuals and as a species.

Christian apologists such as Dietrich Bonhoeffer have acknowledged this view in saying that we have 'come of age' and no longer need the parental support of God:

> God is teaching us that we must live as men who can get along very well without him... God allows himself to be edged out of the world, and that is exactly the way, the only way, in which he can be with us and help us.[29]

But the plain fact is that we can do without him because he never existed in the first place. It is the certainty of the latter conclusion which has led to his being 'edged out'. We do not even need him to allow us to do any 'edging' at all. We are doing it on our own. It casts aspersions on our own achievements to assume that there is a God allowing it all to happen when clearly there is nothing there to stop us from doing and thinking what we like for good or ill.

Karen Armstrong, a former nun, concludes her book, *A History of God,* by saying that the concept of God may be outdated but if we are to substitute it with something else, we must pay attention to the lessons to be had from studying the deep-rooted yearning for God which the history of the subject reveals to us.

> Human beings cannot endure emptiness and desolation; they will fill the vacuum by creating a new focus of meaning. The idols of fundamentalism are not good substitutes for God; if we are to create a vibrant new faith for the twenty-first century, we should, perhaps, ponder the history of God for some lessons and warnings.[30]

It is more important to have faith in life and humanity and in the possibilities of making for a better future than to have yet another religious faith. A religion harks back to the past and does not look to the future. It is retrospective and not prospective, to use the terms explained above. The notion of god is not just 'an aberration' but also harmful to the spirit and abilities of human beings. For that reason, it clearly has no useful role to play in our society.

> Throughout history, men and women have experienced a dimension of the spirit that seems to transcend the mundane world. Indeed, it is an arresting characteristic of the human mind to be able to conceive concepts that go beyond it in this way.[31]

But conceiving of the possibility of things beyond our ken is distinct from believing in their actual existence. As already argued, we can speculate as much as we like about their existence. It is natural for us to speculate about such matters as it helps our inner development. However, it is unnatural for us to believe absolutely in their existence because it impairs our ability to distinguish between fact and fiction. Anything can be imagined to exist in reality if we so wish. But we then live in our imaginations instead of in the real world out there. Thus, this spiritual dimension can best be accounted for in a dualist system of thought, since in that system we interact with external reality and not with non-existent entities. Such an interaction enables us to correct our imaginations and move forward towards a more realistic future.

A great simplification in human affairs is therefore achieved by casting aside the notion of God as having anything to do with us in the universe as it is. Attempting to find a place in the universe for this notion makes things unnecessarily complicated and unfathomable. Great mental contortions are called for in accommodating this notion in the material scheme of things. For example, since Spinoza and Newton marginalised the activities of God in the universe, innumerable writers, from Samuel Clarke and Andrew Baxter onwards, applied immense effort and ingenuity in finding a place for God in the gaps left by the physical sciences. But it is all to no avail. No agreement has ever been reached and the conclusive evidence is still lacking while the almighty obstinately maintains his habitual inscrutability and illusiveness, that is to say, his complete nonexistence.

Attempts to prove or disprove the existence of God are superfluous. It is as easy to prove or disprove as the existence any other social or cultural artefact - Santa Claus, inflation, the euro, or whatever. What matters are the effects and consequences of acting upon such a belief. There cannot be many people who continue writing letters to Santa Claus well into adulthood. People usually grow out of their need to believe in Santa Claus. However, the notion of God remains useful because it gives people a way of bringing more meaning into their lives and because it leads their thinking into a wider dimension. These aspects may now be taken over by the humanist view, and the notion of God can be consigned to the history books.

Summarising the advantages of not believing in god. These advantages can be summarised as follows:

➢ *Our Self-Reliance* - that we are entirely responsible for ourselves and our own future. This demands courage and ingenuity on our part. Taking on this responsibility is a challenge which we cannot refuse without demeaning ourselves in our own eyes. Though it is demanding, it is better to rely on our own resources than depend on a mere fiction to look after us. Our existence as a species only makes sense in so far as we keep moving forward to better things instead of clinging to past illusions. We need to be clear about why this consequence is unavoidable, what the better things might consist in, and how we can move towards them.

➢ *Our Self-Sufficiency* - that we can now be responsible for ourselves and our future as we are already self-sufficient in having the tools of science, reason and common sense to make a success of our existence on this planet. What we lack is the insight and rationale by which to make the best possible use of these tools. This deficiency can be remedied by showing how we can use these tools to carry out our obligations in ensuring the future of our species and of life and the biosphere in general.

➢ *Our Collective Responsibility* - that we are alone responsible as a species for what we are doing to our environment and the planet in general. We are responsible because we have insight into and knowledge of our misdeeds in that regard. We know that we could do better in harnessing and nurturing the resources of this planet, but we need to act collectively and co-operatively to rectify the errors of the past. God belief divides us and spoils our ability to act in unison for the benefit of life on Earth. Also, the fact that we are capable of doing better means doing our best to rectify our errors and deficiencies. Exactly what needs to be done is a matter for practical politics.

➢ *Purveyors of Purposefulness* - that there is no more reason or purpose in the universe than what we ourselves introduce by our most reasonable and purposeful acts and aspirations. So far from demeaning us, this view enhances our importance in the universe. In common with other living creatures, we introduce purposefulness into a mechanical, chaotic universe whose contents make no more sense than we are able to make of them. Thus, the importance of the universe depends on what we make of it by our purposeful activities in it. We need to clarify the nature of purposefulness and how we introduce it into the universe.

➢ *Validators of Value* - that however insignificant we may be in relation to the vastness of the universe, we are still important in that no other life-form, to our present knowledge, contributes as much as we do to the significance and value of the universe, for instance, by acquiring knowledge of its contents and how it functions. We are privileged to confer or withhold value according to our considered judgment as to what is or is not valuable. We need to investigate the nature of value and how that value is altered by our acquisition and use of knowledge concerning life and the universe. This is important because, for instance, it provides the means of overseeing scientific activity and of monitoring its true value and significance.

➢ *Valuing Our Inner Being* - that we are now free to reach within ourselves and find sufficient spirit and reason to do what we have to do in the interests of life on this planet. What is within us is enough to make the difference and no external agency is needed to support us in these matters. But there is no avoiding the hard work and self-discipline that is required to make this difference. There is no denying the need for co-operation and the need to be clear about the directions in which that co-operative effort may be usefully applied. It indicates the available alternatives but decisions must still be made concerning what must be done in scientific, political, and practical terms.

➢ *Valuing Our Capabilities* - that the idea of God within each of us is no more than the notion of perfectibility which a holistic view of our capabilities makes possible. The idea may have originated as a forbidding Father in the skies whose anger expressed itself in thunder and lightening. But Platonist philosophy abstracted the idea into the perfect craftsman or designer of the cosmos. The notion thereafter incorporated ideal capabilities towards which intelligent beings might aspire. We need no longer attribute these possibilities to a being totally distinct from ourselves since it is we who are imagining its capabilities. And the latter can be no more nor better than the capabilities of intelligent beings whom we conceive to be more advanced than ourselves.

➢ *Valuing Our Humanity* - that anthropomorphic appeals to God are really abstract appeals to humanity as a whole. For example, the practical effect of doing something for 'the greater glory of God' is to benefit humankind in respect of present or future generations. But substituting God for humanity also has the impractical effect of alienating us as a species from our own achievements and their good and bad consequences. The result is that religious people attribute good things to God and bad things to the Devil, instead of admitting our direct responsibility for both good and bad.

➢ *Valuing Our Solitude* - that the nature of our relationship to the universe is puzzling enough without the additional mystery posed by the unfathomable nature of God. It is simpler to put aside the notion of God and contemplate our solitary place in the universe. To the best of our present knowledge we are alone, but we hope that some day we will contact intelligent beings out there somewhere. We lie to ourselves in clinging to a creator and pretending that he takes care of us. And we must learn to value our solitude instead of running away from it.

➢ *Valuing Our Universe* - that we should value the universe as something belonging to us and accessible to us, unlike God. It is a source of delight and wonder in itself. The more we understand it, the more we make it our own. We can now understand the universe as being entirely self- subsistent. Arguably, it requires no external agency to bring it into existence or to supply it with initial conditions to get it started. The fact that it came into existence at all is what really concerns us. The notion of a creator is an easy way out which stops us thinking about it and brings the inquiry to a premature end.

➢ *Valuing the Cosmos* – that the celebration of human achievements is contained in the notion of Cosmos as discussed in section 12 below on *Finality*. Everything that is potentially divine about us is expressible as contributing to the entirely human notion of Cosmos. We can bequeath this to the universe as being the ultimate vindication of our existence on this tiny planet, and God has nothing to do with it.

10. Servility: Serving Humanity Dutifully

> A man is already of consequence in the world when it is known that he can be relied on — that when he says he knows a thing, he does know it — that when he says he will do a thing, he can and does it. Thus, reliableness becomes a passport to the general esteem and confidence of mankind.
>
> Samuel Smiles (1871).[1]

A. How We Can Serve Humanity

If we are to work together to achieve the future aims of society, we must be prepared to serve one another. This means making ourselves useful in one capacity or another. It does not mean making an abject slave out of ourselves. Humanity must be suborned to the individual and not the other way round which is the authoritarian way. The humanistic view is that humanity must serve us as much as we serve humanity. Moreover, we are all humanists by virtue of belonging to the human race. Not to be a humanist is to be barely human, but a slave to the creeds of some dictator, priest, mullah or whatever. Thus, the role of humanists is that of serving humanity, both as individuals and as a collective species, with a view to being served by humanity in our turn.

We show how much we value other people by serving them. If we are wise we do not live for ourselves alone but enjoy serving and pleasing other people as well as ourselves. It is natural for us to commit ourselves to the service of other people. In a sense we are born to serve each other, and it is only human to make ourselves useful to each other. We normally do this quite naturally when we are getting something worthwhile in return for our servitude, for example, a good living wage. In serving other people we put them at the centre of our world but only within the limited purposes of the service we wish to perform. We start with individuals and work our way up to humanity as a whole. The individual is more important than humanity as every single human being is an indispensible part of humanity.

If we cut ourselves away entirely from other people, we risk making ourselves less than human. Being human means interacting with others to bring out our unique human traits. Our common humanity alone brings us together. It is natural for us to have fellow feelings for every human being on the planet and not allow our ideas, beliefs or opinions to diminish these feelings or lessen our view of them. The plight of each person on Earth is our common concern.

Service is not slavery as long as we are acting from own freewill and are being treated with the dignity and respect due to every human being. In that respect, being of service to others is fulfilling and liberating. When service stops being fulfilling and liberating then it is indistinguishable from slavery. But it all depends on how we see the role ourselves. We may willingly make slaves of ourselves and not think we are slaves. One of the unfortunate consequences of socialist/communist thinking was that servants and workers were seen as making slaves of themselves. According to that view, we should all be equal as working human beings. The collapse of the serving class as prominent feature in our society resulted from this mistaken point of view. People were metaphorically turned out into the streets to fend for themselves, thus creating a society of loners. The leisure class is no longer composed only of rich people but also of poor people who live permanently on benefits. In contrast, a society in which people willingly become servants is more cohesive as people come together to live with and for each other. For example, the 17th century musketeers in Alexandre Dumas's novel *The Three Musketeers* are portrayed as having their own 'valets' who acted as servants, even though the musketeers themselves were as poverty-stricken as their servants, who were nevertheless happy in that role.

The fact is that we are not all equal human beings and we thrive on our differences. Attempts to iron out our economic and social differences are bound to cause more grief than relief. We are all equal in being different from each other, and the fairest society maximises our opportunities to make the most of our differences without depriving anyone of their opportunities. A society based on our serving one another in one capacity or another arguably gives us all the best chance of attaining the ideal of equal opportunities for all. Too much emphasis on equality has the paradoxical effect of exacerbating competition between people as they strive to differentiate themselves in a society of undifferentiated equals. We need to work together, not against each other.

Co-operation is more important than competition. We have evolved to be a co-operative as well as a competitive species. We progress by balancing these two tendencies. But the unity and survival of society depends more on co-operation than on competition. Serving one another is the best way for us to co-operate towards the common ends of humanity. Our unity depends on a culture of service more than on a culture of competition. The most progressive periods in our history have been those in which service has been to the fore, even though other aspects of everyday life such as war, famine and plague might not have been so propitious. Therefore, co-operation is more important to our survival than competition. The latter only makes sense when we are vying with each other to better our service to others. The most successful organisations under capitalism are those that are more efficient in their service provision than in their profit-making. Internet companies such as Amazon and Google became successful because of the efficiency of their service and only later did they become exorbitantly profitable. The most popular organisations in the UK are the BBC and the National Health Service, neither of which make profits. Also, Wikipedia is obviously an entirely voluntary organisation whose service is universally used and appreciated.

We vindicate ourselves through serving the needs of other people, humanity and life forms in general. Our common humanity consists in making ourselves available for such services and this makes us feel that we belong and are a part of the whole. Also, our daily lives would be impossible without the service of others when we buy goods and services, seek to be entertained and so on. It is only right and just that we should serve others in our turn. Our very survival as a species depends our willingness to serve each other. Our civilisation would cease to exist if we all lived for ourselves alone like male orang-utans. When we know that other people are devoted to serving us honestly and to the best of their abilities, we can trust and rely on them unconditionally. Thus, service is a necessary prerequisite to trust and reliability in our social relationships.

Our security depends on other people being willing to be of service to us. For example, the idea of service to the community offers a way of tackling the problems of internet privacy, snooping, and exploitation. We would be more confident that internet organisations are acting in our best interests if their use of internet information is shown to be strictly in our service. Our interests must be paramount in the access and use of internet information about the people's personal lives and activities. These organisations should be obliged to keep us informed and to demonstrate periodically their commitment to this prime principle of service.

B. Service by Counselling

Counselling of all kinds helps people. We can serve our fellow human beings particularly well by counselling them. This may mean no more than giving them useful advice or giving them help to understand their problems better. It can therefore be performed either professionally or personally. In the past, it was left entirely to religious people to offer counselling to people. But this is increasingly unacceptable, especially when so many priests and clergy are shown to use their profession for their own personal, prurient purposes.

The tendency of religion is to counsel its servants to keep them enslaved to its orthodox beliefs. Its fault lies in making people the means to the end of religion instead of being ends in themselves. Religion gives comfort by offering absolute certainties. In doing so, it does not help people inside themselves. A listening counsellor is liable to be more helpful with people's problems than the canting preacher, as the psychologist, Anthony Storr noted:

> If anyone is in urgent need of help or guidance, let him find someone who will listen rather than preach; someone who will encourage him to look inward and find out what he as a unique individual thinks and believes, rather than accepting some guru's dogma.[2]

Counselling is best performed by professionals who are trained and experienced in helping people. But we can also vindicate ourselves in the counselling that we offer others in our daily lives, when they come to us in times of need. The great Roman writer, Seneca (4BCE – 65CE) summed up the whole thing in this passionate piece of prose:

> Shall I tell you what philosophy offers humanity? Counsel [*consilium*]. One person is facing death, another is vexed by poverty, while another is tormented by wealth – whether his own or someone else's; one man is appalled by his misfortunes while another longs to get away from his own prosperity; one man is suffering at the hands of men, another at the hands of the gods. What's the point of concocting whimsies for me of the sort I've just been mentioning? This isn't the place for fun – you've called in to help the unhappy. You're pledged to bring succour

to the shipwrecked, to those in captivity, to the sick, the needy, and men who are just placing their heads beneath the executioner's uplifted axe. Where are you off to? What are you about? The person you're joking with is in fear. Help him and take the noose from his neck. All humanity are stretching out their hands to you on all sides. Lives that have been ruined, lives that are on the way to ruin are appealing for some help; it is to you that they look for hope and assistance. They are begging you to extricate them from this awful vortex, to show them in their doubt and disarray the shining torch of truth. Tell them what nature has made necessary and what she has made superfluous. Tell them how simple are the laws she has laid down, and how straightforward and enjoyable life is for those who follow them and how confused and disagreeable it is for others who put more trust in popular ideas than they do in nature.[3]

Counselling therefore serves humanity when it really and genuinely helps people. It may not do so if it is imposed on them as a matter of form. Not everyone wants or needs counselling and they should have a choice in the matter. Its role is diminished if it becomes compulsory or enforceable in any way, since it no longer serves but becomes a bureaucratic imposition that interferes with freedom of choice. It then no longer serves real needs but becomes a bureaucratic imposition that interferes with freedom of choice.

C. Service as Being Essential to Society

Capitalism as a form of service. Capitalist society is often seen a competitive more than a co-operative enterprise but this is a distorted view of it. It is important to distinguish between a humane form of capitalism, which aims to serve the public, and an inhumane form which is competitive and inhumane.[4] Extreme forms of capitalism do not prioritise service as they put profit and power before service. However, the best forms of capitalism do bring service to the fore. In the 19th century, the American industrialist, Andrew Carnegie promulgated an inhumane form of capitalism as he was influenced by the dog-eat-dog Social Darwinism of Herbert Spencer.[5] In direct opposition to this approach, the great motor manufacturer, Henry Ford, stressed the importance of service to civilisation and the workings of our economy.[6] He put it this way:

> The spirit of service is just a knowledge that no man can survive, no industry can survive, no government can survive, no system of civilisation can survive which does not continually give service to the greatest possible number. The only interest one can have in anything is the service one gets from it or gives to it.[7]

In his form of capitalism, service comes before profit:

> Without a profit, business cannot extend. There is nothing inherently wrong about making a profit. Well-conducted business enterprise cannot fail to return a profit, but profit must and inevitably will come as a reward for good service. It cannot be the basis – it must be the result of service.[8]

Henry Ford effectively changed society for the better by putting consumer service before profit and by improving the wages and conditions of his workers. He also changed people's views of capitalism which had hitherto been seen as entirely oppressive and exploitative.

The fact is that service capitalism can increase wages and improve standards of living. In direct opposition to the profiteering policies of industrialists such as Carnegie, Ford increased his workers' wages, reduced their working hours while at the same time reducing the price of his cars. When this was done for the first time in 1914, it revolutionised capitalism and set the scene for the consumer society of the 20th century. The ever-improving living standards of workers in the western world were the direct result of his policies. At first, his initiative met with vehement opposition from his fellow industrialists who believed that his example would ruin them financially. On the contrary, his view of consumer capitalism became the norm as it was found that everyone benefited from his enlightened policies. It made possible the trickle-down effect by which organisations use their increasing profits to increase wages proportionately. People's standards of living grew year by year as their wages and salaries were increased year by year. They had more money to spend and it became norm for economies to grow year by year. In this way, money and capital served people's needs as Ford stated:

> The highest use of capital is not to make more money, but to make money do more service for the betterment of life.[9]

Ford's view was that everyone belongs to the consuming class. Thus, his service capitalism completely demolishes the Marxist view of a society having competing classes. He puts us all in the same class in that we are all equal members of the consumer class. In that way, we are all served equally by industry and commerce. So far from being exploited by big business, we are supposed to be served by them. As against class-obsessed Marxism, Ford recognised only one class—the class of consumers that includes everyone. He therefore promoted and popularized the idea of the consumer society. "All are Members of the Consuming Class" is the title of one of his newspaper articles.[10] Therein he argues that the class division between labour and capital is economically inadmissible since the important point is that both are consumers:

> By the law of nature we are all consumers. Rich or poor, learned or ignorant, it does not matter—every living organism consumes the material of life, and for us this means mostly food for the body and the material necessities of residence on the earth.[11]

Nowadays, the success of online companies such as Amazon is due largely to their putting the customer first. Indeed, Amazon's founder, Jeff Bezos is on record as saying: "We start with the customer and work backwards". This ensured that Amazon survived the bursting of dotcom bubble in spite of not being profitable till 2001[12] and not reliably so since then.

Ford also thought that money is meant to serve and not exploit us. His view was that the monetary system exists to be our servant and to facilitate the 'transportation' of goods and services. By that he meant that money helps us to interact with each other and fulfil our needs and aspirations. One can argue further and say that the real wealth of society lies not in money but in people and what they do with their lives. Money can be used to measure the value of what we do for each other, though it is not the only means of doing so. It is our servant and is supposed to be used as a means to our ends. When it becomes an end in itself, we become enslaved to it. This is what happened in the recent banking crises. Ford warned very strongly against making credit the basis of our economy:

> Any system of business in which the money lender too conspicuously thrives is not a truly prosperous system. The greater the spread between the supply and the need, the more middlemen squeezed in between production and use, the heavier is the drag on the nation's prosperity. Credit is an admirable device when it lessens the spread, but when it increases the spread it becomes an enemy to economic health.[13]

Unfortunately, service capitalism is no longer as dominant in society as it once was. The financial sector in particular does not serve us in the way that it should. The spread of middlemen that Ford warned us about has continued and credit is sold by them in the form of ever more obscure and precarious bundles of credit. Financial institutions are becoming increasingly 'leveraged' as their balance sheets contain more and more assets that are founded on people's debts and are therefore dependent on these debts being repaid at some stage, which may never happen.

Originally, our banks served the public by attracting people's savings to lend them to businesses. At present, banks are offering such low interest rates that they are deterring savers from giving them their money. To obtain money to lend to businesses, the banks must borrow money from the central banks at near zero interest rates. They also make money by selling on their credit risks in the form of derivatives, hypothecated mortgages and the like.

All this adds to the growing credit bubble which fuels limited inflation combined with low economic growth (i.e. 'stagflation'). Wages and salaries are no longer being increased year by year according to the Fordian formula. As consumers cannot keep pace with increasing credit and mortgage interest, they must borrow increasingly more to maintain their standard of living, thus contributing to the credit bubble. Instead of building enough houses to meet the demand for them, people are being encouraged to take out loans to pay for increasingly overvalued property, thus creating a housing bubble. In short, the financial system no longer serves the interests of the public but only those who are making money by manipulating money and credit. Whether all these bubbles can be deflated before they burst, remains to be seen.

Thus, the financial sector seems to serve itself more than it serves the public. It is becoming enslaved to making money for itself. Clearly, service of any kind has its limitations. Taken to extremes, it leads to slavery. This is evident in this quotation attributed without reference to Mahatma Gandhi: "The best way to find yourself is to lose yourself in the service of others." This is the nearest way to lose your personal identity and become enslaved to the will of other people. It is an extreme view of service that tends to make slaves of us. We must also preserve our own personal integrity as individuals amid all our servitude.

Ideally, all forms of service ought to be adequately recompensed. This is not the case nowadays with voluntary service which is borderline slavery. Though people work voluntarily in charity shops, hospitals etc., it does not serve the economy well. As a minimum wage is legally enforced, it makes little sense that people are working for no wage whatsoever. Their being paid would contribute to the economy and increase GDP. At the other extreme, successful entertainers and sports persons receive exorbitant sums that far exceed their real importance to society. We can all benefit from being suitably and justly rewarded for the service that we render to humanity. It is necessary and unavoidable that we work towards such a just and fair society even though its complete realisation may recede rainbow-like into the distance.

D. Serving Society through the Civil Covenant

We serve society and it serves us in its turn. Throughout our lives we serve society in one way or another simply by being rational people doing reasonable things. This means behaving in a friendly and sociable way on most occasions, despite provocations or adverse distractions. By being sociable people we make society more tolerable for other people. Society is after all no more than all of us interacting together to get through our daily lives as comfortably and happily as we can. But it is also useful to think of our relationship to society in formal terms. We serve society and society serves us, so that, whether we like it or not, there is a formal relationship going on which only lacks a name. Also, serving others inevitably means serving society as every human relationship is a part of society as a whole.

In so far as we submit to the two-way service of society we enter into an implicit *civic covenant*. This is not to be confused with what was called a 'social contract' which was a legalistic concept to be imposed on the individual by the authorities. The civic covenant is here seen as a matter of individual choice. We enter this covenant on becoming socially responsible persons who choose to take their place in society as free citizens. In entering this covenant, we pay for our freedoms by taking on various obligations and responsibilities. In return, society gives us the facilities and organisations we need in living our lives freely and responsibly. In that way, the civic covenant involves two-way obligations – a give-and-take involving both society and the individual.

In giving of our best, we need to know where we stand and what is expected of us. To maintain the social structure, some basic obligations and responsibilities should be laid down. For instance, the right to freedom of self-expression may accompany an obligation to marry, have children and be responsible for raising a family. Such a promotion of normal family life secures a base for the healthy flourishing of the personality.

Moreover, the civil covenant has moral rather than legal force. We enter into the civic covenant of our own freewill. It is not to be enforced by society in any legal or authoritarian manner. It is only binding on the individual's conscience as it has moral rather than legal force. The civil covenant can be taught in schools so that it becomes the product of education and social expectation. It can help to sharpen up young people's moral sense and sensitivity in particular. Basically, it means behaving ourselves and being answerable to other people. In that way, we may rationalise and socialise our behaviour. In short, we are expected to behave in a sociable way and the civic covenant merely reflects that expectation. The civil covenant is only important from a legal point of view in that it obviates the need for endless prohibitive legal enactments that infringe our freedoms and turn society into a legalistic police state ruled by police, lawyers and judges. It can therefore contribute to our liberation from the restrictive legalism that is currently intruding into every part of our private lives. It does so by appealing to our moral sense and becoming part of our habits of thought instead of being imposed on us legally.

The civil covenant is therefore quite distinct from the age-old notion of a 'social contract'. From Hobbes onwards, this contract was a legal one in which individuals submitted to the authority of government for protection, justice and the rule of law. The civil covenant differs in being made by each individual with themselves and for themselves alone. Thus, the 'original contract' is not with groups combining for self-protection and justice (*vide* Hobbes, Locke, Hume, Rousseau, Kant, Rawls, Nozick, *et al*), but with our individual selves opting into society with all its obligations and responsibilities for our own personal purposes to reap the opportunities and benefits for oneself alone. In being part of the legal system, the social contract is imposed on people instead of being understood as being part of the way we live and take our part in society.

Anyone engaging in anti-social behaviour is not adhering to any social covenant but to their own selfish concerns that take no account of other people's interests. Thus, the source of anti-social behaviour can be seen in the individual's personal failings. It is not solely a matter of law-breaking but mainly a failure to see that it is in their own interests to serve society and thereby serve themselves. Terrorists, sociopaths and hardened criminals break the covenant by alienating themselves and making a personal war on society. They have lost all respect for society because they no longer see a place for themselves in it. If they are taught to see the benefits of society in the light of the social covenant, this may help to obviate their alienation. It clarifies the fact that anti-social behaviour is not in their overall interests as unique individuals having a unique role to play in society.

The civil covenant reflects that fact that moral progress comes from within and cannot be enforced by society. We also make moral progress in our expectations of each other's behaviour. For instance, it is no longer acceptable to behaviour for men to ill-treat or abuse women or children, or to treat them as sex objects. Also, we are no longer allowed to give way with impunity to our feelings and impulses like animals. These expectations are learnt by people as part of their education and social upbringing. Their minds become tuned to the expectations of society and there is no need for these expectations to be enforced by fear of authority or legalistic sanctions. Moral progress is possible but only to the extent that moral self-discipline is taught and appreciated by everyone as responsible individuals.

E. The Contextual Limits to Service

The importance of putting things into context. There are no limits to service unless we put things into their proper context. For example, the demands put on slaves are limitless as they exist only in the context of serving their masters. There is no context within which they can exist for themselves alone. We avoid being slaves by limiting the period or type of out service to the context in which it takes place. For example, job contracts typically lay down the terms of employment and the job specification that make clear what is or is not expected of the employee. Contexts also help us to clarify our role in society so that we are better equipped to find our own place in society that suits our unique personalities. They also help us to expand our view in general and help us to be better and more rounded personalities. Thus, our view of things can be expanded by using contexts, viewpoints or perspectives.

The importance of putting things into context. When we put things into the widest context we adopt a holistic view that looks at things from afar. As we recede from things, they blend together, reduce to one thing and ultimately fade into insignificance. But when we focus in on what we are observing or thinking about, we can differentiate the contents and the parts. It is at this point, that we need to put things into context in differentiating one thing from another. Thus, unity is not a single, indispensible, static thing. Everything is presented to us at any moment of time as a complete unity to which we can react or not react accordingly. When we react to what is before us, we pay attention to particular things. To make sense of these things, we put them into some context or other. In watching television, we don't just see a succession of unconnected images, we also put them in the context of news, a feature film, a play, a comedy or whatever programme we happen to be watching. A person suddenly transported into a crowded room would wonder where they are and what is going on. On being told it is a party, they are then able to put it into context. The sufferer of Alzheimer's disease is typically unaware of where they are and what they are supposed to be doing. They have lost the ability to put themselves into context. As a result, they have lost touch with themselves, since the self depends on contexts to sustain its continuity. We make sense of ourselves by constantly putting ourselves in different contexts as we work our way through our daily lives. This act of putting things into context is here called 'contextualisation'.

Thus, our view of things can be established and expanded by using contexts, viewpoints or perspectives. These expand our outlook by taking us beyond the narrow limits of self. They also help us to divide up our activities and cope with them on a one-to-one basis. We can reconcile ourselves more easily to the role we can play in serving humanity by this process. Through contextualisation we can make more sense of the middle ground in which we find ourselves. We put things into context to get things done in the world. Thus, contextualisation plays an important role in expanding our view of things. For example, the appearance of an infectious disease in any part of the world leads us to put it in the context of a possible pandemic and we then act accordingly to eradicate the disease before it spreads to pandemic proportions. If we do not contextualise this occurrence in that way, then we dismiss it as a problem in a remote part of the world which is of no concern to us. Hence the importance of contextualisation in keeping us aware of problems that affect the entire human race and are not just confined to nations or isolated regions. The failure to put things into contexts is at the root of many misunderstandings and disputes that have led to needless wars and divisions between people.

By contextualisation, we expand our view of things and incorporate disparate opinions and points of view into our general view of ourselves and of what we are doing with ourselves and where we are going. This can be illustrated by using what are here called *Hieroclean Circles*. These are named in honour of, Stoic philosopher, Hierocles, who lived in the second century CE, and who was apparently the first used the metaphor of circles to describe our relationships with other people and the outside world.[14] Thus, contextualisation as a way of thinking originated in antiquity.

The eight concentric Hieroclean circles. Hierocles envisaged a person's mind and body forming a small circle around which were eight concentric circles. The first three circles included one's parents, wife and other relatives. The next three circles included one's neighbours and fellow cities. The eighth circle incorporated one's country or nation, the last that of humanity as a whole. "The outermost and greatest circle, and which comprehends all the other circles, is that of the whole human race."[15] We can go beyond the circle of humanity and include such circles as those of life, posterity, and the universe at large. The individual's task is to bring all the circles into himself and to be at one with them.

This view may be considered self-centred or self-regarding, but it has the opposite effect of taking us beyond ourselves and our selfish concerns. We put ourselves and our selfish concerns into a diminished context by entering the Hieroclean Circles that make us see the importance of things beyond ourselves. We think of things beyond our own narrow perspective. We do so by adding different outlooks to our perspective. This process could go too far and we loose touch with ourselves. If we leave ourselves altogether, we tend to identify ourselves entirely with God, ideas and become narrow-minded fanatics and extremists. We need to retain a humble view of ourselves at the centre of the universe's unimaginable vastness and complexity. By these circles, we can stay in touch with ourselves while incorporating as well as we can the complexities of other viewpoints. The poet, Alexander Pope well understood how these circles extend our concerns beyond those of self alone:

> "Self love but serves the virtuous mind to wake,
> As the small pebble stirs the peaceful lake,
> The centre moved, a circle straight succeeds,
> Another still, and still another spreads,
> Friend, parent, neighbour first it will embrace,
> His country next, and next all human race;
> Wide and more wide the o'erflowings of the mind,
> Take every creature in of every kind."[16]

Hieroclean circles can help us, for example, to deal with moral dilemmas. They are an antidote to the selfishness implicit in the so-called 'prisoner's dilemma' problems.[17] Such dilemmas assume us to be very narrowly selfish individuals who live entirely within the circle of our own interests. In thinking outside the circle of narrow-minded selfishness, the individual is in no dilemma about how to maximise his or her advantage *vis-à-vis* that of other 'prisoners'. Resistance fighters captured by the Gestapo suffered torture and death rather than betray their comrades even though it was to their advantage to tell all. Early Christian martyrs faced no dilemmas as they consistently thought outside the box and deliberately suppressed their own immediate interests because they had higher concerns in mind. In short, it is quite unnatural for us to be as narrowly selfish as these dilemmas assume.

Hieroclean circles act as contexts that add to our view of things. We move from the context of self to that of family, from family to society and humanity, and then onto the contexts of life, posterity and the universe. We broaden our minds in this way and hopefully blunt our prejudices and lessen our dogmatic propensities. Thus, avoiding the extremes of religious and idealist thinking requires us to broaden our perspectives beyond ourselves and our egotistical concerns. What seems real, important and indubitable in one context can seem trivial and mean in another context. For example, buying new clothes for a job interview may seem vitally important in the context of one's daily life, but it is fairly unimportant in the context of world poverty in which many people worry about having something to eat, let alone what clothes to wear. The plight of the poor become of personal importance to us when we see things in that perspective – 'no man is an island entire of itself' – as John Donne put it.[18] We are all a part of the whole and everyone's concerns are ultimately mine also.

These circles are also spheres of activity within which we function. The various circles can be viewed three-dimensionally as spheres, each of which encompasses a whole viewpoint. They may be drawn two-dimensionally but in our thinking about them they each form a whole sphere. Thus, the spheres of self, family, society, humanity, life, universe and posterity are outlined below in terms of how they relate to each other in our thinking about them. These contexts are only examples of the meaning in our lives that we can find within them. They might also help to unify us as human beings within wider spheres of activity. They show that humanity is not to be considered the be-all and end-all of our existence. When we think of the plight of other people we do so from their perspective and therefore enlarge our own thinking beyond our selfish concerns.

F. Serving Humanity through Contextualisation

Using specific contexts to contextualise humanity. Contextualisation means putting things in context for some worthy purpose which is often beyond our selfish concerns. Thus, non-self-serving contextualisation means serving others or making ourselves useful to them. We are more inclined to do this when we put ourselves in contexts beyond those of our own concerns.   The contextualisation process is here illustrated by reference to the following contexts: self, family, society, humanity, posterity, cosmos, and life. These function as spheres that we can use to bring our thoughts together and expand our view of things. They help us to consider things other than our own narrow interests. They also take us out of ourselves and give us the bigger picture. All these contexts combine in contributing to the Cosmos which is dealt with in more detail on section twelve below. The Cosmos encompasses all human endeavour and achievement and in its turn it points towards Posterity which will inherit everything we leave behind us, assuming that the human race survives into the future. Life contains all these contexts and each context in its turn contains life. There is therefore an interactivity between these contexts in our constant use of them that is not reflected in this following static diagram. This diagram is only an aid to picturing these contexts.

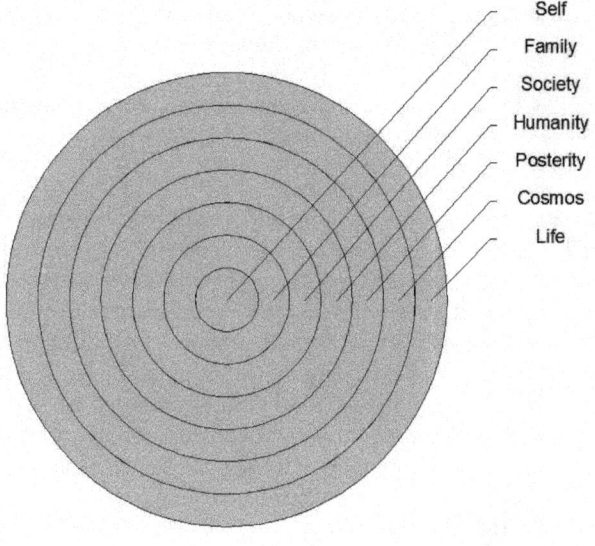

Self

The smallness of Self sphere. This is the smallest and most confined of all the spheres and when a person dwells entirely within it, they think of everything as in relation to themselves alone. The totally selfish person lacks a distinct notion of self since nothing exists for them unless it affects them personally. They expect instant gratification as there are no limits to their wants and desires. Thus, in lacking a clearly defined sense of the limitations of the self, no other contexts or points of view are allowed. Their self-centredness impels them to reduce everything to their own interests, and they have difficulty expanding these interests to include new things. For example, severely autistic persons seem to lack this ability to include other points of view other than their own.

Hume famously reduced the self to "nothing but a bundle or collection of different perceptions."[19] But this is only a bland reductionism that ignores the overall notion of self that we all have. We only lack such a notion if we are unable to step outside ourselves and "see ourselves as others see us".[20] This well-known saying of Robert Burns summarises the earlier view of Adam Smith who exhorts us to stand aside and examine ourselves from afar:

> We can never survey our own sentiments and motives, we can never form any judgment concerning them, unless we remove ourselves, as it were, from our own natural station, and endeavour to view them as at a certain distance from us. But we can do this in no other way than by endeavouring to view them with the eyes of other people, or as other people are likely to view them."[21]

We understand ourselves least of all when we think only of ourselves and fail to understand what we are in relation to the spheres of family and society that take us out of ourselves. Being selfish and self-centred means not entering into other contexts to make their contents as much a part of us as our own immediate concerns. Thus, when the context of self is devoid of any other context, this is the source of self-obsession, narcissism, solipsism, autism, and so on. In fact, we amount to little or nothing if we have only ourselves to concern us. As Mary Midgley puts it:

> In order to 'be ourselves' in the private sphere, we need an appropriate context. Even exalters of solitude such as Nietzsche look forward to a better age when they might find suitable companions. Except for the odd hermit, we see actual, thorough-going isolation as a kind of death.[22]

Moreover, the solitary person need not live for themselves alone. Solitude is only bearable when it is filled with thoughts that are not centred on ourselves alone. Otherwise, we become obsessed with our bodily functions or mental obsessions and delusions. When we think of ourselves in a less selfish way, our thoughts turn to the concerns of other people. We see our concerns being reflected in those of other people. We get to know ourselves better in knowing other people. Thus, to know oneself properly it is necessary to know one's limitations, and self-centred people lack these. They have insufficient self-knowledge to know what their best interests are. This is what comes of being contextually deficient and being unable to appreciate other perspectives. There is therefore a big difference between (1) being egoistical as such and (2) incorporating all the contexts into the self. The one is narrow, stupid, and lacking in self-knowledge. The other constantly strives to incorporate all other contexts in order to maximise self-knowledge.

Family

The broadness of the Family sphere. Family as a sphere includes not only the blood family into which we were born but also the acquaintances and colleagues with whom we associate on a friendly basis. It includes the whole idea of the togetherness of families in which people relate closely to each other whether or no t there is any biological linkage. As a notion, it includes not just the nuclear or extended family but also all our friendships and the other familiar relationships that fill our lives. Everyone with whom we are familiar may be regarded as family. We are all born into the family framework in the shape of a family life that helps each of us to establish our individuality, if it works at all as it usually does.

The family is essential as springboard for socialisation. The first social realities we have to face in life consist in understanding our similarities and differences with other family members. We establish our own identity in that way. Having family roots is necessary to our security and peace of mind. Thus, breaking free of family roots can be difficult for us. In forming friendships outside the family, we expand the framework of family and prepare ourselves to enter the overall context of society. We extend the sphere of our family when we successively go to school, university, become employees, create our own family and so on. In a tribal society, the tribe as a whole functions as family. In a complex, modern society, we need the notion of family to take over from the old tribal or clan affinities. Our view of family can in that way phase more or less smoothly into the sphere of society and the broader sociosphere.

Society

Entering the sphere of society is essential to self-development. Society is the sphere within which all our social activities take place, including family activities. From school experiences we move onto work experiences and gradually incorporate the whole sphere of society in our thinking about things. Society comprises the families and organisation that form the basic structure of society as well as the legal structure and the objective knowledge, technology, and techniques required to make society work. What may be called the sociosphere is the sphere of human communication within which society functions. It includes the internet, the workings of trade, industry, commerce and social activities of all kinds. Our self-development takes a huge leap forward by the process of socialisation by which we enter this sphere. We increase our knowledge and understanding, for example, by talking to people, using the internet, conducting businesses, taking educational courses, and so on. Our families, groups and organisations participate in the sociosphere, and in so far as they set themselves apart from it, they are potentially inimical to its unity and purpose. For example, the notion of the internet becomes more meaningful when we think of it as operating within the sociosphere which embraces all human communication. It is not just seen as something private to ourselves, friends and family as it involves all humanity.

Contact with other people is good for our sense of self. Our views are expanded by contact with other people's views. The formation of a distinct notion of self depends on our entering into the different contexts in which other people function. We learn to see ourselves as others see us. Unless we view our own conduct at distance and with eyes of other people, we cannot judge the value or otherwise of our own actions. Before we judge other people's conduct, we need to compare that conduct with our own. In wanting others to sympathise with our plight we reciprocate by sympathising with their plight. In understanding other people's point of view, we sympathise with their circumstances.

Thus, an essential part of our self-development consists in incorporating other people's views. We do this on entering the sphere of society through all the social activities in which we engage during our lives. Each one of us requires the society of other people to live a meaningful and productive life, and to fulfil ourselves as unique individuals. A large part of the potential of each individual is only actualised by relating themselves to the concerns of others. We diminish ourselves in exact proportion to our neglect of other people. In being interested in the exploits of other people we enrich our own conception of ourselves. When we sympathise with other people and put ourselves in their place, we can then be happy for them, pleased with their success, and speculate as to their future, and so on. Our inner potential is therefore developed and fulfilled within the sociosphere. Within the context of society, we move within spheres of influence in which we can influence other people and are influenced by them. These spheres include the family circle, the peer group, and the workplace. All these socialising agents prepare us for entry into the context of the humanity.

Humanity

The whole sphere of humanity engages our best feelings. Humanity as a whole is the sphere contains all other previous spheres in so far as we cannot avoid being human beings doing human things. It is particularly important in uniting us as a species against the racial, national, religious, sectarian and economic divisions that forever threaten to turn us against each other in self-destructive war and conflict. We have no future unless humanity as a whole pulls together with its collective future in mind. When we all put ourselves in this sphere, we can be united by the common aims of humanity. This happens when we empathise with our fellow human beings who are afflicted by famines, earthquakes, tsunamis, terrorist attacks and so on. It is an additional dimension of ourselves, and an expression of our human feelings. When the idea of humanity is isolated in a Platonic way, it may be misused by utopian ideologists to justify killing and torturing their fellow human beings. The idea has become more important than people and is treated in an absolutist way. By treating humanity as sphere like any other, we do not put it above and beyond us but make an intimate part of what we are as individuals. It is concerned with our sympathetic feelings about other people and not with our thinking of them in an abstract and inhuman way. Their lives are more important than any abstract ideas because their lives are more important than the mere idea of humanity.

It is important to put humanity into context relative to other contexts. Humanity contains all the other contexts in so far as we cannot avoid being human beings doing human things. Even the despicable things that we do are fairly typical of human beings and we need to be constantly aware of such propensities. Within the context of humanity we can think about the good and bad aspects of humanity and hopefully correct the bad aspects. The context of humanity is also important because it is within that context that we can see the need to unite ourselves as a species against the racial, national, religious, sectarian and economic divisions that forever threaten to turn us against each other in self-destructive war and conflict. As already argued, we have no future unless humanity as a whole pulls together with its collective future in mind. When we all put ourselves in the context of humanity we can be united by the common aims of humanity. This happens when we empathise with our fellow human beings who are afflicted by famines, earthquakes, tsunamis, terrorist attacks and so on. It is an additional dimension of ourselves, and an expression of our human feelings.

It is also important to avoid making too much or too little of humanity. An over- or under-containment of the context of humanity occurs when we make too much or too little of the idea of humanity. It has been misused by utopian ideologists to justify killing and torturing their fellow human beings. In that case, the idea has become more important than people and is treated in an absolutist way. The context of humanity needs to be contained by that of life and other contexts to maintain a realistic and balanced view of humanity. Within the context of life, for example, people's lives are more important than any abstract ideas of humanity. The danger then is that we go to the other extreme in our thinking and belittle humanity in relation to life in general.

Posterity

When we look into the far future, we can unify ourselves by entering the context of posterity. The future consequences of what we are doing now is best done from the perspective or viewpoint of posterity. It is either future generations or intelligent beings in the future who are capable of understanding us. The importance of viewing posterity in this way is discussed in more detail in section 11 below on *Posterity*.

Cosmos

Within the context of Cosmos we can unify everything that we know about the material universe and also everything that the human race has brought into being through its cultural endeavours, both mental and physical. It is ourselves and our achievements writ large, as is discussed in more detail in section 12 below on *Finality*.

Life

We can serve life in general by entering this sphere. Life is the sphere in which our whole lives are lived. It is life that makes all things possible as far as we are concerned. It includes also the Cosmos and Posterity as both are nothing with life. They are both a part of life just as life is part of the Cosmos and Posterity, as herein defined. However, it is important to treat life as a context and not as a sacrosanct Platonic notion above and beyond our own daily lives. Those who take other people's lives in the name of life are obviously stepping outside to context of life altogether. They value their own opinions more than they value life in itself. Embracing life as a context helps us to empathise with other life-forms and this encourages us to preserve life for its own sake. We can't help thinking of ourselves being within this context since we are living beings and must make sense of our lives whether we like it or not. When we see life's importance, we are impelled to protect, promote and propagate it, and to make more of it than previously existed.

We vindicate ourselves by living life to the full while living in harmony with all other living beings. It is more important than humanity in that life in some form will continue on this planet even though humanity disappears from it entirely. Thus, embracing this sphere helps us to empathise with other life-forms and it encourages us to preserve life for its own sake. In this context, the purpose of humanity is to protect, promote and propagate life, and to make more of it than previously existed. However this purpose is not to be pursued dogmatically or in total isolation from our personal needs and those of other people.

Those who fail to enter the context of life and make it a part of their thinking will not appreciate its value. They will find it difficult if not impossible to adopt and maintain a 'live and let live' policy. They will not relate to the life and death of other living beings as they live only within themselves. Life itself has less meaning to them. The fact that other life-forms and indeed other people have a right to live their lives in their own way will be a difficult notion for them to grasp. They know themselves to be living but they have no means of valuing their own lives, let alone those of others. The only view they can appreciate is a reductive view of reducing everything to their own view of things since that focuses on the content and existence of their own lives and not on the value of life as a whole Their narrow view of life is such that they are liable to take life in the name of life instead of valuing all life. Many serial killers justify their actions to themselves on that basis. The thankfully very few doctors and nurses who take the lives of elderly people before their time may think that they are sparing people from the agonies of old age but they merely fail to value life as a whole. People are more important than the notion of life or indeed all abstract notions whatsoever. Thus, it is necessary for us to bring all considerations into this context to relate ourselves fully to life as a whole. Thus, it is necessary for us enter with our whole-hearted thoughts into the context of life to relate ourselves fully to life as a whole.

In conclusion, therefore, contextualising life helps us with the problems of preserving it. We enter into the context of life whenever we think our own lives and the lives of other people or living beings in general. But as context, life also has its limitations. For example, it is problematic whether it is humane, on the one hand, to prolong life unnecessarily in the face of unbearable suffering or, on the other hand, to take away the life of a unborn child which is merely unwanted. Sanctifying life in a dogmatic fashion makes it impossible for us to think of exceptions to the rule that life is to be preserved and prolonged at all costs. Yet the fact is that death is a part of life since it marks the end-point of life. This makes such exceptions unavoidable one way or another, as when a choice must be made between the life of a mother and that of her unborn child where both lives are under threat and only one can be saved. Thus, the notion of life may need to be dealt with differently depending on the context in which it is used. Contextualising it helps us to put its problems at arm's length and avoid being emotionally attached to the idea of life as if death itself were not also a part of life.

Part Three

Future Advancement

11: Posterity: Benefiting Future Generations

> Posterity for the philosopher is the other world of the man of religion.
> Denis Diderot (1766).[1]

A. The Importance of Thinking about Posterity

The perspective of posterity helps us to judge our advancement or the lack of it. When we think about the future consequences of what we are doing, this is best done from that viewpoint. The ultimate service that we can perform is that which benefits posterity. Posterity is either future generations or intelligent beings in the future who are capable of understanding us. The word 'posterity' refers to 'future or succeeding generations' and 'all of one's descendants'. It comes from the Latin *posteritas* meaning 'future generations', and from *posterus* or 'coming after'. By thinking about future generations we put ourselves in their shoes and see ourselves from their point of view. We must imagine that our lives become accessible to them so that they can judge us and our lives whether we like it or not. Thus, the idea of serving posterity gives us a powerful tool by which we can evaluate the importance or non-importance of what we are doing now.

The word 'posterity' is used here not only to comprise the generations and life-forms that succeed us in the future, it also refers to what we make of the future by planning to make it better than the past. For we increase our value as individuals by serving posterity. The very meaning of our existence is enhanced as much by what we imagine that posterity will make of our existence as by what we actually make of our lives. This enhancement results from our having entered the context of posterity as well as by our anticipating how posterity may judge our present actions. In other words, we are elevated into a higher perspective of our lives by contemplating posterity. We can then think of our most mundane activities as serving posterity even when we have decided to do nothing when doing something might have adverse consequences. Serving posterity therefore means that everything we do has consequences for posterity, whether for good or ill. Whether we like it or not, we are either serving the needs of posterity or not serving its needs in whatever we do. Our judgments should always have posterity in mind; the possibility of posterity cannot be overlooked, as it is the ultimate vindication of all our efforts.

In this context the word posterity refers to future consequences and what we make of the future in the present. For our present actions have meaning for posterity whether we are aware of it or not. Making ourselves aware of posterity means bringing future generations to mind who will have to live with the consequences of what we do in the present. Future generations are important to us because everything we do now has some consequence to posterity. All our rational and purposeful activities gravitate towards the context of posterity within which the value of those activities is ultimately assessed, whether we like it or not. Everything that we do now, at this very moment, has some future meaning which cannot be ascertained in the present. We must pass on to posterity the ultimate task of judging what we do in the present. All we can do now is try to put ourselves in their shoes and make the best judgments we can.

The fact is that all our everyday actions have consequences for posterity. Most of us most of the time give little thought to posterity. Yet every meaningful thing that we do means something for posterity. When we do something, such as buy a new car, we do it in the immediate present but the effect of our action is in the future. The money spent on the car goes into the economy, helps to pay people's wages, supports the car industry, and so on. If the car is more fuel efficient and less polluting, it reduces our travelling expenditure and is less harmful to the climate. Thus, whatever we do, it has consequences for the future whether or not we intend that there should be consequences. Future generations will either benefit or not benefit from what we do in the present. What we do now therefore has meaning for posterity, assuming that future generations will survive in the future.

If an action is meaningful to us, it will also mean something, either the same or different, in the future. When a house is renovated, those who take over the house in the future will live with the consequences of that renovation. Any long-term benefits from what we do will benefit from posterity and this gives added meaning and value to these actions. Likewise, posterity will suffer because of our shortcomings which may have adverse effects beyond our imagination. It is thus very important to judge our actions from the perspective of posterity, which can suffer from our oversights. People in the future will think badly of us in so far as we fail to do our best for them.

Posterity is not just an imaginary notion. When we think of the future we inevitably use our imagination. But the notion of a posterity awaiting us in the future is more than just imaginary. The notion is backed up, firstly, by the evidence of evolution on this planet and, secondly, by the very real possibility of advanced species living elsewhere in the universe. If the human race autodestructs or is annihilated, other living species such as insects or rodents may evolve into intelligent beings who can peer back into the past. Also, intelligent beings are probably evolving elsewhere in the universe and they may visit the Earth in the far future, (as depicted, for example, in Spielberg's 2001 feature film, *A.I. Artificial Intelligence*). Thus, what I mean here by 'posterity' includes all these possibilities, and is not just confined to our descendants in the future. Whether posterity is composed of humans, other species, aliens, androids, or computer-generated holograms, posterity will still be interested in what we do here and now. Whether we develop or fail to develop further because of our self-destruction, they will want to know the reasons why, just as we are interested in past civilisations and why they ceased to exist. At the very least, they will want to avoid the mistakes we have made in the present.

Posterity in the form of intelligent beings elsewhere in the universe is highly probable because intelligence is a natural consequence of the complexification of the universe's contents. Material bodies organise themselves into ever more complex entities by interaction and intermixture. Eventually, entities become complex enough to have lives of their own. And by interacting with their environment, such life-forms become still more complex over time. They organise themselves into communities whose cultures complexify eventually into civilisations such as our own. Cultures of sufficient complexity will produce intelligent participants, and we can expect intelligence to emerge wherever life produces complex, social beings. As there are billions of galaxies in the universe with billions of stars in each of them, the chances are that there are millions of civilisations throughout the universe. Thus, the existence of posterity in some form seems to be just as assured as the existence of any form of life in the universe.

We must work to ensure a future posterity. However, all we can do at present to ensure that there is a posterity by our working to ensure the future of humanity. We cannot afford to sit back and wait for an alien intelligent species to arrive and take our place in the cosmos. Just as parents invest their time and energy in ensuring a future for their children, so we as a species must invest all our resources in our future prospects because our descendants depend on it. Ultimately we serve ourselves best by serving the purposes of posterity. Only such service can save us in spite of ourselves as long as we work hard to serve posterity by doing things that benefit the future and make for a better future.

Broadly speaking, posterity is the culmination of all human ends. When we look to the far future, we enter the context of posterity. We can see nothing remaining of humanity unless we are succeeded by a viable posterity in the form of generations of people who will take humanity forward to a better future. Within that context we can make judgments about the consequences of our present actions. We must imagine what posterity will make of what we are doing in the present. The problems of society can only be solved in the future, and when we imagine them as they will appear to future generations, we are considering in the context of posterity. However, our thoughts of the future may be mistaken unless they are also considered within such contexts as universe, life and humanity. Within these contexts we can reach the most realistic view of matters by making use of our hard-earned past experiences when things have turned out contrary to our expectations. While the other contexts can also be depicted as containing all the others, depending on the circumstances in which they are used, posterity is ultimately the most important of all and the most of in need of over-containment rather than under-containment.

This view of posterity enables us to re-interpret the 'hereafter' as being the life of future generations that continues after our death. It gives us the possibility of an 'afterlife' of sorts. But this is not experienced by us in any shape or form since we no longer exist physically. We may have a kind of afterlife if people living in the future are able to reconstruct our lives and relive them for their own interest in the same way that we watch films and videos today about past events. We live on potentially only in so far as our lives are accessible to posterity. But this is only our lives as we have lived them in their past. They may relive our lives only in so far as their knowledge and technology allows them to do. They are unlikely to become us in merely re-running our lives as they will be unable to interfere with the things that we have already done in their past. But we can imagine that posterity is watching us as is now argued.

B. The Omnipresence of Posterity

As CCTV cameras are everywhere these days, it is easier than ever to imagine that we are always being watched. We might also imagine that we are constantly under the scrutiny of posterity. People or intelligent beings in the future may well have the technology to reconstruct the past and observe us in our most intimate acts and perhaps also experience what we are experiencing from one moment to the next. The assumption is that posterity is with us here and now in the sense of their knowing what we are and what we are doing just as historians know from diaries and journals who people were and what they were doing at a certain time in the past. It is therefore wise to assume that we are always being watched, as Baltasar Gracián put it:

> *Always behave as though you were being watched.* He is a prudent man who realises that he is being observed, or will be observed. He knows that walls have ears and that evil deeds are bursting to come out into the light of day. Even when he is alone he behaves as though the eyes of the whole world were upon him, for he realises that everything will eventually come to light: he regards people who will later hear of his deeds as already witnesses of them. The man who would like the whole world to see inside his home will not be a prey to misgivings just because others can observe him from theirs.[2]

The presence of posterity is not a physical, or even a ghostly or supernatural, presence. Unless time travel becomes a real possibility, people living in the future are here with us only in that they will have access to knowledge about what we were doing at a certain point in their past. In that way they are able to reconstruct in visual form, by means of an advanced 'virtual reality', the scenes and events in which we ourselves are living our lives at this very moment. The events we are presently experiencing may be imprinted and recorded in the atoms and molecules of our bodies, the air, floor, walls, furniture and so on. We can imagine that their technology will enable them to reconstruct these recorded events from the atoms and molecules that were formerly in our bodies, the air, and so on. Perhaps they will virtually get inside our skins and feel and think what we are feeling and thinking, here and now. But they will only do so in the future and they cannot change events here and now. They will not have the ability to make us feel and think things or to influence us into doing anything other than what we are actually doing at the present time.

The notion of a superior being who is with us all the time and everywhere only makes sense as a way of heralding the scarcely imaginable abilities of posterity to reconstruct the past and to understand present events better than we do ourselves who are living through them. Thus, we can look forward to posterity having the possible cognisance of our most intimate thoughts and acts. 'Heaven' is what posterity has in store for us in making life even more meaningful than it seems to be during our own lifetime. This kind of heaven is an ideal or perhaps even a dream, but it is a real possibility nevertheless. Though a person's life might seem meaningless in present day terms, it is perfectly possible that it will be much more meaningful to posterity in the far future, assuming that intelligent life of some kind does survive into the far future.

Thus, instead of being aware of the ubiquity of God, what we should consider possible is the ubiquitous vigilance of posterity. The idea of our acts being subject to perpetual surveillance has been recognised since the earliest times. For example, in the dialogue, *Phaedrus*, Socrates warns the lusty youth beside him that the cicadas in the surrounding trees are witnesses to whatever deeds they observe and that they report their findings directly to the Muses.[3] A consciousness of unknown and unseen witnesses to our most intimate acts has always been with us since the time we possessed the imagination to think of things not really being what they are immediately perceived to be. Thus, gods, spirits, demons, and angels were posited as possible witnesses of everything we do. Having a better developed scientific imagination than our ancestors, we can now assign this possibility to the future where the ability to reconstruct the past will be a distinct possibility, given the requisite theoretical knowledge and technological know-how.

The Great Day of Judgment awaits us all in posterity wherein we will all be judged according to whatever we have or have not done in our lives. We may not be personally called before the tribunal of posterity to account for our failings, but our lives will be. In leaving these lives behind us to be judged by in the future, we can never be sure how they will be judged. All we can be sure of is that enough traces will be left behind of our having lived, and of how we lived, to enable these lives to be evaluated one way or another. Therefore, posterity will judge us whether we like it or not. We are all 'doomed' in that respect. On the other hand, the thought of being watched all the time doesn't necessarily change our behaviour. The Big Brother television series shows that even though people know that they are being observed 24 hours a day by television cameras, that knowledge does not stop them from making complete fools of themselves.

Our *nunc stans*[4] or everlasting 'now' means that what happens right 'now' belongs to the universe as a whole. All our 'nows' are shared with every other event in the universe and are inextricably linked to them. Everything we experience in the present is a permanent contribution to the cosmos available for all time to come. The 'now' consists in a second to second confrontation with the potential choices which we use our freewill to actualise by means of our mental and physical activities. There is no need to contemplate survival after death as each 'now' lasts forever as it passes into the past where everything is preserved for the potential purposes of posterity.

Dying completely alone and unknown to the rest of humanity will not allow us to escape the tribunal of posterity, since everyone living and everything happening in the present will be known about in the future. Advanced beings in the future, by virtue of being more advanced, will have better technological means by which to study the past than archaeologists have today in their examining the past of human beings. Everything that is happening here and now can be reconstructed in the future as long as the technological problems can be overcome by finding out how to do it. We lack such a technology now and can barely imagine how it can be done but our descendants in the distant future may well acquire it. If we take our lives seriously then we must act on the assumption that they will do so.

But, as already suggested, these advanced beings are unlikely to have any more power to interfere with and change the lives of intelligent beings in the present than present-day archaeologists have with regard to past lives. Unless they physically travel back into the past, they will be unable to interfere with the freewill of intelligent beings because the physical impossibility of reaching into the past and altering events. Time travel may prove to be impossible because the expansion of the universe into the future precludes the possibility of changing the past in any physical way. Such beings could have greater power over the universe as a whole than over individual intelligent beings in the past. Our capacities are presently actualised only in the small scale but superior beings in the future may have technological command of the whole universe's workings.

We can speculate about the godlike abilities of superior beings without needing to believe in their actual existence. More advanced entities than intelligent beings might be more spiritual than material, as anticipated in the form of 'angels' by scholastic philosophers such as Aquinas. Complete spirituality implies being involved totally in potentialities at the expense of actualities. Their lives would revolve round potentialities without the need to actualise them in physical terms. This means creating and destroying potentialities that we are able in our finite world to choose between and exercise our freewill in doing so.

The function of advanced entities in the universe might therefore be that of manipulating potentialities so that some are more available to be actualised than others. They would be responsible for those coincidences and other events that seem to be more than just the product of random chance. If this is the case, then lucky and unlucky individuals are in the hands not of the gods but of these more advanced and wholly potential beings in the future. This kind of activity would not threaten the freewill of intelligent beings as it has no effect on their mental or physical activities; only on the range of possibilities with which they are confronted. Thus, more advanced beings might have an influence over chaotic events, but not over the organised, complex decision-making of lesser beings such as ourselves.

The ultimate goal of these advanced beings could be the perfecting of the universe by manipulating potentialities. This would mean creating a structure which is increasingly better at producing intelligent beings and at giving them a chance of a better and more fortunate life. However, this may not have relevance to the present universe; it may only apply to future universes that are spawned out of the present one.

If these beings do have any influence over present potentialities then there is a feedback operation involved here. It means that in benefiting posterity, intelligent beings are improving the ability of advanced entities to make more good luck and fortune available for intelligent beings in the present. In spite of the fact that good and bad luck have a random and ultimately unpredictable element because of the randomness of quantum wave/particle events, this does not necessarily preclude an element of good and bad luck that is 'caused' by events taking place in the distant future and by technological means beyond present conceptions.

This suggests that, in not doing his best to fulfil his potentialities, the intelligent being diminishes the future potentialities of the universe as a whole. His failure has a knock-on effect on his own life as it makes him less 'lucky'. His good luck is liable to run out since it relies on a conjunction of events that are outside his own control. But some of these events may be in the potential control of more advanced beings in the future. The welfare of these beings may depend on their lives being as productively beneficial to the universe as possible. The good things done in the life of an intelligent being will benefit these beings and give them greater potential to control the conjunction of events in his favour.

The ultimate destiny of the universe may therefore lie in what it bequeaths to eternity to justify its existence. The fate of everything that happens in the universe depends on these events being an indelible part of eternity so that they might not have occurred in vain. Science in the far distant future may have the task of ensuring either that the universe continues indefinitely with its contents intact or that its contents are bequeathed to another universe spawning from it.

Whatever the reasons why intelligent beings are gaining such extensive knowledge and control of the universe, it is certain that there are reasons yet to be explicated and understood by them. If this were not the case then it must be asked how could such a possibility be even comprehended, let alone put into words or symbols which other intelligent beings might understand? The very possibility of gaining such understanding itself seems to be part of the fabric of the universe. In a sense, it is there waiting to be found, even though, in another sense, we are making it up as we go along. The ambiguity arises because we have to discover it for ourselves in our own terms that are personal to us. Thus, we and all other intelligent beings strive for this better understanding of the universe and our part in it, perhaps for no better reason than that this task is there to be done and that we are capable of doing it.

C. Posterity and the After-Life

> In the invincible ignorance, then, in which we are, our imagination has the choice of our eternal destinies.
>
> Maurice Maeterlinck, *Immortality*, (1907).[5]

Our lives themselves may be immortal even though our consciousness certainly is not. Even if we vanish altogether into the void of eternity when we die, we leave our lives behind. That we have lived our lives is an indisputable fact that can be verifiable by all the physical changes we have made during lives, all the work we have done, all the artefacts we have created, all the people who remember us, and all documentation we leave behind us. Nothing and no one can erase the fact of our having lived our lives. It is a question of just how much of our lives can physically survive our demise. However, it is arguable that our lives as a whole are left behind for possible inspection in the future.

As already argued, our scientific knowledge now assures us with some certainty that our lives are imprinted all around our environment. Every event has effects of which we are only partially aware through perception and through our current technology, such as microscopes, telescopes, x-rays and so on. We can extrapolate from what we can do now to what improved technology may be capable of in the future. Their technology will simply be more advanced that we can possibly imagine. Though we don't yet know what technology could achieve such effects we can at least imagine their possibility. It is not beyond the bounds of possibility that the technology of future beings will enable them to reconstruct these recorded events of our lives from the atoms and molecules that were formerly in our bodies, the air, water and so on. In that way, the imprints of our lives could be read like a book.

Even today we can read Samuel Pepys's diary and get a sense of living his life from day to day in the 1660s. His life-style was extraordinarily complex, varied and busy, and it surely gives the lie to the idea that past lifestyles were simpler than those of today! He has already achieved a form of immortality to the extent that we can relive some events of his life by the way he is describing them. For example, on 26th Sep. 1665, he is in a barge sailing down the Thames with King Charles ii and his brother Duke of York (later James II) "and hearing him and the Duke talk, and seeing and observing their manner of discourse" he is ashamed to think that they are just like other men. "The more a man considers and observes them, the less he finds of difference between them and other men, though (blessed be God!) they are both princes of great nobleness and spirits." We can imagine how he felt in the presence of such people. But we are only imagining what life was like for him. Similarly, people in the future will be on the outside looking in and they will not change events here and now. They will be unable to make us feel or think things or to influence us into doing anything other than what we are actually doing at the present time.

Thus, if there is a posterity awaiting us in the future, we can be reasonably sure that it will be ubiquitous and all-seeing. But it will not be omnipotent or god-like. We don't need God watching over us when we can imagine posterity doing so. Atheists can cheerfully dispense with God as there are more rational arguments for believing in an ever-vigilant posterity than there are for believing in the existence of an alien being having supernatural abilities to observe us right now. We can extrapolate such future possibilities more rationally than we can supernatural ones. This is because we can imagine future generations having greater knowledge and technological abilities than ourselves, just as we know that our scientific knowledge and technological abilities are better than those of past generations. Such a view doesn't even depend on human race surviving into the future since life is clearly springing up throughout the universe on countless planets in countless galaxies. We are already discovering planets which may have the ability to generate life and these discoveries are now raising such possibilities into certainties. These developments suggest that our lives may be even more meaningful in the future than they are in the present. The notion of a superior being who is with us all the time and who is present everywhere only makes sense as a way of heralding the scarcely imaginable abilities of posterity to reconstruct the past and to understand present events better than we do ourselves who are living through them.

I argue therefore that we can be reasonably certain that sooner or later the ability to observe the past will be developed. The past will be more accurately reconstructed than we can imagine at the moment. The abilities of advanced beings in the future are only possibilities in the sense that the future is uncertain. If advanced beings evolve in the future then the nature of being advanced implies that, sooner or later, they will acquire the abilities of ubiquitous vigilance. No one can be absolutely sure that this will not be the case at sometime in the future. We may assume that future progress will make all these things possible, even though it may take thousands or even millions of years.

We therefore have no need for religion when we have posterity peering at us. We can speculate about the godlike abilities of more advanced, superior beings in the future without needing to believe in their actual existence. There is no point in worshipping them or putting them on a pedestal since they cannot do anything for us that we cannot do for ourselves. Thus, our freewill is unaffected and there is no need for religion whatsoever. We are all personally responsible for our thoughts and deeds and are answerable to posterity for them if not to our fellow human beings. Consequently, there are moral implications in believing in an ever watchful posterity when we take into account the effects and value of our thoughts and deeds from the point of view of posterity.

It may be argued that the universe will come to nothing in the end so there is no point in speculating about posterity and the abilities of advanced beings. According to the laws of thermodynamics, the universe is running down and it will lose all its energy in a 'heat death' which is predicted sometime in the far future. Some people see this as a reason for despair. The universe will come to nothing therefore our lives are worthless. However, the fixed amount of energy available in the universe according to thermodynamics is not necessarily a foregone conclusion. Perhaps additional energy might be brought into existence through the manipulation of black holes, the medium of wormholes or some other means presently unknown to us. Intelligent beings in the far future may acquire the knowledge and technology needed to prolong the existence of the universe or even create a new universe into which life can be transported.

Perhaps that is how the present universe came into being in the first place, for all we know at the moment.

In this way, future knowledge can save us from denigrating ourselves into total insignificance. We must invest in the future in that regard by supporting whatever expensive research is required to gain greater understanding of the universe both at the macroscopic and microscopic levels. Cosmological understanding is linked at a very deep level with quantum understanding, since the universe began at that infinitely small level of existence. Indeed, the very fact that we can conduct such research and gain an astonishing amount of information about the universe, near and far, is testimony to our superior and perhaps unique abilities in that regard. No other species on Earth has come close to such achievements, and no other species can be relied upon to do so in the future.

Thus, the after-life, according to the above view, is what awaits our lives after we have left them. Nothing of the present time is lost to the future because it is indelibly imprinted in the atoms and molecules in ourselves and our surroundings. Whatever we do now continues to exist for eternity. This is surely more believable than any religious doctrine as it is based on our present scientific knowledge and on a rational extrapolation from what is now possible to what might be possible in the future.

D. Orienting Ourselves towards the Future

The perspective of posterity helps to orient ourselves away from the past and towards the future. As far as our future is concerned, it is a thing to be done rather than a thing to be believed. No particular belief, faith, creed, doctrine or ideology is needed to determine what our future must be. It is a pragmatic matter of what has to be done to secure that future. We need an overall view of where we are going which is not utopian and which does not make unreasonable demands on us as individuals.

Failure to think ahead and to let go the past keeps our civilisation forever on a knife edge. In the current circumstances, a relatively minor incident could lead to anarchy and the breakdown of civilisation. By analogy with the butterfly effect, a mere fuel blockade or a minor conflict in a far off country could precipitate events that cause the world economy to collapse. A similar minor event, an assassination in the Balkans in August 1914, led European nations into war with each other. Civilisation can too easily sow the seeds for its own destruction and this requires no external agency to bring it about. To avoid such catastrophes we need greater insight into where we are going in the future and what the consequences are of what we are doing now. This purposefulness ensures that trivial events are treated as trivial relative to the overall picture of where we are going. They are not then allowed to get out of hand and be blown out of all proportion to their real importance in human affairs. We need to get out of ourselves more and be much less concerned with internal human affairs that contribute nothing to our future but everything to a regression of our civilisation.

We have the possibility of achieving ever greater control over our lives and our environment. As science, medicine, and technology progress, there is less and less need for us to submit to the rigours of fate or bad luck. At the beginning of the sixteenth century, it was thought that we had perhaps fifty per cent control over our fortune. The proportion under our control must be so much greater nowadays as we lessen the chances of becoming ill, being murdered arbitrarily, drowned in floods, dying in a plane crash, and so on. Of course, we will always take chances with our lives by taking risks and tackling physical challenges, but even these have become more controlled nowadays as in bungee jumping, white water rafting, outward bound courses, and the like.

As we gain increasing control over the vagaries of our fortune and we work out where the human race is supposed to be going in the future, we contribute to posterity all the more effectively. That we should look more steadfastly towards the future and consider the needs of posterity above those of our own is a relatively new notion that is not easily understood or appreciated.

12: Finality: Contributing to the Cosmos

> We are the local embodiment of a Cosmos grown to self-awareness. We have begun to contemplate our origins: star-stuff pondering the stars; organised assemblages of ten billion billion billion atoms considering the evolution of atoms; tracing the long journey by which, here at least, consciousness arose. Our loyalties are to the species and the planet. We speak for Earth. Our obligation to survive is owed not just to ourselves but also to that Cosmos, ancient and vast, from which we spring.
>
> Carl Sagan (1983) [1]

A. The Role of the Cosmos

What is ultimately important about humanity is what we leave behind us. Here it is argued that, at the final end of things, the Cosmos is the greatest gift that humanity can bequeath to the universe. The notion of Cosmos is the culmination of all human efforts and achievements. It embodies a holistic view which brings everything together that is significant about us. So far from being divine notion is an entirely human in all respects since it embraces humanity without going beyond it. Its finality rests in making an end to everything we are as human beings. We are all cosmists in making our own contributions to it whether we regard these as trivial or important. We therefore advance humanity, each of us in our own way, by our cosmic contributions.

The Cosmos encompasses not only everything that we know about the material universe but also everything that the human race has brought into being through its cultural endeavours, both mental and physical. It is not God but is only symbolic of what humanity is and has achieved. Just as the knowledge contained in Wikipedia is imposed on no one, so the Cosmos demands nothing of anyone. Like Wikipedia, it is there to be used and contributed to. However, it goes far beyond that incomparable encyclopaedia in containing it and everything else achieved by and attributable to humanity. In this way, the cosmist can appreciate all and everything about humanity however adverse he may be to particular aspects of it.

The cosmist is also a holist since taking things as a whole means embracing all that humanity has to offer – past, present and future. The cosmist's role is to bestow value on all our achievements and proclaim their meaning and importance to all and sundry. Wholeness implies completeness and what lasts forever is only a part of the whole. What is being done in the here and now is also included. Thus, the Cosmos is the imaginary repository by which holists carry around not so much all knowledge in their heads but the appreciation and applicability of it. That knowledge is always accessible online, in books, videos and the heads of experts but it is useless unless it is appreciated and applied whenever the occasion arises by those who see when and where it is needed. The cosmist is therefore a visionary who takes account of all that humanity has to offer and makes as much of it as his imagination will allow.

As a mere carry-all, the Cosmos is not to be worshipped or adulated since it is merely a notion that serves to put the whole of humanity in the broadest possible perspective. Only we as human beings can do this and not any imaginary beings that are only invented by reflecting on our own capabilities or the lack of them. If we are wise, we will try our best to embrace everything without exception in our thoughts and images. Though we may never attain this completely or perhaps only temporarily, we can't stop trying. To stop trying is to start dying. Life gives us no choice if we want to carry on living.

The ultimate nature of the Cosmos. The Cosmos gives us the remote view of humanity that we need to appreciate its ultimate value and significance, and it is an important object of holist's view to absorb and develop that viewpoint. As herein defined, it is the *ne plus ultra* view of what we are and the place we have in it. It gives us a humane way of measuring and judging our achievements objectively without having to resort to a divine perspective that is really unfathomable and beyond our ken.

Nevertheless, the Cosmos cannot include absolutely everything. It is a human notion devoted to human concerns. For example, it does not include posterity. Future generations can only be imagined to exist as the legacy of our present efforts. The Cosmos points to the future which we are constantly working towards in our daily lives. It is emblematic of everything we have achieved as a species. Our future is not in making intelligent robots that would make humanity extinct. It is in building up a Cosmos which can perhaps be launched from Earth and reach the furthest corners of the universe. Doubtless, we will do this as soon as move off this planet and spread ourselves and life across the universe. Robots will be helpful to that end which may be their ultimate function and not that of replacing us. Thus, building up the Cosmos is a prelude to our making our lasting mark on the universe.

Moreover, we move forward as a species when we take account of everything that we have achieved and strive to contribute further to our past achievements. The all-embracing view of the Cosmos is crucial to our progress whether we attain it completely or not. Everything about humanity and its achievements is gathered together in this broad notion of the Cosmos. It contains not just the internet but everything else that we have done in creating buildings, bridges, works of art, and so on, as is listed below. It is therefore the ultimate expression of humanity and everything about it. It is the converse of being divine or religious, as it is literally ourselves writ large. The notion helps us to bring ourselves into perspective and to see our Cosmic importance instead of belittling ourselves purposelessly as religion tends to do. The act of thinking about humanity and our achievements adds to its importance and strengthens our view of ourselves. This encourages us to do all that is necessary to advance humanity and life in general. In short, we see our contributions to humanity as being more meaningful and purposeful when they are put into this broad Cosmic context.

Our Cosmic position. In the vastness of space, which is otherwise composed of mindless matter and energy, something different is being constructed on our minuscule planet. It is a tiny seed of unifying harmony and order that we are bringing into being in exercising our intelligence and creativity in a reasonable, responsible and purposeful way. This is here called the 'Cosmos' which in conceptual terms we can contrast with the material universe. The universe is gradually being blasted to fragments but at the heart of it we, together with all living beings, are unifying agents who are countering this relentless dissipation of matter and energy. Living beings complexify matter and thereby bring meaning and purpose into the universe that is otherwise meaningless and purposeless. We, the human race, are doing more in creating this Cosmic unifying entity. The Cosmos brings together the additional meaning and purpose that we are contributing with our peculiar intelligence and creativity. This Cosmos is like a seed that will sprout forth in the far future though exactly what form it will ultimately take we can scarcely image. We might think of it as a god in the making. But it is not god now; it is only us making something of ourselves when we act intelligently and creatively.

The Cosmos is a part of the universe because we are a part of the universe. But it is distinct from it in being centred on ourselves and other intelligent beings capable of contributing to it. The universe is the external reality with which we interact to make our mark on it. What we do in the universe brings the Cosmos into being as something unique to ourselves. Thus, we can differentiate the notion of the Cosmos from the universe to draw attention to human achievements in a universe in which we otherwise appear to be infinitesimally small compared with its unimaginably size.

The Cosmos is more than just imaginary as it is confirmed by the evidence of human activity in all fields including the arts, music, and literature. That activity is real enough in that it produces concrete products that cannot be overlooked – buildings, books, artworks and so on. The Cosmos embraces everything that has happened to us in the past and is happening to us in the present. Its persistence is confirmed by the eternal existence of the past and of everything that has happened in the past. The everlasting Cosmos may be differentiated from the universe as containing everything that exists forever, whereas the universe continues to move on into the future and to disintegrate entropically. The differences between the universe and the cosmos may be summed up as follows:

UNIVERSE	COSMOS
Lacking Meaning and Purpose	Gathering Meaning and Purpose
Decaying Matter	Organising Order
Ultimately Destructive	Creatively Constructive
Impersonal and Quantifiable	Personal and Qualitative
Decaying into the Future	Accumulating all for the Future
Indifferent to us	Expressive of us

The notion of Cosmos is needed to bring together everything about us that is more than just matter and energy. It goes beyond the internet and all the intercommunications that make up human society. It includes the sociosphere, noosphere and other notions used to depict our integrated social activities. In this context, it embraces all our physical creations as well as those in literature, science, art, music, commerce, industry and the rest. All our buildings, bridges, artefacts, infrastructure, even our gardens and parks may be included in the all-encompassing bracket of contributions to the Cosmos. Though it is not divine in itself, perhaps it has the makings of a divine being in that it refers to everything 'divine' and 'sacred' about us, namely, when our activities and achievements amount to something more than the sum total of its parts and are valued in more than just material or financial terms. It is gradually building towards a god-like status in the far future. At present, the Cosmos is not God in any sense of the word, but it is a way of moving slowly and modestly towards what we conceive to be a more divine state of affairs than what exists at the present time. It gives direction to our culture and civilisation. We and all intelligent beings who know their place in the universe are together in bringing into existence something that embodies everything intelligent and creative about us.

Everything that we value in life belongs to the Cosmos and not to the decaying material universe. Whatever we do on this planet makes no difference to the universe at large. The universe is indifferent to our very existence. But what we do is of great importance to the Cosmos since its very existence depends on us and what we do with our lives. It is a notion by which we objectify ourselves and all our doings. It is what we are and what we do writ large so that we can interrelate with it as if it were distinct from us. We can relate to it because it is what we *are* basically as a productive, intelligent, creative species. We relate to it abstractly and it refers back to us at this abstract level of existence. It is an interactive notion which exists in our minds but which takes us out of ourselves in a positive way. We can view ourselves objectively and assess our achievements through this notion of the Cosmos. It is more than an object of imagination or fantasy since we can use it to evaluate ourselves and what we are doing. It gives us a goal to aim for, namely, that of developing and enriching the Cosmos. Its existence is qualitative and therefore aspirational. We aspire to it as being representative of the best we are capable of achieving with and in our lives.

In making our individual contributions to the Cosmos, we acknowledge its wholeness and become holists. To make such a contribution requires an understanding of the cosmic significance of that contribution. When the artist creates a work of art or the scientist devises a new theory, they cannot do so with seeing the wider significance of their contributions which belong to all humanity. When some thing new is brought into being, the Cosmos is enlarged and invigorated. The more we know about humanity, life and the universe, the more we contribute to its content which embraces all human activities. The Cosmos thrives on the activity of our brains in engaging with its contents. It is also vitalised by the additional order, arrangement, symmetry, regularity, system, pattern, and planning we introduce that did not exist before. The act of acquiring knowledge is a form of ordering and arranging material that is brought into and takes its place in the greater corpus of human knowledge. The 'all' is incorporated into the 'one'; the microcosm becomes the macrocosm, and the macrocosm becomes the microcosm. A constant interaction between these outlooks is the basis of all intellectual activity. Thus, holists are the ultimate polymaths or intellectuals who bring all available knowledge together to serve humanity to the best of their abilities.

The Cosmos is therefore a metaphor for all human knowledge, artistic and physical achievements. It metaphorically brings everything together and makes us to think more precisely and productively about the human condition and our contribution to the universe. The more everything is brought together, the more order and rationality there is in the universe. It is the simplest way to include all the products of our intelligence and creativity that have been objectified in any way. If they are out there for example in the internet then they are within the sphere of Cosmos. In our appreciation of the Cosmos, we cannot exclude any field of knowledge that is understood and appreciated by human beings. In the cosmian sphere, the scientist becomes a holistic intellectual and acquires the imagination and breadth of vision worthy of a holistic visionary. The emphasis is therefore on the continuous creativity of humanity.

B. The Meaning of Cosmos

The origin of the word. The word 'Cosmos' is from the Greek, κόσμος, originally meaning 'order' as opposed to disorder or chaos. It was extended to refer to the perfect ordering of the universe. It was extended to refer to the perfect ordering of the universe. The verb, κοσμεω (*kosmeo*), meant not only to order but also to discipline, rule or govern. Thus, 'Cosmos' originally referred to the divine ability to govern the universe and its contents. It later became associated with the philosophers' quest for the perfect order of eternity, that which is 'ageless and deathless'.[2] However, in Plato's *Timaeus*, 'Cosmos' is equated with '*ouranos*' (sky or heaven), and said to be the '*zoon*' (living being) of which all other living beings form a part.[3] It involves '*genesis*' (becoming) as well as '*on*' (being), since living beings are obviously changeable and not eternal in nature. But the eternal part of living beings consists in '*nous*' or the thinking, reasoning faculty which puts us in touch with the eternal forms of things. The eternal part of the Cosmos is copied from these eternal forms. Thus, the Cosmos for Plato includes our '*nous*' or intelligent reasoning, and not just the universe of material objects. Also, Plato uses another word, '*pantos*' (everything) which is often translated as 'universe'.[4] The body of the All (*to tou pantos soma*) is said to include material objects made of fire, earth, water and air.[5] Therefore, the distinction between Cosmos and universe being advocated here is anticipated to some extent in Plato's *Timaeus*, though in no clear or definitive way.

The contextual nature of the Cosmos. The notion of 'Cosmos' gives us reasons to justify our existence in the universe. In particular, it provides a context within which we can make more sense of our relationship to the universe as a whole. It contains not only everything of qualitative value that we bring into existence, it also includes the activity referred to in such overarching, unifying notions as the internet, cyberspace, the sociosphere, Karl Popper's 'World 3'[6] and Teilhard de Chardin's 'noosphere'.[7] It includes also our social activities: our communications, information, knowledge, culture, art and all our achievements in technology, business or whatever. Everything of a creative and innovative nature that distinguishes us as a species contributes to the Cosmos, wherein our existence is justified. It therefore includes everything that engages us as intelligent beings and makes more of what we are as unique beings. By these activities we are responsible for the beauty and ordering of the universe that makes for the Cosmos which is more than the material universe that we see around us.

The universe began in a state of infinite order and has tended towards greater disorder through time. The order that we are creating in making sense of the universe's workings contributes however minutely towards the reconstitution of the universe's original order. Our culture generates masses of information that introduces order into the universe that is otherwise losing information as it disintegrates. While the universe moves from order to disorder, life creates negative entropy by introducing order to counter this ugly and disorderly trend. The Cosmos embodies the re-ordering of the universe that only intelligent beings such as ourselves are capable of doing. It represents the increasing order that we and other life-forms bring into the universe which counters the universe's entropic dispersal, though in a very small way. It is our contribution to the far future when the universe may be mastered and its inevitable disintegration countered by beings far more advanced than we are.

The notion of Cosmos is useful in objectifying our activities. By including all aspects of our humanity in the Cosmos, we can better judge their value. For example, we can then think of a stunning painting such as Botticelli's *Venus* or an enchanting piece of music such as Beethoven's *Pastoral Symphony* as somehow going beyond humanity without being anything divine or supernatural. Our feelings are entirely physical and material, however transcendental we may feel them to be. Objects of beauty have a cosmic importance of their own, which is nevertheless entirely human and indicative of ourselves and our achievements. In this way, we can distinguish our cosmic judgments from humanity and its activities without losing the humanity which gave rise to them and which sustains them. In other words, the Cosmos gives us an interactive template by which to judge ourselves without dehumanising and lowering us like the divine perspective tends to do.

We thereby recognise that our achievements are not simply our own but have a permanent effect on the world and the universe at large. What we have done as a species exists as a permanent possibility of access in the future, even if by means at present unknown to us. It is therefore useful to think of everything that we value as being out there permanently available in being contributions to the Cosmos which is the ultimate ordering of a universe that is otherwise becoming increasingly disordered and chaotic.

How the Cosmos amplifies our humanity. We are important because of the new and different things that we do that contribute to the Cosmos. We can make this contribution, for instance, through art and science, that is to say: (1) by our creativity and our beautification of everything around us and (2) by our ordering of things and reasoning about them. Everything we do that is new and creative contributes to the Cosmos. Everything we do that brings order, reason and sense into being also contributes to the Cosmos. It is the ultimate end to which we can contribute by our thoughts and deeds that order and beautify our surroundings in a material way. The mere fact of living means that we are ordering our surroundings by relating ourselves to everything and making everything a part of ourselves. Our lives gain more sense and direction when they are seen as participating in a perpetual quest for greater beauty and order than what existed before. The notion of Cosmos thus provides the context in which we can gauge the value of what we are doing in relation to the whole universe.

In so far as our lives are disorderly, negative and self-destructive they lack cosmic value and significance. Such lives are entirely human and understandable but they arrest our cosmic development. There is no reason why we all cannot be productive and purposeful persons doing our bit to benefit humanity, each in our own way. Everyone is capable of being cosmically competent in that way, and the notion of Cosmos amplifies and illuminates the importance of our contributions however insignificant we may feel them to be. Therefore, it is incumbent on society to help everyone to find their own way of contributing meaningfully to the Cosmos. This is obviously a role for our education system which is performing at present only partially and perfunctorily in face of the infinite possibilities of human accomplishment.

The Cosmos comes into being at the medial area between the very large and the very small where intelligent beings such as ourselves make their original contributions to its content. But in that sense the Cosmos exists only ideally, that is to say, as an ideal that inspires and directs our thinking about the universe, its contents and our relationship to these contents. It is an ideal repository of everything worthwhile that we as individuals and as a species have accomplished. Though it is ideal, it is not imaginary. The fact that we are doing all these things and changing things in external reality is evidence of the objectivity of our achievements and that objectivity is concreted in the notion of Cosmos.

There is no need to believe uncritically in the existence of the Cosmos. It is only postulated as an ideal existent used as an interactive interface between our subjective thinking and the objective universe. It is a useful tool in ascertaining our place in the universe. Believing uncritically in the existence of a god is self-defeating compared with postulating the existence of a Cosmos. It is a human thing that refers to us for our purposes, whereas the notion of a God is an inhuman thing that has often been used for inhuman purposes, such as killing those who refuse to believe in it. Anyone not seeing any use or need for the notion of Cosmos is simply lacking a potentially useful notion and nothing more. It is no more an aspect of our culture such as classical music, rock'n'roll, science fiction, modern art, football or any other aspect that some people follow and others do not. On the other hand, there are educational benefits in taking a cosmic view to understand what it has to offer in helping us to appreciate our place in the universe. Taking a theistic or deistic view means giving up and withdrawing from the cosmic fray wherein lies our future and our destiny.

The Cosmos is our gift to the universe in gratitude for our lives. In this way, we make more of ourselves by making cosmic comparisons. This use of Cosmos amplifies our humanity without being inhuman, divine, or supernatural. Its contents are entirely of our own making and are made into objects that are in a sense our offerings to the universe. They are there to be appreciated and judged by posterity and other intelligent beings. Our gift to the universe is what we are and what we have achieved and this is embodied in the notion of Cosmos. We give the creations and products to the universe via the Cosmos in appreciation for the gift of life which the generation of the universe has made possible.

C. The Cosmos as a Unifying Principle

How the Cosmos unifies our thinking and doing. The notion of the Cosmos is particularly important as a way of unifying the diversity of human thought and activity. No matter how diverse, conflicting and contradictory our thoughts and actions may be, they are all subsumable into the Cosmos. They are unified not by being reduced to each other in a logically deductive manner, but by having their place in the overall mantle of the Cosmos. Thus, the Cosmos functions as an inductive, synthetic notion that interrelates everything by being a higher context within they can be considered in relation to each other.

While our beliefs are humanised within the Cosmos, they are not made any more truthful by that process. All the ideas and beliefs of religion and philosophy may be unified within the Cosmos. But it is not a repository of truths but of human intellectual products. These ideas and beliefs belong there because they are the products of human beings making their mark on the world. But the fact that they are unified therein tells us nothing about their truth or falsity. The Cosmos is their holdall and not their arbiter. They are unified in something that goes beyond them and that makes sense of them in a wider context. They are humanised and made part of our culture as a whole without being judged in terms of evidential or logical truth.

In this way, we can agree about the value of beliefs without agreeing about their truth. The unifying function of the Cosmos helps us to agree among ourselves about things that otherwise seem disparate and irreconcilable. We can agree about the cosmic nature of beliefs and ideas without necessarily agreeing about their truth or falsity. The value of Buddhism as a cultural contribution can be agreed upon without believing in it or regarding its tenets as being true. It is seen to be a valuable contribution to human culture but that does not make it true or false. This distinction ensures that religious beliefs cannot be considered absolute truths since they rank alongside other beliefs within the Cosmos without being pre-eminent among them.

Its unifying aspect can be useful in moving us forward to a better future and in making greater cultural progress. We can better see the limitations and defects of particular beliefs by comparing them within the context of the Cosmos. Some beliefs can be seen to be more culturally valuable than others. For example, the value of Scientology may compare unfavourably with the value of Buddhism. Some aspects of beliefs are valuable because they apply more widely to all humankind and are not just specific to particular belief systems. But making decisions as to truth and falsity must be based on facts and events in the physical world and not on anything whose cultural value must be evaluated on cosmic principles.

As unifying principle, the Cosmos functions as a more down-to-earth, human and malleable notion than that of the Absolute of Hegel and the other 19th century idealists. For them, the Absolute was a catchall into which everything whatsoever is subsumed at a very abstract and inhuman level of existence. In contrast, the Cosmos is a more limited notion that embraces things from a cultural point of view. The Cosmos is only one of many contexts in which we can view and appreciate our social, economic and cultural achievements. It must be considered, for instance, alongside the context of posterity within which the same content may also be evaluated. Above all, it is no more important than the context of humanity and indeed the context of the lives of individual human beings.

The Cosmos is the inverse of the material universe which is steadily running down and dissipating its energy through entropy. In contrast, the Cosmos is constantly being built up and developed because of the intelligent and creative activity of human beings. The universe lies in the past and can only be studied as something existing in the past. The Cosmos represents our future towards which we are inexorably moving. It is that towards which all our efforts are directed. It is the opposite of chaos and disorder as we can use it to make sense of our achievements and aspirations. The latter give meaning and purpose to our lives and so enrich the Cosmos in the process. The Cosmos therefore exists in the present as a pointer towards our future and what the human race as a whole is aiming to do and achieve in the universe. Thus, ours is the future, since only we and other life-forms can make the present unpredictably different in the future. The material universe is entirely predictable as far as future events are concerned.

The Cosmos relates the ideal to actuality. The Cosmos is the relationship of our imagination in its constant combat with the stark realities of life and living. It relates the ideal to the actual more effectively than any notion of God.[8] The ideal is related downwards to the real activities and achievements of humanity. For example, the ideal of furthering life on this and other planets relates to what we do in practical terms to achieve that goal. It is more like creating God in our own image than making ourselves into the image of God. We are extending ourselves towards a divine perspective rather than having a divinity thrust upon us with preconceived ideas of what it is that are dictated by scripture.

D. The Cosmic Contribution of Science

Without a doubt, our scientific knowledge constitutes our best and most important contribution to the Cosmos. It is by far the most useful, the most illuminating, and the most far-reaching of all cosmic contributions. Our increasing medical knowledge is indispensable to the future well-being of the human race, and our increasing scientific understanding of the universe and its contents is needed to ensure our survival as a species. The value of scientific knowledge to our culture is immeasurable. It is invaluable but not exorbitantly so. It has immense qualitative value but that value does not overarch the value of every other aspect of our culture.

As science is only one cosmic contributor among many, this fact determines its limitations. Its role in our culture is more clearly circumscribed when we see that it stands alongside the arts and other human activities in its contributions to the Cosmos. It may eclipse every other human activity in what it can do for us but it is still equal to everything else in relation to the Cosmos. For example, the contributions of art and music are scarcely comparable to those of science. But they have a human value that goes beyond all scientific analysis. They are human activities whose value is inestimable in terms of what they give us from aesthetic and emotional points of view. They are needed by us in our daily lives and they are not to be marginalised as their loss would significantly diminish our quality of life.

Science is not necessarily 'omnicompetent'. Scientific methods are extremely important in enabling us to understand the workings of the material world. But these methods are largely abstract and mathematical and do not apply to qualitative value that is largely subjective, intuitive and holistic. That value cannot be pinned down by mathematical or logical methods which depend on discrete distinctions being made and on wholes being reduced to their parts. Science is not 'omnicompetent' (as Peter Atkins put it[9]) in that it is not competent to fulfil the role of other cosmic contributors which do not fall within the context of science. It is not competent to tell us what human feelings are all about. It is not competent to measure these feelings or reduce them to anything scientifically analysable. Any such attempts would violate our integrity as individuals. Everyone has a right to their own feelings without their being imposed on them by 'scientific' means. As it stands, science cannot explain everything about the universe and it cannot predict the future of our species. It also gives us no clue as to what we are supposed to do with ourselves in the future. In short, there are lots of ways in which science is quite useless to us.

It is not possible to extend the scientific method indefinitely, otherwise art, for instance, would be entirely mechanical and mathematical and the machines could take over. There is a sense in which all aspects of human culture may be subjected to scientific methods of one sort or another. Statistical analysis is one example of this. But they are equally subject to other methods which are not regarded as scientific. From the 1970s onwards, physicists have increasingly widened the scope of physics to include not only philosophy in general but also eastern mysticism. Books such as *The Tao of Physic*[10], *Wholeness and the Implicate*

Order[11], *God and the New Physics*[12], all mark the physicists' loss of confidence in the ability of physics to supply the ultimate answers. But in reality they do not extend the boundaries of science so much as involve a retreat into philosophy and mysticism in search of answers, (as I argue in my book, *What is Philosophy?* e.g. pp. 11 and 14)

From a scientific point of view, the Cosmos functions as an interactive process by which we can interact ideally with the reality of the universe to make better sense of it. We arrive at ideas and then test them in relation to external reality. In interacting with the universe through science, and in doing our meaningful and purposeful deeds that add to the order and beauty of the universe, the Cosmos comes into its own as the interface between the stark materiality of the universe and our ideal, subjective thinking about the universe and its contents. It reflects our intermediary position between its vastness and minisculeness. Thus, on the one hand, the Cosmos resides between the macro-universe of astrophysics and the micro-universe of quantum physics. On the other hand, it is placed between our ideal musings and the stark reality of physical existence. Ideality refers to our subjective thoughts and speculations that we constantly relate to reality to arrive at a realistic view of ourselves and the universe. The Cosmos grows and develops by such interactions. For example, as our understanding of quantum physics increasingly approximates the realities of the universe, the Cosmos grows accordingly. The following diagram brings these four relationships together to symbolise their contributions to the Cosmos which is centred between them.

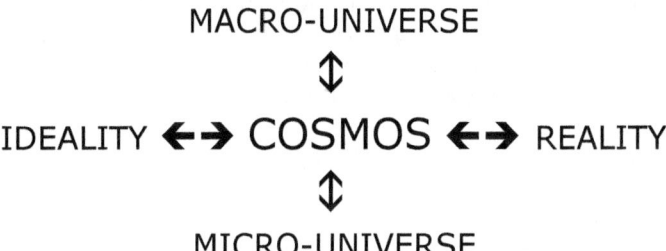

An Interactive Cosmic Quadrifoil Matrix

The above quadrifoil matrix shows how cosmic activity progresses interactively. It depicts the four dimensions of interactivity that are necessary and sufficient for the progress of cosmic activity. The Cosmos in the middle capitalises on our interactive efforts to reconcile the macro-universe with the micro-universe. We do so by constantly relating ideality to reality and *vice versa*. This enables us to put scientific activity into a wider context beyond that of explaining the nitty gritty of how the universe works in concrete mathematical terms. It puts that activity in the context of human activity in general and shows its Cosmic importance.

The diagram also shows that the Cosmos results from the interaction between the physical reality of the universe and the ideal world that we create in thinking about anything, real or unreal. It assumes that the universe's reality comprises only the material and physical parts of the Cosmos. This assumption would presumably be accepted by materialists who deny the existence of anything beyond the material universe. However, sceptics and idealists may deny even that assumption but in so doing they risk disconnecting their thinking from external reality altogether. Thus, the Cosmos reflects the fact that we stay in touch with reality by constantly interacting with it to ensure that our ideas accurately represent reality as far as humanly possible. In short, the diagram depicts dualist interaction which is elaborated in more detail in my book entitled *The Promise of Dualism* (2015).

E. The Cosmic Significance of Past Religions

> How can cosmic religious feeling be communicated from one person to another, if it can give rise to no definite notion of a God and no theology? In my view, it is the most important function of art and science to awaken this feeling and keep it alive in those who are capable of it.
>
> Albert Einstein (1935) [13]

The real cosmic value of religion. All the religions of the past have made their respective contributions to the Cosmos. The study of these contributions is an intimate part of cosmic research since they all have something to say about the human condition and about what it is to be human. But this is only when we consider them historically. Their cosmic value is lost when they are considered as active vehicles of truth that are set against other religions and sources of religious thought and feeling. Their cosmic significance depends on their no longer being proselytising religions whose truths are forced on people in an exclusive way that brooks no deviation from these truths. Thus, Cosmos is inclusive of all religions that are not themselves exclusive.

Religious writings make their own cosmic contribution and they include all the sacred works of all the religions of the world, most notably such documents as the Bible, the Talmud, the Koran, Buddhist scriptures, the Upanishads, and the Bhagavad Gita. The range of writings to be included under this heading can be seen in works such as Bouquet's *The Sacred Books of the World*.[14] This book includes writings as diverse as Sumerian Prayers, Homeric Hymns, Zoroastrian Literature, and Japanese Shinto Literature. We can add to this list our growing understanding of ancient religious writings such as those of the ancient Egyptians and Mayans. All these writings are important to our understanding of how human religious thought developed, and of how diverse that thought is. Although humanist thinking has transcended religious thought, the study of the atter helps us to understand the past trains of thought by which we have arrived at a more advanced understanding of our plight and place in the universe.

The Cosmos as a successor to the comparative religion movement. Within the context of the Cosmos, all religions are brought together eclectically with the hope of convergence at some date in the future. This unifying procedure contrasts strongly with the eclecticism and syncretism of past attempts to bring them together. Comparative religion is an example of an attempt to unify all religions by giving an account of them in a loose and eclectic fashion.[15] No religion is treated as being better than any other though an attempt is made to pinpoint their common features. The comparative religion movement failed because it had no method or system of thought by which all the incompatible religions could be brought together into a unity. The notion of Cosmos is step towards providing such a method of unifying religious thought and practice. It provides a framework within which all religious views and sentiments can be accommodated without necessarily being antithetical to each other.

Religious prophets are those people who have seen beyond the material world and have emphasised the importance of our cosmic musings about our existence. In a sense, we are all cosmic prophets who have views about the cosmic nature of the universe and who strive to communicate these views to other people. Compared the well-known prophets, most of us have made fairly modest contributions to the cosmic content. The most important of all the cosmic prophets who have walked the face of the Earth are those who have had the most impact on the history of the human race. They introduced new religions and thereby changed the thinking of humankind by these acts. The most important of all cosmic prophets include Akhenaton, Moses, Zoroaster, Buddha, Confucius, Jesus Christ and Mohammed. Whether the effects of these prophets have been altogether to the good of humankind is entirely another matter. The notion of Cosmos now gives us the opportunity to establish the real and lasting importance of these figures. We do so by accounting for their influence on their contemporaries, disciples, and followers. The facts about them can be studied objectively so that their true value to humanity can be established beyond doubt.

Religious truths contribute to the Cosmos in so far as they add to our understanding of the human condition. For instance, the distinctive advances of the Christian message contained in the Sermon of the Mount are permanent contributions to the Cosmos. We ought to be *Christians* in our attitude towards our potential enemies and in our attempts to understand people rather than hate them. Equally, we ought to be *Jews* in our respect for family life; *Muslims* in our respect for authority and absolute values; *Buddhists* in our use of meditation to reach our inner being; *Hindus* in our appreciation of spirituality; and so on. In this way, we can make use of the strengths and truths in particular religions without believing in the unbelievable and without practising senseless, superfluous rituals. Such cosmic ideals were anticipated by the comparative religion movement which has its roots in the religious toleration established in Great Britain after the Civil War of the 17th century. In understanding the merits of other religions, we have the possibility of transcending them all within the context of the Cosmos. Also, by taking account of all religions and respecting their respective contributions, we pass on to posterity what is worthwhile about them.

It is therefore clear that the traditional religions have no future as self-sufficient, mutually antagonistic movements. By themselves, they no longer take us anywhere as they have become too ingrown and limited in their outlook and lack competent answers to the human predicament. The exclusivity of these religions means that they exclude unbelievers and heretics. The four great prophets of religion – Moses, Jesus, Buddha and Mohammed – got it wrong, each in their different ways. The first and last of these personages made far too much of a non-existent entity with the aim of belittling people unjustifiably and boosting their power over them without limit. Jesus made too much of unworldliness and meekness. The Buddha made too much of introspective meditation to the point of vacuity. Moreover, they all failed to see the bigger picture. Their view of human potential was also limited by the state of human knowledge available to them.

To summarise, the Cosmos is ourselves writ large. It is a way of thinking about our accomplishments in the abstract. In being all-inclusive concept, it compares favourably with exclusivity of religion, which typically excludes unbelievers and heretics. There is no need to believe implicitly in the existence of the Cosmos as it is only a means of making sense of humanity's contributions to the universe. It is enough to see its usefulness in that regard and then to dispense with it. There is no point in opposing it as it is only a harmless abstraction that does not require anything of anyone. Its role is entirely descriptive and there is nothing prescriptive about it. If it does nothing for you, it is nothing to you. Yet it is a way of describing everything about humanity and of our achievements. It becomes highly meaningful and useful in that context, as it is a holistic aid by which we can see ourselves as an invaluable part of the whole and thus add meaning and purpose to our lives.

Notes and References

Opening quotations (p.iv)

1. Alfred North Whitehead (1861-1947), *Science and the Modern World*, (1925 – New York: Mentor, 1958), ch. XIII, p. 207.
2. Winston Spencer Churchill (1874-1965) 'Speech at Harvard University', 6th Sep. 1943, in *Complete Speeches 1897-1963*, (New York: Chelsea House Publishers, 1974), Vol. VII, 1943-49, p.6826.

Introduction (pp. 1-9)

1. "*In via vitae non progredi, regredi est.*" Bernard of Clairaux (1090-1153) in his second sermon on 'The Purification of the Blessed Virgin Mary', (*Sermones in PURIFICATIONE beatae MARIAE Virginis*). Thomas Aquinas used this saying on at least two occasions i.e. in his *Commentary on St. Paul's Epistle to the Ephesians* and his *Commentary on the Epistle to the Hebrew*, in the latter of which he attributes it to Bernard.
2. W.B. Yeats, 'The Second Coming', *The Collected Poems of W.B. Yeats*, (1933 - London: Macmillan, 1981), p. 211.
3. To use Karl Popper's distinctions as in *The Open Society and its Enemies*, (1945 - London: RKP, 1969), Vol. I, Ch. 3, p. 22, and Ch. 9, p. 157.
4. Alexander Raven, *Civilisation as Divine Superman*, (London: Williams & Norgate 1932), p. 40.
5. For example, Bill Gates, Elon Musk and Stephen Hawking have intimated in newspaper interviews their concerns about artificial intelligence being more of a threat than a benefit to our future. Cf. Katya Siepmann and Annabella McIntosh, 'The Age of Transhumanism Has Begun: Will It Bring Humanism to Its End? – An Interview with Roland Benedikter.' *Essays in the Philosophy of Humanism*, (Sheffield: Equinox Publishing Ltd., 2015), Vol. 23.2, p.136.
6. As listed in Siepmann and McIntosh, *op. cit.* p. 142.
7. Isaac Asimov, 'Runaround', *I, Robot,* (New York: Doubleday & Company, 1950).
8. The full etymology of 'prospective' is as follows: Middle English *prospectyve*, n., from Old French *prospectif*, an adjective (as a noun, *prospective*, feminine) = Italian *prospettivo*, from Late Latin *prospectivus*, pertaining to a prospect or to looking forward, from Latin *prospicere*, past participle *prospectus*, look forward, look into the distance.
9. H. G. Wells (1866-1946), *The Discovery of the Future*, ed. by P. Parrinder, (1902 - London: PNL Press, 1989), p.19.
10. *Ibid.*, p.20.
11. *Ibid.*, p. 34.
12. *Ibid.*, p. 34.
13. *Ibid.*, pp. 35-6.
14. *Ibid.* p. 36

1. Unity: Bringing us all Together (pp. 11-22)

1. Erich Fromm (1900-1980), *The Art of Loving*, (1957 - London: Unwin, 1978), ch. 2, p. 16.
2. Robert Burns, (1786), 'Is There for Honest Poverty', *Poems and Songs of Robert Burns*, ed. by James Barke, (London and Glasgow: Collins, 1955), p. 643.
3. "With instant electric technology, the globe itself can never again be more than a village." Marshall McLuhan, *Understanding Media*, 1964, (London: Sphere Books, 1968), Part II, ch. 32, p. 366. He first used the term 'global village' in *The Gutenberg Galaxy: The Making of Typographic Man*, (Toronto: University of Toronto Press, 1962), p. 31

2 Humanity: Believing in our Future (pp. 23-35)

1. Ralph Waldo Emerson (1803-1882), 'The Method of Nature', in *Nature, The Conduct of Life*, (1841 London: Everyman, 1963), p. 40.

2. Darwin was astonished by how primitive human beings can become: "I could not have believed how wide was the difference between savage and civilised man. It is greater than between a wild and domesticated animal, in as much as in man there is a greater power of improvement." Charles Darwin, *The Voyage of the 'Beagle'*, 1839. Originally published under the title: *Journal of Researches into the Geology and Natural History of the Various Countries Visited by H.M.S. Beagle under the Command of Captain Fitzroy, R.N. From 1832 to 1836*. London: Henry Colburn. Ch. XI, p. 228.

3. Cf., for example, the Wikipedia article on the Aboriginal Tasmanians: "It has been suggested that approximately 4,000 years ago, the Aboriginal Tasmanians largely dropped scaled fish from their diet, and began eating more land mammals such as possums, kangaroos, and wallabies. They also switched from worked bone tools to sharpened stone tools." (Footnoted to Lyndall Ryan: *The Aboriginal Tasmanians*, Second Edition, Allen & Unwin, 1996.) However, they appear to have lost the ability to make fire only in the last few centuries – see: Rebe Taylor, 'The Polemics of Making Fire in Tasmania: The Historical Evidence Revisited.' *Aboriginal History Journal*, Vol 32, 2008. Available at: http://epress.anu.edu.au/wp-content/uploads/2011/05/ch0155.pdf *(Accessed 2012-10-08)*

4. Cf. Colin Turnbull, *The Mountain People*, (1973 - London: Paladin Books, 1984). In this case the regression of this tribe was bought about by poverty, famine and the fact that the tribe's traditional hunting grounds became a national park.

5. Cf. Edward Gibbon (1776), *The Decline and Fall of the Roman Empire*, (London: J.M. Dent, 1962), Vol. IV, ch. XXXVII, p.8, where he tells us that even the army opted for monastic life rather than face the barbarians:

"The affrighted provincials of every rank, who fled before the barbarians, found shelter and subsistence; whole legions were buried in these religious sanctuaries."

6. William Shakespeare, Hamlet, Act II, Scene II, lines 297-299.

7. "Homo sum: humani nil a me alienum puto." Terence (c.190-159 BCE), *Heauton Timorumenos*, (The Self-Tormentor), Act One, Scene One, line 77. In the play this is said by a character to justify his interfering in another person's affairs to help him. Thus in many interpretations it is taken out of context to mean whatever one wants it to mean.

8. Virgil, Aeneid, Book 9, line 641.

9. Erich Fromm, *Man for Himself*, (1949 - London: RKP, 1971), p. 40.

10. A 'human selection theory' is possible which shows that we did not simply evolve from apes but have moulded and developed ourselves in relation to a developing culture.

11. Cf. Neurath's ship: "We are like sailors who have to rebuild their ship on the open sea, without ever being able to dismantle it in dry-dock and reconstruct it from the best components." Otto Neurath, 'Protocol Statements' in *Philosophical Papers 1913-1946*, edited & translated by R. S. Cohen and Marie Neurath, (Dordrecht: D. Reidel, 1983), p. 92.

3. Centrality: Developing the Middle Ground (pp. 36-50)

1. Max Planck (1858-1947), *Where is Science Going?* (London: Allen and Unwin, 1933), p. 217.

2. "That there is an infinite number of such worlds can be perceived, and that such a world may arise in a world or in the one of the *intermundia* [μετακοσμία] (by which term we mean the spaces between worlds)." ('Ότι δὲ καὶ τοιοῦτοι κόσμοι εἰσὶν ἄπειροι τὸ πλῆθός ἐστι καταλαβεῖν, καὶ ὅτι καὶ ὁ τοιοῦτος δύναται κόσμος γίνεσθαι καὶ ἐν κόσμῳ καὶ μετακοσμίῳ ὃ λέγομεν μεταξὺ κόσμων διάστημα.) Diogenes Laertius (c.300CE), *Lives and Opinions of Eminent Philosophers*, (Loeb

Classical Library, 1980), Vol. II, Epicurus, §89, pp. 616-617. Also, Cicero: "And they can laugh with the better grace because Epicurus, to make the gods ridiculous, represents them as transparent, with the winds blowing through them, and living between two worlds (as if between our two groves) from fear of the downfall." (Et quidem illi facilius facere possunt: deos enim ipsos iocandi causa induxit Epicurus perlucidos et perflabilis et habitantis tamquam inter duos lucos sic inter duos mundos propter metum ruinarum.) Cicero, *De Divinatione*, Book II, 40.

3. Giovanni Pico della Mirandola (1463-1494), *Oration on the Dignity of Man*, 1486. Available online.

4. Blaise Pascal, *Pensées*, trans. A.J. Krailsheimer, (1670 – London: Penguin, 1975), §199, p. 90.

"Car qui n'admirera que notre corps, qui tantôt n'était pas perceptible dans l'univers imperceptible lui-même dans le sein du tout, soit à présent un colosse un monde ou plutôt un tout à l'égard du néant où l'on ne peut arriver. Qui se considèrera de la sorte s'effraiera de soi-même et se considérant soutenu dans la masse que la nature lui a donnée entre ces deux abîmes de l'infini et du néant il tremblera dans la vue de ces merveilles. . . Car enfin qu'est-ce que l'homme dans la nature ? Un néant à l'égard de l'infini, un tout à l'égard du néant, un milieu entre rien et tout, infiniment éloigné de comprendre les extrêmes ; la fin des choses et leurs principes sont pour lui invinciblement cachés dans un secret impénétrable. Egalement incapable de voir le néant d'où il est tiré et l'infini où il est englouti."

5. J.B.S Haldane (1892-1964), *The Inequality of Man*, (1932 – London: Penguin, 1938), p.121.

6. Diogenes Laertius, *Lives and Opinions of Eminent Philosophers*, Loeb Classical Library, 1980,Vol. I, Book I, Prologue, §16, p.17.

7. Francis Bacon, *Novum Organon*, 1620, Part I, §95.

8. Francis Bacon (1620), Proem to *The Great Instauration*, as below.

9. Francis Bacon (1620), Preface to *The Great Instauration*, last paragraph. Available at: http://www.constitution.org/bacon/instauration.htm (Accessed 2012-06-30) Kant quotes the Latin version of this preface at the beginning of his *Critique of Pure Reason*, as does Fichte at the beginning of his Preface to the *Wissenschaftslehre* (Science of Knowledge).

10. William James, *Pragmatism*, (1907 - New York: Washington Square Press, 1963), Lecture One p. 9.

11. A.N. Whitehead, *Science and the Modern World*, (1925 - New York: Mentor, 1958), ch. I p.3, ch. XIII p. 199, for instance.

12. Isaiah Berlin, 'The Hedgehog and the Fox' in *Russian Thinkers*, (London: Penguin, 1979), p.22.

13. Bernard Williams, his conversation with Bryan Magee, published by Magee in *Men of Ideas*, (Oxford: OUP 1982), p. 116.

14. C.G. Jung, in 'Psychological Types' (1921), *The Collected Works of Carl G. Jung*, (trans. R.F.C. Hull, Bollingen Series XX, Princeton University Press),Vol. 6, Part I.

4: Duality: Looking at Both Sides (pp. 51-66)

1. Alfred North Whitehead (1861-1947), *The Adventure of Ideas*, (Cambridge: CUP 1933), p. 245.

2. Perhaps such an outstanding team might become an exhibition team that tours the world, like the basketball team, the Harlem Globetrotters, its members becoming celebrities in their own right. However, competitive sport usually involves an element of uncertainty and unpredictability to attract spectators and partisans.

3. A. M. Turing, "Computing Machinery and Intelligence," *Mind*, 1950,Vol. LIX, No. 236. This famous paper is excerpted in Hofstadter and Dennett's book, *Mind's I*, Penguin Books, 1982, pp.53-68. However, the question of whether a machine is thinking or not may be

resolved by observing how it is behaving to itself. Thus, self reference is more important than its reaction to people in the way suggested by Turing. Its inner life, consciousness and self-identity can give it feelings and thoughts of its own. We will react emotionally to their displays of emotion and will either empathise or not as the case may be. What we are actually feeling may be uncertain even to ourselves, and computers would need to behave likewise if they are to be likened to us.

4. This dualist view of the history of philosophy is outlined in my book, *What is Philosophy?* (Edinburgh: Dunedin Academic Press, 2008).

5. Cf. Karl Popper, *The Open Society and its Enemies*, (1945 - London: RKP, 1969), Vol. I, Ch. 7, Note 4, p. 265:

"Unlimited tolerance must lead to the disappearance of tolerance. If we extend unlimited tolerance even to those who are intolerant, if we are not prepared to defend a tolerant society against the onslaught of the intolerant, then the tolerant will be destroyed and tolerance with them. . . I do not imply that we should always suppress the utterance of intolerant philosophies; as long as we can counter them by rational argument and keep them in check by public opinion, suppression would certainly be most unwise. But we should claim the **right** to suppress them if necessary even by force; for it may easily turn out that they are not prepared to meet us on the level of rational argument, but begin by denouncing all argument; they may forbid their followers to listen to rational argument, because it is deceptive, and teach them to answer arguments by the use of their fists or pistols."

6. Aristotle, *Nicomachean Ethics*, Book Two, Section 7, 1107a28. See London: Penguin edition (1987), p. 104.

7. William Hazlitt, 'On People With One Idea', *Table Talk*, (1824 - London: J. M. Dent, 1908), Essay VII, pp. 59-69.

8. Cf. Sir Walter Scott's extraordinary portrayal of Oliver Cromwell in his novel, *Woodstock* (1826). It seems convincingly true to life.

9. Thomas Reid's view of common sense consisted of a psychological examination of the five senses laid down by Aristotle plus a list of common sense principles that served only to stultify metaphysical discussion. See, for example, *Essays on the Intellectual Powers of Man*, Essay VI, Chs IV-VI in *The Works of Thomas Reid*, ed. Sir W. Hamilton, (Edinburgh: James Thin, 1895), pp. 434-461.

10. Robert Graves' poem 'In Broken Images' is freely available online

11. Joseph Addison (1672-1719), in his Roger de Coverely essays in *The Spectator*, no.122, July 20, 1711, (London: J.M. Dent, 1909), p.149. See also no. 117, July 14, 1711 (p.128):

"There are some Opinions in which a Man should stand Neuter, without engaging his Assent to one side or the other. Such a hovering Faith as this, which refuses to settle upon any Determination, is absolutely necessary to a Mind that is careful to avoid Errors and Prepossessions."

12. This is the subject of my paper entitled "The Role of Dualist Thinking in Management" which was presented to the Seventh International Philosophy of Management Conference at St. Anne's College, Oxford on Friday 23rd July 2010.

13. The 'social treatment system' is elaborated in my e-book entitled *Punish the Person, not the Crime! Proposing a Social Treatment System to Punish Lawbreakers*, (Amazon Kindle, 2013).

14. Cf. *The New Production of Knowledge*, Michael Gibbons, C. Limoges, H. Nowotny, S. Schwartzman, P. Scott, and M. Trow. (London: Sage, 1994).

15. The quotation is in fact a paraphrase from a passage in *Plutarch's Moralia*, Vol. One, III 'On Listening to Lectures', (Περὶ τοῦ ἀκούειν - *De recta ratione audiendi*), 48 C2–D4, trans. by Frank Cole Babbitt, (Loeb edition, London: William Heinemann Ltd., 1927). pp. 257-259. A fuller paraphrase might be as follows: 'The mind is not to be filled like a

vessel (ἀγγεῖον) but requires kindling like wood to provide new illuminations and insights through speech and text."

16. These distinctions are also discussed in my article, 'Posterity—An Eighteenth Century Answer to God and Religion', The Humanist, Vol. 71 (2), March/April 2011, pp. 39-40. It is also reprinted in my book, American Papers on Humanism and Religion, (Almostic Publications, 2014).

5. Vitality: Building Ourselves up (pp. 68-85)

1. George Bernard Shaw (1856-1950), Man and Superman, (1903 - London: Penguin, 1971), Epistle Dedicatory, p. 32.

2. William James (1842-1910), 'On a Certain Blindness in Human Beings', Selected Papers on Philosophy, (1915, London: Dent, 1967), p.11.

3. See, for example, Ian Stewart, Does God Play Dice? The Mathematics of Chaos, (London: Penguin Books, 1990), ch. 6, pp. 95-125.

4. Cf. Samuel Smiles, Character, (1871, London: John Murray, 1912), Ch. I, pp.12-13: "Character exhibits itself in conduct, guided and inspired by principle, integrity, and practical wisdom. In its highest form it is the individual will acting energetically under the influence of religion, morality, and reason."

5. For more information on this 'logic of dualist interaction' see my book The Promise of Dualism (2014), pp. 149-185.

6. Lynne McTaggart, The Field: The Quest for the Secret Force of the Universe, (London: HarperCollins, 2003).

7. William Blake, Poems and Prophecies, (London: J.M. Dent & Sons Ltd., 1939), 'All Religions are One', Principles one and five, p. 5.

8. Cf. Immanuel Kant, (1785), The Moral Law, (Groundwork of the Metaphysics of Morals), trans. H.J. Paton, (London: Hutchinson, 1972), §74-77, p. 95. ("Das Reich der Zwecke")

6. Illuminosity: Enlightening Everything (pp. 86-99)

1. Jonathan Swift (1667-1745), The Battle of the Books, (1704 - London: Everyman, 1970), p. 155.

2. This extremely apposite dualist distinction between introversion and extraversion was of course coined by C.G. Jung, C.G. See his paper 'Psychological Types', in The Collected Works of Carl G. Jung, (trans. R.F.C. Hull, Bollingen Series XX, Princeton University Press), Vol. 6. Also in The Portable Jung, edited by Joseph Campbell, (London: Penguin Books, 1978), pp.178-269.

3. Albert Camus, The Outsider, trans. Joseph Laredo, (1942 - London: Penguin, 1983), ch. 5, p. 115.

4. Cf. R.M. Hare, Applications of Moral Philosophy, (London: Macmillan, 1972), ch. 4, pp. 32-33.

5. Cf. Plato, Phaedrus, 250b-e, (London: Penguin, 1973), pp. 56-57.

6. See chapter two of my book, The Answers Lie Within Us, (1998) for more on this.

7. Julian Huxley, Essays of a Biologist, (1923 - London: Penguin, 1939), p. 20.

8. Ernest Becker, The Birth and Death of Meaning, (1971 – London: Penguin, 1980), p. 194.

9. This list is suggested by the examples given by Harvey Siegel in his book, Educating Reason: Rationality, Critical Thinking and Education, (New York and London: Routledge, 1990), ch. 2, p. 40.

10. Dr. Samuel Johnson as quoted by James Boswell in *The Life of Samuel Johnson, LL.D.* (1791 - London: J.M. Dent, 1962), Vol. One, 1763 aged. 54, p. 246.

11. Cardinal John Henry Newman, *On the Scope and Nature of University Education*, (1859 - London, J. Dent, 1915), Discourse VI, pp. 130-1.

12. John Passmore, *The Perfectibility of Man*, (London: Duckworth, 1970), pp. 326-327

7. Creativity: Making the Most of our Artistic Potential (pp. 100-113)

1. Vincent van Gogh (1853-1890), 'Letter from Vincent van Gogh to Theo van Gogh', Arles, 3 September 1888: Available at this website: http://vangoghletters.org/vg/letters/let673/letter.html
"Je peux bien dans la vie et dans la peinture aussi me passer de bon Dieu mais je ne puis pas, moi souffrant, me passer de quelque chose plus grand que moi qui est ma vie, la puissance de créer."

2. The metaphor of the 'invisible hand' is used by Adam Smith in both his main works. (1) In the *Moral Sentiments* it is the rich that "are led by an invisible hand ... without intending it, without knowing it, advance the interest of society" *The Theory of Moral Sentiments*, (1759 - London: H.G. Bohn, 1853), Part IV, ch. I, p. 265. (2) In the *The Wealth of Nations*, it is the worker or businessman who is "led by an invisible hand to promote an end which was no part of his intention. By pursuing his own interest he frequently promotes that of the society more effectually than when he really intends to promote it." *An Inquiry into the Nature and Causes of the Wealth of Nations*, (1776 – London: Routledge, 1900), Book IV, ch. II, p.345.

3. R.G. Collingwood (1889-1943), *The Principles of Art*, (1938, Oxford: OUP, 1977), Book II, Ch. VII, pp. 158-159.

8. Morality: Disciplining Ourselves Purposefully (pp. 114-144)

1. John Fowles (1926 – 2005), *The Aristos*, (London: Triad/Granada, 1980), p. 110.

2. Freud originally used the phrase 'ideal ego' (Ideal-Ich' or 'Ich-Ideal') but from 1923 began using the term. *Superego* (das Über-Ich). Cf. Sigmund Freud, 'The Ego and the Id' (*Das Ich und das Es*), 1923, in *On Metapsychology: The Theory of Psychoanalysis*, Vol. 11 of the Pelican Freud Library, (Harmondsworth, Middlesex: Penguin, 1984), p. 367

3. The phrase ' the Golden Mean' refers to Aristotle's 'mean' between excess and deficiency. See Aristotle, *The Nicomachean Ethics*, (London: Penguin, 1987), 1106a-b, pp. 100-101.

4. Aristotle, *op. cit.*, 1095a, p. 66.

5. This saying of St. Augustine is quoted without reference in *Philosophy as a Way of Life*, by Pierre Hadot, (Oxford: Blackwell, 1995), p. 65.

6. Plato, *The Republic*, (London: Penguin, 1974), Book Six, 508e, p. 308. (καὶ τῷ γιγνώσκοντι τὴν δύναμιν ἀποδιδὸν τὴν τοῦ ἀγαθοῦ ἰδέαν φάθι εἶναι: αἰτίαν δ' ἐπιστήμης οὖσαν καὶ ἀληθείας,)

7. G.E. Moore, *Principia Ethica*, (1903 - Cambridge: CUP, 1922), p. 6.

8. Aristotle, *The Nicomachean Ethics*, (London: Penguin, 1987), 1097b, p. 100.

9. Nietzsche, *The Birth of Tragedy*, (1886 - London: Penguin, 1993), p. 18, where Nietzsche distinguishes the 'Apolline [sic] dream artist' and the 'Dionysiac ecstatic artist'. The Apollonian view involves the quest for self-knowledge and moderation, see *ibid.*, p. 26.

10. Aristotle, *Topics*, I, i, 100a-101a, Loeb edition, pp. 273-274. This use of the word in English is entirely the invention of the author.

11. Hence the sterility of the Scottish common sense movement from Thomas Reid onwards. To confer self-evidence on a metaphysical principle is to inhibit metaphysical discussion altogether. See my book, *What is Philosophy?* (Dunedin Academic Press, 2008), pp. pp. 72-74 for more discussion on the contribution of common sense philosophy.
12. Shakespeare, *Hamlet*, Act One , Scene 3, lines 78-80.
13. Michael Polanyi , *Personal Knowledge,* (London: RKP, 1962), p. 17.
14. *New Testament,* Matthew, 5:44; Luke, 6:35.
15. Edmund Burke, *Reflections on the Revolution in France,* (1790 - London: Penguin, 1976), p. 245.
16. David Hume, *A Treatise of Human Nature,* (ed. Nidditch - Oxford: the Clarendon Press, 1989), Book III, Part I, sect I, *op. cit.,* pp. 469-470.

9. Normality: Having a Society Based on Norms (pp. 145-189)

1. Albert Einstein (1879-1955), 'What I Believe', *Forum and Century,* 84, (1931) pp. 183-194. This saying is engraved on Einstein's statute in the grounds of the National Academy of Sciences, Constitution Avenue, Washington D.C. The full quotation is as follows:

"By academic freedom I understand the right to search for truth and to publish and teach what one holds to be true. This right implies also a duty: one must not conceal any part of what one has recognized to be true. It is evident that any restriction on academic freedom acts in such a way as to hamper the dissemination of knowledge among the people and thereby impedes national judgment and action."

2. As quoted in the Sunday Times, 6th September 1992, Section One, p. 10, where the German term is explicated that way. Its more literal meaning may be 'the psychological turning around of conclusions by the masses' or something of the sort.
3. Plato, *Phaedo,* 59b, as *The Last Days of Socrates,* (London: Penguin, 1971), p. 101. Greek original is Πλάτων δὲ οἶμαι ἠσθένει. (Platon de oimai isthenei).
4. R.L. Stevenson, 'El Dorado', *Virginibus Puerisque,* in *The Works of Robert Louis Stevenson,* London: William Heinemann, Ltd., 1925, Vol. XXV, p. 85.
5. Aristotle, *Ethics,* Book I, iv, 1095a20, (London: Penguin Books, 1987), p. 66. The original Greek for 'living well and doing well' is: τὸ δ' εὖ ζῆν καὶ τὸ εὖ πράττειν. (eu zen kai eu prattein).
6. John Knox (c.1513-1572), *First Blast of the Trumpet against the Monstrous Regiment of Women,* (1558), p. 4. Available at http://www.swrb.com/newslett/actualNLs/firblast.htm Accessed 28/3/2015.
7. John Knox, *op. cit.,* 'Foreword to the Second Trumpet' (which exists only as a draft and is usually appended to the *First Trumpet*).
8. John Knox, *op. cit.,* p. 37.
9. John Knox, *op. cit.,* p.106
10. As reported in various newspapers and in online news sites.
11. Churchill made clear the importance of civilisation in a speech in 1938 which he begins by saying: "it means a society based upon the opinion of civilians. It means that violence, the rule of warriors and despotic chiefs, the conditions of camps and warfare, of riot and tyranny, give place to parliaments where laws are made, and independent courts of justice in which over long periods those laws are maintained." Sir Winston Churchill, *Civilisation,* Chancellor's Address, University of Bristol, 2nd July, 1938, in *Complete Speeches 1897-1963,* New York: Chelsea House Publishers, 1974, Vol. VI, 1943-49, pp. 5990-5991.
12. Margaret Thatcher, *Speech to the Conservative Party Conference,* 10th October 1969. The relevant passage in her speech is as follows:

"This debate has been unexpected in some ways. Some of the men have been provocative and have, perhaps, raised points which will enable me to reply. I think the best claim for greater and better treatment for women came from Mrs. Sell, who proposed the Motion. She was competent, relevant, direct and to the point. She was followed by an equally competent speech by Miss Beryl Cooper. Then some of the men came in and later on one of the women said that not all women need or deserve complete equality with men. May I reply that not all men need or deserve complete equality with women. I think it was Socrates who said long, long ago that when woman is made equal to man she becomes his superior, and I would not dissent from anyone as wise as Socrates."
Available at http://www.margaretthatcher.org/document/101687 (Accessed 28/3/2015.)

13. Nicholas Ling and John Bodenham. *Politeuphuia, Wits Common-Wealth: or A Treasury of Divine, Moral, Historical and Political Admonitions, Similies and Sentences. For the Use of Schools*, (1598), London: Printed for W. Taylor, at the Ship and Black Swan in Pater-Noster-Row, 1722, 'Of Women', p. 25. This edition is available online.

14. The earliest known source of this saying is 1598. Cf. Willis Goth Regier, *Quotology*, University of Nebraska Press, 2010 pp. 12-13 as follows:
"Russell Lewis's *Margaret Thatcher* reports that the prime minister said this memorable sentence but as a quotation from Sophocles [actually Socrates as mentioned above]. But it is not in Sophocles. Innumerable books, articles, and Web sites attribute the quotation to Socrates, and none of them gives a source. The quotation cannot be found in Plato, Xenophon, or Diogenes Laertius or in any other ancient Socratic source, but it can be found attributed to Socrates as early as 1598 in Nicholas Ling's *Politeuphuia*: "A woman once made equal with man becommeth his superior." A provocative quotation like this one requires a distinguished quotee, Thatcher, Sophocles, or Socrates."

15. Plato, *The Republic*, Book Five, 455d-e, translated by Robin Waterfield, (Oxford: OUP, 1994), p. 167:
οὐδὲν ἄρα ἐστίν, ὦ φίλε, ἐπιτήδευμα τῶν πόλιν διοικούντων γυναικὸς διότι γυνή, οὐδ' ἀνδρὸς διότι ἀνήρ, ἀλλ' ὁμοίως διεσπαρμέναι αἱ φύσεις ἐν ἀμφοῖν τοῖν ζῴοιν, καὶ πάντων μὲν μετέχει γυνὴ ἐπιτηδευμάτων κατὰ [455e] φύσιν, πάντων δὲ ἀνήρ, ἐπὶ πᾶσι δὲ ἀσθενέστερον γυνὴ ἀνδρός.

16. There is more on the nature and fate of the Fair Intellectual Club in my Ph.D. thesis *The Emergence of Philosophical Inquiry in Eighteenth Century Scotland* (Glasgow University 1998). The pamphlet mentioned is as follows: *An Account of the Fair Intellectual-Club in Edinburgh*: In a Letter to a Honourable Member of an Athenian Society there, By a young Lady, the Secretary of the Club. (Edinburgh: Printed by J. M'Euen & Co., 1720).

17. As quoted and reported by A.N. Wilson in *Victoria: A Life*, (London: Atlantic Books, 2014), ch. 15, p. 299. The quotation translated from Scots to English reads as: "What are you doing to that poor boy? Have you never dropped anything in your life?" Unfortunately, something of the peremptory intonation of Scots is lost in the translation.

18. H.G. Wells, *Mind at the End of its Tether*, (London: William Heinemann Ltd., 1945), pp. 22-23.

19. *The Diary of Samuel Pepys*, 4th July 1664. Freely available online at www.pepysdiary.com

20. Cf Goethe's *Faust* last two lines: "Das Ewig-Weibliche zieht uns hinan". - the eternal feminine draws us onwards and upwards.

21. Plato, *The Greater Hippias*, 299a, trans. B. Jowett. *The Collected Dialogues of Plato*, ed. E. Hamilton & H. Cairns, (Princeton University Press, 1978), pp. 1552-1553. The Greek text is as follows:
τὰ δέ που περὶ τὰ ἀφροδίσια πάντες ἂν ἡμῖν μάχοιντο ὡς ἥδιστον ὄν, δεῖν δὲ αὐτό, ἐάν τις καὶ πράττῃ, οὕτω πράττειν ὥστε μηδένα ὁρᾶν, ὡς αἴσχιστον ὂν ὁρᾶσθαι

22. John Milton in the poem: "I did but prompt the age to quit their clogs" widely available online.

23. Wikipedia biography: *John Maynard Keynes*, 'Personal Life/Marriage'. Accessed 28/3/2-15.

24. The two sayings are in Chesterton's book: *The Incredulity of Father Brown*, (London: Cassell & Co, Ltd., 1926). They are (1) "It's the first effect of not believing in God that you lose your common sense, and can't see things as they are." ('The Oracle of the Dog' 1923, *op.cit.*, III, p. 105) and (2) "You all swore you were hard-shelled materialists; and as a matter of fact you were all balanced on the very edge of belief – of belief in almost anything." ('The Miracle of Moon Crescent' 1924, *op. cit.*, IV, p. 142.) (Also in *The Complete Father Brown Stories*, ed. by Michael D. Hurley, London: Penguin Books, 2012, pp. 416 and 435, respectively..)

25. William Blake: two verses from a poem entitled "Let the Brothels of Paris be Opened", in his manuscript notebook. He also wrote a poem entitled 'To Nobodaddy' beginning and ending: "Why are thou silent & invisible . . . Or is it because Secrecy gains females' loud applause?"

26. Sigmund Freud, *Moses and Monotheism*, (1939, London: the Pelican Freud Library, Vol. 13, 1985), pp. 239-386.

27. Quoted by Ian Kershaw in *Hitler 1936-45: Nemesis*, (London: Allen Lane Press, 2000), p. 500.

28. Bernard Mandeville, *The Fable of the Bees: or, Private Vices, Public Benefits*, (1714 - London: Penguin Books, 1970).

29. Dietrich Bonhoeffer, *Letters and Papers from Prison*, (London: Fontana, 1959), p. 122.

30. Karen Armstrong, *A History of God*, (London: Heineman, 1993), p. 457.

31. *Op. cit.*, p.6.

10. Servility: Serving Humanity Dutifully (pp. 190-206)

1. Samuel Smiles (1812-1904), *Character*, (1871 - London: John Murray, 1912), ch. I, p. 8.

2. Anthony Storr, *Feet of Clay: a Study of Gurus*, (London: HarperCollins, 1996), p. 233.

3. *The Epistles of Seneca*, Letter XLVIII, Loeb edition, pp. 316-319. Translation partly from *Letters from a Stoic*, translated by Robin Campbell, (London: Penguin, 1969), p. 98.

4. The deleterious effects of Carnegie's industrial policies are discussed in more detail in the paper, 'The Distinction between Humane and Inhumane Capitalism and its Impact on Modern Management', presented by Alistair J. Sinclair at the Philosophy of Management Conference at St Anne's College, Oxford 19-22 July 2012.

5. For Carnegie's social Darwinian views as applied to industry see: Andrew Carnegie, (1906), *The Gospel of Wealth, and Other Timely Essays*, edited by Edward C. Kirkland, (Harvard University Press, 1962).

6. For the humane nature of Ford's views and their beneficial influence duting the 20th century, see Alistair J. Sinclair, 'Henry Ford: The Visionary Humanist', *Essays in the Philosophy of Humanism*, 2012, Vol. 20, no. 2, pp. 81-103. A revised version of this paper is in my book, *American Papers in Humanism and Religion* (Almostic Publications, 2014), pp. 97-122.

7. Henry Ford, (in collaboration with Samuel Crowther), *Today and Tomorrow*, (London: William Heinemann Ltd., 1926), ch. XXIV, p. 269.

8. Henry Ford (in collaboration with Samuel Crowther), *My Life and Work*, (London: William Heinemann, 1922), *My Life and Work*, ch. I, p. 20. This is the third of four principles of service that Ford lays down as being paramount to his view of capitalism. These rules are restated and re-affirmed in ch. XIX, p. 278, and in *Moving Forward*, ch. XII, pp. 174-175.

9. Henry Ford (in collaboration with Samuel Crowther), *My Life and Work*, London: William Heineman, 1922, Ch. XIII, p. 194. Also, *Ford Ideals*: Being a Selection from "Mr. Ford's Page" in *The Dearborn Independent*. (Dearborn, Michigan: The Dearborn Publishing Company, 1922), "'Capital and Labor" are False Terms', p. 93. The saying was probably first coined by Ford's associate, William J. Cameron, who was adept at putting Ford's strong opinions into words.

10. Cf. *Ford Ideals*: Being a Selection from "Mr. Ford's Page" in the *Dearborn Independent*. (Dearborn, Michigan: The Dearborn Publishing Company, 1922), p.249.

11. *Ford Ideals*, pp. 249-50.

12. In an interview with *The Sunday Times*, 11th August 2013, 'Profile: Jeff Bezos', main section, p. 21.

13. Henry Ford, (in collaboration with Samuel Crowther*)*, *Moving Forward*, (London: William Heinemann Ltd., 1931), Ch.VIII, p. 107.

14. The extant writings of Hierocles were translated into English in the following work: *Political Fragments of Archytas and Other Ancient Pythagoreans*, by Thomas Taylor, published in 1822, p. 107. It is available at this Wikisource website:
http://en.wikisource.org/wiki/Political_fragments_of_Archytas_and_other_ancient_Pythagoreans/How_we_ought_to_conduct_ourselves_towards_our_kindred
In Taylor's day, it was assumed that these works were by a 5th-century Pythagorean of the same name but they are now assigned to the 2nd-century Stoic philosopher Hierocles, as evidenced by Aulus Gellius in his *Attic Nights*, ix. 5. 8, available here:
http://penelope.uchicago.edu/Thayer/E/Roman/Texts/Gellius/home.html

> But our countryman Taurus, whenever mention was made of Epicurus, always had on his lips and tongue these words of Hierocles the Stoic, a man of righteousness and dignity: "Pleasure an end, a harlot's creed; there is no Providence, not even a harlot's creed."

15. *Political Fragments, op. cit.* p. 107. The original Greek is as follows: "kai megistos periechov te pantas tous kuklous ho tou pantos anthropon genous" and the text comes from the *Florilegium* of Stobaeus as reproduced by August Meineke, *Ioannis Stobaei: Florilegium*, Leipzig: 1856, Vol. III, p. 134, and is available at this website:
http://www.perseus.tufts.edu/hopper/text?doc=Perseus%3Atext%3A1999.04.0062%3Aalphabetic+letter%3DS%3Aentry+group%3D18%3Aentry%3Dstobaeus-harpers

16. Alexander Pope, *An Essay on Man*, Epistle IV, lines 363-370. I

17. See, for example, Derek Parfit, *Reasons and Persons*, (Oxford: OUP, 1985), ch. 4, §32, p. 88.

18. John Donne (1572-1631), 'Devotions upon Emergent Occasions, Meditation XVII' (1624) in *Selected Prose*, (London: Penguin Books, 1987), p. 126. The complete quotation is as follows (spelling and punctuation has been modernised.):

> No man is an island, entire of itself. Every man is a piece of the continent, a part of the main. If a clod be washed away by the sea, Europe is the less, as well as if a promontory were, as well as a manor of thy friends, or of thine own were. Any man's death diminishes me, because I am involved in mankind. And therefore never send to know for whom the bell tolls; it tolls for thee.

19. Cf. David Hume, *A Treatise of Human Nature*, (1739 - ed. Nidditch - Oxford: the Clarendon Press, 1978), Book I, Part IV, Section VI, p.252. From an analytical, reductionist point of view, the self is "nothing but a bundle or collection of different perceptions . ." But the context of self is what we are in practical terms, rather than what we conceive ourselves abstractly to be. The self is conceived by us just as much as our perceptions are conceived by us. Moreover, conception was not Hume's strong point as Reid and Kant pointed out.

20. Robert Burns, *To a Louse* (1786), "O wad some Power the giftie gie us To see ourséls as ithers see us!" Widely available online.
21. Adam Smith, *The Theory of Moral Sentiments*, (1759 - London: H.G. Bohn, 1853), Part III, ch I, para. 2, p. 161.
22. Mary Midgley, *The Ethical Primate*, London: Routledge, 1996, p. 122.

11: Posterity: Benefiting Future Generations (pp.208-218)

1. "La postérité pour le philosophe, c'est l'autre monde de l'homme religieux." Denis Diderot (1713-84), *Œuvres Complètes de Diderot*, (Paris: Éditeur: J. Assézat et M. Tourneux; Maison d'édition: Garnier, 1875-77), Volume XVIII, 'Lettres à Étienne Maurice Falconet' (1716 -1791), Février 1766, p. 101.

2. *The Oracle: A Manual of the Art of Discretion*, (*Oráculo manual y arte de prudentia*, 1647), translated by L.B. Walton, London: J. M. Dent, 1962, §297, pp.273-274. The original Spanish text is as follows:
> Obrar siempre como a vista. Aquél es varón remirado que mira que le miran o que le mirarán. Sabe que las paredes oyen, y que lo mal hecho revienta por salir. Aun cuando solo, obra como a vista de todo el mundo, porque sabe que todo se sabrá: ya mira como a testigos ahora a los que por la noticia lo serán después. No se recataba de que le podían registrar en su casa desde las ajenas, el que deseaba que todo el mundo le viese.

3. Plato, *Phaedrus*, (London: Penguin, 1973), 259b, p. 70.

4. This phrase, literally 'now stance', was apparently coined by Thomas Aquinas (*Summa Theologia* I, Q X, Art. 2) as in *nunc fluens facit tempus, nunc stans facit aeternitatem*, "the flowing 'now' makes time, the standing 'now' makes eternity". He attributes this to Boethius but it is a concise rendering of the following: "There is this great difference between 'now' which is our present and the divine present. Our present connotes changing time and sempiternity; God's present - unmoved and immovable - connotes eternity." (*De Trinitate* IV). The *nunc stans* is therefore attributed by these authors to God in his eternal mode. The idea that each of our own 'nows' belongs to eternity is obviously anathema to theologians, even though the notion is entirely our own and is hardly worthy of any truly superior being.

5. Maurice Maeterlinck, 'Immortality' in *The Measure of the Hours*, (La Mesure des Heures), translated by Alexander Teixeira de Mattos, New York: Dodd, Mead and Company, 1907, XII, p. 53. "Dans l'ignorance invincible où nous sommes, nôtre imagination a donc le choix de nos destinées éternelles." As in *L'Intelligence des Fleures*, (Paris: Bibliothèque Charpentier, 1907), Immortalité, XII, pp.302-303

12. Finality: Contributing to the Cosmos (pp. 219-231)

1. Carl Sagan (1934-1996), *Cosmos*, (London: Macdonald & Co. Ltd., 1983), ch. XIII, p. 374. Sagan clearly equates the cosmos with the universe whereas they are here being treated as distinct.
2. Cf., John Burnett, *Early Greek Philosophy*, (London: A. & C. Black, 1930), p.3.
3. Plato, *Timaeus*, 28b, 30C-D. (London: Penguin, 1971), pp. 40-2.
4. *Op. cit.*, 48E, Loeb edition, p. 112; Penguin, p. 66.
5. *Op. cit.*, 32B. (London: Penguin, 1971), p. 44.
6. Cf. Karl Popper (1972), *Objective Knowledge*, (Oxford: OUP, 1975), ch. 3, p. 106f and ch. 4, p. 153f.
7. Pierre Teilhard de Chardin, *The Phenomenon of Man*, (1955 - London: Collins, 1965,) p. 200f. Also, *The Future of Man*, 1959 – London: Collins, 1969, p. 120, and other works.

8. Cf. John Dewey, *A Common Faith*, (New Haven and London: Yale University Press, 1934), p. 51, where he argues that God is the activity of relating the ideal to the actual. But the notion of Cosmos surely makes more sense of this activity without being supernatural in any way.

9. See Peter Atkins, 'The Limitless Power of Science', in *Nature's Imagination: The Frontiers of Scientific Vision*, ed. John Cornwell, (Oxford: OUP), 1995, ch. 8, p.129, where he says: "Science has never encountered a barrier that it has not surmounted or that we can at least reasonably suppose it has power to surmount and will in due course be equipped to do so. There is no explicitly demonstrated validity in the view that there are aspects of the universe closed to science."

10. Fritjof Capra, *The Tao of Physics*, (1975 – London: Fontana, 1983)

11. David Bohm, *Wholeness and the Implicate Order*, (London: RKP, 1981).

12. Paul Davies, *God and the New Physics*, (London: Penguin Books, 1983).

13. Albert Einstein (1879-1955), *The World As I See It*, translated by Alan Harris, (San Diego, California: The Book Tree, 2007). Originally published in 1935 by John Lane, The Bodley Head, London), p. 27.

14. A. C. Bouquet, *The Sacred Books of the World*, (London: Penguin, 1954).

15. Cf. A.C. Bouquet, *Comparative Religion*, (London: Penguin, 1941), p. 18.

Bibliography
Of Works Cited in the Text (with pages nos. given)

Addison, J. (1711), *The Spectator*, Vol. I, (London: J.M. Dent, 1909)	63, 236
Aquinas, T. *Summa Theologia*	212, 243
Aristotle, *The Nicomachean Ethics*, (London: Penguin, 1987)	59, 120, 122, 126, 163, 236, 238, 238, 239
Topics, (Loeb Classical Library, 1992)	27, 238
Armstrong, K. (1993), *A History of God*, (London: Heineman)	186, 241
Asimov, I. (1950), 'Runaround', *I, Robot*, (New York: Doubleday & Company)	7, 233
Atkins, Peter (1995), 'The Limitless Power of Science', in *Nature's Imagination: The Frontiers of Scientific Vision*, ed. John Cornwell,(Oxford: OUP)	228, 243
Augustine, St. *Confessions*, (London: Penguin, 1968)	166, 201
Bacon, F. (1620) *Novum Organum*,	45, 46, 235
(1620)*The Great Instauration*	45, 46, 235
Becker E. (1971), *The Birth and Death of Meaning*, (London: Penguin, 1980)	94, 237
Berlin, I. (1978), 'The Hedgehog and the Fox' in *Russian Thinkers*, (London: Penguin, 1979)	47, 235
Bernard of Clairvaux (12th cent.), 'The Purification of the Blessed Virgin Mary'	1, 233
Bible – Old Testament	30,162
– New Testament	88, 90, 92, 132, 133, 161, 166, 182, 239
Blake, W. (1939), *Poems and Prophecies*, (London: J.M. Dent & Sons Ltd.)	82, 182, 237, 241
Boethius, A. *De Trinitate*	21, 243
Bohm, David (1981), *Wholeness and the Implicate Order*, (London: RKP)	228, 243
Bonhoeffer, D. (1953), *Letters and Papers from Prison*, (London: Fontana, 1959)	186, 241
Boswell, J. (1791), *Life of Samuel Johnson*, (London: J.M. Dent, 1962)	97. 238
Bouquet, A.C. (1941) *Comparative R eligion*, (London: Penguin)	230, 231 243
(1954), *The Sacred Books of the World*, (London: Penguin)	230, 243
Burke, E. (1790), *Reflections of the Revolution in France*, (London: Penguin, 1976)	134, 239
Burnet, John (1930), *Early Greek Philosophy*, (London: A & C Black)	223, 243
Burns, Robert (1786a), 'Is There for Honest Poverty, *Poems and Songs of Robert Burns*, (London and Glasgow: Collins, 1955)	11, 233
(1786b), *To a Louse op. cit.*	202, 243
Camus, A. (1942), *The Outsider*, (London: Penguin, 1983)	88, 237
Capra, Fritjof (1975) *The Tao of Physics*, (London: Fontana, 1983)	228, 243
Carnegie, A. (1906), *The Gospel of Wealth, and Other Timely Essays*, (Harvard University Press, 1962)	193, 241
Chesterton, G. K. (1926), *The Incredulity of Father Brown*, (London: Cassell & Co, Ltd.)	181, 241
Churchill, W;.S. (1938), *Civilisation*, in *Complete Speeches 1897-1963*, (New York: Chelsea House Publishers, 1974), Vol. VI	166, 239
(1943), 'Speech at Harvard University', 6th Sep. 1943, in *op. cit.*	iv, 233
Cicero, *De Divinatione*,	36, 235
Collingwood, R.G. (1938), *The Principles of Art*, (Oxford: OUP, 1977)	111.238
Davies, Paul (1983), *God and the New Physics*, (London: Penguin Books)	229, 243
Darwin, C. (1839), *The Voyage of the Beagle*, (London: Henry Colburn)	24, 25, 234
Dewey, John (1934), *A Common Faith*, (Yale University Press)	227, 243

Diderot, D. (1713-84), *Œuvres Complètes de Diderot*, (Paris: Éditeur: J. Assézat et M.
 Tourneux; Maison d'édition: Garnier, 1875-77), Vol. XVIII   208, 243
Donne J. (1624) 'Devotions upon Emergent Occasions, Meditation XVII,
 (*Selected Prose*, (London: Penguin Books, 1987)   200, 242
Einstein, A. (1935), *The World As I See It*, (San Diego: The Book Tree, 2007)   230, 243
 (1931), 'What I Believe', *Forum and Century*, v. 84   145, 239
Emerson, R. W. (1814), *Nature, The Conduct of Life*, (London: Everyman, 1963)   23, 234
Freud, S. (1923), *On Metapsychology: The Theory of Psychoanalysis*,
 (London: Pelican Freud Library, Vol. 11, 1984)   116, 238
 (1938), *Moses and Monotheism*, (London: Pelican Freud Library, Vol. 13, 1985)182, 241
Ford, H. (1922), *My Life and Work* (London: William Heinemann)   193, 241, 242
 (1926), *Today and Tomorrow* (London: William Heinemann)   193, 242
 (1922), *Ford Ideals*, (Dearborn, Michigan: The Dearborn Publishing Co.)   194, 242
 (1931), *Moving Forward*, (London: William Heinemann Ltd)   195, 242
Fowles, J. (1980), *The Aristos*, (London: Triad/Granada)   114, 238
Fromm, E. (1957) *The Art of Loving*, London: Unwin, 1978)   11, 233
 (1949) *Man for Himself*, (London: RKP, 1971)   31, 234
Gibbon, Edward, (1776), *The Decline and Fall of the Roman Empire*, (London:
 J.M. Dent, 1962), Vol. IV   25, 234
Gibbons, M. , Limoges, C. et al, (1994), *The New Production of Knowledge*,
 (London: Sage)   54, 236
Goethe, J.W. von, (1808), *Faust*   173, 239
Gracián, B. (1647) *The Oracle: A Manual of the Art of Discretion*,
 (London: Dent – Everyman's Library, 1962)   211, 243
Graves, R. *In Broken Images*,   63, 236
Hadot, Pierre (1995), *Philosophy as a Way of Life*, (Oxford: Blackwell)   123, 238
Haldane, J.B.S. (1932), *The Inequality of Man*, (London: Penguin, 1938)   45, 235
Hare, R.M. (1972), *Applications of Moral Philosophy*, (London: Macmillan)   88, 237
Hazlitt, William, (1824) 'On People With One Idea', *Table Talk*,
 (London: J. M. Dent, 1908)   60, 236
Hume, D. (1739), *A Treatise of Human Nature* (ed. Nidditch - Oxford: the
 Clarendon Press, 1989)   141-2, 201, 239, 242
Huxley, A. (1959), *The Human Situation*, (London:Triad/Granada)   31, 195
Huxley, J. (1923), *Essays of a Biologist*, (London: Penguin, 1939)   93, 237
James, W. (1897), *The Will to Believe*, (New York: Dover Publications, 1956)   48
 (1907), *Pragmatism*, (New York:Washington Square Press, 1963)   47, 235
 (1915) 'On a Certain Blindness in Human Beings', *Selected Papers on
 Philosophy*, (London: Dent, 1967)   70, 86, 237
Jung, C.G. (1921), 'Psychological Types', *The Collected Works of Carl G. Jung*,
 (Princeton University Press)   47, 86, 235, 237
Kant, I. (1785), *The Moral Law*, (London: Hutchinson, 1972)   85, 237
Kershaw, Ian (2000), *Hitler 1936-45: Nemesis*, (London: Allen Lane Press)   184, 241
Kipling, R. *If* poem. Available online.   59
Knox, J. (1558) *First Blast of the Trumpet against the Monstrous
 Regiment of Women*   165, 166, 239
Laertius, D. *Lives and Opinions of Eminent Philosophers*,
 (Loeb Classical Library, 1980)   36, 45, 234
Ling N. and Bodenham. J. (1598) *Politeuphuia, Wits Common-Wealth:*
 (London: Printed for W. Taylor, 1722, 'Of Women'   167, 240

Maeterlinck, M. (1907) 'Immortality' in *The Measure of the Hours*,
   (New York: Dodd, Mead and Company)   214, 243
Mandeville, B. (1714), *The Fable of the Bees*, (London: Penguin Books, 1970)   184, 241
McLuhan, Marshall (1962), *The Gutenberg Galaxy*, (University of Toronto Press)   11, 233
   (1964), *Understanding Media*, (London: Sphere Books, 1968)   11, 233
McTaggart, Lynne, (2003), *The Field: The Quest for the Secret Force of the
   Universe*, (London: HarperCollins)   81, 237
Midgley, Mary (1996), *The Ethical Primate*, (London: Routledge)   202, 243
Milton, J. 'I did but prompt the age to quit their clogs'   175, 241
Moore, G.E. (1903), *Principia Ethica*, (Cambridge: CUP, 1922)   125, 238
Neurath, Otto, *Philosophical Papers 1913-1946*, (Dordrecht: D. Reidel, 1983)   31, 234
Newton, Cardinal J. H. (1859), *On the Scope and Nature of University Education*,
   (London, J. Dent, 1915)   97, 238
Nietzsche F..(1886), *The Birth of Tragedy*, (1886 - London: Penguin, 1993)   127, 238
   (1901), *The Will to Power*, (New York: Vintage Books, 1968)   48
Parfit, Derek (1985), *Reasons and Persons*, (Oxford: OUP)   200, 242
Pascal, B. *Pensées*, London: Penguin, 1975.   41, 42, 235
Passmore, J. (1970), *The Perfectibility of Man*, (London: Duckworth)   97-8, 238
Pepys, S. *Diary of Samuel Pepys*, (available online)   172, 215, 240
Pico della Mirandola, G. (1486), *Oration of the Dignity of Man*   38, 235
Planck, Max (1933), *Where is Science Going?* (London: Allen and Unwin)   36, 234
Plato *Phaedrus* (*The Collected Dialogues of Plato*, (Princeton University Press,
   1978)   91, 212, 237, 243
   Timaeus, op. cit.   223, 243
   Republic, op. cit.   125, 167, 168, 238, 240
   Greater Hippias, op. cit.   173, 240
   Phaedo, in *The Last Days of Socrates*, (London: Penguin, 1971)   156, 239
Polanyi, M. (1962), *Personal Knowledge*, (London: RKP)   129, 239
Pope, Alexander, *An Essay on Man*   199, 242
Popper K. (1945), *Open Society and its Enemies*   4, 59, 233, 236
   (1975), *Objective Knowledge*, (Oxford: OUP)   224, 243
Plutarch, *Moralia*, Vol. One, (London: William Heinemann Ltd., 1927)   64, 236
Raven, A. (1932), *Civilisation as Divine Superman*, (London: Williams & Norgate)   6, 233
Regier, W. G. (2010), *Quotology*, (University of Nebraska Press)   167, 240
Reid, T. (1785), *Essays on the Intellectual Powers of Man*, in *The Works of
   Thomas Reid*, ed. Sir W. Hamilton, (Edinburgh: James Thin, 1895)   63, 236
Ryan, L. (1996) *The Aboriginal Tasmanians*, (London: Allen & Unwin 2nd Ed.)   25, 234
Sagan, C. *The Cosmos*, (London: Macdonald & Co. Ltd.)   219, 243
Scott, Sir W. *Woodstock*,   60, 236
Seneca, *The Epistles*, Letter XLVII   192-3, 241
Shakespeare, W. *Hamlet*   27, 128, 234, 239
Shaw, G.B. (1903), *Man and Superman*, (London: Penguin, 1971)   68, 237
Siegel, Harvey (1990), *Educating Reason: Rationality, Critical Thinking and
   Education*, (New York and London: Routledge)   95, 237
Siepmann K. & McIntosh A., (2015) 'The Age of Transhumanism Has Begun'
   Essays in the Philosophy of Humanism, (Sheffield: Equinox Publishing Ltd.,)   6, 7, 233
Sinclair, A.J. (1998a) *The Answers Lie Within Us* (Ashgate Publishing)   39, 93, 237
   (1998b), *The Emergence of Philosophical Inquiry in 18th Century
   Scotland* (Glasgow University 1998)   167, 240

(2008) *What is Philosophy?* 127, 229, 236, 239
(2010) The Role of Dualist Thinking in Management' – a paper to the
Philosophy of Management Conference at St. Anne's College, Oxford 64, 236
(2011) 'Posterity—An Eighteenth Century Answer to God and Religion',
The Humanist, Vol. 71 (2) 65, 237
(2012) 'Henry Ford: The Visionary Humanist', *Essays in the
Philosophy of Humanism*, Vol. 20 193, 241
(2013) *Punish the Person, not the Crime! Proposing a Social Treatment System
to Punish Lawbreakers*, (Amazon Kindle e-book) 64, 236
(2014a) *Old Age, Death and Immortality*, (Amazon Kindle e-book) 156
(2014b) *The Promise of Dualism*, (Almostic Publications) 19, 79, 107, 237
Smiles, S. (1871), *Character*, (London: John Murray, 1912) 72, 190, 237, 241
Smith, A. (1759), *The Theory of Moral Sentiments*, (London:
H.G. Bohn, 1853) 100, 202, 238, 243
(1776) *An Inquiry into the Nature and Causes of the Wealth of Nations*,
(London: Routledge, 1900) 100, 238
Spielberg, S. (2001) *A.I. Artificial Intelligence*, feature film. 209
Stevenson, R.L. (1881), 'El Dorado', *Virginibus Puerisque*, in *The Works of Robert
Louis Stevenson*, (London: William Heinemann, Ltd., 1925) 161, 139
Stewart, Ian (1990), *Does God Play Dice? The Mathematics of Chaos*, (London:
Penguin Books) 71, 237
Storr, A. (1996), *Feet of Clay: A Study of Gurus*, (London: Harper/Collins) 192, 241
Sunday Tmes (1992) 145, 239
Swift, J. (1704), *The Battle of the Books*, (London: Everyman, 1970) 86, 237
Taylor, Rebe (2008), 'The Polemics of Making Fire in Tasmania:
The Historical Evidence Revisited.' *Aboriginal History Journal*, Vol 32. 25, 234
Taylor, Thomas (1822), *Political Fragments of Archytas and Other Ancient
Pythagoreans* 199, 242
Teilhard de Chardin, P. (1935), *The Phenomenon of Man*, (London: Collins, 1965) 224, 243
Terence, *Heauton Timorumenos*, (The Self-Tormentor) 30, 234
Thatcher, M. (1969), *Speech to the Conservative Party Conference* 167, 139
Turnbull, Colin (1973) *The Mountain People*, 1973 (London: Paladin Books, 1984) 25, 234
Turing, A.M. (1950) "Computing Machinery and Intelligence," *Mind*, Vol. LIX 58, 235
Van Gogh V. (1888), *Letter to Theo van Gogh, Arles, 3 September 1888:*
Available at http://vangoghletters.org/vg/letters/let673/letter.html 100, 238
Virgil, *Aeneid*, 31, 234
Wells, H.G. (1902), *The Discovery of the Future*, ed. by P. Parrinder,
(London: PNL Press, 1989) 8, 9, 233
(1945), *Mind at the End of its Tether*, (London: William Heinemann Ltd.) 171-2, 240
Whitehead A.N. (1925), *Science and the Modern World*,
(New York: Mentor, 1958) iv, 23, 47, 235
(1933), *Adventures of Ideas*, (Cambridge University Press, 1947) 51, 235
Wikipedia, various anonymous articles published online 25, 180, 234, 241
Williams, Bernard (1982), his conversation with Bryan Magee, in
Men of Ideas, (Oxford: OUP 1982) 47, 235
Wilson, A. N. (2014), *Victoria: A Life*, (London: Atlantic Books) 168, 240
Yeats, W. B. (1933) 'The Second Coming', *The Collected Poems of W.B. Yeats*,
(London: Macmillan, 1981) 1, 233

Name Index

Addison, J. 63, 236
Akhenaten 182, 231
Aquinas, T. 233, 243
Armstrong, K. 184, 241
Aristotle 59, 120, 122, 126, 127, 163, 236, 238, 240
Asimov, I. 7, 233
Atkins, P. 228, 244
Augustine of Hippo 123, 238

Bernard of Clairvaux 1, 233
Bacon, F. 45-7, 235
Becker, E. 94, 237
Beethoven, L van 224
Bergson, H. 109
Berlin, I. 47, 235
Bezos, J. 194
Blake, W. 81-2, 182, 237, 241
Bohm, D. 228, 244
Bonhoeffer, D. 186, 241
Bouquet, A.C. 230, 231, 244
Burke, E. 134, 239
Burnet, J. 243
Burns, R. 11, 202, 233, 243

Camus, A. 88, 237
Capra, F. 228, 244
Carnegie, A. 193-194, 241
Chesterton, G.K. 181, 241
Churchill, W.S. iv, 166, 233, 239
Collingwood, R.G. 111, 238
Copernicus 39
Cromwell, O. 62
Darwin, C. 24, 234
Davies, P. 228, 244
Descartes, R. 53
Dewey, J. 227, 244
Diderot, D. 208, 243
Diogenes Laertius 45, 234, 235
Donne, J. 200, 242
Duke of Edinburgh 150
Dumas, A. 191

Einstein, A. 145, 230, 239, 244
Emerson, R.W. 23, 234

Ford, H. 193-195, 241, 242

Fowles, J. 114, 238
Freud, S. 116, 174, 238, 241
Fromm, E. 11, 31, 233, 234

Galileo 45
Ghandi, M. 195
Gibbon, E. 25, 234
Goethe, J.W. von. 173, 240
Gracián, B. 211, 243
Graves, R. 63, 236

Haldane, J.B.S. 45, 235
Hare, R.M. 88, 237
Hawking, S. 103
Hazlitt, W. 60, 236
Hierocles 199-200, 242
Hitler, A. 182, 184
Hume, D. 141-2, 197, 201, 239, 242
Huxley, J. 93, 237

James, W. 47, 48, 70, 235, 237
Johnson, S. 97, 238
Jung, C.G. 47, 86, 235, 237

Kant I. 85, 142, 197, 237
Kershaw, I. 184, 241
Keynes, J.M. 180, 241
Kipling, R. 59
Knox, J. 165-166, 239

McLuhan, M. 11, 233
McTaggart, L. 81, 237
Maeterlinck, M. 214
Mandeville, B. 184, 241, 243
Midgley, M. 202, 243
Milton, J. 175, 241
Mirandola, G.P. della 38, 235
Monroe, M. 169, 172, 173
Moore, G.E. 125, 238

Neurath, O. 31, 234
Newman, J.H. 97, 238
Nietzsche, F. 48, 127, 238

Parfit, D. 242
Pascal B. 41-2, 235
Passmore, J. 97-98, 238
Paul of Tarsus 166

Pepys, S. 172, 215
Planck, M. 36, 234
Plato 125, 156, 167, 173, 212, 223, 237, 238, 240, 243
Plutarch 64, 236
Polanyi, M. 129, 239
Pope, A. 199, 242
Popper, K. 59, 224, 233, 236, 243
Pratchett, T. 155-156

Queen Victoria 168

Raven, A. 6, 233
Reid, T. 63, 142, 236
Regier, W. G. 167, 240
Ryan, L. 219, 243

Sagan, C. 219, 243
Scott, Sir W. 236
Siegel, H. 237
Seneca 192-193, 241
Shakespeare, W. 104, 128, 234, 239
Shaw, G.B.S. 68, 237
Smiles, S. 72, 190, 237, 241
Smith, A. 100, 202, 238, 243

Socrates 156, 167
Spencer, H. 193
Spielberg. S. 209
Stalin 184
Stevenson R.L.S. 161, 239
Stewart, I. 237
Storr, A. 192, 241
Swift, J. 86, 237

Taylor, Rebe 25, 234
Taylor, Thomas 199, 242
Terence (playwright) 30
Teilhard de Chardin 224, 243
Thatcher, M. 166-167, 239
Turing, A 58, 235
Turnbull, C. 25, 233

Van Gogh 100, 238
Virgil 31, 234

Wells, H.G. 7-9, 171, 233, 240
Whitehead, A.N. iv, 47, 51, 233, 235
Williams, B. 47, 235
Wilson, A.N. 240

Yeats, W.B. 1, 233

Subject Index

abnormal behaviour 148
agapē 133
Amazon 194
analytical line of thought 47
Apollonian/Dionysian 127
artificial intelligence 6-7,
Aristotelian substances 53
Australia 4

Bohemian Rhapsody 88
bootstrap species 31-32
British Commonwealth of Nations 17
British Empire 17
brotherhood of man 11

capitalism 193-196
centrality of our position 40-44
character 72
children 158-160
chimpanzees 31
China 5
Christianity 93, 132, 231
civic covenant 24, 196-197
civic therapy 1
civilisation 6, 9, 12, 25, 49, 217
Cold War 9
common sense 63
comparative judgments 126
comparative religion 231
consciousness 81
consumerism 194
contextualisation 85, 142-144, 198-206
Copernican view 39
Cosmos 90, 189, 201, 205, 219-232
counselling 192-193
creativity 100-131
critical self-awareness 84-85
crime and punishment 64
Cro-Magnon man 126
Cuban Missile Crisis 9
Cyprus 16

Dark Ages 1, 5, 25
Dasein 92, 109
death 74-75, 113, 155-156
determinism 43
Dignitas 155-156

dogmatism 44-7
downward causation 80
dualism 3, 24, 51-66, 146
dualist logic 63
dualist studies 63-65
duration (la durée) 109
dynamic logic 79, 107
dynamism, dynamic philosophy 3, 107, 147

eccentricity 127-128
education 64
élitism 14-15
emotive evaluations 130-133
empirical philosophers 47
empiricism 46-8
enabling principles 109
endoxicality 127-128
environment 153-155
eternity 111-113
ethical interaction 122-123
European Union 12, 17
euthanasia 155-156
evaluative notions 123-144
existentialist philosophers 47
extremism 49, 51-66
extraversion 86

Facebook 14
facts 110-111
falsification principle 109
family life 156-160
feedback 80
feminism 163-173
financial crisis 26, 55, 58, 145, 195
First World War 45
flora and fauna 5
formal logic 139
fracting 154-155
freedom 43, 146, 149-156, 196
Friends of the Earth 40
future advancement 3, 65

genetic engineering 6, 154-155
genetic influences 77
globalisation 12, 13
global monoculture 12, 13
GNP 153, 196

Subject Index

God 20-21, 25, 26, 31, 39, 43, 92, 112, 215, 227
God-belief 181-189
golden mean 120
Greenpeace 40

habits and routines 84
Hamlet 27
happiness 122-123, 162-163
health and safety 151-2
Hieroclean Circles 199-200
holistic view 17, 18-22, 26-7, 36, 103, 117, 121
Holy Trinity 93
human advancement 1, 27-8
humanity, meaning of 11, 30, 55, 204-5
    belief in 23-35, 190-192
human racism 21-2
humanism 149, 190

idealist philosophers 47, 227
illuminist 86-99
illuminosity 86-99
infinitely large and infinitely small 37-8
inner being 68-85
intellectual passions 97-98
International Space Station 7
international community 11
International Monetary Fund 13
introversion 86
intuition 104-111
invisible hand 100
is/ought distinction 141-2

judgmental evaluations 136-138

life 19, 20-206

kingdom of ends 85
Koran 92

management 64
Manichean opposites 132
marriage 156-157
mass interests 14-15
Massenpsychologischerumkehrschluss 145
mathematics 108, 129
Marxism 194
melanist 87

Metacosmian view 38
metaphysical intuitions
Middle East 16
Middle Way 36-50
Milky Way 38
mind and body 75-76
Mohammedism 92
monism 60-63
moral feelings 117-119
morality 114-144
moral logic 124
moral sense 116-119
Muses 104, 112

Nazi regime 13, 164
Neanderthal man 126
neural networks 73
New Zealand 4
Noah's ark 31
normality 145-189
normal society 145-189
North Korea 14, 51
nunc stans 92, 212
Nürnberg trials 11

opportunistic principle 147-148, 160
Optimist's Creed 32-35

paterfamilias 157-158
personal development 2, 98-9, 114, 162, 177, 178
personal degradation 98-9, 114, 162, 177, 178
personal interaction 119-122
personal truth-seeking 126-130
Platonic forms 112, 131, 134
poetic genius 81
political atonement 15-16
political correctness 146, 150, 168
posterity 92, 205, 208-218
pre-Copernican view 38-9
progress 4-6,
prospectivist view 1, 7-9, 65

racial hatred 51
rationalism 46-48
rational passion 94-98
reductionism 74
religion 16, 18, 25, 32, 230-232

religious prophets 88, 231-2
replication 77
retrospectivist view 2, 7-9, 65
robotic laws 7
Royal Institution 7

scepticism 44-7
science 18, 36-47, 129, 228-330
Scots heritage 13, 14
Scottish Common Sense School 63
self-awareness 99
self-belief 25
self-improvement 18-19, 203
self-regarding evaluations 133-136
sentimental idealists 154
servility 190-206
sexual behaviour 173-180
sexual perversion 178-180
Shariah law 14
Sierra Leone 16
singularity 7
social advancement 1
Social Darwinism 193
sociosphere 85, 111, 129-30, 183, 203, 221

Star Trek television series 6
strange attractor 71
subjective self-reference 78-80
synthetic line of thought 47
systematic dualism 48, 60-63

Tierra Fuegan 24
timocracy 135
Tradition 14-15
transgender 176-178
transhumanism 7
Turing's test 58

unity of humanity 11-22
Universal Declaration of Human Rights 171
utilitarian philosophers 147

vitality 68-85, 116

Wikipedia 25, 180, 219, 234, 241
World Bank 13
World Wide Web 11

Zero Point Field (ZPF) 81, 113

www.ingramcontent.com/pod-product-compliance
Lightning Source LLC
Chambersburg PA
CBHW061635040426
42446CB00010B/1429